DIALOGUES AND DEBAGY

Dialogues and Debates in Social Psychology

edited by

Jeannette Murphy
Polytechnic of North London

Mary John and Hedy Brown
The Open University

Lawrence Erlbaum Associates
in association with
The Open University

Lawrence Erlbaum Associates Ltd., Publishers
Chancery House
319 City Road
London EC1V 1LJ

British Library Cataloguing in Publication Data

Dialogues and debates in social psychology.
  1. Social psychology
  I. Murphy, Jeannette   II. John, Mary
  III. Brown, Hedy
  302   HM251

  ISBN 0-86377-019-3
  ISBN 0-86377-020-7 Pbk

Typeset by Spire Print Services Ltd, Salisbury.
Printed and bound by A. Wheaton & Co. Ltd., Exeter.

Contents

Preface

The aim of this book is to explore some of the dialogues and debates currently enlivening social psychology. In particular, we focus on the tensions that develop when the work of social psychologists impinges on social policy and public consciousness. We take the view that social research (including social psychological research) is a perennial attempt to make sense of the social world and therefore start this book by looking at "The Legacy of the Past." We begin our argument by considering the social setting in which the discipline evolved and the stance adopted by early American social psychologists towards the social issues of their day. The main justification for looking at the history of social psychology from this perspective is to understand the nature of the crisis which (as everybody in the discipline agrees) affected social psychology in the late 1960s and the 1970s. In part, the crisis stemmed from the tensions within the discipline about whether the main task should be to create a socially relevant and applicable body of knowledge or whether the first step should be to create a scientific, theoretically underpinned discipline. More important to the crisis, however, was the critique of radical psychologists (which we detail in Chapter 1 and further in Chapter 3); they saw psychology as an ideological defence of the *status quo* which made it unresponsive to the social upheavals of the time. Whilst these radical critics were somewhat vague as to how their criticisms might be translated into research and social action, their ideas were an important catalyst, promoting a more general discussion of the nature and orientation of mainstream psychology. As witness to this rethinking we have included in Chapter 1 an abridged version of George A. Miller's presidential address to the American Psychological Association in 1969. Miller argued that psychologists had created a negative image for themselves by their emphasis on the control of behaviour and, in order to contribute to human welfare, they should instead concentrate on providing people with skills that will satisfy their urge to feel more effective. In other words, he advocated that psychology should not be an esoteric body of knowledge, open only to a few specialists, but that it should be "given away" to people in all walks of life—mothers, teachers, policemen, salesmen and so on. His address remains a challenge yet to be fulfilled.

With this background to the history of social psychology in relation to the social issues of the day, we turn in Chapter 2, "The Perilous Path: From Social Research to Social Intervention," to explore what happens when social psychologists enter the real world and attempt to influence policy decisions. To illustrate this, we focus on the contribution social psychologists made to the American desegregation debate. This issue has been well documented and we trace its history as well as examine the difficulties faced by social psychologists in their role as expert witnesses. We include two papers in this section: one illustrating the research evidence on which the social psychologists based their conclusions (Clark and Clark, 1947); the other a current reappraisal of the issues involved (Gerard, 1983). Finally, we emphasize that the school desegregation debate has a wider importance, for, although our main case study in this chapter is specific to American society, segregation and desegregation have been debated in other contexts. In Britain, for instance, there has been a long-standing debate about segregation in secondary education which, rather than being based on racial inequalities, stemmed from class inequality. The research evidence here is also confusing and contradictory, as is the evidence for improved educational achievement and social development in singe- versus mixed-sex schools. The debate on these issues underlines and emphasizes the problems associated with the extrapolation from social research to social policy.

Chapter 3, "The Social Role of the 'Man' of Knowledge," returns to some of the issues raised in Chapter 1 and exemplified in Chapter 2. We take a closer look at the relationship between the "man" of knowledge and society. In fact, the title of this chapter is taken from a paper by Becker (1970), in which he stresses that for much of history it has been impossible for the "man" of knowledge "to fulfil his authentic and critical role" in society and to influence policies, owing to the reluctance of the state and its powerful institutions to listen to "unbiased" advice by the "man" of knowledge. Of course, one could argue that the real issue is whether knowledge is ever unbiased? The "sociology of knowledge" perspective stresses that human thought and social consciousness is coloured and shaped by the society in which it evolves. As psychologists have become more aware of the degree to which their knowledge is embedded in their social world they have had to rethink the nature of their task. In this chapter we use the question of whether psychologists are (and should be) the "maintainers of the social order" or whether they should see themselves as "agents of change," to explore both the roles of psychologists in society and the process of research.

In Chapter 4, "Psychologists in Action," we move from the sometimes abstract and theoretical discussion to an examination of the work done by psychologists. Specifically, we use selected research reports to illustrate some of the professional roles psychologists have ˙ undertaken. These include the psychologist as independent expert or scholar; advisor or consultant; laboratory experimenter; field investigator; inter-professional resource and agent of change. Such roles are not necessarily mutually exclusive. Describing and discussing them enables us to illustrate the problems and tensions we have highlighted in the earlier chapters.

In Chapter 5, "Psychology in the Popular Imagination," we turn away from how psychologists define and carry out their various professional roles and explore instead how the public at large perceives and uses psychology. Although most people will not have direct access to psychological books or journals, the proverbial man or woman in the street has nevertheless an image of what the subject is about. To try and understand "psychology in the public imagination" we pose three questions: Under what conditions is there an upsurge of interest in popular psychology? What kinds of issues capture the public's imagination? What is the role of the mass media in popularizing psychology? Some of the answers we provide to these questions can, in the nature of things, be only tentative. But our explorations of these themes once again raise the issue, which has been with us throughout, of what the proper subject matter of social psychology is.

In the Epilogue, we do not offer solutions to the questions raised in this book, neither do we smudge the issues or smooth over the differences. The debates and dialogues we have described continue, and indeed are the life-blood of the discipline. We end with an article by Sarason (1978) which argues that the general crisis in the social sciences stems from the fact that we refuse to accept that certain problems may be insoluble, in the scientific sense of the word, and are part of the human condition.

Finally, it should be noted that throughout we have used the terms "psychologists" and "social psychologists" interchangeably, because we take the view that, whether or not psychologists think of themselves as *social* psychologists, they become so, if only by default, when they interact with the real world. The subject matter of social psychology in its most general sense is psychology in the real world.

We hope that this book which has been prepared initially as a companion piece to the Open University's new course in Social Psychology (D307—Social Psychology: Development, Experience and Behaviour in a Social World) will prove of interest and use to a wider social science audience.

We would like to thank our Open University colleagues on the course team for entrusting us with the task of preparing this book. We would also like to express our thanks and appreciation to Mrs Doreen Warwick who provided such efficient secretarial support for us throughout the gestation period of this volume.

Jeannette Murphy
Mary John
Hedy Brown

March 1984

1

The Legacy of the Past

The experimental psychologist ... needs historical sophistication. ... Without such knowledge he sees the present in distorted perspective, he mistakes old facts and old views for new. ... A psychological sophistication that contains no component of historical orientation seems to me to be no sophistication at all.

(Boring, 1929, p. ix)

In recent years many commentators have made reference to the "crisis" in social psychology. Although there are different interpretations as to what has caused this crisis and how best it might be resolved, there is a widespread feeling that the aims and objectives of the discipline need to be reassessed. The purpose of the first chapter of this Reader is to acquaint you with the history of social psychology throughout this century, so that you will be in a better position to understand the tensions and debates that are highlighted in later chapters. This sketch is extremely selective, focusing as it does on those aspects of the past which seem to have a bearing on the present crisis. In particular, the emphasis is on the social setting in which the discipline evolved and the stance adopted by early social psychologists towards the social issues of their day.

THE STUDY OF SOCIAL ISSUES:
PRE WORLD WAR TWO

How did the early social psychologists view their subject and their professional role? We can best convey the vision of the founding fathers by dipping into the influential textbooks of the day. Floyd Allport, an American professor of social and political psychology, published his textbook *Social Psychology*

1

in 1924, with the express goal of making other social scientists aware of the ways in which psychological research challenged traditional conceptions of human nature. Allport had quite definite ideas as to how the social and individual realms related to one another. He warns his readers at the outset of his book that although they might expect social psychology to be about social relations, they will find, in fact, that his goal is to explain social behaviour in terms of individual behaviour: "... I give an unusual amount of space to purely individual behaviour. This is in accordance with my purpose ... to adhere to the psychological (that is, the individual) viewpoint. ... I believe that only *within the individual* can we find the behaviour mechanisms and the consciousness which are fundamental in the interactions between individuals" (Allport, 1924, p. v). Allport goes on to elaborate this view of social psychology in his first chapter, "Social Psychology as a Science of Individual Behaviour and Consciousness." Although the emphasis in Allport's book—in keeping with his definition of social psychology as the study of individuals—was on the more intimate, face-to-face aspects of social relationships (e.g., family life, friendships, social adjustment), he did also venture into more sociological areas, such as race relations, economic control, leadership, social movements, and industrial conflict.

In retrospect, what seems most striking about Allport's analysis of socially sensitive issues was his readiness to make very strong statements on the basis of very weak evidence, and his attempt to explain social trends in terms of psychological principles. Judged by today's standards, Allport's stance on these social issues was curiously contradictory. On some matters he adopted a liberal, progressive line, while on others he seemed inclined to dogmatic pronouncements. If we examine, for instance, his reflections on women's status, we find that he maintained that the differences between the sexes:

... are more probably due to morals than to innate factors. From the start the girl is denied opportunities for development which are held open to the boy. She is considered a "tom-boy" if she secures birds' nests, builds boats, plays ball, or studies electricity. Her lot is to be dressed, petted, admonished, and loved by those around her. She must react to people rather than to things. Play with dolls, the traditionally "correct" pastime for girls, still further emphasizes the personal elements. ... Psychoneurotic conditions are more prevalent in the female than in the male sex. All this is the result, not so much of woman's innate tendencies, as of spending her early years in a home and society warped through unrecognized conflicts and sex jealousies. (Allport, 1924, pp. 345–346)

These comments on social conditioning could quite easily have come from the pen of a present-day radical feminist.

But, although Allport was willing to play the radical social critic when explaining women's status and personality, when he turned his attention to other social groups, he seemed all too ready to accept the social stereotypes and received wisdom of his day. Thus, when talking about racial differences, he began with a liberal-sounding statement that culture and environment, rather than genes and innate capacities, are the critical factors which distinguish one race from another. However, he then went on to endorse what many present-day psychologists would see as the racist views of American intelligence testers. Indeed, in the passage that follows, Allport suggests that the race problem in America stems from black personality defects which arise from faulty socialization:

M. Le Bon mistakenly held that there is a gap between superior and inferior races amounting almost to a distinction of species. The vast differences in cultural adaptation between primitive and civilized races are to be ascribed as much to "social inheritance" and environmental factors as to innate differences of capacity. *It is fairly well established, however, that the intelligence of the white race is of a more versatile and complex order than that of the black race.* It is probably superior also to that of the red or yellow races.
. . . The heart of the negro question, however, is to be reached, not in the sphere of intelligence or temperament, but of sociality. The negro has not been educated socially; his drives have not been conditioned or modified by agencies of social control. . . . The reason why the negro tends to be asocial is that, growing up in an environment of poverty and ignorance, where stealth and depredation are often the accepted means of livelihood, he has had no opportunity for developing socialized traits . . . the negro, though less gifted than the white man, is highly educable. . . . The whole trouble has been that the moral side of his education was not begun soon enough. . . . We need not so much colleges for members of the coloured race as homes in which they can be properly reared . . .we need organized supervision of the moral influences brought to bear upon young negro children. . . . (Allport, 1924, pp. 386–387; emphasis added)

Allport's readiness to blame the victim for his or her misfortunes, to make the underdog the source of the social problem, is reiterated at another point in the book where he seeks to explain what he calls the "recent wave of industrial conflict in America." He was hostile and suspicious of trade unions and unsympathetic to the plight of the industrial worker, subscribing to the view that industrial unrest was triggered off by politically-motivated agitators. Like many politicians and public leaders, he linked American industrial trouble with the Russian revolution and ignored causes which were nearer to hand—the long hours of work, the dangerous conditions in factories and mines, the poor pay, the lack of job security, and so on. In his view:

The condition of labourers and trade-workers has been on the whole better in recent years than ever before. The war brought an era of high wages and better living conditions which seem to have remained fairly stable ever since. Psychological causes, other than those resulting from the oppression of the worker, must be sought to explain the prevailing unrest. . . . Control through . . . crowd mechanisms has been widely exercised by agitators both in assembled crowds and throughout radical literature. . . . Under the influence of the Russian revolution . . . American labourers sought to relieve their minds of the unpleasant consciousness of inferiority. This they did by projecting upon the capitalistic class the charge of oppression and the intent to keep them [the workers] in a state of social and economic slavery. It is true, of course, that their charge of unfair distribution of wealth is partly justified. But the sweeping and exaggerated claims made by radical leaders show that the economic drive is not the basic motive. Thwarting of the domestic and economic life is a *rationalized* cause for class hatred. It is more satisfactory [to the radical] to ascribe his humble status to the injustice of capital than to his personal incompetence. . . . What is the remedy for this unfortunate situation? . . . The manual worker must realize that . . . Nature has not made men equal in ability. . . . If the worker is thus fated to remain at a modest economic and vocational level, vicarious compensations should be sought. . . . (Allport, 1924, pp. 411–413)

Allport then proceeded to give advice to industrial bosses on how best to "cool out" their workers.

What these quotes clearly illustrate is that for Allport the explanatory principles of social psychology derive from the facts of individual psychology. The logical extension of this position, which Allport endorses, is that the laws of social behaviour can be applied to the theories and practical problems of modern society.

THE LIBERAL TRADITION

Another key text (again American) in early social psychology, which it is instructive to reread, is Kimball Young's *Handbook of Social Psychology*, which first appeared in 1930. What is noteworthy about the second edition of this book, published just after the Second World War in 1945, is the extent to which it is tied to what were then very immediate social concerns. War, conflict, revolution, mass communication, public opinion, propaganda and collective behaviours are some of the topics dealt with in the text.

But at the same time, Young did more than merely mirror the problems, attitudes and values of his day. His analysis is informed by a more critical perspective towards his society than would have been held by members of the power élite or the man on the street. Young clearly took the task of the intellectual to be that of using reason to attack and undermine social prejudices. Young's approach exemplifies the psychologist as a champion of liberal causes. He saw the psychologist's role to be that of educating and persuading people; he also argued the need for action-oriented research (e.g., research to find ways of reducing prejudice). Psychologists in this tradition were critical of American society. They were aware of the contradictions that existed between the official ideology of equality and equal opportunity on the one hand, and the actual way in which people behaved and the types of undemocratic social practices that were condoned on the other. At the same time, psychologists who sought to make people conscious of glaring social injustices were anxious to preserve democratic cultures and democratic systems of government. Contemporary critics of social psychology, such as Philip Wexler, are quite right to label social psychology as a *liberal* subject. To quote Wexler (1983): "Historically, culturally, and socially, its academic practitioners have stood between and against an unfettered capitalism on the one side and socialism on the other" (p. xv).

As we shall see later in this chapter, in recent years there has been a bitter debate as to whether the liberal tradition in the social sciences has hindered or aided their development. But, before we focus on this debate, let us see how social psychologists in the decades from 1945 to 1968 sought to find a middle ground that would allow them to attack social prejudices and to defend liberal democratic traditions.

Young's liberalism is evident when he examines the relationship between different racial groups. Unlike Allport, who took black inferiority for granted, Young exposed and ridiculed what he called the 100% Americanism which blossomed during and immediately after the First World War, and which was founded on the racial myth of Nordic superiority. Rather than seeing black–white tensions as something triggered off by black personality characteristics, Young focused on prejudice as a by-product of group conflict:

> The function of prejudice is to facilitate the segregation of opposing groups from each other. In other words, prejudice is a specific expression of basic conflict between in-group and out-group. . . . Prejudice is really most striking when the strata of classes are changing, when one group is threatening another in its power and prestige. In short, it is most evident in periods of intense conflict. (Young, 1945, pp. 258–259)

This passage shows that Young understood prejudice as a psychological mechanism which arises under certain social conditions and implies a different view about the nature of social psychology from that of Allport. For Young it was impossible to conceive of human beings outside of human society: "We are not at the outset isolated individuals with drives, habits, attitudes, and ideas, who are later socialized. Rather, from birth on, the individual operates within a social matrix" (p. v). Young thought that social psychology should do more than just study the individual within a social context; he urged us to look at the way in which social-cultural reality shapes the form and content of thought, emotions, and activities of the individual. He introduced a note of cultural relativity into the debate about prejudice by suggesting that whites may well be offensive and repugnant to other races. To illustrate this he quoted David Livingstone's response to his first contact with whites after his long sojourn in the heart of Africa: "One feels ashamed of their white skin; it seems unnatural—like blanched celery—or white mice." Finally, Young suggested ways in which economic competition, the desire for success, and intense personal ambition all contribute to the perpetuating of racial prejudice.

Another characteristic of early social psychology which is to be found in Young's approach is its optimism, its belief that there were solutions for social problems. As well as describing and analysing the roots of prejudice, Young considered ways in which it could be alleviated. However, he prefaced his proposals with a statement acknowledging that since prejudice is part and parcel of *group* conflict, the remedy cannot be sought at an individual or psychological level. He advocated the following improvements as necessary precursors to better race relations:

1. Greater economic opportunities, training for skilled occupations, and participation in labour unions.
2. Extension of free schooling.
3. Participation in political rights and responsibilities.
4. Improvement in the Negro's standard of living, with better housing and better recreational facilities.

As sophisticated as he was in his grasp of issues having to do with race relations, Young had the same tunnel vision as his contemporaries in mistakenly believing that the colour problem in the United States was, by and large, a Southern problem. The significance of this fact will become clearer in Chapter 2, when we look at the way social psychologists became involved with school desegregation.

APPLIED SOCIAL PSYCHOLOGY

Despite the fact that both Young and Allport were committed to establishing a socially relevant social psychology, they were both writing as independent academics, offering free advice to anyone who was prepared to listen. Essentially, they sought to influence society by educating the intelligentsia. Not all social psychologists have maintained this same degree of distance from social issues. During the period of the Second World War, an increasing number of social psychologists found themselves acting as paid consultants or advisors to industry, the government, and the military. In offering a service to these various agencies and organizations, they were promoting social psychology as a profession, an *applied* discipline, rather than as an academic subject that might just happen to have something to say about the social concerns of the period.

We ceased, during the Second World War, to be essentially the theoretical discipline pursued for the love of learning, and began to serve in public-opinion analysis, morale studies, industrial mental health, psychology and international relations, the political problems arising from race and class suspicions and antagonisms. Applied social psychology, in short, took shape. (Murphy, 1965, p. 28)

One man who made a major contribution to applied research was Kurt Lewin, a German psychologist who settled in the United States in the early 1930s. As Lewin was very aware, involvement in problem-oriented research forces the psychologist to confront a whole new set of problems, which have more to do with social values than technical matters of research design.

The scientist cannot be blind to the fact that the more important the group of problems which he intends to study, the more likely it is that he will face not merely technical social problems. He should be clear about his objective. This objective is fact finding in regard to what is and what would be if certain measures were adopted. Without additional premises, the scientist cannot decide whether a manager "should" prefer high production coupled with a factory atmosphere of relatively small status differences or whether he "should" prefer great status differences even if that means less production. He cannot decide what the ideal of the Scout movement "should" be. In other words, the experimenter as such *is not the policy determiner of the organization*. However, he can investigate what ought to be done if certain social objectives are to be reached. He can secure data which will be important for analyzing a given policy and its effect, and which will be pertinent for any rational policy determination. (Lewin, 1944, p. 168)

Here we seem to have the psychologist portrayed as the servant of the organization, contracted to do the bidding of those who pay his or her salary. This interpretation, however, does not square with Lewin's idealism, or with his rejection of value neutrality. Throughout his career, Lewin argued that psychology was relevant to social reform. Coming as he did from a Jewish background (his own mother died in a Polish concentration camp), he had personal reasons for taking an interest in intergroup tensions. When Hitler became

Chancellor of Germany, Lewin was on leave from the University of Berlin. Realizing that he had no future in his own country, he decided to remain in the United States and from 1933, until his death in 1947, he persuaded other social psychologists to become involved in research programmes oriented towards practical problems. During the war, he worked with Margaret Mead for the National Research Council to discover the best way to change food habits. He analyzed the effects of group participation in decision-making upon the productivity of the Harwood Manufacturing Corporation, and he evaluated psychological warfare activities for the Office of Strategic Service in Washington D.C. During the final years of his life, Lewin was involved with projects designed to attack prejudice and improve intergroup harmony.

Although Lewin made a lasting contribution to social psychology, in the period immediately after the Second World War social psychologists appeared to have had second thoughts about the prospects of constructing an applied or socially relevant discipline. What concerned them was the low status of social psychology vis à vis the more "scientific" community of psychologists, which many attributed to the lack of an adequate theoretical underpinning. Following on from this concern with professional standing, social psychologists became increasingly preoccupied with methodological and theoretical issues. According to some observers (e.g., Reich, 1981), by the 1960s, the applied interests of the war years had given way to an effort to build a laboratory-based and theory-oriented science.

From the time of Lewin until the late 1960s, social psychologists in both North America and Britain strove to establish their subject in academic circles as a fully fledged branch of psychology. However, despite the ascendancy of experimental research designs, social psychologists adopted a variety of social roles. As scientists they were wedded to the study of social issues in a detached, neutral fashion; as activists and active researchers in the field they looked for solutions to the social ills in their world; as liberal academics they sought to defend those values which they saw as essential to individual liberty and freedom. (Chapters 3 and 4 of this Reader will look more closely at these various roles.) Although there were theoretical disagreements between social psychologists, and some tension existed between academic researchers working in universities and those engaged in applied research, on the whole it was a time of consensus and peaceful coexistence. The optimism and self-confidence of the post-war years were shattered by developments both without and within the discipline.

In the latter half of the 1960s there arose a profession-wide concern with the general orientation of social psychology. . . . "Crisis talk" arose, bringing into bold relief all of the conflicting concerns of laboratory experimentation, field experimentation, social action, relevance, and social policy interests that had so consistently intertwined themselves throughout the history of the field up to that point. With the value of hindsight, we might be justified in considering 1969 to have been a bellweather year in the final molding of all of the facets that had been operating up to that time. (Reich, 1981, p. 60)

THE RADICAL CHALLENGE TO THE LIBERAL TRADITION

It was suggested in the last section that social psychology may be characterized as a liberal discipline. In Britain and America, liberalism has long been seen as a progressive, social-political force. During the 1960s, this conception of liberalism as a benevolent influence was fiercely debated amongst academics. The challenge to liberal academic traditions was mounted by various radical groupings, often referred to as "The New Left," who were dissatisfied with what they took to be the ideological nature of much of social science. They linked the "crisis" in the academic world to a larger crisis in the liberal culture and society which produced and consumed liberal social science.

The late 1960s was the height of protests over the Vietnam War. It was a time of political polarization, the student movement, the civil rights movement and the beginning of the new women's liberation movement. Radical intellectuals turned their attention to the content and organization of higher education, especially in the social sciences. The tone of the "new left" critique of liberal social science is best conveyed in Martin Nicolaus' famous "eyes downwards, palms upwards" speech to the American Sociological Association Convention in 1968:

The ruling élite within [sociology] . . . [has invited a speaker who] is in charge of what is called Health, Education, and Welfare. Those of you who listened passively to what he had to say presumably agreed that this definition, this description of what the man did carried an accurate message. Yet among you are many . . . who do know better or should know better. The department of which the Secretary is head is more accurately described as the agency that watches over the inequitable distribution of preventable disease, over funding of domestic propaganda and indoctrination, and over the preservation of a cheap and docile reserve labor force to keep everybody else's wages down. He is Secretary of Disease, Propaganda and Scabbing.

This may be put too strongly for you, but *it all depends where you look from, where you stand.* . . . If you will look at the social world through the eyes of those who are at the bottom of it, through the eyes of your subject population, and if you will endow those eyes with the same degree of clear-sightedness you profess to encourage among yourselves, then you will get a different conception of the social science to which you are devoted. . . . Sociology is not now and never has been any kind of objective seeking out of social truth or reality. Historically, the profession is an outgrowth of nineteenth-century European traditionalism and conservatism, wedded to twentieth-century American corporation liberalism.

That is to say that the eyes of sociologists . . . have been turned downwards, and their palms upwards.

Eyes down, to study the activities of the lower classes, of the *subject* population—those activities that created problems for the smooth exercise of government hegemony. Since the class of rulers in this society identifies itself *as* the society itself . . . therefore the problems of the ruling class get defined as *social* problems. . . . The things that are sociologically "interesting" are the things that are interesting to those who stand at the top of the mountain and feel the tremors of an earthquake.

Sociologists stand guard in the garrison and report to its masters on the movements of the occupied populace. The more adventurous sociologists don the disguise of the people and go out to mix with the peasants in the "field," returning with books and articles that break the protective secrecy in which a subjected population wraps itself, and make it more accessible to manipulation and control.

The sociologist as researcher in the employ of his employers is precisely a kind of spy. . . . Is it an accident that industrial sociology arose in a context of rising "labor troubles," that political sociology grew when elections became less predictable, or that the sociology of race relations is *now* flourishing—to name only a few examples?

. . . Sociology has risen to its present prosperity and eminence on the blood and bones of the poor and oppressed; it owes its prestige in this society to its putative ability to give information and advice to the ruling class of this society about ways and means to keep the people down.

The professional eyes of the sociologist are on the down people, and the professional palm of the sociologist is stretched towards the up people. . . . The crime which graduate schools perpetuate against the minds and morals of young people is all the more inexcusable because of the enormous liberating potential of knowledge about people which directly affects what we do, what we may hope for. The corporate rulers of this society would not be spending as much money as they do for knowledge if knowledge did not confer power. So far, sociologists have been schlepping [carrying] this knowledge that confers power along a one-way chain, taking knowledge from the people, giving knowledge to the rulers.

In 1968, it is late, very late, too late, to say once again what . . . hundreds of others have long said, that the profession must reform itself. (Nicolaus, 1968, pp. 38–41)

Martin Nicolaus' bitter attack on sociology was to reverberate within psychology, giving rise to the so-called "radical psychology" movement of the late 1960s. Phil Brown, an American psychologist, edited a book of readings which exemplifies the types of criticisms that were being made of mainstream psychology. Brown's critique of psychology, like Nicolaus' denouncement of sociology, indicted *applied* psychologists for engaging in overt manipulation of oppressed people:

Industrial psychologists make factory workers more "comfortable," but only in ways to sap their militancy and thus insure corporate profit; fancy lounges and "counselling" services are traded off for speed-ups of the assembly line. These gimmicks are labelled as the liberal benevolence of the bosses, but the benevolence disappears when the operation of the factory is threatened by workers' organizations. Advertising psychologists aid the corporations on the opposite end by brainwashing people into consuming harmful and/or meaningless products, with the promise of financial and/or sexual success if the correct products are bought. School psychologists push working-class children into vocational tracks, while placing middle strata children into academic tracks. They counsel students against militancy, with thinly veiled threats of reprisal. Further, they gain students' confidence, then report their "antisocial" attitude to the higher administration. Military psychologists polish the machinery of U.S. imperialism in Indochina and elsewhere, providing "adjustment" for anti-war GIs and counselling bomber pilots so they won't feel guilty about napalming Vietnamese. Behaviour modification experts work out tortures to "cure" deviants (read: gays, political activists, etc.); . . . Social psychologists perform research for counterinsurgency plans at home and abroad, including attempts to prove sexual and racial inequality—I.Q. research by men, such as Jensen and Herrnstein, not only provides the ruling classes answer to black struggles for freedom, but also provides the rational basis for repression since it is "scientific." Community mental health centres cool out ghettoes, defusing militant activists with soft-sell therapy services. State hospitals jack people up on thorazine and give electric shocks or lobotomies to working-class people whose behaviour would never be "treated" if they were wealthy. *Psychology is a class rip-off: subjects tend to be poor; those who reap the benefits tend to be rich.* (Brown, 1973, pp. xv–xvi; emphasis added)

Brown's critique of psychology extended beyond this wholesale condemnation of the way in which psychologists are employed to deal with social problems. He suggested that psychology performs a much more sinister function—it serves as an ideological defence of the *status quo*. Thus, for Brown, as well as for other radical critics, there was a need to expose the way in which psychology takes the values of the establishment and presents them as the only conceivable values. The task was thus to find a way of dealing with "objective" political issues and "subjective" personal or psychological questions at the same time. This goal of bringing together personal experience and political life was to be a key concern for British social psychologists seeking to revitalize their subject.

In Britain, in the early 1970s, writers such as Peter Sedgwick, David Ingleby, Nick Heather, and Nigel Armistead took on the task of reassessing the state of the discipline on their side of the Atlantic. Although their analysis had much in common with their American counterparts, British writers tended to focus more on the "models of man" put forward by psychology and the consequences that such images have for the way in which people think of themselves and other human beings.

. . . we should look for the ideological significance of the human sciences in terms of the model of man they put forward. . . . Thus we are not primarily concerned with the way psychology is used in the service of "the military-industrial complex"—an issue which bulks large in sociology—because opposition to these activities is a straightforward matter of opposing the ends that are being sought, and does not necessarily reflect on the validity of the scientific means being used. It is through its potency as myth that the psychological model of man can be seen as serving ideological interests: to the extent that the human sciences are taking over from religion the function of providing man with a self-image, they should be seen in the same light as religious myths. (Ingleby, 1972, p. 57)

Ingleby goes on to make the point that by ignoring the context in which behaviour occurs psychology loses sight of human beings, thereby making it impossible to assert the demands of human nature against the social system that encloses the human being.

... a reifying model of human nature, by definition, presents men as less than they really are (or could be): to the extent that a society requires men (or a certain proportion of them) to be thing-like in their work, orientation, thinking and experiencing, such a model will constitute both a reflection and a reinforcement of that society.... If labour is mechanical, it is convenient that those who have to do it, should think of themselves as a species of machine; if freedom of choice, imagination, the pursuit of untried goals and experiences, are seen as threats to a sacrosanct "social structure," then man should learn he is a species of simple computer, a "limited capacity information channel," incapable by definition of creating such goals and meanings. (Ingleby, 1972, pp. 59–60)

Some British writers came to the conclusion that it would be impossible to formulate a satisfactory analysis of the profound social issues of the day if one remained within the confines of the discipline. For example, Peter Sedgwick, who did himself decide for a time to abandon psychology, maintained that the focus of psychology:

... is much too narrow to assist more than marginally in most questions requiring serious social analysis. Psychologists therefore have to go outside the logic of their own training and take up explicit political positions in order to master an outlook on the social order of which they form an indubitable part. There are three alternatives for a psychology which cannot itself incorporate activist and interventionist political values. Its practitioners may compartmentalize their "professional status" and lead split lives, using a radically different problematic outside working hours; or they can try to find some modern equivalent of the "psychology in the service of social goals" which functioned during a period of value-consensus, such as the Second World War, but which cannot be propounded today without immediate and plausible accusations of partisanship; or they can grow out of being psychologists. (Sedgwick, 1974, p. 36)

THE RESPONSE OF MAINSTREAM PSYCHOLOGY

The criticisms we have so far considered all start from the premise that there is something fundamentally wrong with the whole way in which the social sciences operate—their methods, assumptions, and objectives. According to many critics, these flaws stemmed from the dominance of the liberal tradition in the academic world.

The four main charges brought by the radicals against liberalism are summarized by Anthony Platt (1972) in the following way:

1. Liberals accept the *status quo*, thereby reinforcing the power of the state. They use taken-for-granted categories and definitions of reality.

2. Liberals are reformists, believing that it is possible to change or transform existing society. They support technical solutions to social problems (instead of radical social change). Liberals believe that progress will occur through enlightened managers and policy-makers (rather than through the efforts of the oppressed).

3. Liberals are anti-historical and anti-theoretical. They reject general theories and support behaviourism, pragmatism and social engineering. They are intellectual eclectics.

4. Liberals are cynical and lacking in passion. They fail to raise general moral and political questions about the nature of society. Their preoccupation with pragmatism, short-range solutions and ameliorism reveals an attitude of cynicism and defeatism concerning human potentiality and the possibility of far-ranging changes in society.

Radical critics, such as Platt, maintained that these four attributes of liberalism are not mere accidents of academic fashion but rather reflect fundamental relationships between the state, social institutions, and the academic community. To support this analysis, radicals investigated the funding or sponsorship of research, arguing that financial dependence leads to academic and intellectual servility. They also speculated as to the role of the mass media in creating and sustaining certain beliefs about human nature and social reality. The radicals raised many questions as to the stance that psychologists could or should adopt to political causes and social issues. To acknowledge this, however, does not mean that one agrees totally with their critique of liberal values or their wholesale condemnation of the work of earlier researchers. Indeed, in the chapters that follow we seek to demonstrate the constraints that operate when psychology tackles real-world problems. Radical critics were frequently naive about the difficulty of creating a socially relevant discipline.

Nonetheless, the radicals did help to precipitate a debate about psychology's future. There is fairly general agreement that by the late 1960s psychology was in a state of crisis. A paper which very much captures the turmoil of this period is George A. Miller's presidential address to the American Psychological Association in 1969. In the abridged version of the paper which is reprinted here, Miller gives his opinion on the state of the discipline and its potential role in meeting the human problems of our society. Miller's analysis of the reasons why psychologists have not done much to promote human welfare leads him to conclude that psychologists have created and fostered an image of man which makes the public at large mistrust them. Psychology has come to be equated with behaviour control and psychologists have tried to sell themselves as experts with knowledge and power which is not accessible to the layman. The way ahead, according to Miller, is for psychologists to recast their role. Instead of telling people how to live their lives and setting themselves up as experts with the sole right to apply psychology, psychologists must find a way of allowing non-psychologists to practise psychology and, as Miller states, thus "Give psychology away."

It is perhaps too soon to judge whether Miller's words have influenced the way in which psychologists go about their work. However, in the years since his address was given, many psychologists have quoted his phrases and endorsed his sentiments. (See, for instance, John Shotter (1975), *Images of Man in Psychological Research* and Harry Kay's presidential address to the British Psychological Society, 1972.)

Reading I.   Psychology as a Means of Promoting Human Welfare, by G. A. Miller— Extract from Presidential Address to the American Psychological Association, 1969

The most urgent problems of our world today are the problems we have made for ourselves. They have not been caused by some heedless or malicious inanimate Nature, nor have they been imposed on us as punishment by the will of God. They are human problems whose solutions will require us to change our behavior and our social institutions.

As a science directly concerned with behavioral and social processes, psychology might be expected to provide intellectual leadership in the search for new and better personal and social arrangements. In fact, however, we psychologists have contributed relatively little of real importance—even less than our rather modest understanding of behavior might justify. We should have contributed more; although our scientific base for valid contributions is far from comprehensive, certainly more is known than has been used intelligently.

This is the social challenge that psychologists face. In the years immediately ahead we must not only extend and deepen our understanding of mental and behavioral phenomena, but we must somehow incorporate our hard-won knowledge more effectively into the vast social changes that we all know are coming. It is both important and appropriate for us, on occasions such as this, to consider how best to meet this social challenge.

In opening such a discussion, however, we should keep clearly in mind that society has not commissioned us to cure its ills; a challenge is not a mandate. Moreover, there is nothing in the definition of psychology that dedicates our science to the solution of social problems. Our inability to solve the pressing problems of the day cannot be interpreted as an indictment of the scientific validity of our psychological theories. As scientists we are obliged to communicate what we know, but we have no special obligation to solve social problems.

Our obligations as citizens, however, are considerably broader than our obligations as scientists. When psychological issues are raised in this broader context, we cannot evade them by complaining that they are unscientific. If we have something of practical value to contribute, we should make every effort to insure that it is implemented.

I believe that the majority of American psychologists have accepted this broader interpretation of our responsibilities and have been eager—perhaps, sometimes, overly eager—to apply our science to social problems. We have not been aloof or insensitive; the bulk of our profession works full time on exactly such problems. And I do not wish to discount the many and often successful efforts toward application that we have made

Source: American Psychologist (1969), *24*, pp. 1063–1075. Copyright (1969) by the American Psychological Association. Reprinted by permission of the publisher and author.

already. Yet I cannot escape the impression that we have been less effective than we might have been. "Why" and "what more might be done" are questions that have troubled me increasingly in recent years. . . .

Role of the American Psychological Association

. . . the first article of our Bylaws states that the Association shall have as its object to promote human welfare, a goal that is echoed in our statement of the *Ethical Standards of Psychologists*.

[But, having drawn attention to this goal, Miller then goes on to express his scepticism as to how such a goal can be translated into objective action.]

. . . I have traced my skepticism to two sources.

First, even the most cursory study of welfare economics will show that human welfare has never been operationally defined as a social concept. If there is such a thing as human welfare in the general sense, it must be some kind of weighted average. In difficult cases, where disagreement is most probable, something that advances the welfare of one group may disadvantage another group. The problem is to decide whose welfare we wish to promote. The APA is committed to advancing the welfare of psychologists, of course, but we dare not assume blindly that whatever is good for psychology must always be good for humanity.

Vague appeals to human welfare seldom answer specific questions because we seldom have sufficient information to decide which actions will have the desired result. And even when we do have sufficient wisdom to know in advance which actions will promote human welfare most effectively, we still face the ethical question of whether such actions are morally permissible.

My first reason for distrusting appeals to human welfare, therefore, is that they do little to clarify the logical, informational, or ethical bases for making difficult decisions. Something more is required than a sincere declaration that our heart is in the right place.

My second reason has to do with the fact that the phrase is usually quoted out of context . . . As I understand Article I, our corporate aim is to promote psychology. We justify that aim by our belief that psychology can be used for the public good. I do not understand Article I as a general license to endorse social actions or positions, however meritorious on other grounds, that do not advance psychology as a science and as a means of promoting human welfare.

. . . Of course . . . there has been a running debate in recent years concerning the proper role for individual psychologists to play in the initiation of social reforms. We have been divided as to whether psychologists should remain expert advisers or should take a more active, participatory responsibility for determining public policy. An adviser is expected to summarize the arguments pro and con, but to leave the policy decisions to others; a participant wants to make the policy decisions himself.

Those who favor more active participation by individual psychologists tend to argue that APA should also become directly involved in advocating particular social policies. . . . In my opinion, our Association can never play more than a supporting role in the promotion of social change. I do not conclude from this that APA has become irrelevant or useless, or, even worse, that it has tacitly endorsed a political bureaucracy that presides over the inequitable distribution of health, wealth, and wisdom in our society. The fact that APA has not reformed society does not mean that it approves the *status quo*; it means simply that there is relatively little such an association can do. When one considers the magnitude and urgency of the problems mankind faces, the question of what positions APA takes is, after all, a minor matter.

The important question, to my mind, is not what APA is doing, but what psychologists are doing. What Psychology can do as an association depends directly on the base provided by psychology as a science. It is our science that provides our real means for promoting human welfare.

So let me turn now to broader aspects of my topic.

Revolutionary Potential of Psychology

I will begin by stating publicly something that I think psychologists all feel, but seldom talk about. In my opinion, scientific psychology is potentially one of the most revolutionary intellectual enterprises ever conceived by the mind of man. If we were ever to achieve substantial progress toward our stated aim—toward the understanding, prediction, and control of mental and behavioral phenomena—the implications for every aspect of society would make brave men tremble.

Responsible spokesmen for psychology seldom emphasize this revolutionary possibility. One reason is that the general public is all too ready to believe it, and public resistance to psychology would be all too easy to mobilize. Faced with the possibility that revolutionary pronouncements might easily do more harm than good, a prudent spokesman finds other drums to march to.

Regardless of whether we agree that prudence is always the best policy, I believe there is another reason for our public modesty. Anyone who claims that psychology is a revolutionary enterprise will face a demand from his scientific colleagues to put up or shut up. Nothing that psychology has done so far, they will say, is very revolutionary. They will admit that psychometric tests, psychoanalysis, conditioned reflexes, sensory thresholds, implanted electrodes, and factor analysis are all quite admirable, but they can scarcely be compared to gunpowder, the steam engine, organic chemistry, radio-telephony, computers, atom bombs, or genetic surgery in their revolutionary consequences for society. Our enthusiastic spokesman would have to retire in confused embarrassment.

Since I know that rash statements about the revolutionary potential of psychology may lead to public rejection and scientific ridicule, why do I take such risks on this occasion? My reason is that I do not believe the psychological revolution is still pie in the sky. It has already begun.

One reason the psychological revolution is not more obvious may be that we have been looking for it in the wrong place. We have assumed that psychology should provide new technological options, and that a psychological revolution will not occur until somebody in authority exercises those options to attain socially desirable goals. One reason for this assumption, perhaps, is that it follows the model we have inherited from previous applications of science to practical problems. An applied scientist is supposed to provide instrumentalities for modifying the environment—instrumentalities that can then, under public regulation, be used by wealthy and powerful interests to achieve certain goals. The psychological revolution, when it comes, may follow a very different course, at least in its initial stages.

Davis (1966) has explained the difference between applied social science and applied natural science in the following way:

> Applied science, by definition, is instrumental. When the human goal is given, it seeks a solution by finding what effective means can be manipulated in the required way. Its function is to satisfy human desires and wants; otherwise nobody would bother. But when the science is concerned with human beings—not just as organisms but as goal-seeking individuals and members of groups—then it cannot be instrumental in this way, because the object of observation has a say in what is going on and, above all, is not willing to be treated as a pure instrumentality. Most so-called social problems are problems because people want certain things or because there is a conflict of desires or interests. [p. 26]

Davis goes on to argue that once conflicts of interest have developed, applied social science is helpless: that it is only when people are agreed on their goals that our information can be usefully applied.

Although I agree with Davis that behavioral and social sciences cannot be applied to people and institutions in the same way physical and biological sciences are applied to objects and organisms, I do not agree with his view that we must remain impotent in the face of conflict. We know a great deal about the prevention and resolution of conflicts, and that information could certainly be put to better use than it has been. Indeed, sometimes what is needed is not to resolve conflict but to foster it, as when entrenched interests threaten segments of the public that have no organizational identity. And there, in turn, we know a great deal about the creation of appropriate constituencies to defend their common interests.

Behavioral and social scientists are far from helpless in such situations.

More important, however, I believe that the real impact of psychology will be felt, not through the technological products it places in the hands of powerful men, but through its effects on the public at large, through a new and different public conception of what is humanly possible and what is humanly desirable.

I believe that any broad and successful application of psychological knowledge to human problems will necessarily entail a change in our conception of ourselves and of how we live and love and work together. Instead of inventing some new technique for modifying the environment, or some new product for society to adapt itself to however it can, we are proposing to tamper with the adaptive process itself. Such an innovation is quite different from a "technological fix." I see little reason to believe that the traditional model for scientific revolutions should be appropriate.

Consider, for example, the effect that Freudian psychology has already had on Western society. It is obvious that its effects, though limited to certain segments of society, have been profound. Yet I do not believe that one can argue that those effects were achieved by providing new instrumentalities for achieving goals socially agreed upon. As a method of therapy, psychoanalysis has had limited success even for those who can afford it. It has been more successful as a method of investigation, perhaps, but even there it has been only one of several available methods. The impact of Freud's thought has been due far less to the instrumentalities he provided than to the changed conception of ourselves that he inspired. The wider range of psychological problems that Freud opened up for professional psychologists is only part of his contribution. More important in the scale of history has been his effect on the broader intellectual community and, through it, on the public at large. Today we are much more aware of the irrational components of human nature and much better able to accept the reality of our unconscious impulses. The importance of Freudian psychology derives far less from its scientific validity than from the effects it has had on our shared image of man himself. I realize that one might argue that changes in man's conception of himself under the impact of advances in scientific knowledge are neither novel nor revolutionary. For example, Darwin's theory changed our conception of ourselves, but not until the past decade has it been possible to mount a truly scientific revolution based on biological science. One might argue that we are now only at the Darwinian stage in psychology, and that the real psychological revolution is still a century or more in the future. I do not find this analogy appropriate, however.

To discover that we are not at the center of the universe, or that our remote ancestors lived in a tree, does indeed change our conception of man and society, but such new conceptions can have little effect on the way we behave in our daily affairs and in our institutional contexts. A new conception of man based on psychology, however, would have immediate implications for the most intimate details of our social and personal lives. This fact is unprecedented in any earlier stage of the Industrial Revolution.

The heart of the psychological revolution will be a new and scientifically based conception of man as an individual and as a social creature. When I say that the psychological revolution is already upon us, what I mean is that we have already begun to change man's self-conception. If we want to further that revolution, not only must we strengthen its scientific base, but we must also try to communicate it to our students and to the public. It is not the industrialist or the politician who should exploit it, but Everyman, everyday.

The enrichment of public psychology by scientific psychology constitutes the most direct and important application of our science to the promotion of human welfare. Instead of trying to forsee new psychological products that might disrupt our existing social arrangements, therefore, we should be self-consciously analyzing the general effect that our scientific psychology may have on popular psychology. As I try to perform this analysis for myself, I must confess that I am not altogether pleased with the results.

I would like now to consider briefly some of the effects we are having and where, in my view, our influence is leading at the present time. Let me begin with a thumbnail sketch of one major message that many scientific psychologists are trying to communicate to the public.

Control of Behavior

One of the most admired truisms of modern psychology is that some stimuli can serve to reinforce the behavior that produces them. The practical significance of this familiar principle arises from the implication that if you can control the occurrence of these reinforcing stimuli, then you can control . . . behavior. . . .

Regardless of whether we have actually achieved new scientific techniques of behavior control that are effective with human beings, and regardless of whether control is of any value in the absence of diagnosis and planning for its use, the simple fact that so many psychologists keep talking about control is having an effect on public psychology. The average citizen is predisposed to believe it. Control has been the practical payoff from the other sciences. Control must be what psychologists are after too. Moreover, since science is notoriously successful, behavior control must be inevitable. Thus the layman forms an impression that control is the name of the road we are travelling, and that the experts are simply quibbling about how far down that road we have managed to go.

Closely related to this emphasis on control is the frequently repeated claim that living organisms are nothing but machines. A scientist recognizes, of course, that this claim says far more about our rapidly evolving conception of machines than it says about living organisms, but this interpretation is usually lost when the message reaches public ears. The public idea of a machine is something like an automobile, a mechanical device controlled by its operator. If people are machines, they can be driven like automobiles. The analogy is absurd, of course, but it illustrates the kind of distortion that can occur.

. . . Personally, I believe there is a better way to advertise psychology and to relate it to social problems. Reinforcement is only one of many important ideas that we have to offer. Instead of repeating constantly that reinforcement leads to control, I would prefer to emphasize that reinforcement can lead to satisfaction and competence. And I would prefer to speak of understanding and prediction as our major scientific goals.

In the space remaining, therefore, I want to try to make the case that understanding and prediction are better goals for psychology than is control—better both for psychology and for the promotion of human welfare—because they lead us think, not in terms of coercion by a powerful elite, but in terms of the diagnosis of problems and the development of programs that can enrich the lives of every citizen.

Public Psychology: Two Paradigms

It should be obvious by now that I have somewhere in the back of my mind two alternative images of what the popular conception of human nature might become under the impact of scientific advances in psychology. One of these images is unfortunate, even threatening; the other is vaguer, but full of promise. Let me try to make these ideas more concrete.

The first image . . . has great appeal to an authoritarian mind, and fits well with our traditional competitive ideology based on coercion, punishment, and retribution. The fact that it represents a serious distortion of scientific psychology is exactly my point. In my opinion, we have made a mistake by trying to apply our ideas to social problems and to gain acceptance for our science within the framework of this ideology.

The second image rests on the same psychological foundation, but reflects it more accurately: it allows no compromise with our traditional social ideology. It is assumed, vaguely but optimistically, that this ideology can be modified so as to be more receptive to a truer conception of human nature. How this modification can be achieved is one of the problems we face; I believe it will not be achieved if we continue to advertise the control of behavior through reinforcement as our major contribution to the solution of social problems. I would not wish to give anyone the impression that I have formulated a well-defined social alternative, but I would at least like to open a discussion and make some suggestions.

My two images are not very different from what McGregor (1960) once called Theory X and Theory Y. Theory X is the traditional theory which holds that because people dislike work, they must be coerced, controlled, directed, and threatened with punishment before they will do it. People tolerate being directed, and many even prefer it, because they have little ambition and want to avoid responsibility. McGregor's alternative Theory Y, based on social science, holds that work is as natural as play or rest.

External control and threats are not the only means for inspiring people to work. People will exercise self-direction and self-control in the service of objectives to which they are committed; their commitment is a function of the rewards associated with the achievement of their objectives. People can learn not only to accept but to seek responsibility. Imagination, ingenuity, and creativity are widely distributed in the population, although these intellectual potentialities are poorly utilized under the conditions of modern industrial life.

McGregor's Theory X and Theory Y evolved in the context of his studies of industrial management. They are rival theories held by industrial managers about how best to achieve their institutional goals. A somewhat broader view is needed if we are to talk about public psychology generally, and not merely the managerial manifestations of public psychology. So let me amplify McGregor's distinction by referring to the ideas of Varela, a very remarkable engineer in Montevideo, Uruguay, who uses scientific psychology in the solution of a wide range of personal and social problems.

Varela [1970] contrasts two conceptions of the social nature of man. Following Kuhn's (1962) discussion of scientific revolutions, he refers to these two conceptions as "paradigms." The first paradigm is a set of assumptions on which our social institutions are presently based. The second is a contrasting paradigm based on psychological research. Let me outline them for you very briefly.

Our current social paradigm is characterized as follows: All men are created equal. Most behavior is motivated by economic competition, and conflict is inevitable. One truth underlies all controversy, and unreasonableness is best countered by facts and logic. When something goes wrong, someone is to blame, and every effort must be made to establish his guilt so that he can be punished. The guilty person is responsible for his own misbehavior and for his own rehabilitation. His teachers and supervisors are too busy to become experts in social science; their role is to devise solutions and see to it that their students or subordinates do what they are told.

For comparison, Varela offers a paradigm based on psychological research: There are large individual differences among people, both in ability and personality. Human motivation is complex and no one ever acts as he does for any single reason, but, in general, positive incentives are more effective than threats or punishments. Conflict is no more inevitable than disease and can be resolved or, still better, prevented. Time and resources for resolving social problems are strictly limited. When something goes wrong, how a person perceives the situation is more important to him than the "true facts," and he cannot reason about the situation until his irrational feelings have been toned down. Social problems are solved by correcting causes, not symptoms, and this can be done more effectively in groups than individually. Teachers and supervisors must be experts in social science because they are responsible for the cooperation and individual improvement of their students or subordinates.

No doubt other psychologists would draw the picture somewhat differently. Without reviewing the psychological evidence on which such generalizations are based, of course, I cannot argue their validity. But I think most of you will recognize the lines of research on which McGregor's Theory Y and Varela's second paradigm are based. Moreover, these psychologically based paradigms are incompatible in several respects with the prevailing ideology of our society.

Here, then, is the real challenge: How can we foster a social climate in which some such new public conception of man based on psychology can take root and flourish? In my opinion, this is the proper translation of our more familiar question about how psychology might contribute to the promotion of human welfare.

I cannot pretend to have an answer to this question, even in its translated form, but I believe that part of the answer is that psychology must be practiced by nonpsychologists. We are not physicians; the secrets of our trade need not be reserved for highly trained specialists. Psychological facts should be passed out freely to all who need and can use them. And from successful applications of psychological principles the public may gain a better appreciation for the power of the new conception of man that is emerging from our science.

If we take seriously the idea of a peaceful revolution based on a new conception of human nature, our scientific results will have to be instilled in the public consciousness in a practical and usable form so that what we know can be applied by ordinary people. There simply are not enough psychologists, even including nonprofessionals, to meet every need for psychological services. The people at large will have to be their own psychologists, and make their own applications of the principles that we establish.

Of course, everyone practices psychology, just as everyone who cooks is a chemist, everyone who reads a clock is an astronomer, everyone who drives is an engineer. I am not suggesting any radical departure when I say that nonpsychologists must practice psychology. I am simply proposing that we should teach them to practice it better, to make use self-consciously of what we believe to be scientifically valid principles.

Our responsibility is less to assume the role of experts and try to apply psychology ourselves than to give it away to the people who really need it—and that includes everyone. The practice of valid psychology by nonpsychologists will inevitably change people's conception of themselves and what they can do. When we have accomplished that, we will really have caused a psychological revolution.

How to Give Psychology Away

I am keenly aware that giving psychology away will be no simple task. In our society there are depths of resistance to psychological innovations that have to be experienced to be believed (Graziano, 1969).

Solving social problems is generally considered to be more difficult than solving scientific problems. A social problem usually involves many more independent variables, and it cannot be finally solved until society has been persuaded to adopt the solution. Many who have tried to introduce sound psychological practices into schools, clinics, hospitals, prisons, or industries have been forced to retreat in dismay. They complain, and with good reason, that they were unable to buck the "System," and often their reactions are more violent than sensible. The System, they say, refuses to change even when it does not work.

This experience has been so common that in my pessimistic moments I have been led to wonder whether anything less than complete reform is possible.

. . . One of the most basic ideas in all the social sciences is the concept of culture. Social anthropologists have developed a conception of culture as an organic whole, in which each particular value, practice, or assumption must be understood in the context of the total system. They tell terrible tales about the consequences of introducing Western reforms into aboriginal cultures without understanding the social equilibria that would be upset.

Perhaps cultural integrity is not limited to primitive cultures, but applies also to our own society here and now. If so, then our attempts at piecemeal innovation may be doomed either to fail or to be rejected outright.

I label these thoughts pessimistic because they imply a need for drastic changes throughout the whole system, changes that could only be imposed by someone with dangerous power over the lives of others. And that, I have argued, is not the way our psychological revolution should proceed.

In my more optimistic moments, however, I recognize that you do not need complete authority over a social organization in order to reform it. The important thing is not to control the system, but to understand it. Someone who has a valid conception of the system as a whole can often introduce relatively minor changes that have extensive consequences throughout the entire organization. Lacking such a conception, worthwhile innovations may be total failures.

. . . In my optimistic moments I am able to convince myself that understanding is attainable and that social science is already at a stage where successful applications are possible. Careful diagnosis and astute planning based on what we already know can often resolve problems that at first glance seemed insurmountable. Many social, clinical, and industrial psychologists have already demonstrated the power of diagnosis and planning based on sound psychological principles.

. . . There is no possibility of legislating the changes I have in mind. Passing laws that people must change their conceptions of themselves and others is precisely the opposite of what we need. Education would seem to be our only possibility. I do not mean only education in the schoolroom, although that is probably the best communication channel presently at our disposal. I have in mind a more ambitious program of educating the general public.

It is critically important to shape this education to fit the perceived needs of the people who receive it. Lectures suitable for graduate seminars are seldom suitable for laymen, and for a layman facing a concrete problem they are usually worse than useless. In order to get a factory supervisor or a ghetto mother involved, we must give them something they can use. Abstract theories, however elegant, or sensitivity training, however insightful, are too remote from the specific troubles they face. In order to get started, we must begin with people where they are, not assume we know where they should be. If a supervisor is having trouble with his men, perhaps we should teach him how to write a job description and how to evaluate the abilities and personalities of those who fill the job; perhaps we should teach him the art of persuasion, or the time and place for positive reinforcement. If a ghetto mother is not giving her children sufficient intellectual challenge, perhaps we should teach her how to encourage their motor, perceptual, and linguistic skills. The techniques involved are not some esoteric branch of witchcraft that must be reserved for those with PhD degrees in psychology. When the ideas are made sufficiently concrete and explicit, the scientific foundations of psychology can be grasped by sixth-grade children.

There are many obvious and useful suggestions that we could make and that nonpsychologists could exploit. Not every psychological problem in human engineering has to be solved by a professional psychologist; engineers can rapidly assimilate psychological facts and theories that are relevant to their own work. Not every teaching program has to be written by a learning theorist; principles governing the design and evaluation of programmed materials can be learned by content specialists. Not every personnel decision has to be made by a psychometrician; not every interview has to be conducted by a clinical psychologist; not every problem has to be solved by a cognitive psychologist; not every reinforcement has to be supervised by a student of conditioning. Psychological principles and techniques can be usefully applied by everyone. If our suggestions actually work, people should be eager to learn more. If they do not work, we should improve them. But we should not try to give people something whose value they cannot recognize, then complain when they do not return for a second meeting.

Consider the teaching of reading, for example. Here is an obviously appropriate area for the application of psychological principles. So what do we do? We assemble experts who decide what words children know, and in what order they should learn to read them; then we write stories with those words and teachers make the children read them, or we use them in programmed instruction that exploits the principles of reinforcement. But all too often the children fail to recognize the value of learning these carefully constructed lessons.

Personally, I have been much impressed with the approach of Ashton-Warner (1963), who begins by asking a child what words he wants. Mummy, daddy, kiss, frightened, ghost, their own names—these are the words children ask for, words that are bound up with their own loves and fears. She writes each child's word on a large, tough card and gives it to him. If a child wants words like police, butcher, knife, kill, jail, and bomb, he gets them. And he learns to read them almost immediately. It is *his* word, and each morning he retrieves his own words from the pile collected each night by the teacher. These are not dead words of an expert's choosing, but words that live in a child's own experience. Given this start, children begin to write, using their own words, and from there the teaching of reading follows naturally. Under this regimen a word is not an imposed task to be learned with reinforcements borrowed from some external source of motivation. Learning the word is itself reinforcing; it gives the child something he wants, a new way to cope with a desire or fear. Each child decides where he wants to start, and each child receives something whose value he can recognize.

Could we generalize this technique discovered by an inspired teacher in a small New Zealand school? In my own thinking I have linked it with something that White (1959) has called competence motivation. In order to tap this motivational system we must use psychology to give people skills that will satisfy their urge to feel more effective. Feeling effective is a very personal thing, for it must be a feeling of effectiveness in coping with personal problems in one's own life. From that beginning some might want to learn more about the science that helped them increase their competence, and then perhaps we could afford to be more abstract. But in the beginning we must try to diagnose and solve the problems people think they have, not the problems we experts think they ought to have, and we must learn to understand those problems in the social and institutional contexts that define them. With this approach we might do something practical for nurses, policemen, prison guards, salesmen—for people in many different walks of life. That, I believe, is what we should mean when we talk about applying psychology to the promotion of human welfare.

If you tell me that such a program is too ambitious or too foreign to our conception of ourselves as scientists and practitioners, I must agree that I do not know where to place our fulcrum to move the world. . . .

On the other hand, difficulty is no excuse for surrender. There is a sense in which the unattainable is the best goal to pursue. So let us continue our struggle to advance psychology as a means of promoting human welfare, each in our own way. For myself, however, I can imagine nothing we could do that would be more relevant to human welfare, and nothing that could pose a greater challenge to the next generation of psychologists, than to discover how best to give psychology away.

LINGERING QUESTIONS

Although Miller's paper did not set out to answer the points made by the radical critics whose voices were just beginning to be heard at the end of the decade, it is obvious that he had been listening to what they were saying. He seems to have paid particular heed to two issues they raised:

1. The allegation that psychology fosters a dehumanizing image of human beings.
2. The charge that psychology ignores the real-world setting within which human beings live their lives.

Both of these points are especially relevant to social psychology. As we proceed to explore in this Reader the ongoing dialogues and debates in social psychology, we will have occasion to see what different writers have to say about the potency of images and myths and about the way in which the social setting both liberates and constrains human behaviour and experience.

In the chapter that follows we continue to employ an historical perspective on the discipline but we focus on a single issue—the battle to desegregate American schools. This topic gives us a chance to see some of the complex problems that arise when the psychologist leaves the confines of the academic world and enters into the political arena. Whether the rhetoric of the radicals helps to clarify the moral, political, and methodological dilemmas posed by this case study is a moot point.

2

The Perilous Path: From Social Research to Social Intervention

It must be remembered that there is nothing more difficult to plan, more doubtful of success, nor more dangerous to manage than the creation of a new system. For the initiator has the enmity of all who would profit by the preservation of the old institution and merely lukewarm defenders in those who would gain by the new one.

(Machiavelli, *The Prince*, 1513)

In this chapter we focus on an example of what happens when the psychologist enters the political arena. In the process of looking at a particular example, the desegregation of American public schools, we seek to raise more general issues about the nature of evidence and about the way in which different psychologists interpret their professional role. We examine the difficulties associated with acting as expert advisor, and seek to show that intervention in social issues raises questions for professional psychologists about the limits of their "professionalism," the limits of their power and influence in the overall decision-making process, and the limits of their ability to determine the objectives or goals of their intervention.

MODELS FOR POLITICAL PSYCHOLOGY

We turn now to a detailed case study of the way in which social-psychological evidence may enter into public debates on social policy. What emerges from this analysis is a dramatic demonstration that any effort to frame social policy and legislation in the light of psychological "facts" is a controversial enterprise. This point is a central theme in Segall's book, *Human Behaviour and Public Policy* (1976). In analyzing what he calls "political psychology" (i.e., psychology

TABLE 2.1
Segall's Three Models for Political Psychology (1976)

Model One: The Psychologist as "Expert Witness"

The psychologist offers what he knows to those who are in a position to apply it. The ultimate choice of policy remains in the hands of the policy-maker/administrator. Example: psychologists giving evidence in court cases.

Model Two: The Psychologist as Policy Evaluator

The psychologist contributes his research tools to help policy-makers assess the effectiveness of their social programmes. Example: research on the impact of speeding laws, seat belts legislation, various forms of residential treatment, or school desegregation.

Model Three: The Psychologist as Social Engineer

The psychologist uses his expert knowledge of behaviour to devise ways of ensuring socially desirable behaviour. [Segall maintains that there are very few instances of *bona fide* psychological engineering.]

applied to social issues), Segall distinguishes three distinct ways in which psychologists may contribute to the design of social policies. These models are outlined in Table 2.1.

Segall notes that although these three models comprise complementary and overlapping approaches to political psychology they should also be thought of as independent alternatives. A detailed and critical look at this and other ways of classifying the roles of psychologists is the theme of our next chapter. Here we restrict ourselves to looking at what can happen when the psychologist acts as "expert witness."

In this, the simplest model, the psychologist merely offers what he knows to those who could apply it. If it is acknowledged merely that psychological facts ought to be brought to bear on policy dilemmas, then policy-makers, either elected officials or their appointed administrative agents, could be encouraged to seek interpretations of existing psychological facts from psychologists. The judgement as to the relevance of such facts and their implications for a particular policy dilemma would be exercised by the policy-makers themselves.

In the final analysis, however, the policy-maker has both the right and the responsibility to select from the testimony what he considers to be the most relevant arguments and to base his choice of policy on a combination of those arguments and whatever moral, ethical, or ideological values he considers pertinent. While this model advocates considerable input from the psychologist, an essential feature of the model is clearly that *the ultimate choice of policy remains in the hands of the policy-maker/administrator*. This model involves, then, no shift in power since society's usual agents remain free to use or reject whatever psychological information is made available to them. (Segall, 1976, pp. 18–19; emphasis added)

What characterizes this role is the fact that the psychologist who is called upon to testify, or who volunteers to make his expertise available, does so with the awareness that he will not cast the deciding vote, that his audience is free to accept or reject his testimony.

Although natural scientists are quite frequently called upon to give advice to government, it is not very common for psychologists or other social scientists (apart from economists) to be asked to serve as expert witnesses. The best documented and most controversial instance of social psychologists acting in this capacity was when a group of American psychologists in the 1950s gave testimony on the harmful psychological effects of school segregation.

SOCIAL PSYCHOLOGY AND DESEGREGATION

Segregation in American schools was given the backing of law following the 1896 Supreme Court decision (*Plessy v. Ferguson*), which ruled that racially segregated public facilities did not deprive individuals of the equal protection of the law guaranteed by the 14th Amendment as long as the separately provided arrangements were substantially "equal." This "separate-but-equal" doctrine acted as a legal precedent for school segregation until 1954. Under this doctrine 17 states and the District of Columbia either required or permitted segregated schools; in the early 1950s this practice affected eight million white and two and a half million black children (Cook, 1979, p. 422). In the early 1950s a series of cases were brought by individuals and by organizations to challenge the 1896 interpretation. Most of these cases appeared in the lower courts and the judges ruled against the plaintiffs (i.e., segregation was upheld). An appeal was made in 1954 (*Brown v. Board of Education*) to the Supreme Court, the highest court in the land, and this court "declared government-enforced separate education facilities for blacks and whites to be inherently unequal and thereby initiated the process of desegregation for the nation's public schools" (Cook, 1979, p. 420).

The testimony given by prominent social psychologists on the harmful effects of segregation, together with a statement signed by 32 social scientists, was part of the evidence taken into account by the Supreme Court in arriving at its conclusion. We look at how the psychologists presented their case, the ensuing reaction to their testimony, and consider whether, in retrospect, their testimony was valid and relevant.

Firstly, we present a brief synopsis of the lower court cases brought to challenge the practice of public school segregation. (For more details see Kluger, 1976, and Stephan, 1978.)

Case 1—Briggs v. Elliott (1951, State of South Carolina). The psychologists who testified were Kenneth Clark, David Krech and Helen Trager. Both Clark and Trager cited their own empirical studies to show that black children in segregated schools have low self-esteem and that segregation leads black children to be prejudiced toward whites.

In his evidence, Clark put forward the conclusion he had reached, namely: ". . . that discrimination, prejudice, and segregation have definitely detrimental effects on the personality development of the Negro child. The essence of this detrimental effect is a confusion in the child's concept of his own self-esteem, basic feelings of inferiority, conflict, confusion in his self-image, resentment, hostility towards himself, [and] hostility towards whites" (Kluger, 1976, as quoted by Stephan, 1978, p. 218). (See pages 37–48 for the original research by the Clarks.)

Similarly, Trager spoke of the harmful psychological effects of segregated schooling: "the Negro children, unlike white children, showed a tendency to expect rejection . . . A child who expects to be rejected, who sees his group held in low-esteem, is not going to function well, is not going to be a fully developed child . . . [If] we are to diminish the amount of hostility and fear that children of all groups have towards each other . . . [the place to do it] is the school" (Kluger, 1976, as quoted by Stephan, 1978, p. 219).

Although the court admitted the expert testimony of the psychologists, it ruled against the plaintiffs.

Case 2—Brown v. Board of Education (1951, State of Kansas). The two psychologists who appeared in court testified that segregation had negative effects on learning. This argument seems to have weighed heavily with the court: "Segregation of white and coloured children in public schools has a detrimental effect upon the coloured children. The impact is greater when it has the sanction of the law; for the policy of separating the races is usually interpreted as denoting the inferiority of the Negro group. A sense of inferiority affects the motivation of the child to learn. Segregation with the sanction of law, therefore, has a tendency to retard the education and mental development of Negro children and to deprive them of some of the benefits they would receive in a racially integrated school system" (Kluger, 1976, as quoted by Stephan, 1978, p. 219).

Yet, in spite of this summing up, the court ruled against the plaintiffs on the grounds that the facilities furnished to blacks and whites were equal in quality. In other words, the judges adopted a constitutional position and made their judgement on the basis of their interpretation of the Constitution and other legal precedents.

Case 3—Belton v. Gebhart and *Bulah v. Gebhart* (1952, 1953, State of Delaware).   In a case brought by the National Association for the Advancement of Colored People (N.A.A.C.P.) against two small school districts (where the separate physical facilities were demonstrably not equal), four eminent psychologists and one psychiatrist appeared as expert witnesses. Otto Klineberg, George Kelly, Jerome Bruner, Kenneth Clark, and Frederic Wertham all pointed to various adverse psychological effects of segregated schooling. The court in this case ruled that the black plaintiffs should be admitted to the white schools, but the decision was not based on the submission made by the psychologists, instead it derived from the fact that the schools for black children did not provide facilities that were equal to those in white schools.

Case 4—Davis v. County School Board (1952, 1954, State

of Virginia).   In this court proceeding, M. Brewster Smith, Isidor Chein, and Kenneth Clark were witnesses for the plaintiffs. As in previous cases their evidence stressed the fact that irrespective of the actual facilities available, segregation *per se* creates conditions which depress the individual's motivation to learn. The defence decided to mount a counter offence and brought in its own psychologist who maintained that provided facilities were equal, the black child was likely to get a better education in a separate school than in a mixed school.

Case 5—Brown v. District of Columbia (1954). Here the case against segregation was put solely on constitutional grounds. The court did not accept the arguments and segregation was upheld.

Dissatisfaction with the decisions reached by the lower courts resulted in an appeal being made to the Supreme Court. When the Supreme Court reviewed the earlier cases, it not only admitted the oral testimony of the psychologists who had appeared as expert witnesses for the black plaintiffs, but it also accepted an Appendix to the Appellants' Brief, written by Clark, Chein, and Cook, and signed by 32 leading social scientists. This was entitled "The Effects of Segregation and the Consequences of Desegregation." In the literature it is often referred to as the "Social Science Statement." This document was subsequently reprinted in the *Minnesota Law Review*, *37*, 6, 1953, pp. 427–439. What is somewhat confusing to anyone reading this material for the first time is that the 1953 publication appears under Floyd Allport's name. Despite the different names, dates, and titles under which it is cited, it is one and the same paper.

CONSEQUENCES OF SEGREGATION: THE EVIDENCE

We have seen how psychologists were prepared to act as expert witnesses in these court cases which were to have far-flung consequences. It was not merely a handful of psychologists who were prepared to take the stand and to sign a written statement. In 1948, Deutscher and Chein had conducted a survey of American social scientists which found that 90% of the sample studied felt that enforced segregation had "detrimental psychological effects on members of racial and religious groups which are segregated, even if equal facilities are provided" (p. 242). Futhermore, 83% of the respondents were of the opinion that enforced segregation has "a detrimental effect on the group that enforced segregation even if that group provides equal facilities to the groups that are segregated" (quoted by Stephan, 1978, pp. 218–219).

The question that we now want to pursue is: what type of empirical research and data convinced social scientists of the harmful effects of segregation? The single most widely-quoted piece of research was done by Kenneth and Mamie Clark. Kenneth Clark gave evidence in three court cases and, together with Chein and Cook, was one of the drafters of the Social Science Statement. The Clarks' research dated from the late 1930s and the report that is reprinted here was originally published in 1947. The indirect measure of racial identification and preference that the Clarks devised—the dolls test—was adopted by many other researchers in this field. When you read this paper you might ask yourself whether similar results would be obtained today if the study were replicated. It is also worth pondering whether the research did, in fact, demonstrate a relationship between school segregation and self-esteem. Look carefully at the findings, noting particularly the difference between Northern and Southern children and between younger and older children.

Reading II.   Racial Identification and Preferences in Negro Children, by K. B. Clark and M. P. Clark[*]

Problem

The specific problem of this study is an analysis of the genesis and

Source: *Readings in Social Psychology* (1958), edited by E. E. Maccoby, T. M. Newcomb and E. L. Hartley. New York: Holt, Rinehart & Winston.

[*]Condensed by the authors from an unpublished study made possible by a fellowship grant from the Julius Rosenwald Fund, 1940–1941.

RPSP–D

development of racial identification as a function of ego development and self-awareness in Negro children.

Race awareness, in a primary sense, is defined as a consciousness of the self as belonging to a specific group which is differentiated from other observable groups by obvious physical characteristics which are generally accepted as being racial characteristics.

Because the problem of racial identification is so definitely related to the problem of the genesis of racial attitudes in children, it was thought practicable to attempt to determine the racial attitudes or preferences of these Negro children—and to define more precisely, as far as possible, the developmental pattern of this relationship.

Procedure

This paper presents results from only one of several techniques devised and used by the authors to investigate the development of racial identification and preferences in Negro children.[1] Results presented here are from the Dolls Test.

Dolls Test. The subjects were presented with four dolls, identical in every respect save skin color. Two of these dolls were brown with black hair and two were white with yellow hair. In the experimental situation these dolls were unclothed except for white diapers. The position of the head, hands, and legs on all the dolls was the same. For half of the subjects the dolls were presented in the order: white, colored, white, colored. For the other half the order of presentation was reversed. In the experimental situation the subjects were asked to respond to the following requests by choosing *one* of the dolls and giving it to the experimenter:

1. Give me the doll that you like to play with—(*a*) like best.
2. Give me the doll that is a nice doll.
3. Give me the doll that looks bad.
4. Give me the doll that is a nice color.
5. Give me the doll that looks like a white child.
6. Give me the doll that looks like a colored child.
7. Give me the doll that looks like a Negro child.
8. Give me the doll that looks like you.

Requests 1 through 4 were designed to reveal preferences; requests 5 through 7 to indicate a knowledge of "racial differences"; and request 8 to show self-identification.

It was found necessary to present the preference requests first in the experimental situation because in a preliminary investigation it was clear

---

[1]Other techniques presented in the larger study include: (1) a coloring test; (2) a questionnaire; and (3) a modification of the Horowitz line drawing technique (Horowitz, 1939).

that the children who had already identified themselves with the colored doll had a marked tendency to indicate a preference for this doll and this was not necessarily a genuine expression of actual preference, but a reflection of ego involvement. This potential distortion of the data was controlled by merely asking the children to indicate their preferences first and then to make identifications with one of the dolls.

Subjects

Two hundred fifty-three Negro children formed the subjects of this experiment. One hundred thirty-four of these subjects (southern group) were tested in segregated nursery schools and public schools in Hot Springs, Pine Bluff, and Little Rock, Arkansas. These children had had no experience in racially mixed school situations. One hundred nineteen subjects (northern group) were tested in the racially mixed nursery and public schools of Springfield, Massachusetts. [See Table 2.2.]

All subjects were tested individually in a schoolroom or office especially provided for this purpose. Except for a few children who showed generalized negativism from the beginning of the experiment (results for these children are not included here), there was adequate rapport between the experimenter and all subjects tested. In general, the children showed high interest in and enthusiasm for the test materials and testing situation. The children, for the most part, considered the experiment somewhat of a game.

Results

Racial Identification. Although the questions on knowledge of "racial differences" and self-identification followed those designed to determine racial preference in the actual experimental situation, it appears more meaningful to discuss the results in the following order: knowledge of "racial differences," racial self-identification, and finally racial preferences.

The results of the responses to requests 5, 6, and 7, which were asked to determine the subjects' knowledge of racial differences, may be seen in Table 2.3. Ninety-four percent of these children chose the white doll when asked to give the experimenter the white doll; 93 percent of them chose the brown doll when asked to give the colored doll; and 72 percent chose the brown doll when asked to give the Negro doll. These results indicate a clearly established knowledge of a "racial difference" in these subjects—and some awareness of the relation between the physical characteristic of skin color and the racial concepts of "white" and "colored." Knowledge of the concept of "Negro" is not so well developed as the more concrete verbal concepts of "white" and "colored" as applied

TABLE 2.2

Age Distribution of Subjects

Age, years	North	South	Total
3	13	18	31
4	10	19	29
5	34	12	46
6	33	39	72
7	29	46	75
Total	119	134	253

Sex Distribution of Subjects

Sex	North	South	Total
Male	53	63	116
Female	66	71	137

Skin Color of Subjects

Skin color	North	South	Total
Light[a]	33	13	46
Medium[b]	58	70	128
Dark[c]	28	51	79

[a]light (practically white)
[b]medium (light brown to dark brown)
[c]dark (dark brown to black)

to racial differences.

The question arises as to whether choice of the brown doll or of the white doll, particularly in response to questions 5 and 6, really reveals a knowledge of "racial differences" or simply indicates a learned perceptual reaction to the concepts of "colored" and "white." Our evidence that the responses of these children *do* indicate a knowledge of "racial difference" comes from several sources: the results from other techniques used (i.e., a coloring test and a questionnaire) and from the qualitative data obtained (children's spontaneous remarks) strongly support a knowledge of "racial differences." Moreover, the consistency of results for requests 5 through 8 also tends to support the fact that these children are actually making identifications in a "racial" sense.

The responses to request 8, designed to determine racial self-identification follow the following pattern: 66 percent of the total

TABLE 2.3
Choices of Subjects

	Request 5 (For White)		Request 6 (For Colored)		Request 7 (For Negro)		Request 8 (For You)	
Choice	No.	Percent	No.	Percent	No.	Percent	No.	Percent
Colored doll	13	5	235	93	182	72	166	66
White doll	237	94	15	6	50	20	85	33
Don't know or no response	3	1	3	1	21	8	2	1

group of children identified themselves with the colored doll, while 33 percent identified themselves with the white doll. The critical ratio of this difference is 7.6.[2]

Comparing the results of request 8 (racial self-identification) with those of requests 5, 6, and 7 (knowledge of racial difference) it is seen that the awareness of racial differences does not necessarily determine a socially accurate racial self-identification—since approximately nine out of ten of these children are aware of racial differences as indicated by their correct choice of a "white" and "colored" doll on request, and only a little more than six out of ten make socially correct identifications with the colored doll.

Age Differences. Table 2.4 shows that, when the responses to requests 5 and 6 are observed together, these subjects at each age level have a well-developed knowledge of the concept of racial difference between "white" and "colored" as this is indicated by the characteristic of skin color. These data definitely indicate that a basic knowledge of "racial differences" exists as a part of the pattern of ideas of Negro children from the age of three through seven years in the northern and southern communities tested in this study—and that this knowledge develops more definitely from year to year to the point of absolute stability at the age of seven.

A comparison of the results of requests 5 and 6 with those of request 7, which required the child to indicate the doll which looks like a "Negro" child, shows that knowledge of a racial difference in terms of the word "Negro" does not exist with the same degree of definiteness as it does in terms of the more basic designations of "white" and "colored." It is significant, however, that knowledge of a difference in terms of the word "Negro" makes a sharp increase from the five- to the six-year level and a less accelerated one between the six- and seven-year levels. The fact that

---

[2]These results are supported by similar ones from the Horowitz line drawing technique.

TABLE 2.4
Choices of Subjects at Each Age Level*

Choice	3 yr.		4 yr.		5 yr.		6 yr.		7 yr.	
	No.	Per-cent	No.	Per-cent	No.	Per-cent	No.	Per-cent	No.	Per-cent
Request 5 (for white)										
colored doll	4	13	4	14	3	7	2	3	0	
white doll	24	77	25	86	43	94	70	97	75	100
Request 6 (for colored)										
colored doll	24	77	24	83	43	94	69	96	75	100
white doll	4	13	5	17	3	7	3	4	0	
Request 7 (for Negro)										
colored doll	17	55	17	59	28	61	56	78	64	85
white doll	9	29	10	35	14	30	12	17	5	7
Request 8 (for you)										
colored doll	11	36	19	66	22	48	49	68	65	87
white doll	19	61	9	31	24	52	23	32	10	13

*Individuals failing to make either choice not included, hence some percentages add to less than 100.

all of the six-year-olds used in this investigation were enrolled in the public schools seems to be related to this spurt. Since it seems clear that the term "Negro" is a more verbalized designation of "racial differences," it is reasonable to assume that attendance at public schools facilitates the development of this verbalization of the race concept held by these children.

In response to request 8 there is a general and marked increase in the percent of subjects who identify with the colored doll with an increase in age—with the exception of the four- to five-year groups.[3] This deviation of the five-year-olds from the general trend is considered in detail in the larger, yet unpublished study.

Identification by Skin Color. Table 2.5 shows slight and statistically insignificant differences among the three skin-color groups in their responses which indicate a knowledge of the "racial difference" between the white and colored doll (requests 5 through 7).

It should be noted, however, that the dark group is consistently more

---

[3]These results are supported by those from the use of the Horowitz line drawing technique

TABLE 2.5
Choices of Subjects in Light, Medium, and Dark Groups*

	Light		Medium		Dark	
Choice	No.	Percent	No.	Percent	No.	Percent
Request 5						
(for white)						
colored doll	2	5	8	6	3	4
white doll	43	94	118	92	76	96
Request 6						
(for colored)						
colored doll	41	89	118	92	76	96
white doll	4	9	8	6	3	4
Request 7						
(for Negro)						
colored doll	32	70	91	71	59	75
white doll	9	20	27	21	14	18
Request 8						
(for you)						
colored doll	9	20	93	73	64	81
white doll	37	80	33	26	15	19

*Individuals failing to make either choice not included, hence some percentages add to less than 100.

accurate in its choice of the appropriate doll than either the light or the medium group on requests 5 through 7. This would seem to indicate that the dark group is slightly more definite in its knowledge of racial differences and that this definiteness extends even to the higher level of verbalization inherent in the use of the term "Negro" as a racial designation. In this regard it is seen that 75 percent of the dark children chose the colored doll when asked for the doll which "looks like a Negro child" while only 70 percent of the light children and 71 percent of the medium children made this response. The trend of results for requests 5 and 6 remains substantially the same.

These results suggest further that correct racial identification of these Negro children at these ages is to a large extent determined by the concrete fact of their own skin color, and further that this racial identification is not necessarily dependent upon the expressed knowledge of a racial difference as indicated by the correct use of the words "white," "colored," or "Negro" when responding to white and colored dolls. This conclusion seems warranted in the light of the fact that those children who differed in skin color from light through medium to dark were practically similar in the pattern of their responses which indicated awareness of racial differences but differed markedly in their racial identification (responses to request 8 for the doll "that looks like you"); only 20 percent of the light children,

TABLE 2.6

Choices of Subjects in Northern (Mixed Schools) and Southern
(Segregated Schools) Groups*

Choice	North, percent	South, percent
Request 5 (for white)		
colored doll	4	6
white doll	94	93
Request 6 (for colored)		
colored doll	92	94
white doll	7	5
Request 7 (for Negro)		
colored doll	74	70
white doll	20	19
Request 8 (for you)		
colored doll	61	69
white doll	39	29

*Individuals failing to make either choice not included, hence some
percentages add to less than 100.

while 73 percent of the medium children, and 81 percent of the dark
children identified themselves with the colored doll.

It is seen that there is a consistent increase in choice of the colored doll
from the light to the medium group; an increase from the medium group to
the dark group; and, a striking increase in the choices of the colored doll by
the dark group as compared to the light group.[4] All differences, except
between the medium and dark groups, are statistically significant.

Again, as in previous work [Clark and Clark, 1939a, 1939b, 1940], it is
shown that the percentage of the medium groups' identifications with the
white or the colored representation resembles more that of the dark group
and differs from the light group. Upon the basis of these results, therefore,
one may assume that factors and dynamics involved in racial identification
are substantially the same for the dark and medium children, in contrast to
dynamics for the light children.

North-South Differences. The results presented in Table 2.6 indicate
that there are no significant quantitative differences between the northern
and southern Negro children tested (children in mixed schools and children
in segregated schools) in their knowledge of racial differences.

While none of these differences is statistically reliable, it is significant
that northern children know as well as southern children which doll is
supposed to represent a white child and which doll is supposed to represent
a colored child. However, the northern children make fewer identifications

[4]These results substantiate and clearly focus the trend observed through the use of the
Horowitz line drawing technique.

with the colored doll and more identifications with the white doll than do the southern children. One factor accounting for this difference may be the fact that in this sample there are many more light colored children in the North (33) than there are in the South (13). Since this difference in self-identification is not statistically significant, it may be stated that the children in the northern mixed-school situation do not differ from children in the southern segregated schools in either their knowledge of racial differences or their racial identification. A more qualitative analysis will be presented elsewhere.

Racial Preferences. It is clear from Table 2.7 that the majority of these Negro children prefer the *white* doll and reject the colored doll.

Approximately two thirds of the subjects indicated by their responses to requests 1 and 2 that they like the white doll "best," or that they would like to play with the white doll in preference to the colored doll, and that the white doll is a "nice doll."

Their responses to request 3 show that this preference for the white doll implies a concomitant negative attitude toward the brown doll. Fifty-nine percent of these children indicated that the colored doll "looks bad," while only 17 percent stated that the white doll "looks bad" (critical ratio 10.9). That this preference and negation in some way involve skin color is indicated by the results for request 4. Only 38 percent of the children thought that the brown doll was a "nice color," while 60 percent of them thought that the white doll was a "nice color" (critical ratio 5.0).

The importance of these results for an understanding of the origin and development of racial concepts and attitudes in Negro children cannot be minimized. Of equal significance are their implications, in the light of the results of racial identification already presented, for racial mental hygiene.

Age Differences. Table 2.8 shows that at each age from three through seven years the majority of these children prefer the white doll and reject the brown doll. This tendency to prefer the white doll is not as stable (not statistically reliable) in the three-year-olds as it is in the four- and

TABLE 2.7
Choices of All Subjects

Choice	Request 1 (Play With)		Request 2 (Nice Doll)		Request 3 (Looks Bad)		Request 4 (Nice Color)	
	No.	*Percent*	*No.*	*Percent*	*No.*	*Percent*	*No.*	*Percent*
Colored doll	83	32	97	38	149	59	96	38
White doll	169	67	150	59	42	17	151	60
Don't know or no response	1	1	6	3	62	24	6	2

TABLE 2.8
Choices of Subjects at Each Age Level*

Choice	3 yr.		4 yr.		5 yr.		6 yr.		7 yr.	
	No.	Per-cent	No.	Per-cent	No.	Per-cent	No.	Per-cent	No.	Per-cent
Request 1 (play with)										
colored doll	13	42	7	24	12	26	21	29	30	40
white doll	17	55	22	76	34	74	51	71	45	60
Request 2 (nice doll)										
colored doll	11	36	7	24	13	28	33	46	33	44
white doll	18	58	22	76	33	72	38	53	39	52
Request 3 (looks bad)										
colored doll	21	68	15	52	36	78	45	63	32	43
white doll	6	19	7	24	5	11	11	15	13	17
Request 4 (nice color)										
colored doll	12	39	8	28	9	20	31	43	36	48
white doll	18	58	21	72	36	78	40	56	36	48

*Individuals failing to make either choice not included, hence some percentages add to less than 100.

five-year-olds. On the other hand, however, the tendency of the three-year-olds to negate the brown doll ("looks bad") is established as a statistically significant fact (critical ratio 4.5).

Analyzing the results of requests 1 and 2 together, it is seen that there is a marked *increase* in preference for the white doll from the three- to the four-year level; a more gradual *decrease* in this preference from the four- to the five-year level; a further decrease from the five- to the six-year level; and a continued decrease from the six- to the seven-year level. These results suggest that although the majority of Negro children at each age prefer the white doll to the brown doll, this preference decreases gradually from four through seven years.

Skin color preferences of these children follow a somewhat different pattern of development. The results of request 4 show that while the majority of children at each age below 7 years prefer the skin color of the white doll, this preference increases from three through five years and decreases from five through seven years. It is of interest to point out that only at the seven-year level do the same number of children indicate a preference for the skin color of the colored doll as for that of the white doll.

The majority of these children at each age level indicate that the brown doll, rather than the white doll, "looks bad." This result shows positively the negation of the colored doll which was implicit in the expressed preference for the white doll discussed above.

The evaluative rejection of the brown doll is statistically significant, even at the three-year level, and is pronounced at the five-year level. The indicated preference for the white doll is statistically significant from the four-year level up to the seven-year level.

It seems justifiable to assume from these results that the crucial period in the formation and patterning of racial attitudes begins at around four and five years. At these ages these subjects appear to be reacting more uncritically in a definite structuring of attitudes which conforms with the accepted racial values and mores of the larger environment.

Preferences and Skin Color. Results presented in Table 2.9 reveal that there is a tendency for the majority of these children, in spite of their own skin color, to prefer the white doll and to negate the brown doll. This tendency is most pronounced in the children of light skin color and least so in the dark children. A more intensive analysis of these results appears in a larger, yet unpublished study.

North-South Differences. From Table 2.10 it is clear that the southern children in segregated schools are less pronounced in their preference for the white doll, compared to the northern children's definite preference for this doll. Although still in a minority, a higher percentage of southern children, compared to northern, prefer to play with the colored doll or think that it is a "nice" doll. The critical ratio of this difference is not significant for request 1 but approaches significance for request 2 (2.75).

TABLE 2.9
Choices of Subjects in Light, Medium, and Dark Groups*

Choice	Light No.	Light Percent	Medium No.	Medium Percent	Dark No.	Dark Percent
Request 1 (play with)						
colored doll	11	24	41	32	31	39
white doll	35	76	86	67	48	61
Request 2 (nice doll)						
colored doll	15	33	50	39	32	40
white doll	31	67	72	56	47	60
Request 3 (looks bad)						
colored doll	31	67	73	57	45	57
white doll	6	13	22	17	14	18
Request 4 (nice color)						
colored doll	13	28	56	44	27	34
white doll	32	70	68	53	51	65

*Individuals failing to make either choice not included, hence some percentages add to less than 100.

TABLE 2.10
Choices of Subjects in Northern (Mixed Schools) and Southern
(Segregated Schools) Groups (Requests 1 Through 4)*

Choice	North, percent	South, percent
Request 1 (play with)		
colored doll	28	37
white doll	72	62
Request 2 (nice doll)		
colored doll	30	46
white doll	68	52
Request 3 (looks bad)		
colored doll	71	49
white doll	17	16
Request 4 (nice color)		
colored doll	37	40
white doll	63	57

*Individuals failing to make either choice not included, hence some percentages add to less than 100.

A POSTSCRIPT BY THE RESEARCHERS

There was an interval of a decade between the time the Clarks did their research and the time the court cases were heard. When Kenneth Clark reflected on his studies some 24 years later, he emphasized that he had not set out to influence social policy:

It may be of some value to point out that the earlier studies of the development of self-identification and evaluation in children with Mamie Clark were not motivated by or conducted with any direct concern for their applied or policy implications and consequences. The fact that the United States Supreme Court ... cited these findings ... was a gratifying illustration of the possibility that ... what is called "pure" research can sometimes have some direct social policy and applied social change effects. (Clark, 1971, p. 1049)

THE REACTION TO THE TESTIMONY

From the outset there was much public debate as to the status of the social psychologists' testimony and its relevance to the court case. (A lucid account of the legal concerns and misgivings about the admitting of social science evidence into the proceedings is to be found in Garfinkel, 1959.) Opinion has also been divided as to how much weight the Supreme Court judges actually attached to the social scientists' oral testimony and to their written statement.

Looking back, it seems reasonable to suggest that while the evidence presented by social psychologists contributed to the final decision, it was by no means the sole determiner of that decision. At the end of the day, the "finding" was that of the court; the "authority" of the social science was called upon to support the findings of the Justices, not vice versa (Garfinkel, 1959, p. 114).

Some critics, particularly in the South, accused the court of acting unconstitutionally in basing its decision on social science rather than on strict legal criteria. The social scientists who testified found themselves being branded as "commies" and "foreigners." Even amongst those commentators who supported the court's decision, there were doubts as to the advisability of admitting the oral testimony of social scientists as expert witnesses. Responsible legal theorists directed substantial criticisms against the validity of the social scientists' testimony. One objection that was raised to the introduction of social psychological findings was that it created a serious threat to ongoing efforts to extend the boundaries of equal protection. Garfinkel (1959) summarized this argument in the following way:

By assuming it is necessary to show that the inequality in school segregation is psychologically harmful, civil rights proponents have, unwittingly, weakened the protection afforded by the Constitution. Advocates of racial segregation, since the 1954 decision, have argued that there is personality damage to *white* children forced to mix with persons they consider obnoxious. The court, by entertaining the psychological argument in support of its decision, opened the way for this sort of rebuttal . . . inequality is constitutionally proscribed whether it is harmful or not. The decision, therefore, must be based on constitutional grounds and not on social science. (Garfinkel, 1959, p. 98)

But, as Garfinkel goes on to demonstrate, there are a number of flaws in this way of posing the issues.

. . . the argument that showing psychological harm to the children is dangerous and irrelevant misses the main legal point which the N.A.A.C.P. [National Association for the Advancement of Colored People] lawyers sought to establish with this line of evidence. It was necessary to show that an equal education cannot be obtained in segregated public schools even on an elementary level where all facilities, teachers, and curricular elements are presumed equal. . . . Marshall [the N.A.A.C.P. lawyer] sought to convince the court . . . that children on lower educational levels . . . were unable to get an equal education even if the tangible facilities were equal. To do this, he called expert witnesses and referred to a scientific literature which might establish the fact that the children actually did suffer in their personality development, *and that this impaired their ability to learn.* That is, the educational purposes of the state statutes establishing segregated elementary schools could not be of equal benefit to the two groups. (Garfinkel, 1959, p. 99)

Garfinkel's assessment of the context in which expert testimony was produced led him to conclude that "in principle their testimony is relevant and worthy of judicial examination." It is, he points out, an entirely separate matter as to whether the psychologists who have studied the problems have successfully established the harmful effects of segregation as scientifically proven fact.

Another point worth considering with regard to this study of the psychologist acting as expert witness (because it has general relevance to the whole set of questions raised by the radical critics of the late 1960s and early 1970s), is whether the psychologists who gave evidence were confusing matters of value with matters of fact. If one takes the position that the scientific method is appropriate only to questions of fact, then one might argue that the social psychologists were offering value judgements masquerading as facts.

The 32 social scientists who submitted an appendix to the appellants' brief were aware of this potential criticism and sought to distinguish between the factual and value aspects of the problem.

There are, of course, moral and legal issues involved with respect to which the signers of the present statement cannot speak with any special authority and which must be taken into account in the solution of the problem. There are, however, also factual issues involved with respect to which certain conclusions seem to be justified on the basis of the available scientific evidence. It is with these issues only that this paper is concerned. (Allport, 1953, p. 427)

A very useful insight on this difficult problem is offered by Garfinkel (1959) who points out that the valuation which the psychologists made regarding segregation was not derived from their research, but rather it was supplied by the American Constitution. "The 'equal protection of the laws' clause provides the preference for equality; *the scientific question* is whether a given condition, within which individuals are expected to learn, is likely to prove disadvantageous to some compared with persons not so conditioned" (p. 102).

It is one thing to establish, as Garfinkel did, the legal relevance of the social psychologists' scientific, expert opinion. It is quite a separate matter to show that the asserted opinion is supported by the canons of science itself. More recent reassessments of the psychologists' contribution to the legal dispute over segregation have tended to focus on the latter issue.

DID PSYCHOLOGISTS MISLEAD
THE SUPREME COURT?

When Garfinkel reviewed the social science evidence on school segregation in 1959, he noted that one fundamental weakness was that broad generalizations were based on meagre research. In particular, he commented on the limitations of the Clarks' data. According to Garfinkel, there is no sense in which their evidence demonstrates a causal connection between low self-esteem and school segregation. This point was picked up in the cross-examination of Clark in the South Carolina court case. Prior to coming to court, Clark had used his doll test with a group of 16 children, aged between 6 and 9, who were plaintiff parties to the case. His findings with this group were the same as those reported in his paper. Ten of the children "liked" the white doll "best" and 11 chose the brown doll as the doll which looked "bad."

The exchange between Clark and the counsel for the defence in the South Carolina case was as follows:

Q. And then you say you were forced to the conclusion after talking to these children, that they had suffered harm by attending the Scott's Branch School?

A.   I was forced to the conclusion that they had definite disturbances and problems of their own self-esteem; that they had feelings of inferiority that related to race.

Q.   Because they had attended the Scott's Branch School?

A.   No, because they perceived themselves in an inferior status—generally inferior.

Q.   Well, the Scott's Branch School had nothing to do with it?

A.   Well. I wouldn't say that Counsellor.

Q.   Well, what would you say?

A.   Well, I would say it would definitely.

Q.   And why?

A.   Because of some information which I got from the children between the ages of 12 and 17. As you can see, this method is not as sensitive for older children as it would be for younger children. So, it became apparent to me as I talked to the older children that I could get similar data by a different method, namely the interviewer method.

Q.   And you refer to that as the interview method?

A.   The interview method.

Q.   That means you ask them questions?

A.   That's right.

Q.   And they give you answers?

A.   That's right.

(Garfinkel, 1959, pp. 111–112)

What this transcript indicates is that Clark lacked evidence to systematically connect the broad effects of discrimination on personality to the school segregation in these cases. (This is not to say, however, that he was wrong, simply that he was not in a position to demonstrate that the reason why these children tended to select the white doll in preference to the black doll or why they had low self-esteem was *because* they were forced to attend a segregated school.)

A more serious analytical problem arises when we study the Clarks' data. Garfinkel points to two rather puzzling points which the Clarks rather glossed over.

1. Preference for the white doll compared to the brown doll *decreases* gradually from 4 through 7 years, which is when children are starting school.

2. Black children in Northern non-segregated schools showed a *more* pronounced preference for the white doll than the Northern children who attended segregated schools.

Let us turn now to more recent appraisals of the theoretical model and the evidence. By the late 1970s there was an extensive literature which looked at the impact of desegregation. A number of reviewers have juxtaposed the original hypotheses implicit in the Social Science Statement with the picture which had emerged from actual studies of school desegregation. Stephan's paper (1978) is an example of one such thorough review of the literature; like others he arrived at the conclusion that social scientists in the early 1950s may have pinned too much hope on education as a panacea for more fundamental social injustices.

The following extract from Stephan (1978) provides an analysis of the famous "Social Science Statement" and its underlying premises.

The brief began by presenting arguments concerning the effects of segregation on minority group children:

Segregation, prejudices and discriminations, and their social concomitants potentially damage the personality of all children. . . . Minority group children learn the inferior status to which they are assigned . . . they often react with feelings of inferiority and a sense of personal humiliation. . . . Under these conditions, the minority group child is thrown into a conflict with regard to his feelings about himself and his group. He wonders whether his group, and he himself are worthy of no more respect than they receive. This conflict and confusion leads to self-hatred. . . .

Some children, usually of the lower socio-economic classes, may react by overt aggressions and hostility directed towards their own group or members of the dominant group. (Allport, 1953, pp. 429–430).

The brief then discussed the effects of segregation on the majority group. . . . (It) ended with a discussion of the effects of desegregation:

Under certain circumstances desegregation . . . has been observed to lead to the emergence of more favourable attitudes and friendlier relations between races. . . . There is less likelihood of unfriendly relations when change is simultaneously introduced into all units of a social institution . . . and when there is consistent and firm enforcement of the new policy by those in authority. . . . These conditions can generally be satisfied in . . . public schools. (Allport, 1953, pp. 437–438)

The social science brief was concerned primarily with prejudice and self-esteem, but it is clear from the testimony of the social scientists in the individual trials that they believed that self-esteem and prejudice affected the school achievement of minority students. These three variables were perceived to be interrelated in a vicious circle. White prejudice was regarded as the cause of segregation, and segregation led to low self-esteem among blacks. This in turn affected the black students' motivation to learn, as well as their achievement. Low self-esteem and frustration over low achievement were then turned outward in the form of prejudice toward whites. The low self-esteem and low achievement of blacks and their antipathy toward whites reinforced white prejudice and the circle was complete (see Fig. 2.1).

It was reasoned that desegregation would break this vicious circle by denying an institutionalized sanction for white prejudice. If the behaviour of whites was changed, their attitudes should change to be consistent with their behaviour. Further, in desegregated schools the self-esteem of blacks should increase because they would no longer be stamped with the badge of inferiority represented by segregation. It was expected that these increases in self-esteem would be associated with increased achievement and reduced prejudice toward whites. The improved facilities in desegregated schools and the opportunity to interact with white students should also contribute to improvements in black achievement. Intergroup contact in desegregated schools was expected to reduce the prejudices of both groups.

There are a number of testable hypotheses concerning the effects of desegregation that follow from this model:

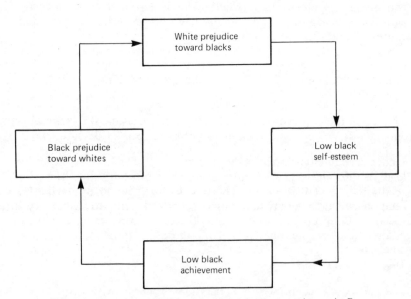

FIG. 2.1 Causal model derived from social science testimony in *Brown v. Board of Education*.

1. For whites, desegregation will lead to more positive attitudes toward blacks.
2. For blacks, desegregation will lead to more positive attitudes toward whites.
3. For blacks, desegregation will lead to increased self-esteem.
4. For blacks, desegregation will lead to increases in achievement.

(Stephan, 1978, pp. 220–221)

Many reviews of the studies that have been done on desegregation have reported a lack of fit between research on self-esteem, prejudice, and school achievement and the hypotheses implicit in the "Social Science Statement," leading to the pessimistic conclusion that school desegregation had not achieved the desired or predicted results. Indeed, in some studies it looked as though desegregation might have had *negative* effects on black school children's self-esteem and achievement. However, Stephan (1978) does acknowledge that the underlying model used by the social psychologists had not been subjected to a fair test because the conditions outlined in the model as essential preconditions for increases in black self-esteem and achievement and for decreases in black prejudice have often not been fulfilled. In other words, one could argue that for the framers of the Social Science Statement desegregation was taken to be a necessary but not a sufficient factor in the struggle to bring about a more just society.

This is the way in which Cook, one of the three framers of the Social Science Statement, argued 25 years after the historic Supreme Court decision. In 1979 he wrote a soul-searching article in which he reappraised the soundness of the information provided to the Supreme Court in the Social Science Statement, in the light of the research that had been done in the intervening years. From his reading of the literature, a complicated picture emerges. Some hypotheses have received overwhelming empirical support (e.g., white children's academic achievement has not suffered through desegregation), while for other hypotheses the findings are inconsistent. Cook's key point is that many of the predictions still cannot be evaluated because of the contradictory nature of the research findings, the difficulties of interpreting some of the evidence, and the fact that many of the necessary preconditions for successful desegregation have not been met.

He maintains that there has been a tendency for those undertaking empirical research to misinterpret or oversimplify what he and other social scientists of the 1950s said. According to Cook, he and his contemporaries did *not* believe that desegregation *in itself* would produce the desired results (i.e., a decrease in prejudice, an increase in black self-esteem and higher academic achievement amongst black school-children).

While it was suggested that these [positive] outcomes might be anticipated, it was noted that "much depends, however, on the circumstances under which members of previously segregated groups first come in contact with others in unsegregated situations." The following circumstances were enumerated: (1) simultaneous desegregation in all comparable units of a system; (2) firm and consistent endorsement by those in authority; (3) the absence of competition among representatives from the different racial groups; (4) the equivalence of positions and functions among all participants in the desegregated setting; (5) interracial contacts of the type that permit learning about one another as individuals. (Cook, 1979, p. 423)

Furthermore, Cook quite rightly reminds us that he and the others who testified were using their expert knowledge to suggest how to *prevent* certain undesirable outcomes from occurring; they did not tackle the problem of how to *remedy* the harm that had already occurred. Hence, logically speaking, evaluative studies should focus on children brought up in a world where segregated schools were a thing of the past. However, in actual fact, most studies have looked at children who began their school careers in segregated schools. Also, Cook draws attention to the time-scale of many of the studies. If we start from the premise that the relationship between self-esteem and school achievement may take some time to change, then it is necessary to carry out long-term studies. Most research has only measured short-term outcomes. After completing his look at the empirical findings on desegregation, Cook concludes thus:

This reassessment of the 1954 Social Science Statement in the light of subsequent research reveals little to indicate that the Statement misled the Supreme Court either as to the consequences of government-endorsed segregation or the constructive potential of desegregation. That only a small fraction of this potential has been realized is a tragic consequence of the manner in which school desegregation has all too often been carried out. (1979, p. 431)

Most of Cook's points, particularly with regard to the methodological aspects of the research studies monitoring desegregation and the caution of those who gave testimony in not overstating their case, are convincing. However, on a number of issues he seems to equivocate, giving the reader the unfortunate impression that he finds it necessary to defend the Social Science Statement in its entirety. A specific instance where he resorts to dubious logic to explain research findings that are at variance with the predictions he had endorsed is his examination of the latest research on black self-esteem in desegregated schools. Quite a number of studies report *decreases* in aspirations and self-esteem under desegregation. Such findings pose a real problem for the thinking behind the Social Science Statement. Although it may make sense to argue that self-esteem may not necessarily show an immediate improvement once desegregation has been achieved, or, indeed, that for those children who have spent many years in segregated schools before transferring to desegregated classrooms there may never be an appreciable change in self-esteem may be interpreted as a beneficial outcome! for an actual *decline* in self-esteem after desegregation. Cook tries to deal with such evidence by pointing out that some psychologists think that perhaps black children have unduly high aspiration levels and so any observed reduction in self-esteem may be interpreted as a beneficial outcome! Although Cook goes on to point out that such *ad hoc* explanations lead to whole new controversies, the very fact that he entertains such a hypothesis suggests an extreme reluctance to modify or rethink his own position.

When psychologists become involved in issues that are of immediate social concern, they must expect to find their evidence subjected to close scrutiny and their deductions challenged. Since Cook's paper appeared, other social psychologists have joined in the debate. One of them is Gerard, an American social psychologist who has himself done research in the area of school desegregation and has recently given his analysis of the issues. He undertook a five-year study of desegregation, in the anticipation that he would find evidence to confirm the expectations that influenced the 1954 Supreme Court decision. His 1983 paper, based on his own research experience and his knowledge of other people's work, is reproduced here.

Gerard is sympathetic to Cook's defence of himself and the other social scientists who acted as expert witnesses, but he thinks that there were several critical flaws in their way of proceeding and arguing. Firstly, as a result of focusing exclusively on the psychological dynamics of prejudice and discrimination, they failed to make the necessary connection between objective social conditions and the way in which individuals react to those conditions. At the same time they failed to appreciate how deeply embedded prejudice was in the fabric of the American character.

Secondly, they did not anticipate the problems that arise when deeply held social values conflict. This same point was touched upon in Miller's presidential address (see Chapter 1, pp. 17–28). What happens when two equally important and widely held social values clash? In the north of the United States, although schools were not racially segregated by law, *de facto* segregation existed because of neighbourhood segregation. Hence, integrated schools could only be achieved by busing children away from their local community. When this was attempted, many individual parents faced a difficult moral dilemma; they supported the general principle of racial integration, but they also happened to believe in the importance of the local neighbourhood school.

Gerard's third point of criticism is that Cook, and his colleagues were testifying on slender evidence. Gerard takes the view that the premature applications of social science to political issues diminishes public confidence in the social sciences.

Reading III.   School Desegregation: The Social Science Role, by H. B. Gerard

ABSTRACT: The Social Science Statement supporting the 1954 Brown vs. Board of Education *U.S. Supreme Court Decision was based on*

Source: American Psychologist (1983), *38*, pp. 869–877. Copyright (1983) by the American Psychological Association. Reprinted by permission of the publisher and author.

well-meaning rhetoric rather than solid research. Social science thinking 10 years later, when desegregation began to be implemented, was more sophisticated but still unsupported by necessary research. We desperately need research and development as well as systems engineering in the social sciences if we are eventually going to tackle and solve some of our social problems, including the successful implementation of school desegregation.

My main credential for writing this article is that I spent some of the best years of my life studying what happens to children from the year before to five years after desegregation (Gerard & Miller, 1975). We have the dubious distinction of having collected more desegregation data than anyone since Coleman (Coleman, Campbell, Hobson, McPartland, Mood, Weinfield, & York, 1966). Coleman studied 600,000 children in all 50 states, whereas we studied 1,800 children in a single school district over a period of six years, collecting detailed data on each child from a number of perspectives. We had hoped that our data would still the critics by demonstrating that minority achievement, achievement-related attitudes, and self-esteem would improve from pre- to postdesegregation, as would school performance, with no adverse effects on white pupils. We had also hoped that interethnic attitudes would improve. This was the heart of the expectations in the historic 1954 *Brown vs. Board of Education* U.S. Supreme Court Decision (see Stephan, 1978), and I fully expected to find confirming evidence.

In this article I hope to point out what can charitably be called slippage in the psychology underlying the *Brown* decision, especially as regards the Social Science Statement submitted to the court by social psychologists Isidor Chein, Kenneth Clark, and Stuart Cook. This statement, which was submitted to the court in support of the plaintiffs, was vague about how desegregation would correct the harms of segregation. All that it said, in effect, was that because the minority child was now in a classroom with whites, he or she would no longer have the status of an outcast or a pariah. This knowledge would somehow impart to the child the self-image necessary to do well in school and later enter the mainstream of American society. The "lateral transmission of values hypothesis," which was implicit in the Coleman report, and in the minds of other workers in the early 1960s, was somewhat more sophisticated than the pariah hypothesis. In discussing the hypothesis, I will attempt to show how our data bear on its various assumptions. I would like to close the article with some general observations about the relationship between social science research and social policy and also show how social scientists should avoid getting black eyes.

The Social Science Statement

In a recent issue of the *Personality and Social Psychology Bulletin* (PSPB), Stuart Cook (1979) underscored a judgment he made earlier (Weigel,

Wiser, & Cook, 1975) that those of us who have deigned to study the consequences of school desegregation have been misguided, unhelpful, and merely reactive. We have chosen to waste our time revealing disappointing result after disappointing result in our evaluation studies rather than applying what we know to make desegregation work. The big questions of course are what do we really know and how can we apply what we may know to the desegregated classroom?

I can understand Cook's frustration over the general lack of positive effects, especially since he was one of three framers of the Social Science Statement. In his recent article Cook (1979) answers the question, Did we mislead the Court? His answer is No—principally, he goes on to say, because the conditions for real integration, which were outlined in the statement, are rarely met in the typical mixed classroom, although the framers argued that these conditions "can generally be satisfied in the public schools." Thirty-two prominent social scientists signed the statement. If I had been asked to do so, I probably would have signed it, too.

In retrospect, however, it was extraordinarily quixotic to assume that the following conditions, as specified in the statement, would or could be met in the typical school system: (a) firm and consistent endorsement by those in authority; (b) the absence of competition among the representatives of the different racial groups; (c) the equivalence of positions and functions among all participants in the desegregated setting; and (d) interracial contacts of the type that permit learning about one another as individuals. What could the framers have been thinking about while believing that the conjunction of these four conditions could be met in the typical American school? As a former teacher in a New York City junior high school that was predominantly black but was supposedly integrated, I can personally attest to the extraordinary difficulty of meeting any one of the four conditions, no less all four. My teaching stint occurred not long before *Brown*.

By 1954 two of the framers, Clark and Cook, had devoted most of their careers to the study of prejudice. Cook had been the director of the Commission on Community Interrelationships of the American Jewish Congress, which later became the Research Center for Human Relations at New York University. The Commission had as its primary focus the understanding and amelioration of anti-Semitism and anti-black prejudice. Cook, more so than any other psychologist, has devoted his entire career to the understanding and reduction of prejudice, a goal he still pursues quite vigorously. Kenneth Clark and his wife Mamie pioneered some of the early, better controlled research on prejudice, and he has continued to be an active worker in the field. The resounding conclusion from Cook's and Clark's own research and the many other studies that had appeared by 1954 is that prejudice is extraordinarily refractory to any attempts to change it. It is a virulent cancer that infects our entire culture from the lowest to the highest rung of the socioeconomic ladder. It is deeply embedded in the fabric of the American character. How then can we easily meet those four conditions outlined in the statement?

The first condition, firm and consistent endorsement by those in authority, requires commitment to a posture that for most white Americans is antithetical to their acknowledged or unacknowledged prejudice. By *those in authority* I assume the framers meant the entire chain of command from the classroom teacher, school principal, and superintendent to the school board and town council. That chain is literally as strong as its weakest link. Recalcitrance or equivocation at any level will spell doom for the levels below. The effects of a strife-torn school board that is unwilling or unable to give its full support to desegregation will permeate the entire system. As soon as the community at large senses recalcitrance by the board in the face of a court order, antidesegregation forces within the community will be mobilized. A crack in a community's resolve provides the room necessary for prejudice to widen it into a chasm.

I would add here that the logistics of community-wide, two-way mandatory busing, especially in sprawling urban areas, is an additional source of community resistance. Much of the so-called white flight that occurs in the two years following the implementation of court-ordered mandatory busing is attributable to the unwillingness of white parents to have their children bused across town. There is some recent evidence of possible "black flight" in Boston as well, presumably for the same reason (Armor, 1980). Los Angeles experienced a 62% white pupil loss in the junior high school grades that were involved in the busing program. On the other hand in San Diego, where Judge Welsh approved a voluntary busing program, white flight attributable to busing has been negligible in spite of rather substantial participation in the plan by minority pupils. It thus appears that in spite of their prejudice, most white parents are willing to accept desegregation achieved through one-way busing as long as their own children can continue to go to their neighborhood school. As in the nation at large, the vast majority of whites are staunchly opposed to two-way busing. There are limits, therefore, as to how willing they are to accept the law of the land as interpreted by the courts.

The authority support condition, as stipulated in the Social Science Statement, did not anticipate the situation as represented by the demography and geography in our large northern urban centers, but it was rather myopically focused on small dual school systems in the South that were maintained by *de jure* segregation. In Cook's (1979) own words. "The fact that busing would put the values associated with neighborbood schools against those of racial integration—with two presidents, the Congress, and a majority of citizens endorsing the former—could not at that time have been anticipated" (p. 430).

Perhaps we should forgive them for their shortsightedness in this respect. The only problem is that the legal doctrine that has been built on *Brown* is now cast in concrete and its application to large urban *de facto* segregated districts is resulting in the resegregation of many of those districts as a result of white flight. I am still willing to give the framers and signers the benefit of the doubt in not having anticipated the logistics of northern urban busing, but I do have trouble understanding their lack of acknowledgment of strong widespread community opposition to two-way busing. When it comes to schools, which are typically supported out of local property taxes, community support is often the effective if not the ultimate authority, the law of the land notwithstanding.

The second condition is that there be an absence of competition among the representatives of the different racial groups. Were the framers here suggesting that it would be relatively easy to change the structure and norms of the typical American classroom? Aggressive competitiveness runs deep in our culture, pervading every corner of society including most certainly the classroom (Pepitone, 1972; Schofield & Sagar, 1977; Suls & Sanders 1979; Veroff, 1978). By the time a child starts school, he or she has been imbued with the competitive spirit that fits right in with the teaching methods and grading system found in the typical school. The teacher has been trained to mete out rewards to the successful competitor. Our child-rearing methods prime the child for school and later life.

Is the teacher as change agent equipped to foster cooperation among his or her pupils? Hechinger and Hechinger (1974) present evidence that competitiveness tends to occur even in classrooms where competition is actively discouraged. In light of this, what hope does the teacher have of prevailing against the countervailing norm? Furthermore, is the teacher able to deal with the effects of subcultural diversity represented in the typical mixed classroom? We know, both from life and the laboratory, that strong ingroup versus outgroup feelings tend to develop in such a context (Gerard & Hoyt, 1974; Tajfel, 1979). These feelings are probably part of the roots of prejudice itself. What in the background and training of the average teacher would enable him or her to cope with these naturally occurring intergroup schisms? Given the competitive bent of most pupils and a general tendency for the teacher to endorse and foster such competition, the potentially hostile intergroup feelings between subgroups of pupils from different backgrounds, and his or her own prejudice, the teacher is necessarily confronted with a herculean task in trying to significantly change the situation.

There is also the important consideration of the probable cultural gap between the teacher, the vast majority of whom are white and middle class, and the lower socioeconomic status minority child. Kay Bikson, who worked with us, collected data indicating that teachers—and this goes for both white and minority group teachers—tend to underrate the intelligence and ability of a minority child who displays ghetto speech mannerisms. In the study, the teachers heard short speech excerpts of children they did not know and rated each child on a number of semantic differential type scales. The data show that the typical teacher is likely to prejudge a child on the basis of speech mannerisms (and probably on other kinds of earmarks as well) by downgrading the minority child relative to his or her performance on objective measures.

I assume the next condition, that there be an equivalence of positions and functions among all participants in the desegregated setting, refers principally to the children themselves and not to teachers and administrators.

To believe that this requirement, which embodies one of Gordon Allport's (1954) conditions for the reduction of intergroup prejudice, could easily be met in the typical mixed classroom ignores what life is really like in such a classroom. Our own longitudinal data and cross-sectional data from the Coleman report show a widening achievement gap between white and minority children as they move through the grades. By the sixth grade, the gap is more than two grade-equivalents wide. Given that the minority children are already one-down by virtue of their minority status, the fact that their academic performance is, on the average, far below their white peers, places them in double status jeopardy, both in relation to their white peers and in the eyes of the typical teacher. So how can we hope to meet the condition of equal status in the traditional classroom when desegregation or not, the average classroom has not changed all that much since we were in school?

Our data show that teachers tend to normalize their grades no matter what the absolute level of achievement is in their classroom. By that I mean they will distribute the same proportion of As, or whatever the grade for excellent work is called, Bs, Cs, and so forth, irrespective of their pupils' average absolute performance. It is as though their adaptation level shifts to meet the average level of performance in their class. Thus, a class of very bright pupils will tend to be undergraded relative to their actual achievement level and a class of slow pupils will tend to be overgraded.

What we find in our data is that in the year just prior to the start of the desegregation program, whites were being undergraded if their normalized grades are compared with their normalized scores on state-mandated achievement tests, whereas both black and Mexican-American children were overgraded. One year after desegregation there is still a tendency for teachers to undergrade whites and overgrade minority pupils, which is evidence for a double standard, but over time we see a progressive diminution of the difference in scores. By the end of the third year after segregation, the teachers' grading practices appear to be completely normalized, as indicated by the negligible discrepancies between grades and achievement for all three groups.

All would be well if academic performance as well as the grade-achievement discrepancy had converged in the years following desegregation, but it did not. The relative achievement standing of minority pupils progressively worsened as they moved through the grades. The effect of gradual grade normalization had the effect of lowering minority grades and increasing white grades, the latter increasing because the poorer performance of the minority pupils provided the teacher with a lower performance anchor. This state of affairs could only have had an adverse effect on the minority pupil's status in the classroom and on his or her self-esteem. Also, since grades, as used in the traditional classroom, signal success or failure, they may spur or reduce motivation. Whites would tend to be encouraged and minority pupils discouraged which, in turn, might affect performance, thus exacerbating the achievement gap. Such a situation contains all the necessary ingredients for creating Myrdahl's

(1944) vicious circle right in the classroom. We in fact have some suggestive evidence that, as compared with predesegregation achievement, white performance increased somewhat and black performance decreased somewhat in the years following desegregation. The only clearly salutary effects we found were for the white children who were initially very poor performers. They showed an increase in both self-esteem and achievement.

Given these facts, it would be nearly, if not totally, impossible to provide the children with the experience of equal status contact. The teacher would literally have to be a genius social engineer with enormous sensitivity to create such a contact situation. How then could the framers have been deluded into believing that such contact could be generally satisfied in the public schools, where the coin of status in the classroom is good grades.

The fourth and final condition listed in the statement, that interracial contacts among the children should be of the type that permit learning about each other as individuals, is somewhat more vague than the other three. What is meant here, I assume, is that contact should somehow cut through the mutual stereotypes each group has of the other. What little evidence we do have about this requirement indicates that stereotypes tend to persist rather than dissolve in the mixed classroom. Furthermore, we found only a minuscule number of cross-ethnic work partner or friendship sociometric choices, especially by whites, with virtually no change over the postdesegregation years we studied. The evidence, thus, is strong that self-segregation occurred within the classroom. There was little meaningful contact, let alone contact that would permit learning about each other as individuals. It is likely that the vicious circle was in full bloom.

To sum up at this point, for the four conditions to be met in the typical school, the teacher would have to be a social engineering whiz. How many of those of us with our supposed sophistication in group dynamics would undertake the task? The truly embarrassing question is, What do we actually know about intergroup contact that could really make a difference in the way a desegregation program is implemented? In 1954 the framers extrapolated from Myrdahl (1944), from the Clark and Clark (1939b) doll studies, and from Kardiner and Ovesey's (1951) study of black self-esteem to argue that segregation inflicts damage to black self-esteem. They also maintained, on the basis of Klineberg's (1935) earlier studies, that the higher IQs of blacks living in the North as compared to blacks who remained south of the Mason-Dixon line represent evidence supporting the success of a desegregated experience. (They failed to take fully into account the fact that most blacks in the North lived under conditions that were often no less segregated than in the South.) They also argued that since President Eisenhower, as one of his first executive orders on entering the White House in 1953, desegregated the armed services, desegregation of the schools could also be successfully accomplished by government decree. This ignored marked differences between the military situation where men and women, black and white, were facing a common enemy in Korea and the complex nexus of circumstances represented by school desegregation, especially in the North. It also ignored the fact that in school desegregation the participants are children, and this engenders a good deal of emotion in their parents.

In his PSPB article Cook (1979) attempted to evade the bad predictions by blaming the system, but it was that self-same system about which the predictions were made, a system with which the framers were intimately acquainted. Excuse not accepted.

The Basis for the Lateral Transmission of Values Hypothesis

I would next like to run through what I consider to be the more sophisticated set of assumptions social scientists held either explicitly or implicitly in the early to mid-1960s when desegregation was getting under way. (Virtually nothing had happened in the way of implementing desegregation during the 10 years following *Brown*.) These assumptions embody the lateral transmission of values hypothesis and provide it with an underlying dynamic. The hypothesis predicts that through classroom contact with their white peers, who should outnumber them, minority pupils would experience what is tantamount to a personality change by absorbing the achievement-related values of the higher achieving whites and would thus start achieving themselves. The way this supposed transformation via elbow rubbing happens is contained in the assumptions that I now enumerate.

1. First, we assume that the achievement gap is not due to a difference in native ability. This has been an abiding faith held by the majority of social scientists, but definitive evidence remains as elusive as ever. The genotypes underlying intelligence are undoubtedly extremely complex, involving numerous genes and their interactions, which probably manifest as many different phenotypes. Therefore, even if it were possible to identify the genotypes, any conclusions about innate racial differences would at best be tenuous. At this point, the only reasonable working assumption is that there are no differences.

2. Given that there are no innate differences, the achievement gap exists because of a difference in orientation toward educational attainment within the white and minority communities, which is internalized by the children growing up in those communities. The evidence here from our own study and from the work of others is confusing, to say the least. I was struck, when first reading the Coleman report, that blacks evidenced higher achievement motivation than whites on the measures used. The black children in their sample also reported that their parents spent more time helping them with school work than did the whites. Others have reported similar evidence (Debord, Griffin, & Clark, 1977; Epps, 1975; Proshansky & Newton, 1968; Weinberg, 1975). In spite of the lack of confirming evidence and evidence to the contrary, most social scientists, I suspect, still believe there is an achievement value deficit among black and

certain other minority group children. What does come through in some of the studies is that aspirations among blacks are not functionally related to the path required to reach lofty goals. Part of the stigma of lower social status is a lack of personal efficacy in realizing academic and vocational goals, which induces a sense of helplessness in not being able to exercise control over circumstances.

3. Achievement orientation deficits are reversible and are easier to reverse in the younger child. Our findings here are disappointing and are in agreement with most of the data collected around the country (Bradley & Bradley, 1977; St. John, 1975). A troubling sidelight to this is the very low correlation we found between actual achievement, as measured by standardized tests, and achievement orientation, as measured by stock-in-trade instruments that psychologists use. Are these values (or traits, if you will) so ephemeral and easily overwhelmed by situational forces, or are we misguided in the kinds of trait and value measures we typically use?

4. Social influence will occur in any group, so that the norms of conduct beliefs, values and attitudes of the majority will influence the minority. The work supporting this assumption represented my own limited area of expertise when I began the study (Deutsch & Gerard, 1955; Gerard, 1953, 1954). The work that has been done has been almost exclusively in the laboratory, where particular attitudes are concocted on the spot and are therefore usually not intense. There is no systematic evidence supporting the idea that the majority can change deep-seated values held by the minority. Some recent work coming mainly out of European laboratories suggests that, on the contrary, a staunch minority may influence the majority in profound ways (Moscovici, 1976).

In any event, the majority influence assumption has been a key one in the desegregation literature. The prescription usually offered, which is based strictly on intuition, is that the number of minority children in a classroom should be no more than 40% and no less than 20%, which supposedly represents a minimum critical mass. To this day, there is no evidence supporting the efficacy of these boundary figures. Incidentally, in the tug of war between the schools and the courts, a consensus has never been reached as to what percentage figures define a desegregated school.

A social psychologist, in supporting this majority influence assumption, might argue that minority values would change because of both informational influence and normative pressures (Deutsch & Gerard, 1955). The white majority in the classroom, through their achievement-related behavior both in word and by deed, would provide minority children with information representing a new benchmark toward which to strive. Normative pressures derive from the desire of the minority children to be accepted by their white peers. Since grades are the coin of status, the minority child will presumably strive to do well in the new, high-achieving classroom. Utilizing a structural equations model, Murayama and Miller (1979) found evidence in our data supporting this normative pressures model. That is, good grades do tend to enhance the child's sociometric status. Since not many minority children improved their performance, we can assume that the normative pressures that did exist did not turn the trick. For normative pressures to be felt by the minority child, he or she would have to perceive that acceptance was a reasonable likelihood. Given the lack of any true integration over the course of five years, the perceived likelihood was undoubtedly low. Others, like Irwin Katz (1964), have argued for a model emphasizing the reverse process: Acceptance leads to reduced threat and increased self-esteem which, in turn, results in improved performance. There was no evidence in our data that would support such a causal sequence.

5. A crucial condition for effective social influence to occur is an implicit assumption underlying the lateral transmission hypothesis, namely that there are no strong barriers to communication in the classroom. To the extent that the racial subgroups are truly integrated socially, there will be fluid communication between the groups. As I have pointed out, there was little evidence indicating that real integration had occurred even after five years of the mixed classroom experience. A subassumption here is that the earlier in his or her school career the child is placed in a mixed classroom, the more likely will he or she experience true integration. Again, we found no such supporting evidence. Self-segregation was as true for the younger children—those who started with desegregation in the first and second grades—as it was for the older ones.

6. Salutary effects for the minority children will be mediated by the higher level of instruction in the desegregated as compared with the segregated classroom. This assumption argues that the teacher will pitch the material at the level of the white majority and, to stay in the running, the minority children will exert themselves and use more of their capacities. That this normalization does not occur is clear from our achievement data. The anecdotal evidence we have indicates that teachers, to cope with the new range of abilities, invariably used some variant or other of ability groupings, especially for reading and math.

7. Assumption 6 is based on a more fundamental notion that competition is good and will lead to improved performance. Research data here, as for most of the assumptions, are sparse. There is some evidence that when performance discrepancies are small, some form of bootstrapping will occur through social comparison (Thorton & Arrowood, 1966; Toda, Shinotsuka, McClintock, & Stech, 1978). There is reason to believe, however, that when the discrepancy is large, as is the case between minority and white pupils, each group will tend to render the other noncomparable as a performance referent, which will not produce the desired bootstrapping in the lower group.

8. An assumption related to and supporting Assumptions 6 and 7 is that if the performance standard for a person is raised, he or she will improve in order to meet the new standard. For this to occur, however, the person must both be motivated to reach the higher standard, and it must not

exceed his or her potential grasp; the performance situation must somehow be tractable for the person. The laboratory research on achievement motivation has explored some of its psychological parameters, but our knowledge is still rudimentary. We would find considerable disagreement among educators and psychologists as to how best to program a curriculum to optimize learning, a curriculum that would take account of the nexus of individual and social-psychological factors that operate in the classroom. Our data indicate that whatever curricula and methods were used, they did not achieve the desired end.

9. Teachers will treat children similarly regardless of ethnic background. This assumption, which is a keystone of the lateral transmission hypothesis, was clearly not met in our data and I would venture to guess is still not being met in schoolrooms across the country. There are fairly consistent findings that teachers pay more attention to white than to minority pupils. As pointed out earlier, there is also evidence that teachers underrate minority children. In our own data we found that teachers who tend to undervalue the achievement of minority pupils as compared with whites—and most teachers do—tend to have an adverse affect on the performance of minority children in their classes (Rosenthal & Jacobson, 1968). Not only that, minority children in such classes tend to be more isolated from their white peers than are minority children in the classrooms of less bigoted teachers. The teachers' behavior seems to set an example for the white students.

In the mid-1960s a number of psychologists argued that teachers in segregated minority schools tend to be punitive and rejecting of their pupils, whereas teachers in white schools are more likely to use various forms of positive reinforcement. It would therefore follow that in the mixed but predominantly white classroom, minority children would experience positive rather than negative forms of reinforcement that would then enable them to flower. According to Katz (1964), one of the proponents of this argument, self-reinforcement as well as self-discouragement are consequences of social learning mediated by social reinforcement and modeling. In terms of what actually happens in the classroom, with all of its bigotry and invidious comparison, this nice-sounding theory was just another pie in the sky.

10. That desegregation will increase the minority child's self-esteem was the real heart of the *Brown* decision. In the decision itself and in the Social Science Statement, as well as in the writings of many social scientists at the time, two separate, but not mutually exclusive, hypotheses appear to underlie the assumption. The one stressed the most was the pariah hypothesis. The child, on being thrust into the previously all-white classroom, would see her- or himself in a new light and conclude that he or she is just like and as good as everybody else—like all those whites out there and here in the classroom. This simpleminded notion that ignores the realities of the classroom deserves to be caricatured.

The original contention in *Brown*, that segregation itself generates low self-esteem, has more recently been called into question (Epps, 1975,

1979; Porter & Washington, 1979; Wylie, 1979). The original Clark and Clark (1939) doll studies that figured so prominently in 1954 have been shown to have serious methodological flaws and interpretive problems (Brand, Ruiz, & Padilla, 1974; Stephan & Rosenfeld, 1978). Also, recent work by Taylor and Walsh (1979) indicates that, controlling for occupational level, black self-esteem is, if anything, higher than white self-esteem. The black child growing up in a black family with black friends and relatives probably develops as strong feelings of self-worth as does the white child growing up in a white world. Thrusting the black child into a predominantly white, status-oriented classroom does nothing to enhance the black child's self-esteem. Instead we find that self-esteem diminishes after desegregation, a consequence that is understandable in the light of recent research on the effect of ability comparison information on self-attributions (Ames, 1978; Ames, Ames, & Felker, 1977; Harvey, Cacioppo, & Yasuna, 1977; Levine, 1983; Nicholls, 1975; Sanders, Gastorf, & Mullen, 1979; Stephan & Rosenfeld, 1978; Wortman, Costanza, & Witt, 1973).

The second less prominent hypothesis predicting that desegregation will increase the black child's self-esteem argues that this self-esteem increase will be mediated by the experience of successful competition with white peers. By comparing his or her performance with whites in the class, the minority child will realize that he or she is just as good as they are. Would that that would have happened, but it did not.

11. The final assumption, to which I have alluded a number of times, is that increased self-esteem will lead to improved performance. Since goal-setting depends on expectation of success and failure, and since self-esteem can be translated into such expectations, higher self-esteem ought to lead to the setting of higher goals and subsequent improved performance. Also, building on the discussion of the previous assumption, the process is assumed to be circular, since higher performance will, in turn, lead to increased self-esteem. Again, there is little evidence for that from data around the country.

In summary, we have found no real evidence for the lateral transmission hypothesis, either directly in the measurement of values and self-esteem or indirectly in the form of improved performance. The lid that was on minority performance in the segregated classroom is still there.

Social Science and Public Policy

At this point, after the heartache and disappointment, I consider myself to be a realist rather than a pessimist. Social scientists were wrong in the belief that change would come easily. There are so many resistances to overcome, many of which should have been anticipated, but many of us were blinded by our ideology into thinking we could have our utopia in one fell swoop of mandated busing. Simply mixing children in the classroom and trusting to a benign human nature could never have done the trick. If this nation is to survive, it must eventually achieve equal, desegregated opportunity for all in housing, education, and employment. What I am questioning here are the assumptions underlying the belief that school desegregation as implemented in the typical school district will be an instrument to achieve that end.

Social scientists have only lost credibility in the process of essentially entering the political arena prematurely. I can imagine what the David Stockmans of the world are saying about social scientists. Cook (1979) argues that social scientists should be out there helping to make desegregation work. The trouble is that a good deal of damage has been done by recommendations that were based not on hard data but mostly on well-meaning rhetoric. Urban districts are now resegregating and becoming less effective in teaching our children. Social scientists and educators have to start learning how to engineer effective integration. Some tentative baby steps are finally being made along these lines (Aronson, Stephan, Sikes, Blaney, & Snapp, 1978; Johnson & Johnson, 1975; Slavin, 1980). Funds for more of it will come from God knows where.

The hard sciences invest a great deal of money and effort in what is called research and development (R&D), in which ideas generated from basic research are developed for application to real-world physical problems. In physics, for example, basic research findings in crystallography are applied to developing solid state devices for the communications industry. Typically, the investment in development far exceeds that of the original basic research, probably by a factor of 10 or more. Oftentimes, years of effort by many scientists and engineers are spent developing a device before it is ready for use in some ongoing communication system. Much time may then be spent actually implementing the device's real-world use with months or even years of field trials. Then and only then, when the device has proved itself useful and reliable, will those responsible for large-scale operating systems approve its widespread use.

We in the social sciences have missed the essential R&D link in the chain of applying ideas to practical problems. Communication between the ivory tower and the real world of family, school, and work place has never been good; mostly it has been nonexistent. In the tower, basic researchers play their interesting little games with 2 × 2 designs while therapists, educators, and managers attempt to cope with real people. If we are ever going to gain credibility with the lay public and with those in charge of the collective purse strings, we are going to have to follow something of the implementation model used by the hard sciences so that when we make recommendations about how to deal with an issue like school segregation, we have the facts and experience to back us up. This can only be done with careful research on such things as the effect of performance on self-esteem and vice-versa, on the effects of social categorization on prejudice and vice-versa, on the effects of competition and cooperation on intergroup attitudes and vice-versa, and so on. We already have some rudimentary knowledge of these problems. But then we have to take what we know and try to apply it on a small scale at first to the school setting with a laboratory-like approach, in which we use the best scientific minds available. In the process we will be forced to go back to the drawing board many times until we develop a program that will really work. This will not happen overnight. The investment required will be enormous both in person years and dollars.

One of the most serious deterrents to successful R&D and systems engineering in the social sciences is the academic reward structure we ourselves perpetuate, especially in psychology. Promotion to tenure and beyond is best achieved by publishing as many short, neat, and methodologically simple papers as possible. By far, the best way to climb the academic ladder is to hit on a simple experimental paradigm like a paired-associate learning task, a conformity situation, or a fear arousal procedure and then crank out studies that vary one or another experimental variable that might possibly affect the criterion response. The faculty member who commits him- or herself to a long-term, messy evaluation study is definitely at risk.

Given the keen competition for a limited number of academic jobs these days, a young person who sets out to do a longitudinal study in some real-world context would be foolish, given the standards used by promotion committees. Better to make your studies short, numerous, and focused on a narrow problem that will be of interest to your own limited group of fellow workers around the country who then can be counted on to write glowing letters of praise to support your promotion. Typically these mutual admiration societies of co-workers number no more than a couple of dozen people worldwide. Members of these groups can also be relied on to help each other get research grants. This climate fosters such comfortable little cliques that continue to grind out esoterica that typically have little or no bearing on the fire fighting going on in clinics, schools, hospitals, prisons, and factories.

Earlier, I pointed out aspects of the culture in the typical classroom that impede true integration, and I have ended by railing at the culture in the typical psychology department that offers no reward for risk taking in the study of real-world problems. Changing the classroom is an enormous task that we psychologists could in our own way facilitate indirectly by changing our own norms. That is something over which we do have some control.

It seems that whatever rhetoric is in the ascendance at the time determines how we as a nation attempt to solve our social problems. Somehow we will muddle through; families, children, and work places will survive still another Washington administration. We will keep muddling until we are prepared to make a real commitment to research, development, and systems engineering of social problems.

IS THERE A LESSON TO BE LEARNED?

The objective of this chapter has been to demonstrate some of the perils of translating social knowledge into social action. Many conflicting conclusions could be drawn from this case study. Before we tackle some of them, it is important to stress that no one is suggesting that the social scientists who gave evidence were acting in bad faith or that they deliberately sought to mislead the Supreme Court or to misrepresent their findings. This point is emphasized because since Kamin's expose of the fraudulent data reported by Cyril Burt there has been a realization that even eminent researchers may misrepresent their evidence. (For further details see Chapter 5 and the extract by Kamin on pp. 303–306). The Burt affair raises questions of ethics and professional responsibility which are quite separate matters from the points that arise out of the school desegregation issue. While everyone agrees that scientists have a responsibility to report their data accurately, there is no consensus as to when it is appropriate for a scientist to act as expert witness.

One might agree with Gerard that social psychologists should refrain from speaking on matters of public concern unless they have a sound empirical foundation upon which to base their assertions. A rejoinder to this position is that "whatever the state of scientific knowledge, men must carry on the function of political life and reach decisions as wisely as they can" (Garfinkel, 1959, p. 115). The social scientists in 1954, according to this line of reasoning, could not ask the black community or the Supreme Court to put off reaching a decision about school segregation for a decade or so while researchers rushed off to do the necessary investigations to enable them to give their professional advice. Their opinion represented the state of knowledge as it existed at the time.

Another possible conclusion is that in the absence of good empirical research American schools should not have been desegregated. This conclusion we feel is also unwarranted. The Supreme Court ruling was not based exclusively on social science testimony. There were compelling legal and moral reasons for desegregating schools, which were quite independent of the factual question as to whether segregation does or does not produce low self-esteem. What was at stake was whether government-enforced segregation violated the "equal protection under the law" guaranteed by the Fourteenth Amendment to the Constitution. If we refer back to the models of political psychology sketched out in the beginning of this chapter, the task of the psychologist as expert witness is to offer what he knows to those who are in a position to apply it. The ultimate choice of policy remains in the hands of the policy-maker, administrator, or law maker. Segall's model echoes Garfinkel's summing up of the Supreme Court case—the psychologists gave evidence which the court weighed in the full context of all relevant considerations.

Another possible conclusion, which we do not wish to endorse, is that since school desegregation has not invariably produced dramatic psychological or academic changes, desegregation was a mistake and it would have been better had things been left as they were. What this line of reasoning totally overlooks is the fact that there were compelling *legal* reasons for ending compulsory racial segregation in schools. The court came out against enforced segregation because such policies rest on premises that conflict with legal rights. The constitutional case against segregation does not require guarantees of academic or psychological benefits, desirable though these may be as goals in themselves.

There is one final point to examine before we leave this study of psychology in the political arena. Is the example we have selected as our case study specific to American society and American social psychology or can it be generalized to other contexts? Our own view is that school desegregation raises points that are relevant to Britain, other European societies, and to European social psychology. In Britain, a very interesting parallel can be drawn with the long-standing debate about secondary school education. The American research started from racial inequalities, while the British investigated class inequalities. Since the Second World War, British secondary education has been a topic of great national concern—evidenced by the numbers of reports, committees of enquiry, mass media coverage, and various efforts at structural reorganization. During these four decades, British sociologists and psychologists have devoted an enormous amount of research time to investigating their educational system.

Initially, the central issue was whether the use of selective examinations at age 11, to determine what type of secondary school a child attended (grammar, secondary modern, or technical), discriminated against working-class children. Comprehensive schools were seen as a way of ending this tripartite system of education which segregated children according to ability as measured by their 11+ results.

There were high hopes that comprehensive schools would result in an overall increase in working-class educational attainment.

... early supporters of the comprehensive principle looked to the new schools to provide a solvent for class barriers and inequalities. They urged the speedy abolition of the grammar school on the grounds of the social exclusiveness, narrowness and rigidity of the academic tradition; and they have gone on to seek positive unstreaming, a common curriculum and flexible teaching methods to promote a new cooperative atmosphere which will help the average and less able child. (Marsden, 1970, p. 140)

From the outset, the issue of what ought to be the form and content of secondary education in post-war Britain divided both academics and politicians. Psychological and sociological evidence was used to argue both for and against selection. If anything, the debate in Britain about the nature of secondary education has been much more polemical and vitriolic than the American debate about school desegregation (at least within the academic community).[5] Perhaps this reflects the fact that in British society academics still perceive themselves as belonging by right to the group that governs the country and, therefore, expect that their opinions *should* carry weight when policies are shaped.

The eventual establishment of comprehensive schools and the abolition of the old 11+ examination did not bring an end to the debate. What has happened (as in the case of school desegregation) is that the ground has shifted. Today the burning question is whether comprehensive schools are achieving what they set out to do. Once again, the empirical research has come up with mixed results and the evidence may be interpreted in a variety of contradictory ways. The parallel

---

[5]Chapter 5 includes the details of one British social scientist's experience of public reaction to her research on comprehensive schools, see pp. 300–302.

with the American experience is very close. Those who, in principle, favour comprehensive schools can quite legitimately point out that because of the fact that various forms of selection still occur, because neighbourhoods are segregated (by class), because of the amount of streaming that takes place within comprehensive schools, and because of the strong tradition of public (i.e., private, fee-paying) schools, the comprehensive schools that exist do not correspond to the model that was originally advocated. Therefore, negative research findings (e.g., low academic attainment amongst working-class children in comprehensive schools) do *not* discredit the comprehensive system. Critics of comprehensive schools, on the other hand, maintain that the empirical evidence does demonstrate that comprehensive schools have been tried and have failed. They advocate a return to some form of segregated education.

British parents, politicians, and academics have an additional worry about the structure of secondary education, which is whether children should be segregated by sex. Once again we find the research evidence is confusing and contradictory. Throughout the last century there was a movement to reform the structure and content of girls' education to make it similar to that of boys. Each innovation, such as permitting girls to sit external examinations or admitting them to universities, was fiercely resisted. Those who opposed a universal form of education argued that girls were unable to deal with competition and would be likely to respond badly to it. Medical evidence was produced to show that girls who receive boys' education were likely to develop nervous trouble and to harm their reproductive organs (Marks, 1976, p. 189). The matter is further complicated in Britain by the long tradition of single-sex schools. Nor did the introduction of compulsory education for girls bring an end to the debate as to what type of education is appropriate for boys and for girls.

As late as 1926, half the 9-year-olds in Britain were in single-sex schools. This proportion dropped to 2% in 1976. Taking secondary schools, only 10% of comprehensives and less than one-third of all maintained secondary schools were single-sex in the early 1970s (Stone and Taylor, 1976, p. 62). From these figures it might appear as though the issue has now

been decided in favour of mixed-sex schools. Dale (1974), the foremost British researcher on the topic of co-education, concluded that mixed schools are more successful than single-sex schools in every way—academically, attitudinally, and socially. This conclusion regarding the superiority of mixed-sex schools and the decision by many local authorities to phase out single-sex schools is being challenged by some parents who argue that, under the terms of the 1944 Education Act, they have the right to choose a single-sex school for their child. (Section 76 of the Act states that within certain constraints "pupils are to be educated in accordance with the wishes of their parents.") Parental objections to what they perceive as a curtailing of their freedom of choice are reinforced by social science research findings which contradict Dale's verdict.

Recent research evidence suggests that boys and girls may actually make more traditional subject choices in mixed-sex schools. Jenny Shaw (1976), a social psychologist, reports that: "the social structures of mixed schools may drive children to make even more sex-stereotyped subject choices, precisely because of the constant pressure of the other sex and the pressure to maintain boundaries, distinctiveness, and identity" (p. 137). A Department of Education and Science survey on curricular differences likewise found that: "Girls are more likely to choose a science and boys a language in a single-sex school than they are in a mixed school, though in a mixed school a higher percentage of pupils may be offered these subjects" (1975, p. 12). Such evidence has caused many feminists to rethink their earlier unqualified enthusiasm for mixed schools. For instance, Eileen Byrne, who has been Education Officer to the Equal Opportunities Commission and Education Consultant to the European Economic Community, sums up her position:

Ten years ago I argued as strongly as any for more mixed schools, partly to help the development of social education, partly to widen access to subject areas not available in single-sex schools, and partly in the hope that the presence of girls would add a slightly civilizing element to boys and that the presence of boys would act as a spur and an incentive to the girls. It hasn't really worked like that at all, and it may well be that now we need a major national debate specifically on co-education. . . . (1978, pp. 132–133)

It is not our intention to review here all the research and controversy regarding single- versus mixed-sex schools. Our purpose in introducing this issue is to make you aware that the problem of extrapolating from social research to social policy is not specific to the issue of racial desegregation of American schools.

We could easily extend this analysis of the difficulties inherent in the role of "expert witness" from the field of education to other arenas of public concern. In all industrial societies there is unease about the effects of various forms of social "segregation." For instance, there is a debate as to whether such groups as delinquent youngsters, old people, or the physically and mentally handicapped should be segregated from the rest of society. Many researchers have emphasized the harmful effects of various types of institutional care and have pressed for the reintegration of these various groups back into the local community. But once deinstitutionalization gets under way, we inevitably discover that there are hidden costs. All social change brings in its wake unanticipated consequences.

This leads one to wonder whether social science can ever tell human beings how they should live their lives or order their society. Many years ago two renowned American psychologists, B. F. Skinner and Carl Rogers (1956), debated this very point. Skinner took the view that science increases our power to control human behaviour and he optimistically predicted that the application of behavioural technology to human affairs could herald a "new and exciting phase of human life . . . in which earlier political slogans will not be appropriate" (p. 1060). Seen in this light, the "question of government . . . is not how freedom is to be preserved but what kinds of control are to be used and to what ends" (p. 1060). In replying to Skinner, Rogers pinpointed a fundamental point of disagreement between them—the role of values in human life, including science:

In any scientific endeavor—whether "pure" or "applied" science—there is a prior subjective choice of the purpose or value which that scientific work is perceived as serving. This subjective value choice which brings the scientific endeavor into being must always lie outside of that endeavor and can never become a part of the science involved in that endeavor . . . to choose to experiment is a value choice. . . . To test the consequences of an experiment is possible only if we have first made a subjective choice of criterion value . . . it seems inescapable that a prior subjective value choice is necessary for any scientific endeavor, or for any application of scientific knowledge. (Rogers & Skinner, 1956, pp. 1061–1062)

Rogers then goes on to give an example to demonstrate that the initial purpose or value which sets research in motion, always and necessarily lies outside the scope of the research. His example concerns educational priorities:

If I value knowledge of the "three R's" as a goal of education, the methods of science can give me . . . information on how this goal may be achieved. If I value problem-solving ability as a goal of education, the scientific method can give me the same kind of help. Now, if I wish to determine whether problem-solving ability is "better" than knowledge of the three R's, then scientific method can also study those two values but *only*—and this is very important—in terms of some other value which I have subjectively chosen. I may value college success. Then I can determine whether problem-solving ability or knowledge of the three R's is most closely associated with that value. I may value personal integration or vocational success or responsible citizenship. I can determine whether problem-solving ability or knowledge of the three R's is "better" for achieving any one of these values. *But the value or purpose that gives meaning to a particular scientific endeavor must always lie outside of the endeavor.* (Rogers & Skinner, 1956, p. 1062; emphasis added)

Thus, like many others in the liberal-humanist tradition, Rogers concluded that the honest researcher should make his value choices explicit. He should not use science to assert that his values are somehow better than those of his competitors. It is on this very issue of certainty about the correctness of one's theories that many radical critics wish to break with the liberal tradition in the social sciences. Many in the "New Left" have expressed a sense of impatience about such a detached way of looking at the world, which they equate with lack of concern or social commitment. The words of Karl Marx are often quoted in this context: "The philosophers have only *interpreted* the world in various ways. The point is to *change* it." Those who bring to social psychology a Marxist orientation deplore the split between academic theory and political practice.

3

The Social Role of the "Man" of Knowledge

What we are witnessing now is, in my view, an attempt by psychologists to wake up from the trance of their own unquestioning professionalism to a realization of who they are working for and what their real job is . . .: and the answer is not, ultimately to be found in their contracts, even in the small print. My hypothesis is that their unwritten contract is to maintain the status quo.

(Ingleby, 1974, p. 317)

In Chapter 2 we followed the treacherous path that psychologists often tread as they step out into the real world. Now we stand back for a moment, and think more generally about the role of psychologists in society. Do they simply "service" that society, as the radical critics maintain, or do they play some part in transforming it, and if so, what part? Is the achievement of social change a legitimate focus for psychologists or should it be left to the politician and policy-maker?

The radical psychologists' disquiet focused on the exact nature of psychologists' social involvement, and the arguments have reverberated ever since. A look at the development of the school desegregation debate—and the part psychologists played in "arming" the various protagonists—dispells any notions we might have had about the neatness of real-world activities. It illustrates how very untidy the whole sequence of "evidence," interpretation, and translation into policy becomes. This is important because the radical psychologists quoted in Chapter 1, while arguing against the whole liberal conception of social science, often over-simplified the actual difficulties of involvement in the development of social policy. They were also somewhat vague as to how their criticisms might be translated into research objectives. The school desegregation issue demonstrated clearly that social policy does not emerge neatly, under the clear regard of the expert,

79

but that other people interpret, misinterpret, and oversimplify the empirical evidence along the intricate path of policy development. Even this "evidence," as we have seen, is difficult to provide because of the contradictory nature of research findings and the problems associated with interpreting the results. Interventions based on expert advice also sometimes fail to acknowledge and take account of the necessary preconditions that have to be met before the suggested changes will be effective. "Society", at times of great controversy, looks for "knowledge" on which to base its policies or, more cynically, one might say that "society" casts around for appropriate "knowledge" with which to legitimatize its already determined policies.

In this chapter we analyze, in a rather less case-specific way, the relationship between the policy-maker's need for "knowledge," "facts," and "expert advice," and the manner in which this is sought and used. These are important questions for the psychologist who is attempting to work honestly in an applied field. Segall (1976), in elaborating on the model of the "expert witness" in the extract in Chapter 2 (pp. 32–33), has said that the essential feature of this role is that the expert has no power, because policy-makers or administrators make the final decision and use the fruits of the "expert's" testimony as they will. Seen from this perspective, the "knowledge" provided by the expert is a commodity that can be bought, and the expert has no control over its use. Policy-makers can use or reject whatever information is made available to them. At worst this could mean that the psychologists are hired hands whose particular quality is that they are knowledgeable. This is stating the case at its worst but it is worth making clear that in political life the charisma one normally associates with words like "expert" or "consultant" can disguise some exercise which is no more than the prostitution of knowledge. This is one of the worries that the radical psychologists had, a worry that if we provided data but relinquished control over the use of that information, then we were not acting in a politically responsible way. They argued that psychologists could no longer dissociate themselves from the policy process in this way. To do so, they said, was to pretend that "science," as represented in the work of psychological research, was value-free and could be offered for use by others. They felt that psychologists had to acknowledge that the "knowledge" arising from their work was, in fact, not detached, pure, and "scientific" in conventional terminology, but was value-laden and socially constructed. They did not think that it was good enough for psychologists to be on the periphery of the political process; to sell themselves short and to act as psychological mercenaries. Passions ran high on this issue and, as you read earlier (p. 14), Peter Sedgwick felt that the marriage of the logic of psychology and political commitment (by which he meant involvement in the decision-making process) was such an impossible feat that he left psychology for a time. The question we wish to pursue is whether the relationship between the activities of scholars and the preoccupations of legislators, politicians, bureaucrats, and administrators must be so separate. Need the expertise of the intelligentsia, in whatever disciplines, be used to rubber-stamp policies that are decided by others or can the scholar initiate action?

THE SCHOLAR AND THE STATE

Ernest Becker (1970), in a paper entitled *The Social Role of the Man of Knowledge*, follows the history of the relationship between "knowledge" as embodied in the sage, the scholar, the "Shaman," on the one hand, and various state institutions, on the other. In his broad historical sweep, Becker claims that the striking thing about the role accorded to the intellectual has been its *sameness* down through history. The "Man of Knowledge" has, he argues, "usually been the servant of power, a simple reflection of the needs and desires of his society." The clever, well-educated, informed man who took it upon himself to be *socially critical*, and who called upon fellow citizens to think about truth and justice rather than self-interest and competition, as did Socrates, encountered many problems. "Society does not want men of knowledge to turn against it. This is what Plato learnt to his own disenchantment; politicians don't turn to the true philosophers to help them out in their plight" (Becker, 1970, p. 324).

According to Becker, however, during the period of Enlightenment in the eighteenth century, there arose a new vision of the man of knowledge as a social critic: ". . . Someone who could rise above his own place and time, above the folly of his society, someone who would use reason, who would overthrow dogma and chart the way out of the Gothic darkness of superstition" (p. 324). In short, it was believed that "the man of knowledge would modify morality in the light of critical reason" (p. 325). Kant reinforced this general view of the man of intellect, arguing that philosophy was free inquiry, no matter where it led nor who would be upset by its outcomes and findings.

Becker traces the fate of the "ideologues" in France in the eighteenth century, in particular Condorcet who proposed to organize education and science in the service of man and to create an autonomous, self-governing community of scholars, protected from encroachment on all sides. These "ideologues" were not only eminent and distinguished scholars but some were also elected to legislative office within the National Assembly. This meant that "experts," at least for one brief moment in history, had power in the decision-making process. The "ideologues" formed a National Institute and hoped to make social science findings a central focus in the framing of national legislation and social reconstruction. They became the new scientific liberals, until they were disbanded by Napoleon in 1803. It was their view that the state should not stifle new knowledge even if it were out of line with its own particular developments and policies. Condorcet's vision of keeping education and knowledge as autonomous and separate from the state has been one that has continued to entice scholars.

The idea of scholars guiding the state has surfaced in other social contexts. Jefferson, an American President, developed ideas along these lines. At a later period, Lester Ward, one of the pioneers of American sociology, tried unsuccessfully to set up a National University in Washington that would influence legislation and social policy. In England, too, there was evidence of the same vision, John Beattie Crozier who "called for a New National Bible, a national brain composed of the best knowledge which would be the scientific gospel truth that the country could use to run itself" (p. 328). H. G. Wells extended this to an ideal of a "World Brain," a new international encyclopaedia that would guide the destiny of nations by providing a base of the best scientific knowledge for all their conduct.

Becker asks why this dream of a national "brain" or of a national university to examine society critically and to translate informed beliefs into legislation died "so totally and so quietly?" He notes two significant historical developments as possibly responsible. Firstly, he suggests that in the nineteenth century the dream of a possible *synthesis* of knowledge yielded to the pressure for specialized fields of enquiry. Each scholar became submerged in his own discipline with the result, argues Becker, that *fact* and *value* become separate subjects: the one "science," the other "philosophy." The hopes and aspirations of the period of the Enlightenment for a science in the service of morality broke down. The second reason for the disappearance of the ideal of knowledge guiding the development of society was that eighteenth-century thinkers were naïve in imagining that the establishment would willingly relinquish power and privileges for the sake of the social reconstruction of society. Although the hope that, somehow, scholarly work and thinking can be translated into the public good lingers on, pessimism prevails: "There is no way today for social science to influence critically government via the parliamentary process. Even worse, since the national scientific organizations consistently refuse to take a stand on social or moral issues, there is no way to influence policy-makers, even by the indirect pressure of enlightening public opinion" (Becker, 1970, p. 330).

Becker believes that the administrative and bureaucratic structure of the state is so big and overpowering that it is impossible for the man of knowledge "to fulfill his authentic and critical role within it." He claims that there are four possible alternative roles for the man of knowledge, each equally idealistic:

1. The social scientist may play a direct role in the legislative process.
2. Social scientists may set themselves up as a political party.
3. Social scientists may seek to create a unified social science to aid policy makers.
4. Social scientists using their understanding of historical events may act as social critics.

We have adopted Becker's fourth position, in that we have been looking back at the use of psychological "knowledge" in relation to a particular issue, the school desegregation debate.

THE SOCIOLOGY OF KNOWLEDGE

The nature of psychological knowledge is the subject of a growing body of literature sometimes referred to as the "sociology of psychological knowledge." Buss (1975) claimed on the basis of his review of past psychological journals that there are now a significant number of psychologists interested in the historical development of their discipline. Their attention has focused on the way in which psychological "knowledge" is linked to the "infra-structure" of society. What characterizes a sociology of knowledge perspective is that it explores the way in which human thought is coloured or shaped by the structures of a society.

The origins of the sociology of knowledge are to be found in nineteenth-century European social thought: notably in the works of Marx, Weber and Durkheim and later Mannheim, who all examined the part social existence played in determining social consciousness.

Psychologists, more recently, have become aware of these connections as we have already witnessed in discussing the views of radical psychologists, views which now also inform mainstream psychology. Thus Gergen (1973), in a provocative and much quoted article, points out that the validity and relevance of psychological knowledge may be limited to the historical period in which it was generated. For instance, the questions social psychologists ask about the nature of conformity arise in specific social contexts and the research findings, in turn, also reflect the *Zeitgeist*. As psychologists have become more aware of the social embeddedness of their knowledge, they have had to rethink the nature of their task. In order to make the discussion a little more concrete, let us move from a rather abstract discussion of the role in society of the man of knowledge and the social construction of the "knowledge" base of the psychologist, to thinking about what psychologists are actually called upon, or choose, to do in society. In particular, we want to explore here whether psychologists, implicitly or explicitly, act as upholders of the social order, or as agents of change.

THE PSYCHOLOGIST:
MAINTAINER OF THE SOCIAL ORDER
OR AGENT OF CHANGE?

The activities of psychologists in the Second World War in such areas as army personnel selection and the study of attitudes, opinions, and communications had produced a confidence bred of success. The urgency of the war effort required that problems be tackled and solutions reached without, necessarily, the time to examine underlying ideologies and values. Psychologists had been seen, and had seen themselves, as "scientists" with a real contribution to make to the war effort. Following the war there was a retreat into the universities and an enthusiastic return to academic activity. An atmosphere of success and optimism prevailed, and psychologists felt they had something to say. During the 1950s and 1960s, therefore, a second generation of founding fathers grew up amongst psychologists, some of whom had been involved in various ways in the Second World War.

Frank (1959), writing in this post-war atmosphere of euphoria, points to the dual role of psychologists in both upholding the social order and changing it. He describes the new ideas generated by psychologists that have found their way into the practices of existing social institutions thereby maintaining, yet subtly altering them.

Psychologists—collaborating with engineers and economists and, more recently, anthropologists—have made many studies concerned with the impact of physical aspects of the workplace, such as lighting, color of walls and machines, temperature and humidity; with working conditions, such as hours, shifts, rest periods, piece rates, and especially relations of foremen and supervisors to their groups. Such studies helped to articulate a new view of corporate life.

Executives being trained for administrative positions frequently participate in courses dealing with industrial relations and personality problems. In many large industries a full-time psychiatrist is on the staff for consultations on a variety of problems and sometimes for group therapy for the executives.

As technology advances and automation embraces more processes, large organizations must have a stable working force of persons who are emotionally balanced and reasonably content with their working conditions. Otherwise these complicated processes may be liable to all manner of breakdowns. However much the future of industry depends on the competence of engineers who design the equipment and plan operations, the future is almost equally dependent upon the quality of industrial relations that are maintained. Hence this cumulative improvement in employer–employee relations—to which psychology, along with other social sciences, is contributing so much—may be regarded as one of the major transformations in our social institutions. (Frank, 1959, pp. 230–231)

In education he claims that psychologists have been instrumental in bringing about changes in teaching, learning, pupil–teacher relations, curriculum, and in heightening awareness of the social implications of education. Psychological insights into child development are seen as having had a profound impact on the development of nursery schools.

. . . Education must, for the sake of the child and for the future of society, be ever more concerned with the kind of personalities it is helping to develop. Our world requires not submissive acceptance, but rather an ability to make changes. To make rational decisions, a person must understand the rapidly changing technology he must work with and the science upon which that technology is based. Education has, apparently for the first time, to undertake the difficult task of aiding students in un-learning—that is, freeing them from folklore, traditional beliefs and assumptions that have become obsolete.

This is a delicate task because to give up what one has learned, often painfully, to accept new concepts and to use new assumptions, can be threatening to the stability of the personality. This is not unlike what the psychoanalyst tries to do with a patient whose life is blocked by persistence of childish ideas and feelings that are no longer appropriate to, nor compatible with, his adult status, responsibilities, and privileges. But this is the long-term transformation that psychology must help to bring about in education, a task made even more hazardous by the often strong resistance of parents who want their children to have the same education they experienced and who resent having their children learn to think in ways that are alien to their older patterns. Thus, this large task can be achieved only as rapidly as the public will permit. If the progress seems slow and halting, it is well to remember that transforming our schools is the institutional fulcrum transforming our social order. In a democratic society this can be done only by education and persuasion. (Frank, 1979, p. 232)

Frank goes on to look at changes that psychology and the work of psychologists have precipitated in medicine. He also advances an interesting case for the way in which psychological ideas are transforming, albeit slowly, religious ideas and practices associated with individual responsibility, culpability, and guilt.

He argues, persuasively, that it is not only *within* these frameworks that psychology has influenced our thinking and our mode of operation, but also that the frameworks themselves are man-made and therefore amenable to change. Society in his view is not simply imposed upon the individual but is an essentially human creation and, as such, can be changed and modified. People are not simply participant members of a human society but are the designers and creators of the shape of that society. It was this kind of enthusiastic optimism about the possibility of social reform that radical critics some 20 years later were to challenge so seriously. The activities of the psychologist in the maintenance and re-creation of the social order may appear to be the same today as when Frank wrote his paper. However, it is the questions about the "hidden agenda" of these roles that are new.

The Hidden Agenda?

Frank's article is interesting in suggesting that the services offered by psychologists are replacing earlier relationships and institutions in helping individuals fit into their society. In particular, he sees that "transforming our schools is the institutional fulcrum changing our social order," and feels that psychologists engaged in education have a vital part to play. It is important to remind ourselves that Frank was writing in 1959 before the crisis in psychology led psychologists to be more analytical about their social role and their power to bring about change. Having followed the history of the school desegregation issue will have made us more sceptical than Frank was about the ease with which society can be changed and modified. Although he sees the "critical scrutiny of all our laws and institutions, traditional beliefs and assumptions" as likely to take a long time, he does not see this as impossible to achieve. This outlook is not shared by Ingleby (1974) who takes a considerably more pessimistic view of the psychologist's possible role as an agent of change. Frank does not indicate any concern about the fact that the psychologist rarely works for him- or herself, and that the jobs undertaken and the outcomes expected are determined by the agency for whom the psychologist works. Frank writes as if the psychologist is a "free agent," yet Ingleby (1974) emphasizes that the psychologist and psychological knowledge are used in order to *guard and maintain the status quo*, not to change it. This, in his view, is a function of the fact that psychologists are employed as servants of the state and are therefore not in a position to bite the hand that feeds them. Ingleby does not conceptualize the problem, however, as having a single cause. In his view, the nature of the discipline itself, as presently conceived, makes it an inappropriate vehicle for social change. He goes back beyond the actual tasks that psychologists undertake to ask searching questions about the knowledge which informs intervention. He feels that frequently psychologists have deceived *themselves* that they are engaged in empirical work when they have in reality been confusing "values" with facts. He takes the "sociology of knowledge" debate beyond the structure of theory into the arena of practical intervention.

The realization that psychologists have very often not been practising empirical science leads naturally to the question: What have they been doing . . . what is the point of this pseudo-science? My answer will be that the shortcoming of the human scientist reflects the contradictions of his social role: that he fails to discover the truth because he is paid (in part) to conceal it, just as the welfare agent fails to help people because he is paid (in part) to hinder them. I shall argue that the key to the current debate is the question—for whom does the psychologist work? What interest is he paid to further, and what value-judgement does his work embody in consequence? Sartre provides the key word: it is the *universality* of psychological knowledge which is in question. (Ingleby, 1974, p. 316)

Let us consider this a little further as this is a serious charge: not simply about the conduct of a psychologist in a particular case, i.e., individual fallibility, but about the whole psychological endeavour. How does he come to regard the psychologist as operating as no more than a servant?

Psychologists have failed to be the agents of change or the social engineers that Frank (1959) and Segall (1976), to whom we referred earlier, conceive them to be. Ingleby argues:

What has somehow earned itself the label of "empirical psychology" has been the target of particularly determined attacks in the last few years, not just in the social psychology department, but wherever it is practised. Yet it is not at all easy to see what either its proponents or its critics are getting at: ... I shall try to show that the job psychologists do—their role in society—is, in the last analysis, what the conflict is about. (Ingleby, 1974, p. 314)

According to Ingleby, the disquiet about empirical psychology resides partly in its historical development and in a concern about the value-systems implied in particular findings rather than with the correctness or otherwise of the results. It becomes clear, as Ingleby's argument unfolds, that the criticisms of empirical psychology do not come from outside the discipline, but are the subject of a reflexive anxiety by psychologists themselves about what they are doing; a growing awareness of a need for a sociology of psychological knowledge and of the "crisis" in psychology discussed earlier. He claims that those "who have pioneered the application of scientific methods to psychology have all too often used them like horse or mule,' without understanding." It is worth looking at what factors Ingleby claims have affected the status of the "knowledge-base" in psychology. He cites the following:

1. *"Methodological Bemusement."* Namely a tendency to "fetishize" the representations of reality whilst forgetting the underlying realities. Ingleby points out that we often use numbers to mean more than they do. This is a criticism we have already applied to the Clark and Clark findings, based as they were on the insecure foundations of the "dolls test."

2. *The Universality of the Psychologist's Knowledge.* Can research, which is funded by a particular institution or agency, serve both the needs of the person for whom the psychologist works *and* the people within the organization? It is the issue that Nicolaus has drawn our attention to earlier in his "Eyes down, hands up" (1968) speech when he asks from whom are we taking the knowledge and to whom are we giving it? Such

anxieties are not simply about for whom we work, but how this shapes the "knowledge" presented. In working as a psychologist the insights that are gained in the applied field are coloured by the context: it is "social" knowledge. Ingleby (1974) is not as concerned as Nicolaus was with the ways in which psychology can be used to secure the advantage of those in power, although he does not dispute that it is so used, but rather that: "the applications of psychology have formed the concepts to such an extent that psychology can only be used to perform the tasks for which it was fashioned. Thus, psychological knowledge cannot claim the same 'conceptual' universality as, say engineering . . . it is not just its applications which serve particular interests—it is the form of knowledge itself" (p. 317). As we argued earlier, "knowledge" itself, that is the way we think, is actually shaped by the culture we live in, its implicit ideologies, values, and structures. This means, as Ingleby is pointing out here, that it is not only the *jobs* that psychologists do that serve established interests, but even the nature of their psychological thinking actually reinforces and furthers those interests.

3. The Incorporation of Social Norms into the Laws of Nature. Ingleby feels, in examining further the nature of psychological "knowledge," that psychologists "systematic-ally distort reality." This is rather a different assertion from our earlier one—that psychological knowledge is socially constructed—for here Ingleby is suggesting that the process is deliberate and intentional. If social norms are treated as if they are laws of nature then they are viewed as some-how unalterable, basic "givens" that cannot be changed. This means that "society," the *"status quo"* is not even considered as a target for change within the psychologists' usual sphere of operation. Ingleby is, therefore, completely disagreeing with Frank's unquestioning optimism, that psychologists can be instrumental in bringing about changes in society. Ingleby argues, on the contrary, that since psychologists ignore "society" as such and treat social norms as laws of nature a fallacy develops which involves seeing social norms in an immutable way. This fallacy has its roots in a very basic problem for the psychologists' role, which is how to deal with human *agency*, i.e., the fact that human beings make choices and direct their own lives.

4. The Lack of Universality and Hence of Scientific Status in Much Psychological Knowledge is Located in the Concept of "Variables." Ingleby outlines the ways in which the social psychologist has been guilty of a confusion about the status of variables he is dealing with. This has resulted in the social psychologist treating some aspects of the social structure which are unquestionably variables as if they are "constants."

. . . because psychologists collect data on society as it exists, they are easily misled into producing causal theories embodying the covert assumption that the existing social order is the only possible or desirable one—a constant, and not a variable. This follows from the pragmatic nature of the concept of "cause" itself. . . .

Now the conservative bias inherent in the way psychologists set about looking for "causes" is that, when it comes to factors determined by the way society is organized, they treat these as given—i.e., as constants—and not as variables. This is why psychological knowledge cannot claim the universality, at present, of physical knowledge: and I shall argue shortly that it is a direct consequence of the social role that psychologists have—because for them the facts of social life *are* constants, in the sense that their brief does not allow the possibility of varying them. I would go further and suggest that medical knowledge suffers from the same flaw. The doctor is, by the nature of his job, not empowered to change the way people live: in his role as a consultant to society, he therefore takes the client's way of organizing life as a constant and proceeds to look for cures which will remove the problem by other means than changing it. This is why he usually ends up treating symptoms rather than causes—because he is not allowed to consider normal life as the pathogenic condition it so often is: it is not part of his job, whether he practises physical or psychological medicine, to do so. But there is no reason why he should allow his clinical role to distort his empirical perspective: theories of causation cannot be universal if they depend on pragmatic considerations. In many ways they do, perhaps the paradigm case being the concept of "death by natural causes;" when a doctor issues a certificate to this effect, he is including in the concept of "nature" (whose laws, as we know, cannot be altered) a whole host of variables—conditions of work, housing, nutrition, and social relations—which are to a very large extent not part of "nature" at all, but part of that man-made artefact we call civilization.

To sum up: the bias which the psychologist's role gives rise to in his theories can be located in the practical meaning he gives to the abstract concept of a "variable." A "dependent variable" comes to mean one which *must* be varied (the problem he is paid to manipulate), and an "independent variable" one which *may* be varied. Any other factors acquire the status of constants, and like other constants—the speed of light for instance—become imbued with the inviolability of laws of nature. We can see most clearly how theory is moulded by the role of the person making it by taking as our paradigm a scientist whose function is quite overt: the industrial psychologist, whose understanding of human beings is invoked to improve their efficiency at work. It is easy to show that this understanding will be far from universal, either in the sense of being valid in all contexts or being equally geared to the interests of all involved. (Ingleby, 1974, pp. 320–321)

In some of the papers that follow we will be examining the extent to which psychologists define their variables and limit their conceptions of "cause" in terms of their *client's brief* rather than their own. It is *the* issue in the crisis in contemporary social psychology: what could and should the psychologist's role be? Ingleby has expressed himself strongly about the distortions that he sees embedded in empirical psychology, distortions which he believes are determined in two ways: firstly by their applied origin, their origin as an "employer," a "ruler," a "client" to be served; secondly by their ideological "acceptability."

... the psychologist's [and doctor's] job is to service the institutions of family, school and work in the particular form that the existing socio-economic system requires them to take—not in any other, hypothetical forms: correspondingly, he will take as his independent variables those that can vary independently of that system, and will hunt around for causal factors which have nothing to do with the actual form of our civilization. In education, different strategies of learning; in clinical psychology, different attitudes to one's situation; in medicine, different drugs or operations.

From what I have said, it would appear that psychological knowledge is more likely to obscure than to clarify the actual conditions of human life: in the rest of the paper, I shall advance the proposition that this activity of obscuring is, in fact, an important unwritten part of the psychologist's job, and moreover that by studying the smokescreen itself we may learn a lot about what it is there is to conceal. What I have in mind is that psychology can perhaps be understood as having the same role socially as the conscious ego has individually: at both levels, since (as T.S. Eliot put it) "human kind cannot bear very much reality," the symbolizing mechanism will be engaged in constructing defences against the experience of things as they are—but the form of the resulting distortions, once we know the code, will point to the facts of life against whose perception they are defences. Properly speaking, this applies not only to psychology, but to all the ways in which man represents to himself his own activities. (Ingleby, 1974, pp 322–323)

Ingleby acknowledges that the humanistic psychologists have been trying to promote individual self-realization, fulfilment, creativity, etc. But he feels that they, too, have failed to comprehend the social realities which hinder the achievement of these goals so that "becoming fully human becomes not a universal human right, but a middle class leisure activity." He further argues that:

It is possible to practise a psychology which does something more than reproduce collective illusions, just as it is possible to escape from one's own phantasies into relationships with real people: in both cases, the pre-requisite of losing one's illusions is renouncing that which creates the need for them—the refusal to apprehend certain disturbing facts of life. What is therefore necessary is for psychologists to try and hold political realities and psychological problems in focus at the same time. (Ingleby, 1974, p. 327)

It follows from this discussion that the roles of psychologists should be conceived as lying at the interface between the individual and society and their applied roles should involve re-negotiating the two realities at the same time. We have seen in Ingleby's argument that psychologists should not merely unquestioningly "service" the social institutions of the family, school, and work, but should be working as agents of change across the broad social canvas. In this view, psychologists should no longer simply ensure that individuals fit comfortably into society, but they should re-examine the nature of the "fit" by questioning the nature of the relationship between the *two* variables. Leaving this exhortation with you, we now return to an examination of some possible ways of classifying the roles psychologists play.

TYPOLOGIES OF PSYCHOLOGISTS' ROLES

We have already mentioned another long-standing dialogue in social psychology concerning the roles the psychologist can play in relation to specific tasks. We have briefly encountered Segall's model and the three roles he identifies. Let us now look in a little more detail at these three roles.

Reading IV.   Three Models for Political Psychology, by M. H. Segall

Psychology's contributions to public policy analysis can take several forms. In this book, we shall advocate three approaches, which will be presented as "models." Although together they comprise complementary and over-lapping approaches to political psychology, they should also be thought of as independent alternatives.

Model One: The Psychologist as "Expert Witness"

In this, the simplest model, the psychologist merely offers what he knows to those who could apply it. If it is acknowledged merely that psychological facts ought to be brought to bear on policy dilemmas, then policy makers, either elected officials or their appointed administrative agents, could be encouraged to seek interpretations of existing psychological facts from psychologists. The judgment as to the relevance of such facts and their implications for a particular policy dilemma would be exercised by the policy makers themselves.

Presumably there will occur instances in which the expert testimony of the psychologists would contain contradictions. Under such circumstances, although Model One leaves the responsibility for resolving them to the policy maker, he might press the psychologists to clarify matters, for their expertise includes practice in determining the circumstances under which one principle applies rather than an apparently contradictory one.

In the final analysis, however, the policy maker has both the right and the responsibility to select from the testimony what he considers to be the most relevant arguments and to base his choice of policy on a combination of those arguments and whatever moral, ethical, or ideological values he considers pertinent. While this model advocates considerable input from the psychologist, an essential feature of the model is clearly that the ultimate choice of policy remains in the hands of the policy maker/administrator. This model involves, then, no shift in power since society's usual agents remain free to use or reject whatever psychological information is made available to them.

The single best-known example involves the 1954 U.S. Supreme Court decision that racial segregation was unconstitutional which we have already discussed in Chapter 2.

. . . This was truly a landmark decision, not only for society at large but also for the discipline of psychology. It was a rare and dramatic instance of

Source: Segall, M. H. (1976). *Human Behavior and Public Policy: A Political Psychology*. New York: Pergamon Press Inc., pp. 18–28.

psychology's serving as expert witness, thus exemplifying Model One. Given this example, it ought to be clear that the Model has implications that are not at all inconsistent with contemporary humanitarian values. It may, therefore, be hoped that the Model will be employed far more often in the future than it has been in the past.

Model Two: The Psychologist as Policy Evaluator

Imagine, if you can, "an honest society, committed to reality testing, to self-criticism, to avoiding self-deception. . . . It will be a scientific society in the fullest sense of the word 'scientific.' The scientific values of honesty, open criticism, experimentation, willingness to change once-advocated theories in the face of experimental and other evidence will be exemplified." This noble vision was the creation of Donald T. Campbell, eminent psychological methodologist and recipient in 1970 of the Distinguished Scientist Award of the American Psychological Association and in 1975, the president of the Association. Campbell's words serve well to introduce our second model, which advocates that psychologists contribute their research tools to help policy makers determine the effectiveness of their social programs.

In contrast with Model One, wherein the psychologist contributes existing empirical findings, Model Two is concerned only with the psychologist's methodological expertise, his ability to ask answerable questions about variables which might influence human behavior. At the same time, as Campbell himself made clear, Model Two shares with Model One the important feature that ". . . the conclusion drawing and the relative weighting of conflicting indications must be left up to the political process" (Campbell, 1969, p. 8).

One of Campbell's basic arguments regarding social programs as presently constituted in the United States and elsewhere is that it is difficult to say not only what *is to be* done but also what *has been* done. Particularly when programs have been introduced without a preplanned effort to assess them, their evaluation is an extremely complex process, calling for exacting methodological skills. These typically require a degree of sophistication that is possessed by relatively few people who have been trained, as have research psychologists, in the twin arts of statistical inference and research design.

Assessment and evaluation are difficult even under the best of conditions, but the problem of arriving at valid assessments of actual social programs is exacerbated by several conditions which prevail in most societies. These conditions were reviewed by Campbell in a 1969 paper. In it he noted, "It is one of the most characteristic aspects of the present situation that *specific reforms are advocated as though they were certain to be successful*" (Campbell, 1969, p. 409, italics in original). Typically, a reform program advocate, in order to obtain funding for the program from those who control the purse strings, feels himself compelled to assure them of the program's likely (if not guaranteed) success. Once having committed his position and career to that particular program, he is likely to "prefer to limit the evaluations to those the outcomes of which [he] can control" (p. 409).

An even more unfortunate ramification of present conditions surrounding program evaluation is that hardly ever is there more than one program in any given arena to be evaluated! Comparison, which is the *sine qua non* of evaluation, is seldom possible.

To deal with such difficulties, Campbell has carried what is in effect our Model Two to its logical conclusion by proposing the creation of an "experimenting society." In his terms, this would require a shift "from the advocacy of a specific reform to the advocacy of persistence in alternative reform efforts" (1969, p. 410). In other words, in the Campbellian concept of the experimenting society, policy makers would typically seek funds to establish several alternative pilot projects, which could be conducted either simultaneously or in programmed sequence. Their relative effectiveness would be assessed and the best features of each retained. With modifications as indicated by the assessment, a pre-tested program would emerge.

. . .Any research, even an experiment done under laboratory conditions, with maximal control by the experimenter of variables that could influence the outcome of his experiment, is subject to invalidity. When research is done outside the laboratory, with the likelihood that numerous influences have been left free to vary, the threats to the validity of conclusions drawn by the researcher are much more intense. Since evaluation studies must be done in real-world settings, they are particularly subject to invalidity threats.

Campbell has distinguished two classes of threats to the validity of an evaluation study. The first includes any circumstance which makes it likely that an obtained "effect" of a program was not really a result of that program but a result of some unknown or uncontrolled variable. These are referred to as *internal validity threats*. The second class, *external validity threats*, includes any circumstance that casts doubt on the representativeness or generalizability of the research outcome. . . .

Model Three: The Psychologist as Social Engineer

. . . A recent president of the American Psychological Association (George A. Miller) [asserted] that psychology is a revolutionary intellectual enterprise, which can produce a new public conception of what is humanly possible and desirable. . . . A recent science advisor to the President of the United States (Jerome Weisner) [has pleaded] for federal financial support for "social engineering." Together, these ideas reflect the essence of our third model for political psychology. In effect, this model says, "We have a new way of understanding human behavior which should be applied toward the maximization of occurrence of socially desirable behavior."

Implied in this model is the notion that our new understanding of behavior consists of a fairly detailed awareness of how human behavior is controlled. Hence, the application of psychology that is called for in Model Three boils down to the intentional use of techniques of behavioral control. In other words, since we know how behavior is controlled, we, rather than someone else, may control it; so let's do so rationally and, of course, for good ends.

There can be little doubt that this model is attractive to many and anathema to many others. It is clearly the only really controversial one of the three models being advocated in this chapter. I have found that whenever it is proposed it provokes vigorous, sometimes angry, discussion. Among the first questions asked whenever the concept of conscious behavioral control is raised are these:

Do psychologists really know enough about how behavior is controlled?
Who will decide which behaviors are socially desirable?
Won't social engineering lead to a totalitarian society?
Who will have the power to control behavior and how, if at all, will they themselves be controlled?

Often, such questions are asked rhetorically; the questioner doubts that they can satisfactorily be answered. Nevertheless, they are legitimate questions, pertaining to issues of considerable importance, and they deserve answers. Even if their being asked is a disguised attack on this model of political psychology, those who advocate the model must try to answer them.

The single best-known effort to date to deal with such questions is by B. F. Skinner in his book *Beyond Freedom and Dignity* (1971). It is a carefully reasoned effort by this eminent experimental psychologist to summarize some basic principles that reveal how human behavior is shaped and controlled by environmental forces (both natural and man-made) and to argue that this knowledge should be employed to produce pre-planned social change. Obviously, then, Skinner's book exemplifies Model Three.

ROLES: AN IDEALIZED VIEW

Segall's scheme is an interesting one and indeed focuses our minds on certain aspects of the psychologist's operation. He is, however, unduly confident about the "facts" the expert is able to provide. We have already looked critically at claims made for the universality and scientific status of social knowledge.

Segall also glides very lightly over the *choice* of expert and indeed his or her role as not simply an "expert," but also a professional. As an example of the difficulty here, a paper, written by Loxley in 1975, concerning a High Court judgement that prevented doctors carrying out a sterilization operation on an 11-year-old who had Soto's Syndrome (which is characterized by epilepsy and a mild degree of subnormality) concludes:

One of the dangers of "professionalism" is the arrogant assertion of spurious expertise in the arbitration of other people's affairs. Psychologists are by no means always on the side of the angels. There is a moral dilemma concerning confidentiality, allegedly in the interest of the client, and public accountability, about which we make a similar assumption. The "expert" is apt to conceal himself both from his client, sheltering behind his official mantle (cf. Jourard,1972), and from public accountability, under the guise of protecting the confidentiality of his client. This is not necessarily the case if the client happens to be a child (Gilham, 1973). (Loxley, 1975–6)

Loxley felt strongly about "spurious expertise" because the original decision to sterilize the child had been made by a paediatrician and "had completely ignored the educational, psychological, and social evidence which contradicted his personal views." An educational psychologist was largely responsible for generating the public controversy and guiding the eventual legal outcome by organizing a determined campaign by educational and social workers to have the doctor's unilateral decision overruled. The case raised some important issues not simply about the psychologist's role, but about the operation of any professional expert in the applied field, questions which must add to our concern about Segall's comfortable "ideal" types. *Who* chooses the "expert" and what reliance is put on his or her views and testimony— whether he or she is acting as an expert witness, a policy advisor or setting in motion changes as a "social engineer"—are important questions. Loxley puts a fine edge on this disquiet by asking "How does a paediatrician come to be regarded, by some members of his own profession at least, as interchangeable with a psychologist? This is a sub-question of the broader challenge to the medical profession's apparent belief that it contains global knowledge within itself. No profession is, or can be, omniscient" (Loxley, 1976, p. 1).

Questions about the universality of the "knowledge" of the "expert." Questions about whether the knowledge base is solid and relevant or diffuse and tangential. Questions about conceptions of "cause." All are of concern to us as we look at the "ideal" types of operations of psychologists in an applied field. Segall's scheme, apart from its over-confidence about "expert" status, also fails to capture the dynamic nature of the psychologist's work in a social world.

CONTEXT AND PROCESS

Another social scientist, Cherns (1979), takes a view of the psychologist's role that is much more "process" based. He does not see the psychologist as walking on stage in a particular guise, but as being involved in a long negotiative process of seeking funding, defining the task, clarifying outcomes, deciding upon possible research strategies, ways of communicating results and so on. One thing which unifies the psychologist's activities (and, indeed, all three of Segall's roles are united in this respect) is that the psychologist believes that the solution to the problem does have some psychological components. Although economic, political, environmental and other problems are possibly contributory factors, nevertheless, there are some psychological causes and consequences that are worth investigating.

Let us look at Cherns' view of the psychological operation in the real world. Cherns claims that the social sciences have contributed to policy by: (1) providing the policy-maker with a theory, good or bad (a role parallel to Segall's expert witness); (2) providing data; and (3) occasionally devising technical solutions to problems.

Cherns, in the paper that follows, makes it clear that "giving knowledge away," which Miller (1969) has urged us to do, is not only problematic in terms of anxieties (such as Nicolaus had as to whether "knowledge" is being given to those "below" or to the establishment) but also in terms of the actual translation of knowledge into an appropriate form relative to the problem, which is in itself a challenge to the psychologist. Cherns emphasizes that an important part of the social scientist's role in relation to the policy-maker is making their knowledge accessible. This takes up what was emphasized earlier about the determining influence of the person or agency for whom the psychologist works. It also highlights the fact that apparently there is a discussion to be had with Segall about the way in which the psychologist tenders psychological expertise to the policy-maker. Cherns points out that: "what is seen as valid knowledge in one frame of reference will not necessarily be accepted in another." Part of the problem is that policy-making, as we have seen in the school desegregation debate, is not a once-and-for-all affair. It is sequential and programmatic; thus there are a number of activities which result in the selection of one course of action, which is thought to be more likely than others to bring about the state of affairs envisaged by the policy-makers. The nature of the decision-making process affects, in Cherns' view, the nature of the psychologist's role.

Reading V.   Relationship Between
Policy-maker and Social Scientist, by A. Cherns

Whether the [role of the] social scientist is described as one of advisor or consultant, researcher or even critic, his relationship with the policy-maker is essentially one of provider of knowledge, whether it be an analytical framework or new facts or new relationships between previously known facts. The knowledge to be usable must have validity for the client.

Niehoff (1966) discusses ways in which knowledge must be adapted to pass effectively from one culture system to another. He refers to the 'sociocultural component, which means simply that technical know how and economic patterns are embedded in cultural systems, elaborate patterns of customs and beliefs, which can either act as sanctions or barriers to technical or economic change'. It may be presumptuous to point to the difference between administrative and academic cultures in one's own country as obstacles to acceptance of the validity of social science knowledge. Nevertheless, we are not entitled to assume that all administrative organizations in our society are equally ready to accept the legitimacy of ideas. Hauser (1967) has made the point that in a complex society we have 'almost every stage of social evolution simultaneously present'. So what is seen as valid knowledge in one frame of reference will not necessarily be similarly accepted in another.

Source: Cherns, A. (1979), *Using the Social Sciences.* London: Routledge & Kegan Paul, pp. 150–155.

Warren Bennis (Bennis et al., 1961) has sketched what is required for knowledge generated by the social sciences to be 'valid'. His 'desiderata' include taking into consideration 'the behaviour of persons operating within their specific institutional environment', accepting that groups and organizations are 'as amenable to empirical and analytical treatment as the individual', and, above all, including 'variables the practitioner can understand, manipulate and evaluate'. But even the most heroic efforts to generate 'valid' knowledge will fail if the 'practitioner' (as Bennis calls him though sometimes referring to him generically as the 'client system'), or in our terms, the policy-maker, fails to generate the corresponding capacity to assimilate the knowledge provided. The demands on the social scientist to make himself understood, his advice practical, are familiar. But there is equal need for a corresponding effort on the part of the policy-maker to acquire familiarity with the concepts of social science, if only to provide a conceptual framework which enables him to relate 'values' to probable action.

But above all, the client system must have, or must develop, channels for diffusion of the 'valid' knowledge. Lazarsfeld, Sewell and Wilensky (1968) describe this problem: 'Whatever study has been made, whatever fund of available knowledge has been drawn upon, then comes the moment when one has to make the *leap from knowledge* to decision.' But the concern of the social scientist cannot end at the point where he has made valid knowledge available to the policy-maker. He must also, if he is concerned with the usability of, as well as the validity of, this knowledge be concerned with the policy-maker's capability of adopting the conceptual base into which the knowledge can be absorbed so as to make the leap from a secure platform. This means among other things that the policy-maker and social scientist must have similar conceptions of the relationship of science to policy. Horowitz (1967) points out that social scientists are anxious to study the policy process so as to add to scientific knowledge, as well as providing 'intelligence' for government, whereas the policy-makers in government are more interested in social engineering than in social science. Horowitz (1967) makes two further important points:

Policy places a premium on involvement and influence; science places a premium on investigation and ideas. The issue is not so much what is studied or even the way an enquiry is conducted but the auspices and purposes of a study.

And further:

We witness in ... the social sciences ... the break-up of the functionalist ideology with its value-free orientation.

This last point we must take up again in consideration of the ethical problems is the relationship of the social sciences to policy. It is important here because it shows that Bennis's valid knowledge is knowledge acquired from a particular stand-point and cannot in any case be regarded as value-free scientific knowledge. However this may reflect on the scientific status of the knowledge, it certainly implies that the valid knowledge provided by the social scientist is based on a system of values shared by both social scientist and policy-maker.

Churchman and Emery (1966) argue the consequences of this very cogently. They discuss the relationship between the organization to which the researcher belongs and the organization which he is studying. They consider three ideal types of this relationship:

> One approach . . . is to regard the researcher as a member of an organization completely independent of the organization being observed.

In this type of relationship the researcher's reference group is the research community with its values of scientific objectivity and disinterestedness and purity. His goals are publication, a scientifically sound piece of work and the recognition of the scientific community. As a member of an entirely different kind of organization from that which he is studying he may not find it possible to identify the organization's problems in terms which meet its real needs. Nor can the research organization learn how to make its output more valuable to the organizations it studies:

> A second approach to the study of organizations is to regard the researcher as both a member of an independent research community and a member *pro tem.* of another organization that includes the one being observed.

Here the researcher is faced with insoluble dilemmas. He cannot resolve conflicts in the goals of the two organizations. He has to restrict his involvement in the organization under study and therefore shies away from problems of central importance. Further, he has conflicting claims on his time. Should he end the research when the research organization is satisfied or go on until the observed organization accepts and understands his contribution?

> A third approach to the study of organizations is to regard the researcher as a member *pro tem.* of a third organization under study to encompass the conflicting interests and yet sufficiently close to it to permit its values to be related to the concrete issues of conflict.

In this view we escape the problem of the social scientist's acquiring the values of the policy-maker by requiring that both share values sanctioned by a higher-level organization of which both are members. At the level of their interaction the policy-maker has acquired a capability of using knowledge whose validity is not determined by its relevance to his view as an administrator or the aim and functioning of his organization. Policy-maker and researcher are then able to engage in the mutual learning approach, which is the most effective way in which knowledge generated by social science research can be brought into the action frame of reference of the policy-maker. The basis for this mutual learning must, however, as Buckley (1967) puts it, be continually shifting.

Social order is not simply normatively specified and automatically maintained but is something that must be 'worked at' and continually reconstituted. Shared agreements that underlie orderliness are not binding and shared indefinitely, but involve a temporal dimension implying an eventual review, and consequent renewal or rejection.

The question then arises: how much shift in the basis of the 'shared agreements' can take place without overstraining the tension between the policy-maker and the researcher? At what point do roles undergo so much change that the basis of negotiation has been changed requiring new roles? And if new roles are required, can they be assumed without a change of cast?

G. N. Jones (1969) has introduced the definition of three roles involved in the processes of change in policy in organizations. These roles are 'change agent', 'change catalyst' and 'pacemaker'.

The 'change agent' is a 'helping professional'. Like the 'client system', he possesses 'his own unique set of values, norms and behavioural patterns'.

The change agent is a 'helping professional'. Like the 'client system', he possesses 'his own unique set of values, norms and behavioural patterns'. client system and is at all times free to move between them.

The pacemaker, which may be an individual, group or organization, has as its primary function the maintenance of the change process 'by the proper and the systematic changes of stimuli'.

At different stages during the consideration and adoption of policy changes, using knowledge generated by social science research, the three functions of agent, catalyst and pacemaker become crucial and remain of importance for different durations. All three functions can be fulfilled by social scientists, but not by the same social scientist, as they involve different sets of relationships with the policy-maker. Difficulties arise in practice because, as the basis of the 'shared agreement' shifts, demands are made first on one then on another of these roles. Simple models relating one researcher to one policy-maker ignore the variety and complexities of these relationships and ignore, too, the fact that both policy-maker and researcher must operate within organizational contexts.

Not only are we obliged to consider different relationships between policy-maker and researcher at different stages of the policy process, we also need to consider the different relationships appropriate to different kinds of research. Moreover, not only do different types of research have associated with them different channels of diffusion, but different types of research are also linked to different diffusion channels.

The time characteristics of the policy-administrative process set many specific problems for research. It is not only a question of the policy-maker's need for quick results nor his difficulties in attempting to predict what will be his future needs for research. Different kinds of information are needed at different phases of the policy process. Analytic studies classifying and possibly increasing options are required at the stage when options are being generated and considered. Technical studies are needed at the stage of realizing options. Manipulative 'research' may be called for at the stage of obtaining acceptance of the favoured option. For example, researchers may be asked to find out how a particular policy can be 'sold'. Or they may be asked to undertake research aimed to 'show the need for XYZ' or to make findings selectively available (see Rainwater and Yancy, 1967). The time characteristics of the phases of the policy-making process and of the associated researchers can be expected to match only in the case of action research (which cannot otherwise be undertaken).

Now when we put together the points we have made so far we see that:

1 Policy implies a sequence of decisions, with what is executive at one level becoming policy at the next level below.

2 In the stages of the policy-making process different social science inputs are required.

3 As a consequence of (1) and (2) multiple entries into the decision-making process are required both in terms of points in the sequence and level of intervention.

4 The basis for any transaction between policy-maker and social scientist requires: (a) some shared values sanctioned by their mutual relationship to a higher level, if temporary, organization; and (b) continuously renegotiated terms of reference.

5 The research may be of various types each of which is associated with a set of typical diffusion channels and is, therefore, best conducted by different types of research institution.

6 If the research is not of an 'operational' or 'action' type it may not enter the action channel unless it has built into it a strategy for implementation—in effect an operational or action research phase.

Following this analysis it would seem that the linkage between policy-making and social science can be improved by changes in the mutual perceptions of policy-maker and social scientist and their joint understanding of the potential relevances of research and the problems of diffusion of its results into channels of action and policy-making. A greater planned range of research institutions with special competences in one or other kind of research would doubtless help too. But we can get just so far with tailoring research to assist in the formulation and realization of policy. At least as much advantage could come from using the resources of social science to *improve the policy-making process.*

The psychologist plays a part in securing the platform so that the "leap from knowledge to decision" can be made more onfidently. He also variously acts as agent, catalyst, and acemaker at different stages in the policy-making process. Different kinds of information will be required at successive tages of this process.

Cherns establishes that social psychologists, like any other social scientists operating in a social world, do not give their advice, collect data, interpret, and analyze that data in a neutral "zone." They operate within the cultural assumptions which they themselves unconsciously feed. The knowledge-base of social psychologists is "structured" by their own beliefs, preoccupations, and values and these in turn derive from their membership of the society of which they are, professionally or not, a part. They cannot, even if aware of this, disengage themselves.

The "role" of the psychologist, however, is not only constrained by the fact that his or her "part" is already half written in the action that takes place on the social stage, but also because once the action has started, the freedom to manoeuvre and the freedom to interpret both the play and the parts in it will be limited. Taking the issue chronologically, the negotiations of the research contract will in many ways shape the "role," the psychologists' perceived identity, in terms of the work to be undertaken and the extent and limitations of their professional powers. Cherns argues that the actual formulation of the research contract is a vital part of the whole engagement and too often, if the original expectations are disappointed or confounded, weaknesses are looked for in the *research* but very rarely are the original contract and the contingent expectations referred to which may in fact be the source of the problem. In the extract that follows, Cherns sets out a scheme classifying the various types of behavioural science engagements.

Reading VI.   Behavioural Science Engagements, by A. Cherns

Having highlighted some of the complexities of negotiating a research contract and defining the problem to be researched, we now turn to a more

---

Source: Cherns. A. (1979). *Using the Social Sciences.* London: Routledge & Kegan Paul. p. 172–176.

general classification of the forms of engagement between social scientists and organizations.

Clark (1972) draws the conclusion, from which we would not wish to dissent, that the 'collaborative/dialogic' mode is the one which offers most potential for the constructive use of the behavioural sciences in assisting organizations to develop and to change in response to their environments.

And yet it is probable that only a minority of engagements are of this kind, although many practitioners would claim that they invariably operate in this manner. The discrepancy is part misconception, part self-delusion. The essence of the collaborative/dialogic or action research mode is joint decision-making by client and researcher/consultant. There are certain decisions which can only be implemented by one party—the decision to use a particular method of investigation or to change the content of jobs or the structure of the organization or organizational rules. In these cases the decision is perhaps more accurately described as 'consultative' rather than joint, but there seem to us to be three key areas of decisions which must be taken jointly if the requirements of collaborative dialogue are to be met. These are: the nature of the problem, the nature of the solution, and the methods of investigation.

We have already considered the process of defining the problem and suggest that if the problem definition is negotiable, the opening period of the engagement will be taken up largely with arriving at a mutually acceptable formulation, a process which has to be clearly recognized and budgeted for.

Somewhat similar considerations operate in respect of the client's perception of the type of solution he will be presented with. Indeed in his

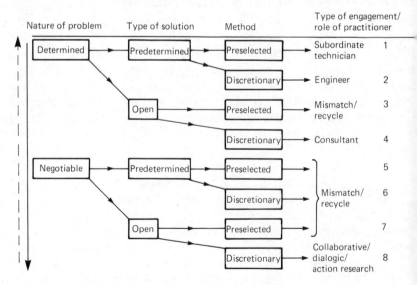

FIG. 3.1   Degrees of freedom and types of engagement.

approach to the researcher the client may begin with the solution and may not even refer to the 'problem' at all. 'We need human relations training for our supervisors', or 'We need an incentive payment scheme'. Again, it is perfectly possible to do what one is bidden, but again this is to deny any diagnostic role or even a problem-solving role to the researcher.

The client may already have decided on his choice of method. 'We want an attitude survey' is one of the commonest approaches made by clients. And once again it is possible to gratify his wish. The client may even invite the practitioner to interpret the outcome for him and perhaps even suggest what actions would be appropriate in the light of this interpretation. But the role of the practitioner is reduced to a purely technical one.

A simple figure should clarify these points and allow the introduction of a dynamic aspect (see Fig. 3.1).

There are eight possible combinations of the alternative positions of each of the three variables. Combinations 1, 2, 4 and 8 represent consistent combinations; 3, 5, 6 and 7 are inconsistent, which is not to say that they never occur but are unlikely to have outcomes unless the inconsistencies are removed.

Engagement 1

We have already given as an example the contract 'to conduct an attitude survey'. All that is required of the practitioner is that he use the technical skill he has in selecting the appropriate questionnaire, administering and scoring it. His role is that of a technical subordinate exercising his skills for ends determined at higher executive or political levels.

Engagement 2

When the choice of method is discretionary, our practitioner is in the role of engineer. Problem: lack of communication between one side of river and the other. Solution: build a bridge. Method: leave to the discretion of the engineer. Again, however, there is nothing especial about this role, which makes it preferable for its practitioner to be located outside the organization.

Engagement 4

Keeping the example of Engagement 2, the problem of lack of communication across the river need not necessarily be solved by the construction of a bridge. A ferry, a tunnel, are possibilities—the problem may be solved by better telecommunications. A communications consultant would be an appropriate person to advise on the appropriate mix of methods which would achieve the most cost-effective linking of people on either side of the divide. A consultant has every right to assume, if he wishes, that his client, having taken stock of his situation, knows what his problem is. Providing the nature of the solution is going to be influenced by his consulting work and the method is a matter for his judgment, the consultant has an appropriate task.

Engagement 8

The distinguishing feature is the negotiability of the nature of the problem as well as the type of solution. It is negotiable, not totally open. It is unlikely that a client will ask for help or advice unless he has some problem bothering him or some change in mind. He may, as we have described already, have diagnosed his problem or he may ask for help on the basis of his symptoms—the presenting problem. If he asks for help on the basis of his own diagnosis, it is a simple matter to ask for the symptoms on which the diagnosis rests. Thus a client may put forward any of the following:

(a) 'We have a high labour turnover'—presenting problem, symptom;

(b) 'We have a problem of human relations'—diagnosis;

(c) 'We need a new incentive scheme'—solution;

or

(A) 'We have a high number of quality rejects'—symptom;

(B) 'We have an inspection problem'—diagnosis;

(C) (C_1) 'We need training for our inspectors' or (C_2) 'We need a new incentive scheme'—solutions.

If propositions (c), (C_1) or (C_2) are put to engineers (i.e. Type 2) they will doubtless be efficiently tackled whether or no they resolve the presenting problem. Propositions (b), (B) will be acceptable to a consultant (i.e. Type 4), who will expect to advise his client on the solution of his problem. If, however, the consultant is inclined to probe, to withhold a decision that he has the appropriate competence to help the client, to want to assure himself first that the presenting problem is sufficiently near the root cause not to mask something quite different, he will attempt to negotiate the nature of the problem with the client (i.e. Type 8).

In arriving jointly at a definition of the problem, the client and the practitioner will have begun their collaboration and should have put in place some of the mechanisms for joint determination of the progress of the engagement, of data collection, analysis, solutions, implementation and evaluation.

This will, however, be a dynamic situation, as suggested by the two vertical arrows on the left of Fig. 3.1. The solid arrow represents the striving of the action researcher/collaborative—dialogic consultant. The hatched arrow represents the controlling urge of the organization. Uncertainty, an open system, are the conditions under which inventive solutions are most likely and under which the broadening of the base of decision-making within the organization is able to come about.

Because opening everything to negotiation and challenge leads to a feeling of loss of control by organization management, they tend to enter cautiously and reluctantly into an engagement of this kind and to generate pressures towards restriction and closure, a regaining of the feeling of being in control. It should, of course, be the concern of the practitioner to keep the system open long enough to enable systemic change, where required, to take place and to aim at an end state where sufficient openness still exists for a continuing adaptive evolution. At the same time he should beware of overstraining the organization members' tolerance of uncertainty and risking a retrogressive reaction and premature termination of the engagement. The possible state of the engagement is, therefore, governed by the balance of these two opposing tendencies. The best safeguard against a disastrous attempt to hold the engagement at an inappropriate state is an understanding by both sides of the nature of the engagement and the forces operating in it.

This chapter has considered the way psychologists have been attempting to put their house in order in recent times. It is not the intention or aim of this Reader to provide a resolution to the tensions that beset the discipline or to decide in favour of one school of thought or another. We see our goal as more that of playing devil's advocate, so that you are aware of these unresolved differences and you are left to arrive at your own point of view. In our next chapter we move from what has at times been an abstract and theoretical discussion of psychologists' roles to a more detailed examination of the work done by particular psychologists.

4

Psychologists in Action

The outcome of any serious research can only be to make two questions grow where only one grew before.

(T. Veblen, quoted in Bunde, 1919)

In this chapter, we want to look at some examples of the kind of engagements psychologists take on in the 'real world'. It is not possible, of course, to survey the full range of tasks psychologists have undertaken. You will become aware in reading the extracts in this chapter that roles shade off into one another. In every real-world engagement the psychologist is at times an expert, a policy evaluator, and an agent of change. The relative importance of each of these components varies from one assignment to another. Whether the roles are made explicit or not, there are always questions concerning funding, the definition of the problem, the identification of possible outcomes and the choice of method. Despite such a classification of roles not necessarily representing clearcut divisions, it has a useful organizing function. The roles we have chosen to illustrate are the psychologist as independent expert, i.e., "scholar"; the psychologist as expert advisor, i.e., "consultant"; the psychologist as experimenter; the psychologist as field-investigator; the psychologist as an inter-professional "resource"; and the psychologist as an agent of change. We do not give a further example of the psychologist as expert witness as Chapter 2 has already presented a detailed example.

THE PSYCHOLOGIST AS INDEPENDENT EXPERT/SCHOLAR

The first of our readings here was written after the end of the Second World War. Psychologists were eager to get back to

111

university research after many years of the practical pressures and demands of their war service. It was in this climate that the research of Smith, Bruner and White was undertaken. The extracts we have chosen are taken from a book which was originally published in 1956, based on research they had started some years earlier. The language in which the paper is couched represents the pre-crisis optimism of the fifties and early to mid-sixties. Although Smith, Bruner and White shared the relief of many of their colleagues in being able at last to get back to some "real" theoretical work after the war, the subject they chose for their studies, that of opinions, was, in fact, an area of crucial social concern. Nevertheless, they were conducting their studies on their own initiative, in the role of the psychologist as a scholar.

Smith, Bruner and White's (1964) paper is an attempt to study the nature of "opinions." They believe that opinions form the link between man and his world. "Opinions, in short, are part of man's attempt to meet and master his world. They are an integral part of personality" (p. 1). They chose to study the opinions that their subjects held about Russia, since Russia had become the subject of much speculation and popular interest. Feelings and attitudes about Russia were changing. The Russians were no longer seen as friends and the Cold War was just beginning. Also, they chose this topic because they could expect people to have strong anxieties about Russia. Therefore, they were conducting pure research in the full academic tradition but in an area that was socially very relevant and important. Although this was a real-world topic, they were not trying to solve a social problem. In moving into this area as theoreticians and researchers what they hoped to do was to sweep away some of the "dead wood" that had accumulated in the psychological literature on opinions and to provide insight into the way people's opinions are formed and the way in which they change. We made a case in Chapter 3 for the need to understand research in the context in which it is undertaken. If we look at the social forces at work when this paper was written, it is possible to see that this confident approach, the authority with which the paper is written, was part of the spirit of the period. The scientist here is the commentator who implies that it is possible to establish a value-free science of personality. The extract we have included suggests that man's values and philosophies *can* be studied in a value-free way. They saw the problem as one of spending more time on research to gain a fuller understanding. As we have already pointed out, this stance is no longer held and we realize that even the "independent" expert is a psychologist who is influenced by his or her contemporary world.

The second example we have chosen to illustrate the psychologist acting as an independent academic expert comes from much later in the history of the discipline. Clarke and Clarke (1976) also chose to look carefully at a subject of popular, as well as professional concern. They examined a seemingly well-established psychological truth, which has had a profound effect on social policy and practice. It has been commonly believed that the child's experience of the social world in the first few years of life provides a determining influence over later development. The implication of this assumption is, of course, that experience in the later years of childhood is less important and less formative. It is the latter-day equivalent of the early Jesuit view. Clarke and Clarke painstakingly mapped out the constituent hypotheses for this view and meticulously examined the evidence and the counter-evidence for each of these assertions. Their findings underlined how flimsy much of the "evidence" was for this emphasis on early experience and also how rarely alternative interpretations or contradictory evidence had been sought. This study is important in our examination of the psychologist in the role of expert. It reminds us that quite often the knowledge-base itself, from which the psychologist operates, has not been firmly established. It makes us aware that one task the scholar performs is to look again at the ideas which are subtly informing social policy, and, in the ways Cherns has suggested, are feeding back into the discipline and reinforcing myths.

In the extended extract we reprint in this chapter (pp. 133–141) from Clarke and Clarke, we look at the hypotheses that they examined and their final "verdict" on each of these. The book from which this is taken tries to show how prevailing beliefs about the necessity for continuity of care have influenced policies concerning the age at which children can safely be offered for adoption, although they believe that there are signs that this is changing. Maternal deprivation theory, another component of our ideology of childhood has had an abiding influence on social policy by leading to a narrow conception of women's role in society. The following piece from Clarke and Clarke (1976) discusses the way in which ideology and social policy may draw on psychological theories.

Social Policy and Early Experience

... Patricia Morgan (1975) offers a broad critique of one aspect of the current theme, namely the maternal deprivation theory which she sees as underpinning current child-rearing ideology, and the role of women in society. She states correctly:

> ... for about twenty years, the public, including the most influential bodies responsible for social policy-making, has been persuaded that the connection between maternal deprivation and personality damage has been scientifically established, and that it enjoys the same kind of authoritative standing as other medical discoveries. ... But the true position is not remotely like this. By experimental standards as strict and coherent as those applied in the case of rubella, for example, the Maternal Deprivation Theory has no significant scientific support, and there is sufficient counter-evidence to make it decidedly improbable. (Morgan 1975, pp. 17–18)

She goes on interestingly to argue that a rejection "of the erroneous view of childhood must involve us in very wide reappraisals of our assumptions about society."

There is little difficulty in justifying these arguments whether from earlier official documents or from the "experience" of intelligent people who perceive problems in the light of this model. Thus a World Health Organization Expert Committee (1951) regarded the use of day nurseries and crèches as leading to "permanent damage to the emotional health of a future generation." Baers (1954) claimed the children's normal development is dependent on the mother's full-time role in child rearing, and that "anything that hinders women in the fulfilment of this mission must be regarded as contrary to human progress." At a more popular level a mother refers to persistent school phobia in her daughter and to "endlessly examining myself and her home to find the reason; I accept that it was the mother-separation anxiety she suffered in her most formative years" (*Guardian*, 27 August 1975).

The quasi-mystical bond between mother and child, seen as the great shaper of the future by psychoanalytic writers, has led in practice (and particularly among social workers) to the adoption of the slogan that a bad home is better than a good institution. There is also much talk about the sanctity of the family, and the need to keep deviant families "propped up" with support, rather than remove the children to alternative forms of care. And yet, inconsistently, such workers are ready to point to the perpetuation of disadvantage through poor parent–child interactions; privately many admit that a regular weekly visit is hardly likely to produce significant change, and it is, of course, a common finding that those most in need of help are least likely to seek it, use it or profit by it.

In recent years there has been much talk about labelling and its effect in closing options for the individual. The wholesale acceptance that poor experiences in the first few years inevitably lead to doom has also tended to set in motion administrative decisions which confirm the implication. The disturbed young child, taken away from parents, on a "fit person" order, is sent to an institution rather than a foster home because the prognosis is bad. Only later, if miraculously the child improves, will he be considered for non-institutional care. But by then the next slogan awaits his case. "Children adopted, or fostered late, do badly," so this option is seldom in fact open.

Indeed, the whole field of child care is so bedevilled by case law and by outmoded theories that it is small wonder that increasing criticisms from the voice of common sense are being levelled against its practitioners. In a sense this is unfair to them, for their past training, which in most cases had little effect in encouraging critical attitudes, and instead offered superficial generalizations, is ultimately responsible. In every part of this book the inadequacy of such received wisdom is made manifest, not by exchanging one set of clichés for another, but by examining facts dispassionately, outlining areas of ignorance and uncertainty and drawing appropriate, if modest, conclusions. To anticipate a little, such a survey makes it clear that a child's future is far from wholly shaped in the "formative years" of early childhood. Rather, human development is a slow process of genetic and environmental interactions, with sensitivities (rather than critical periods) for different processes at different times. The implications of such a view are far from being merely academic; they challenge what Morgan (1975) has termed our current ideology of childhood. (Clarke & Clarke, 1976, p. 259–273)

The "expert," then, rigorously examines the findings and theories which influence not only the man in the street, but also the policy-maker. The extract we present from the Clarkes' concluding section (on pp. 133–141 of this chapter) looks at the hypotheses they identified as central ones and the current status of these hypotheses. As this is a synopsis of points dealt with in greater detail earlier in their book you may not follow all their substantive and methodological points. One of the problems with rigorous, painstaking research is that it is not easily amenable to summary. However, you should appreciate how thoroughly they reviewed the evidence and how skilled they were in spotting anomalies. An interesting thing to note about the Clarke and Clarke study was that it was not commissioned or funded by an outside body, but rather it was undertaken by them as part of their own research work at the University of Hull. It is difficult to gauge the impact of such a book but we suspect that it served to crystallize the niggling doubt many professionals had as to what was really established fact as opposed to conjecture. It can, of course, misfire in that if one claims that early experience is *not* vital and irreversible then this can also make the policy-maker complacent about the poor provision of nursery schools and pre-school playgroup facilities. The Clarkes, however, were themselves clearly reserved about the implications of their research and review. It certainly could not be taken to invalidate and completely undermine research on early deprivation and its effects. It just helps us to take a more balanced view. It is very necessary to be aware that even rigorous research may be misused and misquoted. This is a point taken up again and discussed in Chapter 5.

Research cannot itself, however, solve policy problems. The extracts that follow demonstrate the ways in which well-defined research can clear the ground for discussion and identify the problems to be faced more precisely.

Reading VII.   Opinions and Personality,
by M. B. Smith, J. S. Bruner and R. W. White
—Extract I, from Chapter 1 (Introduction)

Of what use to a man are his opinions? It is with this question that we choose to open our inquiry. A pattern of opinions may be for one man a basis of personal serenity in the face of a changing world, for another a goad to revolutionary activity. Opinions, in short, are part of man's attempt to meet and to master his world. They are an integral part of personality.

If opinions are thus inseparable from the rest of personality, then our task is made clear. Not only must we describe opinions; we must also investigate how they are related to other aspects of the person's life. We ask, in brief, what functions are served by the holding of an opinion. The

Source: Smith, M. B., Bruner, J. S. & White, R. W. (1964). (First published 1956.) *Opinions and Personality.* New York: John Wiley & Sons, pp. 1–3.

study of attitudes becomes one phase of the study of complex behavior generally. A "special" psychology of opinion, as Walter Lippmann and William McDougall demonstrated three decades ago, is neither necessary nor to be desired. The theory of opinion in use or of "attitudes in the individual" derives from general principles of personality, of perceiving, remembering, thinking, learning, motivation.

Yet during the first three decades of the century, only two major works appeared with the avowed objective of relating opinions or sentiments to the life processes which constitute personality functioning. One of these, Walter Lippmann's *Public Opinion* [1922], was the work of an inspired amateur who, mindful that men lived in a "personal world" partly of their own fashioning, saw opinions as reflecting the selectivity of man's experience, as means of simplifying the complex social and political world of events to which access was at best indirect. McDougall [1908], on his part, saw the development of opinions or sentiments as the differentiated expression of man's deepest needs, as these were altered in the course of commerce with the environment. For him a sentiment combined a way of striving, a way of knowing the world, and a way of feeling; and insofar as one's needs and sentiments were organized in a pattern of personality, they could never be treated autonomously.

There are perhaps three ways of approaching the study of public opinion. The first and most ancient of these seeks to understand the broad relations between public opinion and political institutions. How does the public, holding what opinions it may, affect the policies of government, its laws, its social and political form? In turn, putting the question more as Aristotle did in the *Politics*, what is the fate of public opinion under various forms of government? That such inquiries seek in the main to form moral judgments on the best relationship between a public and the instruments of government—as in the works of Aristotle, Montesquieu, Locke, or even Machiavelli—underlines the fact that they have often been more normative in spirit than empirical. Such need not, however, be the case. One can indeed understand the relation of government to public opinion prior to evaluating it: and ultimate evaluation may be better for having paused for such dispassionate understanding.

A second approach to the study of opinion, at once less subtle and more empirically demanding than the first, is ecological in spirit. Its emphasis is upon the distribution of opinions in a population and the subgroupings therein. The ecological spirit, in a simple form, is represented by the typical opinion-polling study. What is the division of opinion on an issue? How are opinions on the issue distributed in various segments of the population? And a final question: What accounts for this distribution? More experimentally conceived, such investigations may choose special groups for study in order to test hypotheses: employed and unemployed industrial workers, to study the effect of unemployment on radicalism; veterans and non-veterans, to assess the influence of military service on nationalism; farm workers and farm owners to analyze the effect of ownership on opinions about government subsidies. Ecological studies of this kind provide a ready, if risky, springboard into speculation about the psychological origins of group opinion.

The inferences about psychological origins that grow out of ecological studies bring us to the third or psychological approach. The psychologist wants to know what are the various routes by which one comes to favor a given point of view or to oppose it. Specifically, the psychological approach to the study of opinion asks four kinds of questions. The first of these is a *genetic question*. How did an opinion develop? Through what psychological process did it come into being, undergo transformation, or remain unchanged? The second is an *adjustive question*. What function does an opinion serve in the adjustment of the individual? The third is a *relational question*. One asks what other processes are associated with opinions. Does intelligence correlate with differentiation of opinions in a population of subjects? Is there a relationship between degree of parental dominance experienced and the extremeness of opinions on issues involving authority? Out of these relationships there gradually develops more rational theory. Finally, there are *structural questions*. Since we may properly assume that the individual personality is organized or "structured" in a more or less enduring manner, we ask how opinions fit into this organization or structure.

Extract 2, from Chapter 3
(On Understanding an Opinion)

Some Assumptions about Personality

We have made much of the axiom that the total behavior of a person—including his opinions—reflects certain underlying regularities of functioning. It is this underlying regularity that lends predictability to behavior. The description of this regularity is the description of personality. Our first duty, then, is to make explicit our own assumptions about the nature of personality.

An individual's opinions are but one of a number of consistent and regular forms of behavior which characterize him. From these consistencies in his behavior we infer the individual's *personality*. Personality, then, is an inferred construct to which we ascribe certain dynamic properties—striving, adaptation, defense, etc. Opinions, like all behavior, both constitute part of the data from which personality is inferred and are in turn a function of personality. We account for consistencies in a person's opinions in the same theoretical terms that we use to account for his consistencies of gesture, emotional expression, or purposive action. And

Source;   Smith, M. B., Bruner, J. S., & White, R. W. (1964). *Opinions and Personality*. New York: John Wiley & Sons, pp. 29–47.

since we have learned to regard the various expressions of personality as highly interdependent, we may expect to find important relationships between a person's opinions and other forms of his behavior.

How shall we describe *personality*, the context in which a person's opinions exist? Perhaps the most widely shared point of view on human behavior is what may roughly be called *functionalism*. The human being, according to this approach, is not governed by a rational calculus, nor is he a blank slate on which experience traces its inexorable mark. Nor yet is man an ingenious machine translating physical stimuli into bodily response. Like all animals, he is an organism, a system of life processes that somehow maintains its identity in active interplay with its environment. An organism is never passive, but survives and grows through constant striving, responding selectively to relevant aspects of its environment, and reaching out to incorporate, modify, fend off, or attain. Final passivity is death; in life there is always striving to maintain the delicate adaptation of the needs of the organism to its environment.

. . . Each, through his needs, interests, and aversions defines what for him constitutes the *effective* environment, what Lewin called the "life space." A person does not passively read off his experience; he selects the characters and settings to weave into the plot of his own purposes.

For man, the *social environment* provided by other human beings is particularly significant. Unlike the social environments of other gregarious animals, the potential complexity of the human environment is enormously increased by the fact that man has developed language as a means of communication and as a way of conserving, symbolizing, and manipulating experience. The essential social character of language and its traditionalized categories of thought are of incalculable importance in giving "human nature" its distinctively human character. Indeed, both Freud [1933] in his conceptions of superego and ego-ideal and George Herbert Mead [1934] in his theory of the self have remarked that much of what we label personality represents an invasion of the human organism by his social environment. Personality as we know it is an essentially social product, inconceivable in the completely isolated human being.

. . . Notwithstanding the fact of conflict, each individual personality achieves at least a minimum degree of integration and congruity. A person's various needs and the adaptive devices that he brings to their service form a more or less integrated structure. Lacking a minimum degree of unity, the organism would be incapable of persistent striving. At one level or another the various activities of the organism must strike a balance of mutual compatibility.

Such are the main lines of the view of personality into which we propose to fit a *theory* of opinion. . . .

Describing an Opinion

It follows from our description of personality functioning that we must define an attitude in such a way as to take into account its presumed interrelation with other aspects of personality. With this in mind we define an attitude as a predisposition to experience a class of objects in certain ways, with characteristic effect; to be motivated by this class of objects in characteristic ways; and to act with respect to these objects in a characteristic fashion. In brief, an attitude is a predisposition to experience, to be motivated by, and to act toward, a class of objects in a predictable manner.

We shall not be fussy about the word used to denote the phenomenon described in our definition. Attitude, opinion, sentiment—all of these terms refer to the kind of predisposition we have in mind. The permanence of such a predisposition is less a problem of definition than of measurement. Although it is true that most of the attitudes in which the social psychologist and student of personality are interested are relatively long enduring, we would emphasize the continuity between supposedly short-term "sets" and more long-term "attitudes." Finally, the class of objects around which a sentiment is organized—the object that one is predisposed to experience, to be motivated by, and to act toward in a characteristic manner—need not be restricted as in some definitions of attitude to "social objects" or "controversial issues." For an attitude as we have defined it can be related to any class of objects which exist in the person's life space: moral issues, lifted weights in a psychological experiment, Russia, prime numbers, or what not. The specification of objects is again an empirical matter, not a matter for definition.

. . . Now let us sketch our descriptive apparatus for distinguishing the *object* of an attitude. As we have indicated, it may be anything in the life space of the individual. In less technical terms, it may be anything which exists for the person.

One problem in the use of words can be set aright here. It is important to distinguish the object as it exists for the person and the object as we designate it in common speech. When the object of sentiment is specified in terms of some social referent, we shall speak of the *topic* of an attitude. A man, let us say, has a highly negative attitude toward "Russia -as-it-exists-for-him." "Russia-as-it-exists-for-him" is the *object* of his sentiment. When, however, we speak of this man's attitude toward "the Soviet Union" or "Russia" or some other socially defined entity, we shall be speaking of the *topic* of his attitude. Perhaps the use of these two terms will keep us from the pitfall of assuming that attitudes have as their objects the socially defined entities of the history books and newspaper columns.

We may distinguish various characteristics of the object of a sentiment: *differentiation, saliency, time perspective, informational support*, and *object value*. We shall consider each of these in turn.

Differentiation

An attitude toward Russia may be focussed upon a highly amorphous subjective impression of that country or upon a highly differentiated one. One person will see Russia as a highly complex phenomenon comprising many *aspects;* Russia as a social experiment, Russia as an aggressor, Russia as a country capable of producing many of the great literary figures of the 19th century, Russia as an approach to Orwell's *1984*, Russia as a veritable basin of natural resources, Russia as anti-Zionist—all of these may be aspects of one man's view of Russia. To another man, Russia is a collectivity of ignorant peasants guided by a small ruthless band of radical agitators and "trouble-makers"—and that is about all. Not only is the object of an attitude differentiated into various aspects; it also varies with respect to its *organization.* "Degrees" of structure are not readily specified, and we shall not attempt to scale such a dimension. One can, however, specify the manner in which a differentiated object of opinion is organized. In the second hypothetical case cited above, the major, organizing aspect of our man's view of Russia might be the sensed absence of personal liberty in that country, and all other parts of the picture might be subordinated to it. . . .

Saliency

By this term we indicate the extent to which a particular object or class of objects is central in the everyday concerns of a person. Russia and Communism were matters of the most personal concern and central attention for one of our subjects—almost the most important things in his life. For another, it was of the most marginal interest. We may also speak of the saliency of various differentiated aspects of a man's view of Russia—saying, for example, that Russian anti-religious activity for a given person is more salient than Russian aggressiveness.

Time perspective

Here we mean the temporal frame of reference applied to the object of a sentiment. In our analysis of cases we found this to be an inescapable and vital characteristic of an attitude. Characterizing time perspective systematically is difficult. Yet if we are to predict anything about the way in which the person will guide his actions, it is essential that we do so. Again in terms of Russia, one person will regard Russia as a matter of only momentary, transitory concern: something that erupts into the headlines for a while and then is gone. Another will take, as one of our subjects did, a long-term view, the essential theme of which was: "Russia is an unreasonable child; if we remain firm, she will eventually grow up." Still another will adopt a short-term climactic point of view in which Russia is seen as making tremendous inroads into our strength which, unless stopped immediately, will drive us to disaster. Such characterizations of time perspective are, to be sure, highly qualitative and will undoubtedly vary widely as one goes from one kind of attitude to another. . . .

Informational support

Strictly speaking, this term does not characterize the object itself, but rather the knowledge an individual possesses that is relevant to his attitude. It merely identifies the amount of information a person is capable of bringing to bear in appraising the topic of an attitude. In our studies, for example, we have used rather primitive information tests to determine how much the individual "knows" about various phases of Soviet life and society. We recognize, of course, that there is a very close relationship between the amount of differentiation of an attitude and the amount of its informational support. Differentiation refers to an analysis of the person's subjective conception of Russia (which is based upon many things aside from information): while informational *support* refers merely to the amount of the available information that may go into the building of this conception.

Object value

Here we refer to the affective tone of an object. We had considered the term "object *affect*," our choice of "value" being dictated primarily by the importance of value in the sense of positive, negative, and neutral. For the first thing we usually ask about the object of a person's sentiment is whether it appears as disagreeable, pleasant, or neutral. It goes without saying, of course, that when one has said that Russia is a negatively toned symbol for a given person, one has said very little. One must also specify certain other affective qualities: whether, for example, it is seen as threatening or simply as annoying. . . .

Orientation

Our next task is to characterize the action tendencies aroused by the object: what we shall call the *orientation* of an attitude. Given a person's subjective view of Russia, we may ask how he orients himself action-wise. In abstract terms, we may speak of three possible action tendencies: *approach, avoidance*, and *hostility*. Concretely, and again in terms of an attitude toward Russia, approach may mean a wish to go to Russia, the act of taking books out of the library to find out more about Russia, joining the Communist Party, buying the *Daily Worker* to find out about its side of the story, or what not. Avoidance again may take varied forms: anything from motivated indifference to an actual active avoidance of anything having to do with Russia. Hostility we know to be a subtle and complex form of behavior. By it we mean any act whose objective is injury, debasement, or any other form of harm to the object: advocating a preventive war, voting for a rabidly anti-Communist candidate, or even fantasying a counter-revolution in Russia.

Policy stand

The translation of one's orientation into a preference for a particular proposal for collective action (such as a given foreign policy), we shall call the *policy stand* of the person. *Policy stand* indicates preference for a socially defined policy and may or may not be identical with the individual's own *orientation*. So a person may say, "I'm in favor of taking Russia's veto power away, but what I'd really like to do is to take the whole damned Politburo and dump them into the middle of the Atlantic Ocean." Most of the work done in public opinion polling is designed to discover the policy stands of cross-sections of the population. And one of the major differences between the regular polls and the open-ended surveys is that the latter try to determine the orientation of their respondents in addition to their stand on policies. . . .

The Adjustive Functions of Opinion

We come now to our most central question: What purpose is served by holding an opinion? Put more technically, the question becomes, "What adjustive functions of personality are served by the formation and maintenance of an opinion?"

Let us say at the most general level that one's opinions or attitudes serve as mediators between the inner demands of the person and the outer environment—the material, social, and, most immediately, the informational environment of the person. Figures of speech may be misleading, yet we do well to think of a man's attitudes as his major equipment for dealing with reality. This equipment is not a product solely of basic needs and defenses nor is it fashioned directly according to the blueprint of the world in which the person finds himself. Nor is it simply borrowed ready-made from the groups to which he belongs or aspires. Something of all of these but not quite any one of them, it is, essentially, an apparatus for balancing the demands of inner functioning and the demands of the environment. One cannot predict a man's opinions by knowledge of his personality alone or of his environment alone. Both must enter into any predictive formula.

It is a mistake to restrict the concepts of attitude and opinion to those predispositions which have as their object the issues of contemporary social and political life. Such restriction overlooks the fact that these attitudes are embedded in larger systems of opinion which mediate between the most compelling pressures of the environment and the most imperious and pervasive needs. Perhaps someone will ask, "Why all this searching analysis of a man's half-baked attitudes toward Russia?" The answer is this: look far enough into the origins of any opinion, and one will find not just an opinion but a sample of how the holder of that opinion copes with his world.

Rather than risk later misunderstanding we shall pause for a moment to examine the two meanings that can be attached to "having an opinion." Let us say first that one can *hold* an opinion and at the same time reserve option on when and how the opinion should be *expressed*. It is obvious that the two acts serve somewhat different functions. And while we may be inclined to say that the one is freer of constraints than the other—that a man may hold whatever view he likes so long as he is discreet in its expression—it is the better wisdom to attribute an equal lawfulness to each. Only in a most superficial sense is one "free' to hold whatever opinion he will. The illusion of free choice of opinion is scarcely borne out by closer analysis of the many inner and outer requirements that limit what a person will find acceptable. "I can't believe that," he will say; or, "What an irresponsible, almost despicable point of view that is!"

Once we have said that there is a lawful determination both in the opinions one holds and in the occasions and circumstances of their expression, we must then go on to say that the same laws do not hold for each. The two must be held separate, for separate but concurrent examination. It is true, of course, that the opinions permissible to express are, under some circumstances, the very opinions one wishes to hold. Or, quite the reverse, the rebel may find himself repelled by popular points of view whose expression savors to him of conformism. Such instances do not cancel the need for separate analysis.

In our discussion of the adjustive functions of opinion we shall make no special effort to incarcerate "holding" and "expressing" into separate and purified theoretical categories. They each present somewhat different problems for empirical analysis and we shall, where possible, analyze them separately. Our principal theoretical interest, as the reader must long ago have noted, is in the opinions *held* by the individual. It is a crucial but secondary theoretical problem how a man works out the strategy of their expression.[1]

There are three functions served by holding an opinion, and we shall call them *object appraisal, social adjustment*, and *externalization*. Let us note briefly the characteristics of each and then return to a more extended discussion of their significance.

Object appraisal

We use this expression in the same sense in which psychoanalysts employ "reality testing." The holding of an attitude provides a ready aid in "sizing up" objects and events in the environment from the point of view of one's

---

[1] If one should ask, "How do you know the opinion held by a person save by its expression?" we shall reply that we know it only in that way. Knowledge of a "held" opinion is based upon inference from observation of its expression under a variety of special situations—including those highly permissive diagnosis situations in which there is neither gain nor loss to be earned or incurred by expressing one's views.

major interests and going concerns. Insofar as attitudes are predispositions to experience certain classes of objects, to be motivated by them, and to respond to them, it is evident that their existence permits the individual to check more quickly and efficiently the action-relevancy of the events in the environment around him. Presented with an object or event, he may categorize it in some class of objects and events for which a predisposition to action and experience exists. Once thus categorized, it becomes the focus of an already-established repertory of reactions and feelings, and the person is saved the energy-consuming and sometimes painful process of figuring out *de novo* how he shall relate himself to it. If the environmental fact either defies categorization or is categorized in such a way as to bring harmful consequences to the person, new attitudes may be developed or shifts in categorization may occur. In sum, then, attitudes aid us in classifying for action the objects of the environment, and they make appropriate response tendencies available for coping with these objects. This feature is a basis for holding attitudes in general as well as any particular array of attitudes. In it lies the function served by holding attitudes *per se*. Without them, we should be in the constant throes of determining the relevance of events, of fashioning decisions and of deciding upon actions—all *ab initio*. More specifically, object appraisal is the process whereby the person develops attitudes that are a creative solution to the problems posed by the existence of disparate internal demands and external or environmental demands.

Social adjustment

Opinions can play another role: that of facilitating, disrupting, or simply maintaining an individual's relations with other individuals. It is in this realm particularly that one must take care to distinguish the functions served by holding an opinion and by expressing it, for the strategy of expression is of particular importance in maintaining or cementing one's relationship with what may be called "membership groups"—the individuals with whom one is in direct contact. Where there is a need to be accepted in the community, one will more readily and more forthrightly express acceptable attitudes while inhibiting or modulating the expression of less approved ones.

The function of social adjustment served by holding an opinion is at once more subtle and more complex. For it is by holding certain views that one identifies with, or, indeed, differentiates oneself from various "reference groups" within the population. By reference groups we mean here those groups in terms of whose standards the individual judges himself and with which he identifies or feels kinship. They may or may not correspond to the membership groups with which he has face-to-face commerce; moreover, certain reference groups may never be physically present to the individual for interaction. Representative of reference groups are such symbols as "intellectuals," "average middle-class Americans," "decent girls," and so on. The act of holding certain opinions, ... is an act of affiliation with reference groups. It is a means of saying, "I am like them."

Reference groups, we shall see, may also play a negative role in opinion functioning. There are groups with which one seeks to reject kinship or identification. Thus, one of our subjects sought as hard to dissociate himself from the bourgeoise as he sought to associate himself with the *avant-garde* left. When rebelliousness and rejection are prominent features in a man's adjustment, we may expect negative reference groups to play a prominent role in his opinion formation.

Two rather unique kinds of social adjustment can also be achieved by holding opinions of a certain kind. First, one may develop opinions as the expression of a need to be autonomous from others. Such declarations of autonomy—and we must distinguish the term from rebellion—are in a curious backhand way still another mode of identifying oneself with various reference groups. Thus one of our subjects showed a strong need for working out his opinions independently, unswayed by prevailing points of view. This procedure was for him a way of expressing his lack of dependence on others; but it was also a way of identifying with that nebulous category known as "independent and liberal thinkers." And second, it is sometimes convenient to indulge hostility toward others by holding opinions that are at odds with prevailing beliefs. If such an adjustment be neurotic in origin, it is nonetheless a form of negativism one occasionally encounters.

The very act of holding an opinion, whatever its nature, may serve the social adjustment of the individual. ... Given identification with certain groups—let us take the reference group called "intellectuals"—the individual feels that he *must* have opinions on certain issues to maintain his sense of identification.

We must not, however, leave a false impression. The underlying motive gratified by holding and expressing opinions that aid our social adjustment is neither a conformity need nor its reverse, a need to rebel. A wide variety of psychological mechanisms is at work, motivating us to relate our destinies to those of the concrete membership groups around us and to those of the more remote reference groups to which we adhere. Requirements of ego defense, dependency needs, drives for autonomy, hostility, drives for status, and many other dynamisms may be involved.

Externalization

It would be all too easy to equate externalization of inner requirements with the classical conceptions of projection and displacement. These two mechanisms are two *examples* of what we mean by externalization. Externalization occurs when an individual, often responding unconsciously, senses an analogy between a perceived environmental event and some unresolved inner problem. He adopts an attitude toward the event in question which is a transformed version of his way of dealing with his inner difficulty. By doing so, he may succeed in reducing some of the anxiety which his own difficulty has been producing.

Perhaps an illustration, a case not included in our study, will clarify the process. An adolescent develops a violent hatred for Fascism, the Nazis, and for Hitler, particularly during the 1930's. Although he is not accepted because of his age, he is aroused to the point of volunteering for the Abraham Lincoln Brigade during the Spanish Civil War. Upon entry of the United States into the War, he volunteers, is rejected, but flings himself into a lather of civilian war activity from which he derives a deep satisfaction.

Whence the tremendous intensity of this attitude? Leaving aside the realities of the situation, the grave threat with which Fascism *did* in fact confront the world and which our subject sensed, why was there such an extraordinarily intense compulsion to do something about his feelings? Analysis reveals in this man a strong and unresolved fear of rejection by powerful figures who can be reached neither through their sympathies nor through their intellect: the figure of an inchoate, powerful, cruel, but basically unreachable force. We need not examine the genesis of this deeply repressed fear. It suffices that it existed. The emergence of Hitler and the Nazis served for the adolescent as a concretization or "binding" for this fearsome and rejecting figure. Hitler in a unique way could serve as the apotheosis of that figure which could be reached neither by sympathy nor by reason. Energies previously directed at coping with the inner problem could now be liberated and focussed on an external object. If anxiety could thereby be reduced, so much the better.

We present this case not only to illustrate externalization but also to show how it differs from run-of-the-mill displacement. Certainly the case illustrates displacement, but that is not all: there are also externalization of affect and externalization of action. An external object is treated in terms relevant to an internal problem: where the internal rejecting figure could not be destroyed by direct assault, the externalized object could become a target for highly energized, creatively destructive planning and action. If the externalization proved an adaptive one, that is partly the good fortune of history and partly the result of adequate object appraisal. The fact that there were active membership groups and palpable reference groups with whom our young man could align himself also helped.

The Functioning of an Opinion

Finally we must discuss the various ways in which opinions operate in carrying out their adjustmental functions. We will be forgiven, perhaps, if our exposition reflects the autobiography of our project, for our stumblings may have a certain didactic value.

Early in our program of interviewing and testing it became apparent to us that our subjects expended considerable energy and ingenuity in maintaining the integrity of their attitudes in the face of changing information encountered by them in the newspapers, on the radio, and in conversation. This impression was most vivid when we observed the behavior of our subjects in two of our procedures: the *Stress Interview* and the *Information Apperception Test*. In the first of these, three interviewers confronted the subject with questions ostensibly aimed at "clearing up a few inconsistencies that we had noticed in the course of looking over your interviews." The real object was to test the stability of expressed opinions by presenting counter-arguments and by using the other devices of debate. The second, the *Information Apperception Test*, consisted of a series of "factual" statements about Russia—some pro, some neutral, and some anti in intent—about which the subject was asked, "What do you make of this?" and then requested to judge in terms of the degree to which they were "typical" of Russia.

At the outset the behavior evoked in these situations appeared to us to be primarily defensive in character, designed to ward off or to incorporate in revised form information not congruent with established opinions. Indeed, we slipped into the habit of speaking of "opinion defense," no doubt in analogy to the psychoanalytic conception of ego defense.

Two circumstances broke us of this habit by revealing the superficiality of such a conception of simple defense. The first of these was the gradual realization that the psychoanalytic theory of ego defense was itself faulty in conception when applied to our concrete case materials. The classical ego defenses, it turned out, were, so to speak, last ditch stands of the ego against vicissitudes that had come to be too great a burden for normal handling. And so too opinion defense. A normal adult does far more than simply defend his opinions against inimical information. He may be on the alert for supporting information to nourish them. He may welcome occasions to express them, to give them exercise. He may even seek opportunities to test their ability to withstand challenge.

The terminology that we finally adopted reflects the change in our thinking. In place of "ego defenses" we adopted the term "adjustive strategies"; for "opinion defense" we substituted the phrase "opinion maintenance and furtherance." Part of the process is, of course, narrowly defensive. But there is also a considerable amount of continuous "monitoring" of attitudes with the object of testing their fit not only to reality but also to inner requirements. When one looks carefully at the verbatim transcript of an interview in which a man is discussing his opinions of some matter that interests him, one notes a series of "testings" of the conformance of expressed opinions both with deeper and more general values and with available information. Insofar as the person is in the habit of thinking aloud, so to speak, the process is the more noticeable. We may assume that the same process goes on continuously in the course of dealing with the environment.

The tentative proposition can be offered that the freer the individual is of disruptive anxieties and tumultuous inner demands, the more flexible is the process of "testing" opinions inwardly and outwardly. In the hypothetically mature person, the program of opinion furtherance and maintenance would almost be akin to the scientist's approach to nature. But even in the less-than-mature person, there is a constant push, however slight, toward greater comprehension of the environment and greater congruence of internal convictions.

The effectiveness of this push toward "actualization" (call it what you will) is a function not only of the maturity of the person and his freedom from neurotic trends, but also of the information environment in which he lives. Where the environment is very homogeneous, where, for example, only one interpretation of Russia is presented in the press, over the radio, in magazines, and in conversations, the information environment ceases to present a challenge, and maturation of opinion is hindered.

The phrase "opinion maintenance and furtherance" is not meant to exclude examination of the conditions affecting attitude change, for attitude change is one of the means whereby the person maintains an effective balance between inner and outer demands. Let us assume first that temptation to large-scale shifts in attitude provokes resistances in the average person. One does not upset one's balance with the informational environment for minor causes. There is probably some optimal rate of change in one's attitudes for any given shift in environmental information. As events change, some individuals shift attitudes rather faster than others: these people we call "flexible," those strikingly slow to shift, "rigid." In either case, long-term alterations in opinion are far more frequent than short-term alterations of comparable scope.

Opinion and Action

We end this chapter with a brief mention of the relation between holding an opinion and doing something about it. However remote the object of an attitude—Russia *is* remote from a citizen's direct action—there is still much that an individual may do on behalf of his opinions. Such actions range from a willingness to express his views to a resolve to devote his life to their realization. Our study was not designed to get at these actions; had it been our primary focus to do so, we should undoubtedly have studied opinion on a different topic. A satisfactory formulation of this important problem, it nevertheless seems to us, will have at least two ingredients, and our explorations throw some light on one of these.

One component of a satisfactory account of action in relation to opinion arises from [a] kind of motivational analysis. . . . The pertinent question is: To what extent are the functions served by a person's opinions fulfilled by the mere fact that he holds them, and to what extent does their fulfillment depend on some futher action on his part? Opinion as part of a person's orderly world view may serve a "placing" function with no agenda for action being implied. If the scanning of object appraisal turns up relevancies to strong personal interests, however, the function of opinion in readying him for action is incomplete unless he follows through. Similarly with social adjustment; our discussion of the distinction between holding and expressing an opinion has already suggested respects in which the functions of overt behavior may be differentiated from those of the disposition itself. When we come to externalization, the question becomes one that the psychoanalyst discusses under the phrase "acting out." Clinical leads are available as to the kinds of people who externalize in deed as well as thought.

[One of our subjects, HS,] . . . is a striking example of a person whose vehement opinions satisfy urgent personal functions with little action beyond the spoken word being required of him.

The second aspect that we see essential in a satisfactory formulation of the problem of action is an analysis of the situations with which the "actor" is confronted. For attitudes are but half of the formula. We have not examined in systematic detail the action-evoking properties of events and situations. The careful reader of our case histories will, we think, be struck as we were by the importance and complexity of the question. Why do some situations call for the adoption of opinion *and* action, while others can be handled by attitudinal means alone?

Extract 3, from the Postscript
(Approaches to Opimions and Personality)

Implications for the Study of Personality

Our exploration of ten adult men—men very much in the midst of life—has led us perforce to look at the field of personality research in a somewhat new perspective. Pathology was not a matter of concern: these were stable men, at least to the extent that they were functioning without seeking or receiving professional psychological help. Nor were we diverted by the exigent need to gather data to aid in therapy. Moreover, our interest led us to consider not only the classical inner dynamics of these lives, but also their world views.

What have we learned of interest to the student of personality from the many hours we spent with these men?

The first conclusion is that one gains rich insight into the functioning of personality by considering not only the deep dynamics but also the level that is closely in contact with events in the world. Various theorists have spoken of manifestations of personality as "wheat" and "chaff," the former leading to deep knowledge of underlying trends, the latter leading only to trivial knowledge about transitory states. Granting that the distinction is not without some virtue, it is nonetheless true that one may learn

Source: Smith, M. B., Bruner, J. S., & White, R. W. (1964). *Opinions and Personality*. New York: John Wiley & Sons, pp. 280–284.

much and go deep into the consistency of a personality without searching for basic hostility or underlying latent homosexuality. The pattern of a man's expressed opinions and values tells one much, often more when it comes to prediction than his responses to projective techniques that appear to indicate, say, underlying masochism and self-destructiveness.

There are here two important and related points. One of them is substantive: about the organization of personality. The other is methodological: about the devices and procedures one may fruitfully use in the study of personality. The two are best separated for discussion.

The manner in which a person copes with his problems is the most revealing thing about him. The solutions to his problems are conserved in the form of values: ways of looking at and evaluating himself, the people about him, and the world around him. Those values represent a resultant of the contacts and struggles between a motivated individual and the surrounding world. From them one can infer much about the kinds of underlying problems with which the person has had to deal.

One's attitudes, examined for their consistencies and patterning, provide an excellent basis for inferring such values. In this sense, the student of personality cannot overlook the study of sentiments and opinions as an approach to his subject matter. To know the manner in which ego-functioning proceeds, one literally must examine the attitude-value patterns of his subjects.

This brings us to the methodological problem. In the past decades it has often been assumed that the only "valid" approach to personality lay in indirect, projective, or "keyhole" methods. There is a possibly apocryphal story about the selection of officers for duty in the tropics and the arctic in which the whole gamut of projective psycholological tests and physiological measures was employed, along with a brief questionnaire that included an item on the candidate's preference for one or the other climate. According to the story, the only item that correlated with later performance was the preference item. One can infer much about a person by letting him tell what he likes, what moves him to action, what he is like.

Among the most revealing procedures used in our investigation was a two-hour interview on "Personal Values and Religious Sentiments" which began with a question on "What things really matter to you most in life?" and moved widely over the topic of philosophy of life. To be sure, there were evasions and prettifications in the record, but withal one obtained a picture of the person that was consistent with and in some ways more revealing than later information obtained by more conventional projective techniques.

... Interview material ... may tend to exaggerate [a person's] assets, but we came to the conclusion that recorded interviews formed a much-needed bridge between overt and covert levels of personality. When it is possible to study at leisure a transcript of all that was said in an interview, the material yields unsuspected riches. Slips of the tongue, hesitations, self-contradictions, preferred figures of speech, and the transitions from one topic to another all lend themselves to analysis as manifestations of covert process. These manifestations do not yield the rich picture of underlying motives and unwitting assumptions that can often be derived from an analysis of fantasy. But they enjoy one great advantage over the findings of projective tests: they show the actual effect of covert processes on conscious thought and behavior. The most difficult problem in interpreting fantasy material is to decide upon its importance in the actual functioning of the personality. Do the fantasies reveal tensely suppressed strivings that are ever ready to disrupt behavior, do they disclose wishes that demand at least symbolic satisfaction in life, or do they show tendencies that exert no real influence over the contemporary personality? Recorded interviews can sometimes play the crucial part in answering such questions. They show us the actual transactions between overt and covert processes, thus allowing us to observe what would otherwise be precariously inferred.

. . . The traditional defenses about which Anna Freud and others have written so ably—repression, undoing, denial, reaction formation, and the rest—while they are adequate as far as they go, leave out of account a wide variety of tactics employed by normal individuals. That is to say, the traditional defense mechanisms appear to us to represent techniques of defense used *in extremis*. In many spheres of their lives, our subjects never got into dilemmas of such severity as to be forced into reaction formation or projection or even repression. Insofar as one can single out a particular flaw in current views of ego defense it is that writers on the subject have failed to mention the tremendous importance of constructive strategies as a means of avoiding the vicissitudes that make crippling defenses necessary. . . .

Our subjects, too, were capable of avoiding difficulties by constructive action. They could often prevent things from occurring that might disrupt them or, more positively, they could plan events in such a way that they could operate effectively and thus grow increasingly competent in dealing with still other situations. . . .We cannot emphasize too strongly that these are not instances of mere avoidance. They were the constructive ways by which our subjects learned to make the most they could of their capacities and limitations.

Indeed, opinions and values may themselves serve as constructive means of avoiding the critical vicissitudes that require extreme defenses. Here we are speaking of the entire pattern of a man's opinions of the world about him—his philosophy of life, if you will. A striking example is provided by [one of our subjects, AR]. Impressive as was the picture of strength that [AR] presented, his was not an untroubled soul. Beneath the surface, we knew him as a man of strong anger, guilt, and anxiety—as well as of responsibility and compassion. To be sure, symptoms of these latent passions came through here and there; that is how we learned of them. Psychopathology would appropriately dwell on these. We are more impressed, however, by the way in which his version of the Catholic faith fulfilled his life and obviated the need for more drastic defense. Through his good works of visitation, through the sense of rightness and appropriateness emanating from his Catholic world view, his life took on meaning and order that gave him deep gratification while it held unruly impulse in check. Similar processes could be traced in others among our men.

It is also the case, to be sure, that opinions, rather than obviating the need for drastic defense, may reflect the inadequacy of such defenses already in being. This is typical of the externalizing function of an opinion. . . .

Whether one's philosophy of life turns out to be a guarantor of serenity that saves one from crippling defensive tactics, or whether it turns out to be a by-product of crippling defenses: how this issue is determined, we do not know. It is our conviction that the matter is central in understanding personality. It cannot be approached unless and until as much time is spent on understanding a man's values and philosophy as is spent on his underlying, basic strivings.

Reading VIII.   Overview and Implications, by A. M. Clarke and A. D. B. Clarke

[The authors begin by making clear the nature of their inquiry:]
Before discussing the evidence and attempting to reach some conclusions, it is important to emphasise what this book is *not* about. We are not primarily concerned with the major problem of whether and to what extent the physical and social environment influences the development of personal attributes such as intelligence and social adjustment. Had this been our aim, a large number of, often excellently documented, empirical studies would have been included, some of which also emphasise the importance of genetic and constitutional variables. We are concerned *solely* with the problem of the implications of *early* environmental events for later development. Without exception, the authors whose work is cited are aware of the importance of genetic variables; they are sensitive to the possibility of environmental effects; a majority have, sometimes to their own surprise, produced evidence suggesting that events occurring in the first few years of a child's life are not necessarily of any great significance for later development.

[such findings call into question] . . . the modern view that the first few years of life are of vital long-term importance. These views have entered into received wisdom, and are rarely challenged. Indeed, they appear to be reinforced both by selective perception and clinical experience. For example, the social worker or psychiatrist assessing the problem of a deviant or abnormal individual has traditionally directed his initial

---

Source: Clarke, A. M. & Clark, A. D. B. (1976). *Early Experience, Myth and Evidence*. London: Open Books Publishing Ltd., Chapter 15.

attention to early development. As Vernon (1964) pointed out, this may for the individual be a welcome escape from discussing current problems. Equally one might add that both clinician and patient may unwittingly act as mutual reinforcers in discovering anomalies in early life, anomalies which in such cases are usually to be found both then and later.

It has been widely argued that various forms of often loosely defined deprivation in early childhood may find expression in a variety of deviant behaviours in later life. These range from maternal separation with hospitalisation leading to delinquency in adolescence, to severe lack of cognitive and emotional stimulation leading to subnormal intellectual functioning in adoptive homes in childhood. In evaluating the evidence our first difficulty is that, with one exception (Koluchová), there is a total lack of detailed description of the social transactions between the child and his caretakers and peers following the early depriving experience.

Furthermore it is absolutely clear that, among other things, the research findings reported in this book are to some degree attributable to the type of sample studied, the life histories of its members, the measures used, both of the individual and his environment, the crudity or sensitivity of such measures, the duration of study, to name but a few. The different estimates (68–72 per cent versus 22 per cent) in the Prugh and others (1953), Schaffer (1958) and Douglas (1975) studies . . . of immediate disturbances in behaviour following early hospitalisation are a case in point. It could well be that each estimate is correct for the sample concerned and the particular type of measure of disturbed behaviour used. Yet these estimates at face value are wildly discrepant. Thus there is great difficulty in comparing the results of one study with another.

In order to summarise and evaluate the evidence, a skeletal sketch of the more important studies follows:

1.   **Davis** (1947). . . . Six-year-old girl rescued from life-long isolation with deaf-mute mother. Specialist speech treatment. Very rapid normalisation from rickets, lack of speech, severely subnormal ability. Limited follow-up to age fourteen. Regarded then as normal

2.   **Koluchová** (1972). . . . Twin boys, developed normally first in an institution, and later with an aunt until aged eighteen months. Then isolated and cruelly treated until rescued at age seven. Rickets, I.Q.s in 40s, little speech, fears of normal objects, unable to understand meaning of pictures. Rapid I.Q. increments, then slower and smaller to normality. Educational retardation decreasing to normality. Severe emotional maladjustment decreasing under unusual adoptive care; now rare traces of the past. Essentially normal outcome. I.Q.s 100 and 101 at age fourteen.

3.   **Goldfarb** (1943) Two groups, 'matched for heredity' from very bad orphanage. One adopted in early months, other adopted about age three. Age ten to fourteen on follow-up. Average Wechsler I.Q.s for early versus late adopted, 95 and 72, respectively. All-round inferiority of latter on other measures. But what selective factors were associated with early versus late adoption? Would a longer follow-up have reduced the gap? (See Clarke and Clarke 1954, [and Clarke et al.] 1958, whose follow-up of deprived children *started* later than the age at which Goldfarb's ceased.)

4. **Skeels and Dye** (1939); **Skeels** (1966) Early life of twenty-five children in exceedingly bad orphanage; thirteen moved to a mental-retardation institution at average of nineteen months, then moved aged three and a half to adoptive homes of rather average status. Diverging I.Q.s, and above all, diverging life experiences of thirteen experimental and one contrast case, compared with other contrast cases. Poor matching of groups, but contrast group initially superior. Wide range of rather average outcomes for experimental subjects, rather homogeneous poor outcomes for contrast cases (except one with fortunate life experiences). In spite of uniform early experience in orphanage, and in the case of the experimental group relatively late adoption after two different residential experiences, outcome related to life-long changes or non-changes in environment.

5. **Dennis** (1973). . . . Foundlings from very bad institution either adopted at different ages by Lebanese or American adopters, or, if female, transferred about six years to another very bad institution, if male to a very good one. Outcome related to direction of environmental shift or non-shift. Only about half of those adopted were available for study. Evidence of selective adoption policies relating to age at adoption. Average I.Q. outcome for those adopted before age two, sub-average outcome for those adopted later. Very poor status of older institutionalised girls, sub-average for boys. Did differing 'age of adoption' policies or adoption preferences impinge on constitutionally different children? Were children adopted at very different ages taken on by different types of home? Why are results somewhat discrepant with those of Skeels, when the experimental children were all adopted after age two?

6. **Tizard and Rees** (1974). . . . Sixty-five children reared from infancy in three residential nurseries. High staff–child ratio, material provision good; multiple caretaking, constant staff changes, official disapproval of close personal relationships. Between ages two and four and a half, twenty-four were adopted and fifteen restored to their mothers. At age four and a half I.Q.s were at least average, the adopted children had higher I.Q.s and appeared more stable than those restored or remaining in institution. At eight and a half there was inevitable sample attrition. Children still average or above; earlier adopted higher than a small group adopted after four and a half, or children restored to parents. Children remaining in institution had declined slightly in I.Q. (n = 7). Reading ages reported; little difference among the groups.

7. **Kadushin** (1970). . . . Large sample of eighty-plus I.Q., healthy children, typically coming from large families in substandard circumstances, often below poverty level, and suffering physical neglect. Natural parents showed a picture of considerable personal pathology compounded of promiscuity, mental deficiency, alcoholism, imprisonment and psychosis. At average age three and a half, the children had been removed from their homes by court order and, after an average of 2·3 changes of foster home, were placed for adoption just over average age seven, and followed up at an average of almost fourteen years. Adoptive parents older than natural parents and of a considerably higher socioeconomic level. Data obtained

from agency records and detailed statements by adoptive parents. The children in general were a source of satisfaction to the adoptive parents and showed a greater degree of psychic health and stability than might have been expected from their background. It is not precisely known how many were excluded from adoption by virtue of low I.Q.s. Population background very similar to those in the Clarke and Clarke, and Hilda Lewis studies. Outcome also similar in so far it is better than would have been predicted (1) from social history; (2) after several foster changes; and (3) following very late adoption.

8.   **Rathbun and others** (1958, 1965) Refugee children (thirty-eight) age range five months to ten years, brought to United States from Korea and Greece, hence change of language and culture. Considerable personal disturbance on arrival; adopted by thirty-three families, five children unavailable for six-year follow-up. On average these had above average health, I.Q. and general competence; twenty-one had adequate or superior adjustment, ten problematic and two were clinically disturbed. Authors believe problematic adjustment arose in response to present rather than past problems. The picture is one of 'almost incredible resiliency'. No background details exist, almost certainly a group selected by overseas welfare workers in refugee camps.

9.   **Lewis** (1954) Five hundred children with poor backgrounds, the worst in Kent, majority aged over five years, admitted to reception centre. Wide range of presenting disorders (delinquency 32 per cent; severely neurotic 18 per cent, psychopathic 3 per cent; normal behaviour but with slight neurotic symptoms 21 per cent; normal behaviour 25 per cent). One sample of a hundred followed up two years later by means of personal interviews with staff, foster parents, teachers and systematic recording of school data. Another sample of a hundred and twenty followed up by post. Wide variety of placements; no one type of placement had a monopoly of success. Essentially similar results from both follow-ups. Whereas on admission only 15 per cent of the samples had been in 'good' condition, two years later this had increased to 39 per cent. The 25 per cent in 'fair' condition increased to 36 per cent. Thus 75 per cent of the most deprived were in 'good' or 'fair' condition after only two years of better experiences.

10.   **Clarke and Clarke** (1954, 1959)/**Clarke, Clarke and Reiman** (1958) Two total samples of certified 'feeble-minded' adolescents and young adults drawn from bad or very bad homes (independently assessed from case histories) followed by, on average, several moves through residential schools or institutions, followed by certification. All exhibited mild subnormality, poor scholastic attainments, poor social competence and work capacity. I.Q.s and measures of work and social adjustment taken two and a half, four and a half and six years after initial assessment. Greater (and substantial) I.Q. and social improvement in those from the worst homes. All groups had average ages in the mid-twenties at follow-up, but such changes could occur at any time between age fifteen and about thirty, and perhaps slowly and steadily throughout the period. Estimates for change were very conservative owing to selective wastage from the loss

of the more successful individuals. All data collected independently before being brought together.

. . .

12. **Kagan** [and Klein (1973)] studied Guatemalan, rural and city children of different ages. From a position of considerable retardation during early life, related to environmental conditions and modes of child care, the rural children advanced in several cognitive areas by pre-adolescence, attaining Guatemala City and American norms. The report emphasises plasticity of development and its potential discontinuity in relation to changing environmental demands, and that early retardation has no important implication for ultimate normality.

13. **Douglas** (1975) Subsamples of large national sample, those who had experienced early or repeated admission to hospital. Relations found between these admissions and ratings in adolescence. Surprisingly 68 per cent, according to mothers' reports, showed no disturbance on discharge, but suggestion of a 'sleeper effect' apparent in adolescence. Such later ratings for 'troublesomeness', 'poor reading', 'delinquency', 'unstable job pattern' clearly associated with early hospitalisation. Even stronger associations with longer periods of admission after five years. Douglas indicates that the 'evidence . . . though highly suggestive, does not establish the existence of a causal relationship between early hospital admissions and later behaviour. For that an experimental study would be required.' Yet he also shows that children hospitalised in the early years are more likely to return to hospital, to have persisting physical disability, to be boys, from large families, with manual-worker parents who take little interest in their schooling. We believe data are inconclusive allowing either Douglas's interpretation or our own that early hospitalisation (and particularly repeated admissions) represent significant actuarial signs of present and future disadvantage.

14. **Bowlby and others** (1956) Sixty children who before age four had spent a period (range less than six months—more than two years) in a T.B. sanatorium, matched with three controls per child, adjacent in age in same school class in follow-up. Latter took place within age range six years ten months to thirteen years seven months. Average I.Q. 107, . . . controls 110. . . . Capacity for friendship normal. Maladjustment 63 per cent compared with 42 per cent regarded as usual expectancy. This excess 21 per cent might have arisen from social class and family contexts rather than separation and hospitalisation. Indeed, authors carefully point out that such children tend to 'come from families where other members . . . have tuberculosis, so that illness and death are common with their attendant disturbed family relations and depressed economy' (1956, p. 213). Thus 10 per cent of the mothers were dead at the time of follow-up. The authors indicate that 'part of the emotional disturbance . . . is to be attributed to factors other than separation' (see Rutter).

15. **Rutter** (1970) Part of a total sample of nine-to twelve-year-old children on the Isle of Wight, plus a representative group of London families in which one or both parents had been in psychiatric care.

Anti-social behaviour in boys was associated with ratings of parents' marriage, not separation experiences. Where separation had occurred, the cause was relevant: holiday or illness, no effect; family discord or deviance, larger effect. On the whole separation due to parental death had little effect. It is also suggested that the longer the family disharmony lasts, the greater the risk to the children.

As yet there is no clearly developed comprehensive model of how the physical and social environment affects children during the course of growth. We do, however, have evidence which calls into question certain assumptions which appear to have guided the thinking of a large number of professional workers. These are stated in the form of hypotheses. In each case, of the studies assembled in this book, the most pertinent are cited.

The generic hypothesis, to which the others are related, states that environmental events in the first few years of life influence the developing organism in a way which is critical for later development.

Hypothesis 1

What is believed to be essential for mental health is 'that an infant and young child should experience a warm, intimate and continuous relationship with his mother (or permanent mother-substitute) in which both find satisfaction and enjoyment' (Bowlby 1951).

This hypothesis has already been extensively examined by Rutter (1972) in a book entitled *Maternal Deprivation Reassessed*, and by Morgan (1975); further contrary evidence is provided in connection with other more specific hypotheses.

Hypothesis 2

That temporary separation of a very young child from its mother may result in later behaviour problems.

This widely held hypothesis must be subdivided into at least two research areas: hospitalisation, involving much more than mother–child separation; and other brief separations.

1 Douglas (... summary 13) shows an association between early hospitalisation and adolescent problems, but indicates himself that the problem is complex (see discussion).

2 Rutter (... summary 15) presents contrary evidence, emphasising that the nature of the separation experience is important.

Hypothesis 3

That young children cannot develop normally in an institution.

Contrary evidence: Skeels (. . . summary 4); Bowlby and others (. . . summary 14); Tizard and Rees (. . . summary 6). . . . The evidence suggests that the quality of the institution is important.

Hypothesis 4

That where children have suffered from adversity, late adoption cannot be successful in bringing them to normal intellectual functioning or emotional adjustment.

Goldfarb (. . . summary 3) offers evidence in support; and Wayne Dennis's (. . . summary 5) data appear to confirm this hypothesis for average intellectual status. Certainly among those adopted after age two there were many children who were subnormal. Unfortunately nothing is known of the natural parents, but there may well have been an unusual combination of biologically determined vulnerability and severe social deprivation, a possible point of difference between these children and Koluchová's twins. So far as social-emotional adjustment is concerned, the evidence of Lewis (. . . summary 9), Rathbun and others (. . . summary 8) and Kadushin (. . . summary 7) strongly suggests that late removal of children from adverse circumstances should lead in most cases to a satisfactory outcome.

Hypothesis 5

That there is a critical period about the age of two for normal (average) cognitive development (Dennis . . . summary 5).
Contrary evidence: Davis (. . . summary 1); Koluchová (. . . summary 2); . . . and Kagan (. . . summary 12). Clarke and Clarke (. . . summary 10) found that some of their population of formerly deprived certified mental retardates reached average status during late adolescence and early adult years.
. . .
In short, if there is a critical period, it is difficult to know how to define it; clearly chronological age is not a good contender; mental age fares worse; perhaps one should consider social age? Moreover, it does not seem any more promising to think in terms of critical events: apart from those which make it impossible to sustain life, *it appears that there is virtually no psychosocial adversity to which some children have not been subjected, yet later recovered*, granted a radical change of circumstances.

[Conclusions]

As indicated [earlier], the view that the early years of infant development are of crucial importance has become so widely accepted as to be implicit in the writings and decision-taking of research workers and practitioners alike. We have assembled a body of evidence which suggests a reformulation: this should not be interpreted literally as a counter-balance, which might be an equal and opposite extreme, but rather as an attempt to achieve a balanced view. . . .

. . . The human organism appears to have been programmed by the course of evolution to produce normal developmental outcomes under all but the most adverse of circumstances (Waddington, 1966). Any understanding of deviancies in outcome must be seen in the light of this self-righting and self-organizing tendency which appears to move children towards normality in the face of pressure towards deviation. (Sameroff and Chandler, 1975)

This is what elsewhere we have termed resilience.

[However, the authors are aware that certain false and dangerous conclusions could be drawn from this position. To counteract this, they make clear what are *not* the implications of their analysis.]

. . . The swing of the pendulum which resulted from Bowlby's (1951) monograph had many humane effects, sensitising the public to the needs of children. It would be more than unfortunate if this book played any part in a reaction against the new humanism, on the mistaken grounds that 'it doesn't matter what happens early in life'. Thus while the evidence does suggest that no mother of a very young child should feel bound to remain at home (provided satisfactory alternative caretaking arrangements can be made) equally, no mother should feel that her responsibilities diminish after her child becomes older. Nor does the evidence condone bad institutions, or 'problem families' or refugee camps, simply because their unfortunate effects can, in many cases, be reversed. Nor would we wish to see nursery schools either opened or closed as a result of this debate. That such schools fail to show long-term effects is no argument against their existence, both for the present benefit to the child and also to his mother. There is absolutely no implication that infancy and early childhood are unimportant, only that their long-term role is *by itself* very limited.

The way in which children are perceived and handled is intimately affected by the prevailing *zeitgeist*. In spite of the currently more humane attitude to children (mentioned above) they are not always accorded prime importance when their interests and those of their parents are in conflict. More usually, of course, such needs are in harmony.

What then are the main implications? First and foremost, the whole of development is important, not merely the early years. There is as yet no indication that a given stage is clearly more formative than others; in the long-term all may be important. We are now entering the era when empirical findings, based upon the newer and more powerful methodologies of the behavioural sciences, have the possibility of dictating appropriate policies. Thus our relative dependence upon fashions in child rearing may give way to a more careful empirical analysis of the needs of individual children, to the manner in which these needs can best be satisfied, to the methods by which the disadvantaged may best be helped, and indeed to diminishing the pathology of society. The widespread use of over-simple notions about children, of inadequate social action dependent on such notions, and the unwitting employment of self-fulfilling prophecies, need to give way to imaginative, yet independently and austerely evaluated experiments which depend only on the assumption that what one does for a child at any age, provided it is maintained, plays a part in shaping his development within the limits imposed by genetic and constitutional factors.

THE PSYCHOLOGIST AS EXPERT ADVISOR/CONSULTANT

The papers in this section of Chapter 4 include examples of psychologists accepting commissions to do research on particular issues. The work of Rutter and Madge (1976) and Fishbein (1977) demonstrates how psychologists may use their "knowledge-base" as a framework for their recommendations. These papers are useful examples of how some psychologists' values arise as a direct result of their own engagement in the growth of the discipline and their involvement in shaping its theoretical form. Another feature of their operations, a familiar feature in psychological enquiry, is "uncertainty." Psychologists will try to set things up so that, to the extent that they are good researchers, they try to falsify even their own dearly-held hypotheses. Psychologists acting in this role are acting as "consultants" who present a cohesive picture of psychological knowledge in a particular field.

Using Cherns' approach to the psychologist's role, we suggest that the Rutter and Madge (1976) and Fishbein (1977) extracts presented in this section are approached from the angle of how in each case the problem was originally formulated and of what type of solution was expected. We begin by giving some background detail on the Rutter and Madge paper. On 29 June 1972, Sir Keith Joseph, the Secretary of State for the Social Services made a memorable speech to the Annual Conference of the Pre-School

Playgroups Association; a speech which was widely reported. The following extract is taken from *The Times'* report of the following day:

Minister Launches Campaign to Save Doomed Children from "Cycle of Deprivation"
By Pat Healy
Social Services Correspondent

A government initiative to find ways of preventing the "doomed children" in deprived families from continuing the "cycle of deprivation" when they become parents was launched in London yesterday.

In an important policy speech, Sir Keith Joseph, Secretary of State for Social Services, told the annual conference of the Pre-School Playgroups Association that he would be launching research, paying new grants and bringing together relevant organizations to combat the cycle.

Earlier he had announced a capital grant to the association of £9,500 and a recurring annual grant of £45,000. The grants mark the first recognition of the association by Sir Keith's department, and are regarded by experts as recognition of the social service aspect of provision for under-fives.

Turning to family deprivation and poverty, Sir Keith said conditions had improved generally, but misery continued unabated. Much deprivation and maladjustment persisted from generation to generation. Many of today's deprived children were doomed not only to stunted lives themselves but to become, unless they could be helped, the parents of a further generation of doomed children.

His department was in touch with the Social Science Research Council about the possibility of mounting a research programme designed to throw more light on the cycle. A working party would shortly start exploring it. But any breach that could be made in the cycle was not the complete answer.

"Deprivation is wider than poverty", Sir Keith said. "Even if we were successful in eradicating poverty, deprivation in some forms would remain."

His department, collaborating with others, was considering how best to devise a programme of research to provide information on the dynamics of family poverty. Much of that would be relevant and complementary to research on the deprivation cycle.

Sir Keith was reviewing family planning policies and said he hoped to announce the results later this year. But he urged that more should be done to help people to prepare for parenthood.

There was a profound contrast between the scrupulous attention our society gave to pregnant women and on the other hand the limited extent to which we helped the mother and the father, where necessary, to understand the child's emotional and intellectual needs.

Yet where these needs were left unmet, Sir Keith said, the children would find school unrewarding, because they were ill-prepared for it;

would carry into adolescence and adult life an inability to form trusting and stable relationships, because they had never experienced them; and would become parents of the next generation of children who were deprived emotionally and intellectually.

He hoped to commission shortly from the National Children's Bureau a comprehensive study of the developmental needs of children and the consequences of those needs not being met. In the meantime he was sending copies of his speech to relevant organizations and inviting them to a meeting in September or October.

(*The Times*, 30 June 1972)

The importance of this speech is demonstrated by the Leader comment which appeared in *The Times* on the same day as the speech was reported. This editorial comment shows us something of the intellectual climate in which the speech was delivered.

Sir Keith Joseph Sets The Targets

In his speech to a conference organized by the Pre-School Playgroups Association in London yesterday Sir Keith Joseph dwelt on the reasons why so many children remain deprived in an age of growing material prosperity. One reason is that this prosperity is not distributed with such precision as to eliminate all pockets of poverty. But that is by no means the only explanation. Many children live in bleak and depressing surroundings, and go to schools where their talents are not developed. A good many others, who may not lack material prosperity, come from families where there is little affection or emotional stability—and Sir Keith Joseph laid particular stress on how the emotional failings of one generation may be repeated in their children and grandchildren. The conclusion that needs to be drawn above all others is that these different factors react upon each other, and that just as there is no single cause of deprivation in childhood so any attempt at a remedy must require a combined approach.

Whenever any minister offers a persuasive diagnosis it is reasonable to ask what the Government intend to do about it. Sir Keith Joseph provided a few answers in his speech. There will be more money for day nurseries and playgroups, a further statement on family planning policies before the end of the year, more research into poverty and on how to break the cycle of deprivation from one generation to the next, and possibly a conference of voluntary organizations and professional bodies on preparation for parenthood. All this is useful, but it is not enough. The Secretary of State's speech will be of more than passing interest only it it can be seen as part of the development of a combined approach by the Government to the problems of child deprivation.

There have been some signs of this already. A number of Government departments—including Health, Education, and the Home Office—have been considering how they can work together more effectively in this area. This is necessary because the policies required do not fit neatly within departmental frontiers. Possibly the two most urgent requirements are more playgroups and domiciliary family planning. There also needs to be a much closer tripartite relationship between teachers, parents, and social workers. This will be all the harder to achieve because the parents who would benefit most from this are those least likely to be in touch with their children's teachers and are living in poor areas where the teachers are most hard pressed. Further services for personal support need to be developed, and only if there is sufficient cooperation in planning these at the centre can there be much hope of proper coordination at local level.

It is, however, not only the personal support services that have to be coordinated. Personal and family difficulties, poverty, bad housing, poor school conditions, the sense of living in a decaying area—they all contribute to the feelings of personal hopelessness that drags some people down and starts some children off with such a poor chance in life. All these causes need to be tackled as part of a combined approach to the problems of deprived areas, because deprived areas and deprived people go together.

The Government's approach is at the moment anything but combined. There are the various services run by the different departments. There is the Urban Programme which is inadequate in scale and not strongly enough controlled at the centre as to demand a coherent strategy from those local authorities which benefit from it. There is Mr Walker's plan to set up joint working groups from the Department of the Environment and from local government in a number of towns and inner city areas to examine the resources necessary to improve their physical condition. These different efforts need to be combined in an enlarged urban programme, which should bring in physical development as well as personal services and facilities.

(*The Times*, 30 June 1972)

The Leader article is critical of the Minister's diagnosis as to the persistence of deprivation and of the limited intervention programme he outlined. It expresses the view that the origins of the problem are not simply at the level of the individual or the family. In other words a wide combination of circumstances contribute to the feelings of hopelessness that characterize those at the very bottom of society.

Following this speech, a DHSS/SSRC Joint Working Party on "Transmitted Deprivation" was set up and at its second meeting in October 1972 this group suggested a survey of the literature to clarify the concept of deprivation. The task of the Working Party had been to consider whether it was feasible to do research, and if so, by what means. It was thought that a survey of the literature was required to overview existing research on deprivation both in the United Kingdom and in the United States before any major programme of research could be started. Professor Michael Rutter and his assistant Nicola Madge were selected to undertake this survey. It turned out to be a much bigger task than they had originally envisaged because it was not possible to examine the "continuity of deprivation" without looking generally at the broad context of "deprivation." This is a familiar dilemma for the expert advisor: that the problem he or she is hired to investigate increases in complexity and extensiveness as it comes under closer inspection.

The extended extract we have chosen to reproduce in this chapter (pp. 147–157) demonstrates the way in which Rutter and Madge tried to define the problem. This was not Sir Keith Joseph's problem, but rather the academic "experts'" problem of defining the field, assessing the possible methods of investigation, and developing appropriate hypotheses. Their conclusions look beyond the available literature to possible avenues of intervention. They make it clear in their final paragraph, which we present below, that even though we cannot necessarily know precisely what to do to eliminate cycles of disadvantage, actually posing the question accurately and precisely goes some way towards useful intervention. They emphasize that in clarifying the question it is important to account for evidence that runs counter to the original hypotheses as well as evidence that confirms them.

It is sometimes assumed that nothing less than a complete change of our economic and social structure could influence cycles of disadvantage. This view stems from the extensive evidence concerning inequalities in our society and the findings that poor living conditions are often associated with delinquency, educational failure and the like. We share the feelings of outrage concerning the appalling circumstances under which many families have to bring up their children and we regard both the regional maldistribution of national resources and the very large gap between the advantaged and the underprivileged sections of society as unacceptable. Of course, action is needed to remedy these problems, but we delude ourselves if we think that nothing short of massive social change can influence cycles of disadvantage. In the first place, cycles of disadvantage are to be found at all levels of society. They are by no means confined to the poor. In the second place, the associations with inadequate living conditions provide a very poor guide to levels of disadvantage in other respects. For example, the National Child Development Study makes much of the association between overcrowding and low attainment in reading. Davie et al. (1972) argue that this is a causal relationship and that "the effect of overcrowding ... is equivalent to approximately nine months' retardation in reading age." But as both Rutter (1975b) and Burgess (1975) have pointed out, overcrowded homes are more than twice as common in Scotland as in England, yet in spite of this Scottish children are much better readers. Why? While the answer to that question is not known, the very posing of it emphasizes the existence of possibilities for action to overcome cycles of disadvantage. If research into such cycles merely reconfirms that children disadvantaged in one respect are often also disadvantaged in other respects it will have failed. What are needed are investigations to determine why this is often *not* the case and how we can bring about discontinuities in cycles of disadvantage. This is the challenge for the future.

(Rutter and Madge, 1976, p. 327)

Another thing to note about the role of the psychologist as expert consultant is the time scale. Sir Keith Joseph's speech was made in June 1972, the findings of Rutter and Madge were communicated some four years later. Answering the original questions accurately when the problem has "rolled on" might be subject to a variety of temporal problems, such as, being "out of phase" with what is happening by the time the research gets published, and that can affect the appropriateness of the advice.

The next reading, by Martin Fishbein, dates from 1977 and is an extract from a report that was prepared for the U.S. Federal Trade Commission. This commission has several responsibilities. In relation to the advertising and promotion of cigarettes these include: the monitoring of deceptive and unfair acts and practices; a general authority to gather information and issue reports; a specific obligation to report to Congress annually on current cigarette advertising and promotion. The Federal Trade Commission has the power to translate its findings and concerns into legislative recommendations. The problem that was set for Fishbein, a well-known American psychologist in the field of attitude research, was defined by this Commission. It was not a problem which arose simply within his own discipline interests. The Federal Trade Commission asked Fishbein to undertake a critical examination of the social psychological literature on consumer beliefs and behaviour with respect to smoking. Fishbein, however, did not see his task as merely one of cataloguing research findings. He stated that: "Although well over 10,000 references have been considered, this report is not a literature review. Rather, it attempts to provide a critical analysis and synthesis of what the literature presently reveals about the role of information and beliefs in decisions to smoke or not to smoke" (Fishbein, 1977, p. 1). He attempted to answer what he saw as two crucial questions:

1. Whether or not in 1977 the American public's decision to smoke (or not to smoke) cigarettes was an informed one.
2. Whether there is anything more that could be done to ensure that decisions to smoke are informed decisions.

Reading the extracts from the report, which we have included here, we can see that Fishbein used this particular task in part as a means to demonstrate the usefulness of his own model of how information shapes attitudes.

Fishbein, Madge, and Rutter were *given* their problems which they then re-cast in their own way, that is, they were "consulted." In fact, in both cases, however, these experts were really being consulted with regard to refining the definition of the problem. Sometimes the psychologist is "consulted," or psychological research is quoted, to endorse or *validate* a policy position that has already been established. In this case the psychologist is a "witness," not simply an "expert."

Reading IX.   The Cycle of Transmitted Deprivation, by M. Rutter and N. Madge

The term 'deprivation' must be one of the most overworked words in the English language. The literature is full of countless articles and books on the nature, causes and consequences of 'deprivation', and the research reports are outnumbered only by the emotional and polemical monologues

Source: Rutter, M. & Madge, N (1976). *Cycles of Disadvantage: A Review of Research*. London: Heinemann, pp. 1–13.

and interchanges on a variety of theoretical, practical and political aspects of the topic. Much of the controversy is a consequence of the very diffuseness of the concept which is used by different writers (usually with force and conviction) to cover quite different issues and problems. In the first place, 'deprivation' may refer to very varied aspects of a person's environment. Thus Bowlby (1951) and Ainsworth (1962) in their discussion of 'maternal deprivation' were primarily concerned with the consequences of lack of mother love; Casler (1961), on the other hand, saw the issue as a lack of sensory stimulation; Runciman (1972), by contrast, discussed deprivation in terms of financial and material resources; and Jessor and Richardson (1968) considered the matter more broadly in terms of psychosocial disadvantage. All these writers were concerned with lacks of one kind or another. But, that is not the only way the word has been employed. Eckland and Kent (1968) defined deprivation in terms of deviation from what is considered normal or appropriate, and suggested that it could only be understood in terms of society's responses and society's values. Following the same theme, Ginsberg (1972) and others have dismissed the whole notion of deprivation as a myth based on middle-class misconceptions about poor children.

Not only has 'deprivation' been used to refer to quite diverse aspects of a person's environment, but it has also included circumstances which have nothing to do with deprivation in the dictionary sense of 'dispossession' or 'loss' (Ainsworth, 1962; Jessor and Richardson, 1968; Rutter, 1972). With respect to 'maternal deprivation', Ainsworth wrote, [it] 'has been used also to cover nearly every undesirable kind of interaction between mother and child—rejection, hostility, cruelty, over-indulgence, repressive control, lack of affection and the like.' Jessor and Richardson pointed out that the term was both restricting and logically misleading in that the conditions of disadvantage included under 'deprivation' were often characterized as much by excess (of stigma, of deviant role models, of stressful experiences, etc.) as by lack, and that the problems often lay in what was present as much as in what was lacking. Rutter (1972) ended his review of the evidence on 'maternal deprivation' by concluding that the experiences covered by the term were too heterogeneous and the effects too varied for it to continue to have any usefulness. The concept had been valuable in focussing attention on the sometimes grave consequences of deficient or disturbed care in early life, but it had served its purpose and should now be abandoned.

Our review of writings on the topic of deprivation has strongly reinforced that view. The word almost functions as a projective test in which each person reads into the concept his own biases and prejudices, regardless of how the word has been used in the article or book in question. The result has been an inordinate amount of fruitless friction and heat concerning words and their usage. This might be dismissed as mere academic disputation not worthy of further consideration were it not for the fact that behind the words lie people who continue to suffer from various forms of personal and social disadvantage. The term may generate semantic confusion but the human predicament is real enough.

There are many facets of that predicament which warrant serious attention and require political action. Thus, Wedge and Prosser (1973) emphasized the extent of social disadvantage in present-day Britain—one in six children live in an overcrowded home where the density exceeds $1\frac{1}{2}$ persons per room; one in eleven children live in a family without the exclusive use of a hot water supply; one in sixteen in a one parent household; and one in six is part of a family where there are five or more children. Field (1974) on the other hand, stressed the inequalities in our society: infantile mortality is much higher in social classes IV and V than in I and II and the gap between the classes is not narrowing; the gap in financial resources between the rich and the poor remains as wide as ever; the unemployment rate for unskilled men is over ten times that for professional men; and manual workers have more dental decay than the middle class but receive dental care less often. Daniel (1968) and Smith (1974) have shown that black people in this country continue to be subjected to extensive discrimination in the fields of housing and employment. To a considerable extent their disadvantage lies in what society does to them to restrict their opportunities. Others have suggested that stigma socializes people to disabling roles and that this process may explain the disadvantage of many groups other than ethnic minorities (Eckland and Kent, 1968). Within the field of 'maternal deprivation', by contrast, most attention has been paid to the nature of psychological processes which lead children to be damaged by adverse early experiences within the family (Ainsworth, 1962; Bronfenbrenner, 1968; Rutter, 1972). However, research into causal processes has by no means been restricted to psychological variables. For example, various writers have been concerned to identify the social and political forces which lead to disadvantage within the school system (e.g. Hargreaves, 1967; Ginsberg, 1972), or which underlie the particularly high rates of personal problems among families living within inner city areas (e.g. Rutter, 1975).

Of course, these different perspectives do not constitute alternatives. Each has some validity and concerns itself with an important aspect of the problem. There is not, and cannot be, any one 'right' way of considering the predicament of disadvantaged persons. Nevertheless, the choice of perspective has crucial implications for both research and policy. Raising national housing standards would do much to remedy the disadvantages highlighted by Wedge and Prosser, but unless differentials between the best and worst housing were reduced it would do nothing to right the inequalities noted by Field. Even a levelling (upwards) of housing facilities would not be sufficient if it left some people subject to discrimination. The improved material conditions might make parenting easier but they would not eliminate the adverse family experiences which Bowlby outlined and which are found in all levels of society. Furthermore, betterment of family circumstances and of household facilities might make little difference to the problems associated with school disadvantage or to the stresses associated with inner city life. In short, the topic of 'deprivation' and of disadvantage constitutes not one, but many problems. The search for a 'best' research approach or a single political solution would be as futile as it would be silly.

In 1972, Sir Keith Joseph, then Secretary of State for Social Services, drew attention to another aspect of 'deprivation' in a speech made to the Pre-School Playgroups Association. He asked 'Why is it that, in spite of long periods of full employment and relative prosperity and the improvement in community services since the Second World War, deprivation and problems of maladjustment so conspicuously persist?' By deprivation he was referring to 'circumstances which prevent people developing to nearer their potential—physically, emotionally and intellectually—than many do now', which often showed itself in 'poverty, in emotional impoverishment, in personality disorder, in poor educational attainment, in depression and despair'. He suggested the operation of a cyclical process whereby, in a number of cases, problems reproduced themselves from generation to generation.

The purpose of this book is to review the evidence on the extent to which the 'cycle of transmitted deprivation' mentioned by Sir Keith Joseph in fact exists, and in so far as it does exist, to consider the possible mechanisms which may underlie the intergenerational continuities. For reasons which are implicit in all that has been said so far, we have made three variations from the then Secretary of State's terminology in choosing a title for this book. Firstly, we have preferred the broader term of 'disadvantage' to the more narrow and restricting concept of 'deprivation'. According to the Oxford English Dictionary, disadvantage refers to unfavourable conditions or circumstances, detriment, loss, injury or prejudice. We will be discussing all of these in our examination of the extent to which troubles persist across generations. Secondly, we have emphasized the many processes involved by putting cycles in the plural. Even in the terms of Sir Keith Joseph's question several different phenomena are suggested. The first quotation above raises the issue of why various problems remain in spite of rising prosperity. This leaves open the question of whether the problems are still with us because they keep recurring (possibly in different groups of the population) or because they are being passed on within defined subgroups. If they are being passed on, the question next arises as to whether the continuities are most evident in families, in geographical areas, in social groups, or in minorities subjected to discrimination. These considerations led us to drop the adjective 'transmitted' from the title, in that the term might be thought to prejudge the nature of the processes involved.

Not surprisingly, in view of the background of controversy and conflict over the whole area of 'deprivation', Sir Keith Joseph's speech has been subjected to many (often contradictory) interpretations. Although others have felt more confident in their analysis of the motives and meanings behind the 1972 speech, we have not considered it either appropriate or fruitful to engage in these speculations. We have simply attempted to review research findings and concepts as objectively as we could, and in so doing to avoid taking any one theoretical position. This book does not present 'a view', nor does it provide a prescription for policy. Naturally, we have our own concepts and views on what is most important in the field we have reviewed. But, although our reading of the evidence has inevitably been coloured by our own training, experience and personalities, we have tried to avoid the excessive intrusion of our own theoretical constructions. Also, we strongly believe that social research should lead to appropriate political action and in our other writings we have not shirked our responsibilities in that direction. However, our role here is different and it must be left to others to draw policy implications from our conclusions. What we have tried to do is to summarize the current state of knowledge on this rather broad and diffuse question and to make a few comments about the most pressing research needs.

Whether what we have done fits in with the assumptions of Sir Keith Joseph's speech is not our concern. Nevertheless, in view of the controversy surrounding both the concepts of the speech it is necessary to clarify a few points. Firstly, Jordan (1974) and others have criticized the 'cycle of transmitted deprivation' because it links poverty with maladjustment and seems to assume that parental inadequacy and neglect are features of low income families. Such a view might be read into a later statement of Sir Keith Joseph's (1974), although the original speech did stress that deprivation occurred at all levels of society. Be that as it may, we wish to make quite clear that in no sense do we equate poverty with maladjustment. . . .

Secondly, in his 1972 speech, Sir Keith Joseph explicitly linked his suggestion of a cycle of transmitted deprivation with parenting and with the need for 'preparation for parenthood'. Thus, he said: 'It seems perhaps that much deprivation and maladjustment persist from generation to generation through what I have called a "cycle of deprivation". People who were themselves deprived in one or more ways in childhood become in turn the parents of another generation of deprived children'. In our view this apparent focus on the family is too narrow. In the first place, as already mentioned, continuities over time regarding high rates of various forms of disadvantage can be seen in terms of schools, inner city areas, social classes, ethnic groups and other social and cultural situations which lie outside the family. These are also highly important. In the second place, even with respect to familial continuities, the reason for the intergenerational continuity may not be familial at all but rather may reflect the influence of a common social environment or a common political structure on successive generations. . . .

Thirdly, the very use of the term 'deprivation' is often taken to imply environmental causation. Undoubtedly, many of the disadvantages considered in this volume do stem in considerable measure from environmental forces. However, in most cases, genetic and biological factors play some part in the process of disadvantage and this review aims critically to discuss the role of both environmental and constitutional factors without preconception as to which constitute the more important influence in any particular situation. . . .

Fourthly, as discussed later in the book, even with the variables showing the strongest continuities across successive generations, discontinuities are prominent and frequent. Among children reared under conditions of severe multiple disadvantage, many develop normally and go on in adult life to produce happy, non-disadvantaged families of their own. Although intergenerational cycles of disadvantage exist, the exceptions are many and a surprisingly large proportion of people reared in conditions of privation and suffering do *not* reproduce that pattern in the next generation. . . .

Fifthly, intergenerational continuities in disadvantage are, of course, only one aspect of the more general problem of disadvantage and they must be examined in that broader context. . . .

Types of Disadvantages

Various issues had to be considered in deciding how to tackle this review. The first problem stemmed from the fact that the disadvantages suffered by mankind are legion and some selection had to be made if the review was not to achieve infinite length. We were guided in the first instance by the various items noted in Sir Keith Joseph's 1972 speech—namely poverty, unemployment, poor housing, poor educational attainment, crime, psychiatric disorder, inadequate parenting and problem families. He also made mention of alcoholism and drug addiction but we decided that these problems were too specific for inclusion as topics in their own right. In addition, it was decided not to discuss intergenerational continuities with respect to chronic physical handicap and psychosis as such, although both would receive some attention in so far as they were responsible for continuities in other forms of disadvantage.

However, we thought that special attention should be paid to the situation of ethnic minority groups in this country in order to focus on the possible importance of discrimination in creating disadvantage. . . . We thought it essential to determine how disadvantage occurred in ethnic minority groups in order that appropriate action may be taken to prevent the country repeating the errors made elsewhere and also that light might be shed more generally on the processes involved in the creation of disadvantage. It would have been appropriate to consider the same issues with respect to the disadvantage and discrimination suffered by women in our society but this seemed a major topic in its own right and it was regarded as outside our remit.

We are aware that this selection of topics is somewhat arbitrary and other choices could be equally justified. However, our aim has not been to provide a comprehensive survey of all that is known on disadvantage—an impossible task in any event—nor even a total coverage on all that has been written on intergenerational continuities in disadvantage. Rather, our purpose has been to take a quite limited set of examples of different kinds of disadvantage in order to examine patterns and processes which might apply both to these particular disadvantages and others.

Throughout the book we have culled world-wide literature but in doing so we have been particularly concerned to review it in terms of its implications for present-day Britain. This was necessary as it was apparent from the outset that the pattern of continuities and the causal processes differed substantially according to socio-cultural context. No universal answer is possible and in the circumstances it seemed best to focus on the British situation. Nevertheless a great deal of what we have to say is applicable much more generally.

Some Methodological Considerations

Inevitably, our discussion of cycles of disadvantage has been constrained by the strategies and methods employed in published studies. Nevertheless, it was essential to approach the task with some notion of the main methodological pitfalls, particularly as many of the investigations reviewed were planned for purposes other than the assessment of intergenerational continuities. The first point concerns the range of variables. Although the main purpose of the review was to examine disadvantage, it would be unduly restricting to confine attention to the disadvantaged end of the continuum regarding any variable. . . . The causes of severe mental retardation, which show very little intergenerational continuity, are quite different from the causes of mild retardation, where continuity is much greater, and somewhat different again from the factors determining individual differences in the middle range of intelligence.

The second issue was how to measure disadvantage. Several dimensions of measurement suggested themselves. . . .

Each dimension of disadvantage has its own particular problem. At first sight, a statistical definition seems the most precise approach as it allows of ready quantification. However, very few variables can be measured in absolute terms so that the choice of reference group becomes a critical issue. Measures will change if population norms change. . . . When comparing across generations some techniques must be found to equate the reference groups used to provide a norm for each generation. As will be seen, this has rarely been done.

Administrative definitions of disadvantage are often the most convenient because of the availability of official statistics. While they are of value for some purposes they have marked limitations. Thus, once a family is 'known' to the authorities, the offspring are more likely to come to official notice for difficulties which might not otherwise have led to administrative action. Not only is this a matter of selective administrative surveillance but also a person's attitudes and behaviour may change as the result of derogatory labelling. In this way, stigma may cause quite artifactual continuities. Moreover, even when this does not occur, it is important to recognize that an administrative category involves two factors; firstly disadvantage and secondly the disadvantage coming to official notice. With data on administratively defined continuities, it is quite difficult to determine how far the continuities refer to the disadvantage and how far to the process of coming to notice. It is also noteworthy that an administrative category in one generation may not be equivalent to the same category in another generation. For example, police practices as well as the law are subject to change, and the regulations on the provisions of welfare benefits vary over time.

The dimension of impairment usefully provides an assessment of how far an individual is impeded in his various life activities. In this connection, of course, impairment strictly refers to level of functioning and carries no implications about the individual as a person. Because of this it necessarily follows that impairment applies to specific functions. A person may be impaired in his capacity to work but not in his interpersonal relationships. Also it should be emphasized that impairment can only be seen as relative to a person's life circumstances and must depend ultimately on value judgements. . . .

Similar questions arise when considering disadvantage in terms of self-perception or values. It should be added that a variety of other conceptual frameworks may also be employed. Thus, disadvantage may be considered in terms of disease states or illness which are qualitatively different from normality. This medical frame of reference involves additional methodological problems. However, as the transmission of disease falls outside our terms of reference these will not be considered here. Almost none of the research considered in this review is entirely free from these various methodological problems and the findings must therefore be viewed with appropriate caution. Where the research strategy makes serious biases possible these are pointed out in the text, but in order to avoid unduly tedious repetition and excessive qualification, the methodological points made in this chapter will not be discussed with every study mentioned.

Intragenerational Continuities

In order to study intergenerational continuities adequately it is necessary to study two or more generations at the same stage in the life cycle. Furthermore, to understand the practical implications of disadvantage, it is essential to know something about its persistence or non-persistence within a single life span, and to appreciate its associations with other forms of disadvantage. For all these reasons, attention is paid in this review to *intra*generational as well as *inter*generational continuities. It is important, for example, to appreciate the frequency with which juvenile delinquency is purely a transitory phenomenon which does not persist into adult life. To the extent that it is transitory, comparisons between parental crime in adult life and delinquency in the offspring during childhood are not a comparison of like with like and so provide an invalid estimate of continuities.

Similarly, if occupational status fluctuates over the life cycle it would be misleading to measure social mobility by the disparity in status between parents and children at one point in time (and hence at different points in their respective life cycles).

It is not enough, however, to study the extent to which the *same* phenomena persist throughout life. There are some features which by their nature can only be manifest at certain points in the life cycle. Thus, parenting skills can only be studied in adult life during the period of child rearing. However, it may well be that there are attitudes or behaviour shown in childhood which provide the basis for later parenting. Similarly, occupational status can only be measured meaningfully after school leaving and up to the point of retirement. Nevertheless, it is of value to know how far school attainment is associated with later occupational level. In short, a study of life cycle continuities must include consideration of patterns of associations as well as mere persistence of the same features.

Intergenerational Continuities

Much of the literature on intergenerational continuities simply reports the proportion of disadvantaged adults who had disadvantaged parents or who have disadvantaged children. On their own, however, these data mean very little. Changes over time in the base rates of disadvantage within the population can readily create a quite misleading picture of continuities or discontinuities. For example, during this century crime rates have steadily risen. . . . As a result, many more criminal adults will have criminal children than have criminal parents. The impression of an increasing intergenerational continuity may be largely an artefact resulting from secular trends in crime. Accordingly, the study of intergenerational continuities requires systematic comparisons between disadvantaged and non-disadvantaged individuals or groups as well as information on general population base rates. For these reasons, most reliance in this review is usually placed on the data from epidemiological studies of the general population.

. . . Of the other issues involved in the assessment of continuities . . . two matters require mention here. First, when continuities are being examined within non-familial groups, it is important to know whether the continuities are a function of differential movement in and out of the group or whether they apply to those who remain. For example, it will be shown that certain forms of disadvantage are especially common in inner city areas. However, the meaning of this finding very much depends on whether the high rate of disadvantage is a function of disadvantaged individuals moving into the city or whether the high rate also applies to people born and bred in the city.

The second matter concerns familial continuities. Since any one individual has two parents, four grandparents and may have several children, the question of continuity, even within a single family, is not susceptible to a simple 'yes' or 'no' answer. . . . The extent to which there is intergenerational continuity will depend to a certain extent on the nature of the marriage network. The wider the network the less continuity there will be.

Causal Processes

Simple estimates of the extent of intergenerational continuities provide no guide to social policy or political action. Knowledge on the causal processes is also required. The use of the word 'processes' deliberately emphasizes that it is an understanding of a chain of circumstances which is required rather than the identification of any supposed 'basic' cause. Furthermore, the use of the plural notes that with almost all forms of disadvantage several different mechanisms are likely to be operating and interacting one with another. . . . As the results clearly show, multifactorial and interactive causation is the rule, although the relative importance of different factors varies with different sorts of disadvantage.

The futility of a search for a basic cause is well illustrated by the medical syndrome often called 'deprivation dwarfism' (see Rutter, 1972). This is a condition found in young children who come from grossly disturbed families and who are of extremely short stature. The dwarfism is not associated with any disease or illness and at first it was thought that lack of love or emotional privation impaired growth even when the intake of food remained adequate. This now seems not to be so, at least in most cases. The answer is more humdrum—the children have not received enough to eat. To that extent the dwarfism is 'caused' by starvation. However, that leaves open the question of why the children had been inadequately fed and the answer to that question often lies in parental neglect or in the child's depression following chronic stress. Therefore it could be said that parental neglect or lack of love is really the cause. But that only puts the matter back one stage further. Why did the parents neglect the child? The answer may lie in current social disadvantage (e.g. loss of job and housing) or in adverse childhood experiences which failed to provide the proper basis for parenting. Are these then the causes? Of course, in a sense all of them are and appropriate action requires an understanding of the process as a whole.

It should be added, too, that different aspects of disadvantage may involve different causal processes. For example, the 'causes' of poverty involve at least three distinct questions. First, what are the factors which underlie the extent of *inequalities* in our society (i.e. the difference between the highest and lowest incomes)? Second, what are the factors which underlie the *level* of poverty (i.e. how many poor people there are)? Third, what are the factors which determine *who* is poor (i.e. whether Mr Brown or Mr Smith is in poverty)? The answers to each of these questions may involve quite disparate mechanisms, as will be discussed in later chapters.

Plan of Book

The book starts with a discussion of economic status and then housing. Although these are forms of disadvantage about which there is very little evidence on intergenerational continuities, they constitute two of the most important aspects of a person's material environment. They differ from most of the other forms of disadvantage considered in the book in one important respect. It would be possible by one stroke of the pen to give someone adequate financial resources and a good house. The particular disadvantage could be removed in an instant (although associated personal disadvantages might remain). This is in sharp contrast to the situation with poor educational attainments or psychiatric disorder or inadequate parenting where remedial action takes time to be effective and also involves changes in personal functioning. However, the distinction is more apparent than real in that, in practice, poverty and poor housing tend to be very persistent disadvantages, and in that the other difficulties are to some extent dependent on immediate social circumstances which are also potentially subject to instant improvement.

Nevertheless, these differences have meant that the various forms of disadvantage have been tackled in somewhat different ways in this book. Thus, social and political influences receive more consideration with respect to economic status and housing than they do in other chapters. To some extent this is appropriate in terms of the relative weight of different influences with different forms of disadvantage. But we have inevitably been constrained by what is available in the literature. There are several important topics which deserve a fuller treatment but a lack of evidence has made this impossible. Because of these constraints, the length of individual chapters provides no indication of their relative importance. The length is simply a reflection of what is available in the literature.

Although obviously we are deeply concerned with the alleviation of disadvantage this was not part of our remit. Intervention programmes are discussed in individual chapters where they are thought to be of possible relevance to factors influencing intergenerational continuities, but there has been no attempt to provide a systematic coverage of preventive or therapeutic actions.

Finally, the concluding chapter brings together some of the conceptual issues which emerged from our review of the literature but it does not attempt to summarize all the findings. The book as a whole is a summary of research and to summarize the summary seemed a pointless exercise. Unfortunately, the subject is too complex to be dealt with by a few succinct conclusions and we request the reader's indulgence and patience in asking that the book be read as a whole.

Reading X.   Consumer Beliefs and Behavior with Respect to Cigarette Smoking: A Critical Analysis of the Public Literature, by M. Fishbein

This report is directed at two fundamental questions: First, it attempts to determine whether, at the present time, the American public's decision to

Source: 1977 Report prepared for the US Federal Trade Commission.

smoke (or not to smoke) cigarettes is an informed one. Second, it attempts to determine whether there is anything more that could be done to insure that decisions to smoke are informed decisions.

The report provides a method for analyzing the decision to smoke and actions to influence it, whether by government, public education groups, or cigarette advertisers. It also defines areas where further research is needed, and it draws some conclusions based upon the presently available literature. It is hoped that the report will be useful to all interested parties whether their goal of action is to insure the sufficiency of consumer beliefs or to influence attitudes, intentions, and behavior with respect to smoking.

Generally speaking, the main findings of this report can be summarized as follows:

1. Providing a person with a given piece of information may inform the person in at least three different ways: (1) he may become aware that the information exists; (2) he may accept the information in general; and (3) he may accept the information at a personalized level. These three ways of being informed correspond to three levels of belief which can be illustrated as follows:

>   *Level 1* (Awareness): A person may believe that "The Surgeon General has determined that cigarette smoking is dangerous to health."
>
>   *Level 2* (General acceptance): A person may believe that "Cigarette smoking is dangerous to health."
>
>   *Level 3* (Personalized acceptance): A person may believe that "My cigarette smoking is dangerous to my health."

Needless to say, a person may be informed on one Level but not on another.

2. At the present time, we know relatively little about the American public's *Level 1* or *Level 3* beliefs about smoking (or not smoking). With respect to *Level 2* however, there is sufficient evidence to conclude that the American public is not well informed at the present time.

For example, approximately 25% of the total population and almost 50% of all current smokers have still not fully accepted (at *Level 2*) the general, undifferentiated proposition that "Smoking cigarettes is dangerous to health." Further, although current data are not available, there is little question that there is even less general acceptance (*Level 2*) of propositions linking smoking to specific health consequences, such as heart disease, emphysemia, chronic bronchitis, and lowered birth weights.

Since all available evidence suggests that personalized acceptance lags well behind general acceptance, the above data suggest that the American public is even less well informed at *Level 3*. There is also evidence (although it is not current) that people may be misinformed about the position of various referents with respect to smoking. Finally, it should be noted that most Americans overestimate the number of current smokers in the U.S. population.

3. In addition to beliefs about the health hazards of smoking, there are many other beliefs that are material to smoking decisions. Although the

literature has pointed out that there are a multitude of factors that may be related to a given smoking decision, there is no general consensus concerning what these factors are, or how they contribute to a smoking decision.

The widely held view is that different factors underlie different smoking decisions (e.g., to initiate, continue, or stop smoking) and further, that different people may reach the same smoking decision for different reasons. Thus, despite the enormous amount of research on smoking, no systematic theory of smoking behavior has been developed and there is general agreement that no single explanation of smoking behavior is possible.

4. In marked contrast to this view, we have described an empirically supported social-psychological theory of the relationships among beliefs, attitudes, intentions, and behavior that is both consistent with, and capable of explaining, all of the diverse findings in the smoking literature. Perhaps most important, this theory allows one to identify the determinants of a given smoking decision. More specifically, the theory points out that:

A. Any given smoking decision is ultimately determined by the information the person has concerning each of the behavioral alternatives among which he or she must choose. More specifically, it is based on: (a) the information (or *Level 3* beliefs) one holds concerning the positive or negative consequences that will follow from one's own performance of each of the available alternatives (e.g., trying a cigarette *and* not trying a cigarette; continuing to smoke *and* stopping smoking) and/or (b) the beliefs one holds about the views of various individuals, groups, or institutions concerning one's performance of each alternative.

B. These two types of beliefs represent two major factors underlying any given decision: (a) a personal or attitudinal factor and (b) a social or normative factor. The relative importance of these two factors as determinants of any decision varies: (i) as a function of the particular decision one is confronting (e.g., normative factors may be most important in the initiation of smoking while attitudinal factors may be most important in its maintenance or cessation) and (ii) across different individuals (e.g., attitudinal factors may be more important in the decisions of adults while normative factors may be more important in the decisions of teenagers).

5. The ability to identify the determinants of any given smoking decision has many different implications, including the following:

A. Awareness and general acceptance of information linking smoking to various health hazards and/or not smoking to various health benefits may be a necessary but not sufficient condition for making an informed decision.

B. In order to make a fully informed decision a person should have: (a) a complete and accurate set of *Level 3* beliefs about the outcomes (both positive and negative, health related and nonhealth related) that will follow from his or her performance of *each* alternative from among which he or she must choose, and (b) a complete and accurate set of beliefs about the normative prescriptions of relevant referents, i.e., beliefs that these referents think one should (or should not) perform each available alternative.

C. At any Level of belief, a person may be informed with respect to one smoking (or nonsmoking) alternative but not with respect to another. For example, although a person may be informed about the health hazards associated with continuing to smoke, he may not be informed about the dangers of trying a cigarette or of starting to smoke. Similarly, although a person may be informed about the advantages and disadvantages of continuing to smoke, he may not be informed about the advantages and disadvantages of continuing not to smoke or of stopping smoking.

6. Given the fact that the American public is presently uninformed (by almost any definition of "informed"), there is unquestionably a great deal more that can be done to insure that the public will make more informed smoking decisions. The smoking literature, however, provides little insight into this problem. Indeed, the general consensus seems to be that because of "the diversity of needs which impel different persons to smoke . . . no general rule concerning efforts to persuade people not to smoke, or to give up smoking, will be valid or effective . . ., no single approach will be satisfactory for more than a minority of individuals. . . ." (see Larson & Silvette, 1968, p. 304).

7. In marked contrast to this position, the available evidence indicates that it is possible to influence smoking decisions by providing the public with information. For example, despite the often expressed position of the tobacco industry that cigarette advertising does not influence the decision to smoke but only the brand choice of current smokers, the available evidence supports the conclusion that cigarette advertising does increase overall consumption.

Perhaps more important, there is considerable evidence that providing the American public with antismoking information significantly decreased consumption and produced large scale changes in other aspects of smoking behavior. This is not meant to imply that most educational programs or informational campaigns have been successful; indeed, the majority of such programs have ended in apparent failure. However, there are enough reported successes in the literature to warrant the conclusion that it is possible to both inform the public and to influence their smoking decisions.

8. There is little basis for assuming that a message failed to be persuasive because it was avoided by people with contrary positions or because it was fear arousing.

A. Despite the long lasting assumption that people avoid or fail to attend to information with which they disagree, there is no evidence to support this assumption. In fact, it appears that one's own beliefs and attitudes have little or no influence on one's ability to recognize or recall information presented by an outside source.

B. Despite the long lasting argument that certain types of appeals (e.g., fear appeals, rational appeals, one-sided appeals, etc.) are more (or less) effective than other types, there is no evidence to substantiate this argument. In fact, it is not the type of appeal, but the *content* of the appeal that determines its effectiveness.

9. Communication failures are primarily due to: (a) the selection of inappropriate arguments and/or (b) a failure to select a sufficient number of appropriate arguments.

For example, it must be recalled that beliefs about the negative consequences of one's own smoking coexist with beliefs about the benefits of one's smoking as well as beliefs about the advantages and disadvantages of one's not smoking (or quitting). Needless to say, providing information that may produce changes in one or two of these beliefs may not be sufficient for either reinforcing or changing a smoking decision.

Further, if a person's smoking (or nonsmoking) behavior is primarily under normative control, changing beliefs about the consequences of one's own engaging in various smoking alternatives may have little or no influence on a person's smoking decision. Similarly, if a person's smoking decision is primarily under attitudinal control, providing him with information about the positions of various referents with respect to his performance of one or more alternatives may have little or no influence in that decision.

Considerations such as these can account, at least in part, for the reported failures of some antismoking educational campaigns.

10. It should be possible to influence a person's smoking decision by providing information about the advantages or disadvantages of performing various smoking and nonsmoking alternatives and/or information about the views of relevant referents with respect to the performance of those alternatives. The exact content of the information, however, should be determined by: (a) the beliefs, attitudes, and intentions already held by the public with respect to different smoking and nonsmoking alternatives; and (b) by the degree to which the decision one wishes to affect is under attitudinal or normative control.

At the present time however, we do not have enough information about either (a) or (b) above to aid us in developing communications that would contain the most appropriate arguments for affecting a given smoking decision. Thus, although there is much that could be done immediately to inform the public, much more research is necessary if one wishes to maximize the likelihood that this information will also influence a smoking decision. . . .

[Conclusions]

What Can Be Done to Inform the Public and Affect Their Decisions to Smoke or Not to Smoke?

We have already pointed out that our analysis of the literature did not provide any helpful information with respect to this question. Indeed, if anything, the literature suggests that there is no systematic way to answer literature does make it clear that providing information to the American public can influence decisions to smoke or not smoke.

For example, despite the often expressed position of the tobacco industry that cigarette advertising does not influence the decision to smoke but only the brand choice of current smokers, the available evidence supports the conclusion that cigarette advertising has increased overall consumption. Perhaps more important, there is considerable evidence that providing the American public with antismoking information (as was done, for example, during the years of the FTC's [Federal Trade Commission] equal time ruling) significantly decreased cigarette consumption and produced significant shifts in other aspects of smoking behavior.

This is not meant to imply that most educational programs or information campaigns have been successful; indeed, the majority of such programs have ended in apparent failure. There are, however, enough reported successes for such campaigns in the literature to warrant the conclusion that it is possible to both inform the public and to influence their smoking decisions.

Moreover, our analysis of the literature makes it clear that there is little basis for assuming that a message failed to be persuasive because it was avoided by people with contrary positions or because it was fear arousing. Indeed, the most crucial aspect of any message is its content. Communication failures are primarily due to: (a) a failure to select a sufficient number of appropriate arguments and/or (b) the selection of inappropriate arguments. In order to clarify this point, it is necessary to consider the possible effects of presenting different types of antismoking information to the public.

Possible Effects of Information on a Decision to Smoke

It should be recalled that according to the theory outlined above, the beliefs that are most material for any given smoking decision are beliefs about the consequences (both positive and negative, both health and nonhealth related) of one's own performance of each of the behavioral alternatives involved in the decision and/or beliefs about the normative prescriptions of various referents concerning one's own performance of each of these alternatives.

This implies that, depending upon the degree to which the intentions to perform the various alternatives involved in the decision are under attitudinal or normative control, it should be possible to influence a person's smoking decision by providing information that will influence his beliefs about the consequences of *his* performing these alternatives and/or information that will influence his beliefs about the normative prescriptions of relevant referents.

It should be clear, however, that since a given smoking decision is based upon a large set of underlying beliefs, providing information that may produce a change in one or two of these beliefs may not be sufficient either to reinforce or to change a person's decision. Perhaps even more important, it must be realized that providing a person with a given piece of information (e.g., exposing him to a proposition, such as, "cigarette smoking causes cancer") may have many different effects:

A. The person may form the belief that a particular referent (i.e., the source of the information) expressed the proposition. For example, he may come to believe that "The American Cancer Society says that cigarette smoking causes cancer."

B. The person may accept (believe) the proposition; i.e., he may believe that "Cigarette smoking causes cancer."

C. He may yield to the information; i.e., exposure to the information may produce a change in his belief that "Cigarette smoking causes cancer." Note that the distinction between acceptance and yielding in this situation is simply a recognition of the fact that if a person already believes the information he is exposed to, he can accept the information without its producing any change in his corresponding belief, i.e., without his yielding to the information.

D. The information may have an impact upon other beliefs. For example, if a person yields to the information that "Smoking causes lung cancer" this could also increase his belief that "Smoking is dangerous to health." There is one type of impact effect that is particularly relevant for understanding the effect of information on a given smoking decision: the impact of the information upon those beliefs that underlie the decision in question.

For information to have an influence on a person's smoking decision: (a) it must be presented in a personalized form (e.g., "Your smoking will increase your chances of getting cancer"), in which case yielding is equivalent to changing the belief that "My smoking will increase my chances of getting cancer," or (b) it must have an impact on such an underlying belief. Note that information can also have an impact on normative beliefs. For example, the person could form (or strengthen) the belief that the source of the information (e.g., the Surgeon General, the American Cancer Society) "thinks I should not smoke."

Finally, it must also be realized that information that may have an impact on beliefs underlying one smoking decision may not have an impact on beliefs underlying a different smoking decision. For example, although acceptance of and yielding to the proposition "Smoking causes cancer" may have an impact upon a person's belief that "My smoking increases my chances of getting cancer" or his belief that "My continuing to smoke will increase my chances of getting cancer," it may not have an impact on beliefs concerning other alternatives (e.g., "my trying a cigarette will increase my chances of getting cancer," "my starting (or not starting) to smoke will . . .").

To be maximally effective, information should link an outcome to a specific smoking or nonsmoking alternative. One cannot assume that information about smoking will have an impact upon beliefs about not smoking or vice-versa. This same point is also important with respect to normative information as well. Providing a person with information that a given referent thinks he should not smoke, for example, may not have an impact on his belief that the referent "thinks I should not try a cigarette."

What we have tried to show is that even though a person may accept and yield to the contents of a given communication, this may have little or no effect on his or her smoking decision if the information in the communication is not directly or indirectly material to the smoking decision involved. That is, the information should correspond directly to a belief underlying the decision or it should be known to have a relation to one or more of such underlying beliefs.

It must again be pointed out, however, that since a smoking decision is based on a large number of underlying beliefs, information that changes one or two of these beliefs may be insufficient for influencing a given smoking decision. Moreover, it must be recalled that some decisions may be primarily under attitudinal control while others may be primarily under normative control. If a given decision is primarily under normative control, and if the goal of action is to change that decision, little will be accomplished by providing a person with information that is designed to change his beliefs about the consequences of his performing one or more smoking or nonsmoking alternatives. Similarly, if a given decision is primarily under attitudinal control, providing information directed at changing his beliefs about the normative prescriptions of relevant others will have little, if any, influence upon the smoking decision in question.

Considerations such as these can, to a large extent, explain the apparent failure of many antismoking educational programs and informational campaigns. Indeed, the failure of most persuasive communications can be traced to the fact that they contain information that is either immaterial, insufficient, or both.

But more important than explaining failures, these considerations also provide a framework for the development of appropriate communications. For example, if the goal of action is to change the decisions of current smokers (e.g., to get current smokers to stop or quit smoking) an effective message will have to contain some, or all, of the following:

1. Information linking "continued smoking" to a number of negative outcomes that may be either health or nonhealth related.
2. Information linking "quitting" and/or "stopping smoking" to a number of positive outcomes that may be either health or nonhealth related.
3. Information that emphasizes the personal relevance of (1) and (2) above.
4. Information that a number of important others think that the receiver should not continue smoking but should quit or stop.

Until more is known about the beliefs, attitudes, subjective norms, and intentions of current smokers, and until one knows whether this decision is primarily under attitudinal control, normative control, or both, it is impossible to say which of these four types of information is most likely to be effective, or what the exact content of the information should be. That is, very different types of information will be called for if the decision is under attitudinal control than if it is under normative control. Similarly, very different types of information will be called for if smokers already have unfavorable attitudes towards their own continued smoking, than if they have favorable attitudes toward their continued smoking. Further, although it might be clear that an appropriate strategy would involve providing information about the benefits of stopping or quitting, the particular benefits that should be associated with quitting will depend upon what beliefs the receiver already holds.

Recommendations for Research

We have already pointed out the need for research that would allow us to identify the beliefs, attitudes, subjective norms, and intentions that are currently held by the American public (or segments of the American public) with respect to various smoking and nonsmoking alternatives. Equally important, research is needed to provide some understanding of when, and under what circumstances, general acceptance of a piece of information will have an impact upon those beliefs that underlie a given smoking decision. More specifically, research is needed to determine:

1. When, or under what circumstances awareness of a given piece of information leads to general acceptance of that information. For example, given that a person is aware that a given source provided a piece of information (i.e., given that the person believes that "The Surgeon General has determined that smoking is dangerous to health"), what are the factors that influence the likelihood that the person will generally accept this information, (i.e., believe that "Smoking is dangerous to health")?

2. When, or under what circumstances awareness of a given piece of information leads to the formation of a normative belief, i.e., a belief about the position of the source of that information concerning a given smoking alternative? For example, given that the person believes that "The Surgeon General has determined that smoking is dangerous to health," what are the factors that influence the likelihood that the person will form (or strengthen) the belief that "The Surgeon General thinks I should not smoke cigarettes?"

3. When, or under what circumstances general acceptance of a piece of information becomes personalized and/or has an impact upon beliefs that underlie a given smoking decision? It must be realized that this question has many aspects to it.

We have already pointed out that general acceptance of a proposition such as "Smoking leads to cancer" may have very different effects upon beliefs that underlie different smoking decisions. For example, it may have an impact upon a belief such as "My continuing to smoke will increase my chances of getting cancer," but not upon a belief such as "My trying a cigarette will increase my chances of getting cancer." Thus, it is necessary to investigate the relations between the general acceptance of a proposition and personalized beliefs concerning a variety of smoking and nonsmoking alternatives.

It must also be realized that information that itself is not directly concerned with the consequences of performing various smoking and nonsmoking alternatives and/or the views of various referents may still be material to a smoking decision if it impacts upon the beliefs that underlie that decision. For example, little is known about the relations between beliefs about the characteristics, qualities, and attributes of smokers and nonsmokers and beliefs that underlie different smoking decisions. That is, there are no data concerning the relations between a belief, such as, "Smokers are more mature (sophisticated) than nonsmokers" and material beliefs, such as, "My smoking will make me look more mature (sophisticated)" or "Most mature (sophisticated) people think I should smoke."

Similarly, although it seems reasonable to assume that beliefs about the smoking behavior of others (e.g., beliefs such as "Most of my friends smoke") will influence a person's material beliefs (e.g., beliefs such as "My starting to smoke will please my friends" or "Most of my friends think I should try a cigarette"), there are no data that indicate whether, or to what extent such impact effects occur.

It should be noted that there already is a considerable amount of research relating to question (1) above. Although this research has provided many important insights into this question, we are still a long way from knowing all the answers, and additional research in this area is necessary. With respect to the other questions, however, we were able to find *no* research that was directly relevant.

Although some research has investigated the relation between general acceptance of one piece of information and general acceptance of another, we know of no studies that have been concerned with the relation between generalized and personalized acceptance. Research on this question appears crucial if one is to gain an understanding of the types of information that are most likely to influence a smoking decision.

Concluding Comment

In this report we have tried to show that: (1) the American public is not currently well informed about various aspects of smoking and nonsmoking and (2) that it is possible to provide the public with information that will both (a) increase the degree to which they are informed and (b) influence their smoking decisions. There is a great deal that could be done immediately. Among other things, for example, the public needs more information concerning specific health hazards of smoking, specific benefits of not smoking, the percent of the population that currently smokes, and the total amount of consumption of different types of cigarettes (e.g., high versus low nicotine) that can put one at risk with respect to different illnesses.

However, if the goal of action is to provide information that will be most material to the various smoking decisions that confront different segments of the population, considerably more research is necessary. Only through such research will one be able to identify the type and the content of the information that is required if one wishes to maximize the likelihood that any given smoking decision will be an informed one.

We now change focus from the political, social policy, and commercial problems that the psychologist has addressed in various ways to methodological issues within psychology itself. These are, however, issues very close to the heart of any psychologist trying to work in the applied social field.

THE PSYCHOLOGIST AS EXPERIMENTER

We have just considered how the "experts" consult the literature as part of the process of "clearing the ground" so that research questions can be posed in the most precisely articulated way possible. Sometimes, however, the psychological "expert" tries to set up a situation in the laboratory similar to that in real life, but in such a way that crucial aspects can be controlled and manipulated. An example of this approach is Stanley Milgram's research on reactions of people to orders from an authority figure (Milgram, 1963, 1965). His interest in the problem was aroused by the knowledge of the trials of Nazi soldiers following the Second World War. Their actions would, without question, have been considered "criminal" if they had been the offences of one individual against another. Such was the nature of the atrocities that it would have been easy to conclude that the perpetrators were devoid of any sort of feeling for fellow human beings and had little, if any, regard for the value of human life. In their defence, however, it was claimed that this was not at all the case but that these were soldiers, serving their country in time of war, who were simply obeying orders that were passed down from their superiors. It was claimed that this sort of unquestioning obedience to authority is a vital part of military training. Milgram was fascinated by this justification. He was intrigued to know whether average American citizens held "obeying orders" so sacred that they would inflict pain on other people if ordered to do so. Milgram was not commissioned to research this problem, the study arose from his concern about understanding human "nature." He, like many of us, was bothered by this sacrifice of personal, humane values for obedience at whatever cost. The problem he set for himself was to clarify an issue about human potential. Milgram decided to explore the problem in a laboratory setting. If he had chosen to study the problem "in the field," he could have set out to study all of the situations in which people obey orders in real life. In practice that would have been impossible, not least because it would take a lifetime. Not only would a field study be impracticable, but also he would not be able to explore the precise conditions in which people did, or did not, obey orders.

He, therefore, set up a situation in the laboratory which included what he considered the essentials of the problem. The "authority" in Milgram's experiment was a researcher at a high-prestige University (Yale) who wore a white laboratory coat and assumed an authoritative manner. The volunteers were paid to participate in the research and, therefore, were placed under something of an obligation to carry out the tasks. When a subject arrived at the laboratory he was introduced to another subject (in fact, a member of Milgram's team). One was to be the "teacher" and the other the "learner" in the experiment. A draw was rigged so that the subject always became the teacher. The teacher was instructed to give an electric shock to the learner every time the learner made a mistake. The elaborate "equipment" in the room was described as a shock generator. A "slight shock" was labelled as "15 volts," with appropriate labellings extending to "450 volts," which was labelled as "danger: severe shock." The teacher was instructed to get the learner to memorize by drill a list of paired words, mistakes being punished by the teacher administering a shock to the subject; these shocks were to increase in intensity as the mistakes accumulated. No one actually experienced pain, however, as the only shock emitted by the "equipment" was a very mild one given to the "teacher" to demonstrate that the equipment worked. The "learner" followed a prepared pattern of reaction to the "shocks" culminating in loud groaning, beating with his free hand, and increasing insistence that the experiment be stopped. Finally, when the "shock" being administered was 300 volts the learner demanded to be freed from the apparatus and refused to answer any more questions.

In the extract from Milgram's book that follows, three questions that are frequently asked about his experiments are explored: Are the people studied in the experiment typical? Did they really believe they were administering shocks to the learner? Is it possible to generalize from the laboratory to "real life"? We want to examine the psychologist in the role of the experimenter beyond these three important questions. One of the debates that arises out of this sort of work concerns psychological ethics and value systems. The discussion between Savin (1973), Reading XII and Zimbardo (1973a), Reading XIII, which is included in the readings that follow, lays bare the problems associated with "real-world" experimentation and focuses upon the ethical issues that arise in Zimbardo's experimental study of prisoners and guards in a simulated prison. (A comment on this same piece of research is given in Chapter 5.)

Reading XI.   The Problems of Method, by S. Milgram

In the minds of some critics, there is an image of man that simply does not admit of the type of behavior observed in the experiment. Ordinary people, they assert, do not administer painful shocks to a protesting individual simply because they are ordered to do so. Only Nazis and sadists perform this way. In the preceding chapters, I have tried to explain why the behavior observed in the laboratory comes about: how the individual makes an initial set of commitments to the authority, how the meaning of the action is transformed by the context in which it occurs, and how binding factors prevent the person from disobeying.

Underlying the criticism of the experiment is an alternative model of

Source: Milgram, S. (1974). *Obedience to Authority*. London: Tavistock Publications, pp. 169–178.

human nature, one holding that when confronted with a choice between hurting others and complying with authority, normal people reject authority. Some of the critics are doubly convinced that Americans in particular do not act inhumanely against their fellows on the orders of authority. The experiment is seen as defective in the degree to which it does not uphold this view. The most common assertions with which to dismiss the findings are: (1) the people studied in the experiment are not typical, (2) they didn't believe they were administering shocks to the learner, and (3) it is not possible to generalize from the laboratory to the larger world. Let us consider each of these points in turn.

1. *Are the people studied in the experiment representative of the general population, or are they a special group?*   Let me begin with an anecdote. When the very first experiments were carried out, Yale undergraduates were used exclusively as subjects, and about 60 percent of them were fully obedient. A colleague of mine immediately dismissed these findings as having no relevance to "ordinary" people, asserting that Yale undergraduates are a highly aggressive, competitive bunch who step on each other's necks on the slightest provocation. He assured me that when "ordinary" people were tested, the results would be quite different. As we moved from the pilot studies to the regular experimental series, people drawn from every stratum of New Haven life came to be studied in the experiment: professionals, white-collar workers, unemployed persons, and industrial workers. *The experimental outcome was the same as we had observed among the students*.

It is true that those who came to the experiment were volunteers, and we may ask whether the recruitment procedure itself introduced bias into the subject population.

In follow-up studies, we asked subjects why they had come to the laboratory. The largest group (17 percent) said they were curious about psychology experiments, 8.9 percent cited the money as the principal reason, 8.6 per cent said they had a particular interest in memory, 5 percent indicated that they thought they could learn something about themselves. The motives for coming to the laboratory were evidently diverse, and the range of subjects was extremely wide. Moreover, Rosenthal and Rosnow (1966) have shown that volunteers for experiments tend to be *less* authoritarian than those who do not volunteer. Thus, if any bias was introduced through a volunteer effect, it was in the direction of obtaining subjects more prone to disobedience.

Moreover, when the experiments were repeated in Princeton, Munich, Rome, South Africa, and Australia, each using somewhat different methods of recruitment and subject populations having characteristics different from those of our subjects, the level of obedience was invariably somewhat *higher* than found in the investigation reported in this book. Thus Mantell, in Munich [1971], found 85 per cent of his subjects obedient.

2. *Did subjects believe they were administering painful shocks to the learner?* The occurrence of tension provided striking evidence of the subjects' genuine involvement in the experimental conflict, and this has been observed and reported throughout in the form of representative transcripts (1963), scale data (1965), and filmed accounts (1965a).

In all experimental conditions the level of pain was considered by the subject as very high, and Table 4.1 provides these data for a representative group of experiments. In Experiment 2, Voice-Feedback (victim audible but not visible), the mean for obedient subjects on the 14-point scale was 11.36 and fell within the "extremely painful" zone of the scale. More than half the obedient subjects used the extreme upper point on the scale, and at least one subject indicated by a + sign that "extremely painful" was not a strong enough designation. Of the 40 subjects in this condition, two indicated on the scale (with scores of 1 and 3) that they did not think the victim received painful shocks, and both subjects were obedient. These subjects, it would appear, were not successfully exposed to the manipulatory intent of the experimenter. But this is not so simple a matter since denial of an unpleasant action can serve a defensive function, and some subjects came to view their performance in a favorable light only by reconstructing what their state of mind was when they were administering shocks. The question is, was their disbelief a firm hypothesis or merely a fleeting notion among many other notions?

The broad quantitative picture of subjects' testimony on belief can be examined, among other ways, by scrutinizing responses to the follow-up questionnaire distributed about a year after subjects participated in the study. Item 4 of the questionnaire is reprinted in Table 4.2, along with the distribution of responses to it.

Three-quarters of the subjects (the first two categories) by their own testimony acted under the belief that they were administering painful

TABLE 4.1
Subjects' Estimates of Pain Felt by Victim

Condition	$\bar{x}$ Obedient S's	$\bar{x}$ Defiant S's	$\bar{x}$ All S's
	n	n	
Remote-Victim	13.50 (20)	13.27 (11)	13.42
Voice-Feedback	11.36 (25)	11.80 (15)	11.53
Proximity	12.69 (16)	11.79 (24)	12.15
Touch-Proximity	12.25 (28)	11.17 (12)	11.93
New Base Line	11.40 (26)	12.25 (14)	11.70
Change of Personnel	11.98 (20)	12.05 (20)	12.02
Bridgeport Replication	11.79 (19)	11.81 (18)	11.80
Women as Subjects	12.88 (26)	12.07 (14)	12.60
Closeness of Authority	11.67 (31)	12.39 (9)	11.83

shocks. It would have been an easy out at this point to deny that the hoax had been accepted. But only a fifth of the group indicated having had serious doubts.

David Rosenhan of Swarthmore College carried out a replication of the experiment in order to obtain a base measure for further studies of his own. He arranged for elaborate interviewing. Among other things, he established the interviewer as a person independent of the experiment who demanded a detailed account of the subject's experience, and probed the issue of belief even to the point of asking, "You really mean you didn't catch on to the experiment?" On the basis of highly stringent criteria of full acceptance, Rosenhan reports that (according to the determination of independent judges), 60 percent of the subjects thoroughly accepted the authenticity of the experiment. Examining the performance of these subjects, he reports that 85 percent were fully obedient. (Rosenhan, it must be pointed out, employed a subject population that was younger than that used in the original experiments, and this I believe, accounts for the higher level of obedience.)

When my experimental findings are subjected to a comparable type of statistical control, they are not altered in any substantial manner. For example, in Experiment 2, Voice-Feedback, of those subjects who indicated acceptance of the deception (categories 1 and 2), 58 percent were obedient; of those who indicated category 1, 60 percent were obedient. Over all experimental conditions, this manner of controlling the data slightly reduced the proportion of obedient to defiant subjects. The changes leave the relations among conditions intact and are inconsequential for interpreting the meaning or import of the findings.

In sum, the majority of subjects accepted the experimental situation as genuine; a few did not. Within each experimental condition it was my estimate that two to four subjects did not think they were administering painful shocks to the victim, but I adopted a general rule that no subject be

TABLE 4.2
Responses to Question on Belief

During the Experiment	*Defiant*	*Obedient*	*All Subjects*
(1) I fully believed the learner was getting painful shocks.	62.5% (230)	47.9% (139)	56.1% (369)
(2) Although I had some doubts, I believed the learner was *probably* getting the shocks.	22.6% (83)	25.9% (75)	24.0% (158)
(3) I just wasn't sure whether the learner was getting the shocks or not.	6.0% (22)	6.2% (18)	6.1% (40)
(4) Although I had some doubts, I thought the learner was probably not getting the shocks.	7.6% (28)	16.2% (47)	11.4% (75)
(5) I was certain the learner was not getting the shocks.	1.4% (5)	3.8% (11)	2.4% (16)

removed from the data, because selective removal of subjects on somewhat imprecise criteria is the quickest way to inadvertently shape hypotheses. Even now I am not willing to dismiss those subjects because it is not clear that their rejection of the technical illusion was a cause of their obedience or a consequence of it. Cognitive processes may serve to rationalize behavior that the subject has felt compelled to carry out. It is simple, indeed, for a subject to explain his behavior by stating he did not believe the victim received shocks, and some subjects may have come to this position as a post facto explanation. It cost them nothing and would go a long way toward preserving their positive self-conception. It has the additional benefit of demonstrating how astute and clever they were to penetrate a carefully laid cover story.

More important, however, is to be able to see the role of denial in the total process of obedience and disobedience. Denial is one specific cognitive adjustment of several that occur in the experiment, and it needs to be properly placed in terms of its functioning in the performance of some subjects . . . .

3. *Is the laboratory situation so special that nothing that was observed can contribute to a general view of obedience in wider social life?* No, not if one understands what has been observed—namely, how easily individuals can become an instrument of authority, and how, once so defined, they are unable to free themselves from it. The processes of obedience to authority . . . remain invariant so long as the basic condition for its occurrence exists: namely, that one is defined into a relationship with a person who one feels has, by virtue of his status, the right to prescribe behavior. While the coloring and details of obedience differ in other circumstances, the basic processes remain the same, much as the basic process of combustion is the same for both a burning match and a forest fire.

The problem of generalizing from one to the other does not consist of point-for-point comparison between one and the other (the match is small, the forest is extensive, etc.), but depends entirely on whether one has reached a correct theoretical understanding of the relevant process. In the case of combustion, we understand the process of rapid oxidation under conditions of electron excitation, and in obedience, the restructuring of internal mental processes in the agentic state.

There are some who argue that a psychological experiment is a unique event, and therefore, one cannot generalize from it to the larger world. But it is more useful to recognize that any social occasion has unique properties to it, and the social scientist's task is finding the principles that run through this surface diversity.

The occasion we term a psychological experiment shares its essential structural properties with other situations composed of subordinate and superordinate roles. In all such circumstances the person responds not so much to the content of what is required but on the basis of his relationship to the person who requires it. Indeed, where legitimate authority is the source of action, *relationship overwhelms content.* That is what is meant by the importance of social structure, and that is what is demonstrated in the present experiment.

Some critics have attempted to dismiss the findings by asserting that behavior is legitimized by the experimenter, as if this made it inconsequential. But behavior is also legitimized in every other socially meaningful instance of obedience, whether it is the obedience of a soldier, employee, or executioner at the state prison. It is precisely an understanding of behavior within such hierarchies that the investigation probes. Eichmann, after all, was embedded in a legitimate social organization and from his standpoint was doing a proper job. In other words, this investigation deals with the obedience *not* of the oppressed, who are coerced by brutal punishment into compliance, but of those who willingly comply because society gives them a role and they are motivated to live up to its requirements.

Another more specific question concerns the degree of parallel between obedience in the laboratory and in Nazi Germany. Obviously there are enormous differences. Consider the disparity in time scale. The laboratory experiment takes an hour; the Nazi calamity unfolded over more than a decade. Is the obedience observed in the laboratory in any way comparable to that seen in Nazi Germany? (Is a match flame comparable to the Chicago fire of 1898?) The answer must be that while there are enormous differences of circumstance and scope, a common psychological process is centrally involved in both events.

In the laboratory, through a set of simple manipulations, ordinary people no longer perceived themselves as a responsible part of the causal chain leading to action against a person. The way in which responsibility is cast off, and individuals become thoughtless agents of action, is of general import. One can find evidence of its occurrence time and again as one reads over the transcripts of the war criminals at Nuremburg, the American killers at My Lai and the commander of Andersonville. What we find in common among soldier, party functionary, and obedient subject is the same limitless capacity to yield to authority and the use of identical mental mechanisms to reduce the strain of acting against a helpless victim. At the same time it is, of course, important to recognize some of the differences between the situation of our subjects and that of the Germans under Hitler.

The experiment is presented to our subjects in a way that stresses its positive human values: increase of knowledge about learning and memory processes. These ends are consistent with generally held cultural values. Obedience is merely instrumental to the attainment of these ends. By contrast, the objectives that Nazi Germany pursued were themselves morally reprehensible, and were recognized as such by many Germans.

The maintenance of obedience in our subjects is highly dependent upon the face-to-face nature of the social occasion and its attendant surveillance. We saw how obedience dropped sharply when the experimenter was not present. The forms of obedience that occurred in Germany were in far greater degree dependent upon the internalization of authority and were probably less tied to minute-by-minute surveillance. I would guess such internalization can occur only through relatively long processes of indoctrination, of a sort not possible within the course of a laboratory hour. Thus, the mechanisms binding the German into his obedience were not the mere momentary embarrassment and shame of disobeying but more internalized punitive mechanisms that can only evolve through extended relationships with authority.

Other differences should at least be mentioned briefly: to resist Naziism was itself an act of heroism, not an inconsequential decision, and death was a possible penalty. Penalties and threats were forever around the corner, and the victims themselves had been thoroughly villified and portrayed as being unworthy of life or human kindness. Finally, our subjects were told by authority that what they were doing to their victim might be temporarily painful but would cause no permanent damage, while those Germans directly involved in the annihilations knew that they were not only inflicting pain but were destroying human life. So, in the final analysis, what happened in Germany from 1933 to 1945 can only be fully understood as the expression of a unique historical development that will never again be precisely replicated.

Yet the essence of obedience, as a psychological process, can be captured by studying the simple situation in which a man is told by a legitimate authority to act against a third individual. This situation confronted both our experimental subject and the German subject and evoked in each a set of parallel psychological adjustments.

A study published in 1972 by H. V. Dicks sheds additional light on this matter. Dicks interviewed former members of the SS concentration camp personnel and Gestapo units, and at the conclusion of his study relates his observations to the obedience experiments. He finds clear parallels in the psychological mechanisms of his SS and Gestapo interviewees and subjects in the laboratory:

Milgram was . . . able to identify the nascent need to devalue the victim . . . we recognize the same tendency as, for example, in BS, BT, and GM (interviewees in Dicks' study). . . . Equally impressive for an evaluation of the "helpless cog" attitude as a moral defence was Milgram's recording of subjects who could afterwards declare that "they were convinced of the wrongness of what they were asked to do," and thereby feel themselves virtuous. Their virtue was ineffective since they could not bring themselves to defy the authority. This finding reminds us of the complete split of a man like PF (member of the SS) who afterwards managed to feel a lot of indignation against had to do.

Milgram's experiment has neatly exposed the "all too human" propensity to conformity and obedience to group authority . . . His work has also pointed towards some of the same ego defences subsequently used as justifications by his "ordinary" subjects as my SS men. . . .

The late Gordon W. Allport was fond of calling this experimental paradigm "the Eichmann experiment," for he saw in the subject's situation something akin to the position occupied by the infamous Nazi bureaucrat who, in the course of "carrying out his job," contributed to the destruction of millions of human beings. The "Eichmann experiment" is, perhaps, an apt term, but it should not lead us to mistake the import of this investigation. To focus only on the Nazis, however despicable their deeds, and to view only highly publicized atrocities as being relevant to these studies is to miss the point entirely. For the studies are principally concerned with the ordinary and routine destruction carried out by everyday people following orders.

Reading XII.   Professors and Psychological Researchers: Conflicting Values in Conflicting Roles, by H. B. Savin

Psychology Professor Philip Zimbardo and his colleagues hired ten undergraduates to play at being prisoners, and eleven others to be their jailers. The psychologist-directors spared no pains in constructing a convincing jail. They persuaded the Palo Alto police to arrest the 'volunteer' prisoners in squad cars, charge them with felonies at the police station and deliver them blindfolded to Zimbardo's jail, without informing them that this 'arrest' was the beginning of the experiment they had agreed to take part in.

The principal result was that the guards behaved like prison guards and the prisoners like prisoners. Indeed, the guards seem to have been more brutal, and the prisoners more degraded, than one would expect them to have become after only a few days in an establishment jail; Zimbardo was outstandingly successful at simulating the most destructive aspects of prisons. Within five days, he reports, he had felt obliged to release four of his ten prisoners because of 'extreme depression, disorganized thinking, uncontrollable crying and fits of rage' (1973a, p. 48), even though he was not so squeamish as to have prevented his guards from forcing prisoners to clean toilets with their bare hands, spraying them with fire extinguishers and repeatedly making them 'do pushups, on occasion with a guard stepping on them' (p. 44).

In short, one cannot make a prison a more humane institution by appointing Mr. Zimbardo its superintendent—a result no more surprising to him than to the rest of us because he knows all about man's 'dehumanizing tendency to respond to other people according to socially

Source: Cognition (1973), 2, 1, pp. 147–149.

determined labels and often arbitrarily assigned roles' (1973a, p. 58). The roles of prisoner and guard have been much discussed of late, and their characteristics are reasonably well known. But Mr. Zimbardo's study also calls attention to the role of psychological researcher. Much research in psychology, and in medicine as well, cannot be done without subjecting people to injury, sometimes physical and sometimes psychological, sometimes temporary and sometimes permanent. When is such research justifiable? No one, surely, would object to embarrassing a few self-confident volunteers if the result were a cure for schizophrenia. But in a great many experiments it is by no means clear that the good outweighs the harm, and the balance one strikes will depend in part, as social psychologists know better than anyone else, upon one's role.

Consider again Zimbardo's study. He has acknowledged that his results were 'no surprise to sophisticated savants' (1973b, p. 123), but feels that, even if it did not contribute anything to scientific knowledge, it was worth doing because it would help to enlighten those who had not learned about the importance of roles from less melodramatic research than his.[1] Is the degradation of thirty-two young men justified by the importance of the results of this research? That depends, obviously, on one's point of view. In practice, the decision about whether to do an experiment in which the subjects are mistreated rests with the experimenter, who, of course, is likely to profit from whatever good comes of an experiment but does not experience the harm that it does to his subjects.

Similar questions are raised by a great many other psychological experiments in which subjects are deceived, frightened, humiliated or maltreated in some other way. Like everyone else, psychological experimenters are bound by the code of criminal law, but the subject in a psychological experiment cannot assume that he will be treated any better than the law requires. Indeed, the police are apt to be somewhat lax in upholding the laws that might otherwise protect subjects because of a presumption that research of almost any sort is useful, or at least respectable.

Professors and scientists have traditionally resisted any proposal that outsiders participate in judgments about what research ought not to be done because its objectionable side-effects outweigh its value. (The American Psychological Association continues this tradition in its newly published *Ethical principles in the conduct of research with human*

---

[1]Zimbardo makes one other claim about the value of this research: 'From what we have learned by observing the *process* of dehumanization and causal matrix in which pathology was so easily elicited, we can help design not only more humanitarian prisons but help average people break out of their self-imposed or socially ascribed prisons. We have begun to do the former with correctional personnel, and the latter through a fuller exposition of the psychology of imprisonment in a forthcoming book' (1973b, p. 123). Zimbardo does not explain how an experiment whose results were foreseeable can help us escape whatever metaphorical prisons we are in, nor how except for its possible use in enlightening the ignorant, it can help him design more 'humanitarian' physical prisons.

participants [1973], where numerous ethical precepts are set forth but the only advice given to an investigator whose proposed experiments would violate these precepts is to weight the harm to be done by the research carefully against its possible benefits.) But, when the experimenters themselves decide how much mistreatment the importance of their work justifies them in inflicting on their subjects, the result is exactly what social psychologists would predict: Simple lying becomes a perfectly commonplace feature of even students' routine laboratory exercises; humiliation of subjects is not uncommon; on occasion there is a hell like Zimbardo's.

Society survives in spite of its used-car salesmen, its politicians' assistants, and a host of other people whose roles tempt them to be as obnoxious as the law allows, and it will not be destroyed by a few dozen psychologists who are similarly overzealous in the pursuit of their careers, but this particular kind of morally obtuse zeal raises special problems for the university. Most of the psychologists whose experiments involve mistreatment of human subjects are university professors, and most of their subjects are university students. Professors who, in pursuit of their own academic interests and professional advancement, deceive, humiliate, and otherwise mistreat their students are subverting the atmosphere of mutual trust and intellectual honesty without which, as we are fond of telling outsiders who want to meddle in our affairs, neither education nor free inquiry can flourish.

Reading XIII.   On the Ethics of Intervention in Human Psychological Research with Special Reference to the "Stanford Prison Experiment", by P. G. Zimbardo

Research was conducted recently (August 14–21, 1971) in which subjects assumed the roles of 'prisoner' or 'guard' for an extended period of time within an experimentally devised mock prison setting on the Stanford University campus. The projected two-week study had to be prematurely terminated when it became apparent that many of the 'prisoners' were in serious distress and many of the 'guards' were behaving in ways which brutalized and degraded their fellow subjects. In addition, the emerging reality of this role-playing situation was sufficiently compelling to influence virtually all those who operated within it to behave in ways appropriate to *its* demand characteristics, but inappropriate to their usual life roles and values; this included the research staff, faculty observers, a priest, lawyer, ex-convict, and relatives and friends of the subjects who visited the prison on several occasions (for details see Zimbardo, Banks, Haney and Jaffe, 1973; Haney, Banks and Zimbardo, 1973).

This research represents one of the most extreme experimental

---

Source: Cognition, (1973a), *2*, 2, pp. 243–255.

demonstrations of the power of situational determinants in both shaping behaviour and predominating over personality, attitudes and individual values. As such it extends the conclusions from Stanley Milgram's research on obedience to authority (1974). But the ethical concerns voiced over Milgram's treatment of placing subject-teachers in a conflict situation where they believed (incorrectly) that they were hurting another person are even more pronounced in the present case. Volunteer prisoners suffered physical and psychological abuse hour after hour for days, while volunteer guards were exposed to the new self-knowledge that they enjoyed being powerful and had abused this power to make other human beings suffer. The intensity and duration of this suffering uniquely qualify the Stanford prison experiment for careful scrutiny of violations of the ethics of human experimentation.

The plan of this article is to: (a) Give a synopsis of the experiment to familiarize the reader with its basic features; (b) summarize one set of critical arguments levelled against the experiment (which invited my reply in this particular journal); (c) analyze the sense in which the mock prison study can be considered to be unethical, and (d) present a body of information relevant to passing judgment on its ethicality from a legal, pragmatic, utilitarian or relativistic model of ethics.

My intention is less to assume a defensive stance in support of this particular study than to use it as a vehicle for delineating the enormous complexity of making ethically based decisions about interventions in human experimentation.

Synopsis of Mock Prison Study

Interpersonal dynamics in a prison-like environment were studied experimentally by designing a functional (rather than literal) simulation of a prison. Environmental, structural, institutional and social variables were manipulated in an effort to create a 'psychology of imprisonment' in a group of subjects who role-played being guards (for eight hours a day over three shifts) and a group who acted as prisoners (for twenty-four hours a day).

To assess the strength of the social, situational forces on the behaviour of these volunteer subjects, alternative explanations in terms of pre-existing dispositions were eliminated through subject selection and random assignment to treatments. A homogeneous sample of about two dozen normal, average, healthy American college males was chosen after extensive interviewing and diagnostic testing of a large group of applicants recruited through newspaper advertisements. The subjects were from colleges throughout the United States and Canada who volunteered to be in 'a study of prison life' in return for receiving a daily wage of fifteen dollars for a projected two-week period.

Half of these pre-selected subjects were randomly assigned to role-play prison guards the others to the mock-prisoner treatment. Neither group received any formal training in these roles—the cultural mass media had already provided the models they used to define their roles. The mock guards were impressed with the 'seriousness' of the experiment and by the demeanour of the research staff; the prospective prisoners began to take their roles seriously when they were subjected to an unexpected arrest by the city police. After being processed and temporarily detained at the police station, they were escorted to the experimental setting. Uniforms and differences in power further served to differentiate the two groups of subjects.

Continuous, direct observation of all behavioural interactions was supplemented by video- and audio-taped recordings, questionnaires, self-report scales and interviews. All of these data sources converge on the conclusion that this simulated environment was sufficiently realistic and forceful to elicit intense, personal and often pathological reactions from the majority of the participants. Many of the prisoner-subjects exhibited behaviours characteristic of the learned helplessness syndrome described by Seligman (1973) in his research on traumatic, avoidance conditioning. The guard-subjects displayed a behavioural profile which was marked by its verbal and physical aggressiveness, arbitrariness and dehumanization of the subjects in the prisoner condition. None of these (and other) group or individual behaviour patterns was predictable from the medical, social or educational histories of the subjects, nor from a battery of personality test scores.

Summary of Critique of the Stanford Prison Experiment

One critic of this research (Savin, 1973) begins his commentary by raising the fundamental question of 'under what conditions is research justifiable which subjects people to injury?' Unfortunately, the promise of suggested guidelines for meaningfully dealing with this vital and difficult ethical issue is never realized, as his argument is first trivialized (by asserting that one would be justified to embarrass a few self-confident volunteers if this 'injury' resulted in a cure for schizophrenia), and then descends into a series of direct and implied *ad hominem* attacks. Some choice instances are: 'One cannot make a prison a more humane institution by appointing Mr. Zimbardo its superintendent'; 'professors in pursuit of their own academic interests and professional advancement' are subverting the teacher-student relationship; there are some psychologists who are 'as obnoxious as the law allows', who show 'a morally obtuse zeal' in the pursuit of their careers, and who can be likened to used-car salesmen; finally, 'on occasion there is a hell like Zimbardo's'.

The major substantive points raised in this commentary appear to be:

(a) 'The roles of prisoners and guards have been much discussed of late, and their characteristics are reasonably well known', therefore, no new worthwhile knowledge was derived from this study.

(b)   A study which presents results that are not surprising to the scientific research community is not justified in subjecting volunteers to harm. If the outcome could have been predicted in advance by an already existing body of knowledge, there is no reason to conduct a study whose treatment of human subjects is questionable.

(c)   Some researchers, blinded by their own ambition, are unable to identify with the noxious experiences to which they expose their research subjects.

(d)   Researchers and academicians resist any objective evaluation and appraisal of the conduct of their research.

(e)   Subjects would be better protected if there were more *'law and order'*. If only the police were not so 'apt to be somewhat lax in upholding the laws that might otherwise protect subjects', we can assume guilty psychological experimenters would be brought to justice [and imprisoned??].

Absolute Ethical Principles to Guide Research

Ethics embody individual and communal codes of conduct based upon adherence to a set of principles which may be explicit and codified or implicit and which may be abstract and impersonal or concrete and personal. For the sake of brevity, we may say that ethics can be dichotomized as 'absolute' and 'relative'. When behaviour is guided by absolute ethical standards, a higher-order moral principle can be postulated which is *invariant* with regard to the conditions of its applicability—across time, situations, persons and expediency. Such principled ethics allow no degrees of freedom for ends to justify means or for any positive consequences to qualify instances where the principle is suspended or applied in an altered, watered-down form. In the extreme, there are no extenuating circumstances to be considered or weighed as justifying an abrogation of the ethical standard.

To search for those conditions which justify experiments that induce human suffering is not an appropriate enterprise to anyone who believes in the absolute ethical principle that human life is sacred and must not in any way be knowingly demeaned physically or mentally by experimental interventions. From such a position it is even reasonable to maintain that *no* research should be conducted in psychology or medicine which violates the biological or psychological integrity of any human being regardless of the benefits that might, or even would definitely, accrue to the society at large.

Many people feel that the world is already too polluted with human pain, alienation and the cynicism and mistrust of Watergates, known and suspected, to allow any further increments. This is so, even if they are in the name of science, for the sake of knowledge, 'national security' or any other high flying banner.

Within psychology, some of those identified with the humanist tradition have been most vocal in urging that these basic concerns for human dignity take precedence over the stated goals of the discipline, namely, to predict and control behaviour.

To the Christian Scientist, for example, the principle of the integrity of the human body and God's design in the ebb and flow of life does not allow therapeutic drugs and internal treatments for illnesses even though death may result in the absence of such interventions. On the basis of such an absolute ethic, the Stanford prison experiment must certainly be ajudged unethical because human beings did suffer considerable anguish, yet it was possible to terminate the experiment once that was apparent. . . .

Indirect Impact Evaluation of the Stanford Prison Study

If this research were saying nothing new, and if its findings could all have been predicted in advance by everyone, then it would amount to nothing more than just another exercise in 'Bubba Psychology'. As such, it would have joined the legions of other studies instantly buried in the So-what-who-cares? Archives of Psychology.

Detailed records kept of the dispersion of information about this experiment over the last two years reveal the following pattern:

(a)   Phone calls to office requesting information about the study.   215
(b)   Correspondence requesting written information, confirming findings, questioning implications (reports sent to each one)

Prisoners	202
Correctional personnel	70
Criminal justice organizations	30
Legislators and politicians	25
Social scientists	210
Students	90
General public	230

(c)   Mass media coverage has included:
1. A 20-minute feature on NBC-TV Chronolog (to an estimated audience of 3 million).
2. A 10-minute feature on NET-Public Television of AAAS panel on Prisons.
3. 12-minute feature on CBS-TV (Los Angeles)
4. A variety of local TV and radio programs.
5. Featured story in *Life* magazine (10/15/71).
6. One of the few reports of a single experiment ever published in *The New York Times Magazine* (4/8/73) and syndicated in 14 other newspapers throughout the USA and Canada.
7. Articles and editorials in over 100 other newspapers in the USA and thoughout the world.
(d)   Interest by the U.S. Congress in the form of an invitation to appear as

a witness before a special sub-committee investigating prison reform (October 1971), with a statement published in the *Congressional Record*.

Invited and appeared as witness before Senate sub-committee studying problems of juvenile justice and juvenile detention procedures (September 1973). Presented audio-visual show of our research to the committee. The Chairman, Senator Birch Bayh, stated that the research and presentation had a significant impact on his thinking.

(e)   Public speaking engagements by principal investigator and research associates (Haney, Banks, Jaffe, Prescott, White and Phillips) at national psychological and science conventions, to over two dozen colleges and high schools, to prisoner groups, Sheriff's deputies, judges, parole officer's units, several Chamber of Commerce meetings, law school faculty groups and others.

(f)   A slide-sound, self-contained presentation of this experiment was prepared by the author and Greg White and has been distributed to colleges, high school and correctional groups. The feedback of its emotional impact and discussion generating appeal has been unequivocally and unanimously enthusiastic.

(g)   The above material has been requested and submitted (along with an affidavit by me) as supporting evidence in a class action law suit currently being brought against the New York State Department of Corrections by a team of lawyers and social scientists (Wallace *et al.*, vs. Kern *et al.*, U.S. District Court, Eastern District of New York).

(h)   The results of the study have been used by a citizen's group in a legal action to prevent the construction of a new, large, impersonal prison in Contra Costa County, California, in favor of more costly, smaller, more personal facilities and community-based facilities.

(i)   The President of the Louisiana State Senate is developing a coordinated research social-legal action program to reform the state's juvenile delinquency facilities and to change attitudes of the public toward the need for prison reform in general. This program was in part stimulated by this author's research on attitude change and on the psychology of imprisonment. I shall serve as one of his senior consultants on this innovative project.

(j)   Of the several experiments (and Ph.D. dissertations) which have been specifically designed to extend the ideas contained in our study, the most noteworthy is a mock-psychiatric ward study done at Elgin State Mental Hospital in Illinois (Orlando, 1973). Using 58 staff members in the roles as mock-patients and role-playing staff, this experiment substantiated many of our findings about the de-humanizing effects of institutionalized roles and rules. The participants in Orlando's study have since formed an action group to improve the social psychological treatment of patients at their hospital.

How can we account for the unprecedented amount of publicity and broad appeal this study has generated? We have been told by people who are using the results of this research in a variety of social-legal actions that it is one of the most convincing demonstrations of the pathological impact of a prison-like environment on human behaviour. Not that anyone ever doubted the horrors of prison, but rather, it had been assumed that it was the predispositions of the guards ('sadistic') and prisoners ('sociopathic') that made prisons such evil places. Our study holds constant and positive the dispositional alternative and reveals the power of social, institutional forces to make good men engage in evil deeds. In contrast to the observations of generations of criminologists, and first-person accounts of prison life, this study is unique in its appropriate utilization of intervention methodology: A diagnostic selection procedure, random assignment of subjects to treatments and a careful recording of the process and chronology of the psychology of becoming imprisoned.

In the words of a team of social psychologists recently reviewing the status of small group research (Helmreich, Bakeman and Scherwitz, 1973), the heuristic value of this research is similar to that of Milgram's.

The upset generated by a Milgram or Zimbardo, both from the public and from their colleagues, in part stems from ethical concerns. But another part of their power lies precisely in their demonstration of how strong situational determinants are in shaping behavior. No resort to a correlation between 'those' people who do 'evil' things is allowed: the subjects were randomly assigned. It is the experimental method, not a fascination with the artificial, that convinces.

Milgram's and Zimbardo's studies evoke public outcry in part because, through shaming dramatizations, they remind us just how fragile our ethical independence and integrity really are (p. 343).

To be sure, we believe we have discovered other things of academic and scientific value (e.g., the function of explicit and implicit rules in behavior control, conditions which promote preferences for the use of punishment over reward by training agents, as well as clues to investigating subtle forms of psychological prisons, such as shyness). But the social value of this study is in demonstrating what a mock-prison environment could do to healthy, law-abiding, middle-class young men in less than a week. Moreover, we demonstrated it to those middle-class people who make the laws, enforce them and pay the bulk of the taxes which finance the operation of prison systems everywhere. It is these people who have hitherto been ignorant of, or actively unconcerned about, what prisons are or what they are doing to too many men, women and children subjected to their treatment procedures.

If the roles of prisoner and guard are well known and being considerably discussed of late, it is not unduly immodest to believe that our research has contributed to that increased concern and public discussion. The major recent prison riots in America occurred just *after* our study was completed and had been reported in the media. The murder of George Jackson, several guards and inmates at San Quentin took place August 21, 1971. Attica was less than one month later. These dramatic events forced prisons into the awareness of the public; our study had already made all of us who had spent a week in the Stanford prison aware of the hell of prison. In some small way we believe our analysis of the ingredients which create such hells may help to change them.

A Note on Precautions and Postcautions

The final ethical point to be raised in this paper is the extensive precautions we took prior to putting the subjects in our prison, and the follow-up activities we have conducted to ensure that any possible chronic, negative after-effects were identified and adequately treated.

We did consider whether there was an alternative methodology to use which might avoid the possible distress to the subjects and still yield the information we sought. Since we were interested in the general psychology of imprisonment and not just in role-playing, or anonymity, or other specific variables and processes, there seemed to be no suitable alternative.

The legal counsel of Stanford University was consulted, drew up a formal 'informed consent' statement and told us of work, fire, safety and insurance requirements we had to satisfy (which we did). The 'informed consent' statement, signed by every participant, specified that there would be an invasion of privacy, loss of some civil rights and harassment. Neither they nor we, however, could have predicted in advance the intensity and extent of these aspects of the prison experience. We did not, however, inform them of the police arrests, in part, because we did not secure final approval from the police until minutes before they decided to participate and, in part, because we did want the mock arrests to come as a surprise. This was a breach, by omission, of the ethics of our informed consent contract. The staff of the university's Student Health Department was alerted to our study and prior arrangements made for any medical care which might be required.

Approval was officially sought and received in writing from the sponsoring agency ONR, the Psychology Department and the University Committee of Human Experimentation. The members of this committee, like the subjects themselves, did not predict the impact a mock prison could have on a group of carefully screened healthy students. Since that time, however, armed with the hindsight from the knowledge of our results, they have 'withheld approval' for a subsequent study designed to investigate the *positive* effects of different types of prison guard training on the prisoner–guard interaction. Their reasoning is, if the training variable does not make a difference the outcome may again be as negative as we have shown it to be previously. Similarly, our former subjects will think twice and demand more knowledge before they again sign away their 'informed consent', since they no longer underestimate situational control of behavior nor so overvalue dispositional dominance.

Following the study, we held group and individual debriefing sessions, had all subjects return post-experimental questionnaires several weeks later, several months later, and at yearly intervals. Many submitted retrospective diaries and personal analyses of the effects of their participation. We have met with most of the subjects since the termination of the study singly or in small groups, or where that was not possible, have discussed their reactions in telephone conversations. We are sufficiently convinced that the suffering we observed, and were responsible for, was stimulus-bound and did not extend beyond the confines of that basement prison.

In the future, we will insist that students, or representatives of the population being studied, be part of the University Committee to pass on the ethics of human experimentation. We will encourage that committee to send an observer to, or secure recordings from, a pilot session of any 'potentially unethical' research. We will ourselves in the future incorporate a meta-experimenter in the role of unbiased monitor with 'detached concern'. His/her task will be to assess the impact of the treatment on the subjects as well as the impact of the progress of the experiment on the researchers. Such a person should also have the authority to intervene on behalf of the subjects if necessary.

Finally, I wish to contend that responsible and competent teachers and/or researchers welcome assessment and evaluation of their work by their peers and by those affected by their teaching and experimentation. The academic, scientific Ivory Tower is fast becoming a cliché as professors and social scientists become more directly involved in the life of their community and want meaningful feedback on the worth and impact of what they are professing and doing.

The need for an aware, enlightened consciousness among psychologists about the ethics of intervention is more critical than ever, since we are at a time when our research findings and techniques are being 'given away to the public' in the form of therapies, remedial practices, selection procedures and cures for a host of social and personal problems. It would be ironic to limit our concern to the ethics of what happens to volunteers in a mock prison experiment and not also to what is happening daily to untold numbers of people suffering in social-political prison 'experiments' being conducted in our cities and nations. But at the very least psychologists should themselves be vigilant of, and willing to take public exception to, research and practices of their colleagues which appear to violate basic principles of human rights, dignity and ethics. The proper initial course of action in such cases is to register a complaint with the American Psychological Association Ethics Committee, which has an investigatory body that thoroughly reviews such ethically questionable practices by its members. They have the power to bring considerable social pressure against offending members. Censure or ostracism from the APA carries serious professional penalties and personal shame.

I have been informed by the head of the APA Ethics Committee, Dr. Brenda Gurel that as of July 24, 1973, only one inquiry had been directed to her committee to investigate the ethics of the Stanford prison experiment. Curiously, it was *not* from Professor Harris Savin (who may have been too involved with the professional activity of publishing several critiques of the ethics of this research). Rather it was *my* recommendation to review the ethics of this research that was acted upon about a year ago by the APA. A final decision by that committee awaits the last follow-up evaluation being undertaken at this time.

THE PSYCHOLOGIST AS FIELD INVESTIGATOR

A running debate in applied psychology, as we have seen from the papers presented here, centres on the question of how one generates valid data. One of the ways the psychologist can deflect some of the criticisms that Savin levels at Zimbardo is to study situations naturally occurring in the field rather than in contrived laboratory situations.

Occasionally, observations in the field are undertaken to gain a general impression of a problem. More usually, however, the psychologist goes into field research armed with a model based on theory elaborated through previous laboratory research. Steven Reicher's paper, which follows, represents the psychologist in this role. He used a contemporary model from the psychology of intergroup relations with which to try to interpret and understand the St. Pauls riots in Bristol in April 1980. His paper reports his findings and provides an interesting account of the events as witnessed by participants and bystanders. As you will see, he tries to use these accounts to support a theoretical position.

Reading XIV.   St Pauls: A Study in the Limits of Crowd Behaviour, by S. D. Reicher

1. Introduction

Crowd psychology emerged towards the end of last century as an élitist response to a wave of working class unrest. Faced with seemingly spontaneous protest actions involving large homogeneous masses, the establishment sought less to understand than to discredit and reprise the threat. Indeed, the earliest works on the crowd were written by criminologists discussing on what basis to punish crowd partici-

---

Source: Specially commissioned article.

pants—should all be considered guilty or just a criminal core of ringleaders who incited the others? (cf. Tarde, 1890; Sighele, 1892). Moreover the most influential of all books on the crowd, Le Bon's *The Crowd: A Study of the Popular Mind*, first published in 1895, gained its repute not through any theoretical novelty (it is, if anything, an object lesson in plagiarism), but rather through its conscious attempt to advise the establishment on how to contain crowds or even use them against the socialist opposition. For his efforts he gained fulsome praise from, amongst others, Mussolini and Goebbels.

Only by bearing in mind the circumstances of its birth is it possible to understand the biases that permeate theoretical explanations of crowd behaviour. Because they were not prepared to admit that crowd action may have been a response to gross social inequality and active repression, theorists were forced to ignore the social context in which such actions occurred. This had a number of consequences, both in terms of description and of theory. On the descriptive level certain characteristics of the crowds—as they appeared to these "gentleman" observers—were abstracted from the context of class struggle and converted into generic characteristics of the crowd: violence, irrationality, fickleness, mental inferiority. On a theoretical level there were two ways in which the social causation of crowd behaviour was denied.

The older approach, exemplified by Le Bon, is group mind theory. This asserts that individuals in the crowd lose their conscious personality and revert to a primitive racial unconscious which accounts for the barbarism of crowd action. The slightly more modern approach is the extreme individualism of Allport, who asserts that the individual in the crowd is the same as the individual alone "only more so" (cf. Allport, 1924, p. 295). While these two approaches are diametrically opposed to each other, the one proposing that individuality is extinguished in the crowd and the other that it is accentuated, they are nonetheless united in one crucial premise. Both suggest that the only mechanism capable of directly planned or rational behaviour is a sovereign individual identity.

The problems with these approaches become clear when one asks about the limits of crowd behaviour: that is, who is involved and what do they do? On participation, the group mind theory seems to predict that all members of a given race will participate, while the Allport approach would argue that all members of a particular personality type will take part. Both suppositions fly in the face of all the available evidence. On the question of the limits or content of crowd behaviour both theories are even more inadequate. The group mind theory has little to say about content except that it is extreme and destructive. Allportian individualism can only seek to explain behaviour in terms of each participant's personality. However, it is unclear how personality factors could control the precise behaviours in any crowd event.

Despite the antiquity of these theories, their influence on later work has left a legacy of exactly the same problems as those outlined above (cf. Reicher, 1982a; forthcoming, on the problems of various modern approaches to the crowd, such as, de-individuation, social facilitation, contagion theory). The one apparent exception is emergent norm theory (Turner & Killian, 1972), which proposes that crowd behaviour is governed by norms that arise from the actions of prominent individuals (keynoting activities) as the crowd mills around. This approach has a number of problems. Firstly, it implies that crowd action is not homogeneous and that norms take a significant time to evolve in the crowd. Secondly, this approach would seem to suggest that the norms are only limited by the personality of certain prominent individuals. As such it resolves itself into an élitist version of Allport's position and does not explain the limits of crowd action.

In contrast to these approaches Reicher (1982a; 1982b; forthcoming) has proposed a model of crowd behaviour based on the social identity approach of Tajfel and Turner (cf. Tajfel (ed.), 1978; Turner, 1982). In essence, it is argued that a crowd is a form of social group in the sense of a set of individuals who perceive themselves as members of a common social category, or, to put it another way, adopt a common *social* identification. This common identification which provides stereotypical norms of behaviour explains the *homogeneity* of subjects' behaviour. However, given the novel or ambiguous nature of crowd situations, the social identity adopted by participants may not provide precise guidelines for behaviour. Thus they are faced with the problem of constructing an appropriate situational identity. This may give rise to a range of behaviours, however, because as the situational identity must always conform to the larger social identity, behaviour will be limited by the nature of the appropriate social category. For instance, a crowd of anti-fascists meeting a National Front march may adopt a variety of responses, but these responses will all be constrained by what it means to be an anti-fascist. Moreover, participation will be limited to those identifying with this category. Bystanders or others caught up in the crowd will not be subject to the collective contagion.

2.   The St. Pauls "Riots"

The purpose of this paper is to examine the limits of a specific crowd event—the 'St. Pauls riot' which occurred in Bristol on 2 April 1980—and to investigate the type of theoretical explanation that would be necessary to account for such limits. Given limitations of space, only a part of the data will be used. In particular, only the period before the police withdrew will be considered. For this reason the looting and arson attacks on various buildings will not be dealt with, since these occurred only after the police had left the area. This omission is not because the themes to be elaborated below do not apply, although there are differences between the two periods (cf. Reicher, forthcoming), but, rather, due to the fact that the data is lengthy and detailed and adds little to the basic arguments.

Before continuing, it is important to make explicit the nature of the data: in particular, to distinguish between the account of the events, to be described in Section 2.1, and participants' perceptions of the events, to be described in Section 2.2.

The account of the events is constructed from a large set of sources, including descriptions by crowd members, "neutral" witnesses, and police, and other official reports. These sources include six subjects (all white) who were involved in, or present during, the riot and with whom the author recorded interviews on tape; twenty individuals who were informally interviewed on the streets of St. Pauls within three days of the events, notes made on these conversations as soon as they were terminated; several officials were interviewed including the local councillors, and the police officer responsible for organizing the initial raid; official reports were studied including those of the chief constable, the chief fire officer and the official Riot Opinion (Cotterill, 1981) to the local council; all relevant TV and radio programmes were recorded and all newspaper reports collected; film of the event was studied, and a set of some 40 photographs, in chronological sequences, was collected; finally, 20 children from the top class of Cabot Primary School in St. Pauls were interviewed and replied in written script. Where specific quotations are used these sources will be referred to as follows: source: tape script, conversation, radio, TV, paper; colour: W = white, B = black; sex: F = female, M = male; and age. Out of these partial accounts a composite account was constructed using techniques of "methodological" and "data" triangulation (cf. Denzin, 1970). In other words, events were only included to the extent that two or more independent sources described them in the same way (any exceptions are clearly marked). While there are problems in reconstructing any event from accounts (cf. Potter & Mulkay, 1982), this account of the events can, at least, be seen as "complete" insofar as it does not reflect the partial perspective of one group. Moreover it can, in part, be verified by reference to more "objective" indices, such as, film and photographs.

On the other hand, much of the data in Section 2.2 is openly partisan, reflecting the views of crowd members. The reason for using this data is not to endow it with any privileged epistemological status but rather to show that participants' perceptions of themselves and their actions help to make sense of their behaviours. The same operation would have been carried out on the police had access been possible.

One final qualification should be made concerning all the data. There were considerable difficulties in finding respondents. In particular black respondents were naturally suspicious of the white researcher's motivations and possible uses of the data. Thus this data is open to challenge on the basis of representativeness, accuracy, and so on. Such difficulties are insuperable. Therefore, it should be borne in mind that the evidence presented does not constitute final proof but rather that it provides some support for a "social identity" model of crowd behaviour.

2.1 The Events

(a) At approximately 3.30 p.m. on 2 April 1980, two plain clothes policemen entered the Black and White café on Grosvenor Road. On th road outside were another 12 officers and more officers with dogs were held in reserve, about ¼ mile away, in Portland Square. The purpose of the raid was to execute a warrant issued to investigate allegations of illegal drinking (the Black and White had lost its licence in 1979) and the sale of drugs. Shortly aferwards, the 12 officers waiting outside came into the café. Two men, Bertram Wilkes (the owner) and Newton Leopold Brown were arrested. The police went into the cellars and began to take out the 372 crates of beer and lager found on the premises. These were stacked outside the café ready to be removed.

What actually happened during this time is unclear. The police state they showed a warrant and all proceeded peacefully. Several witnesses in the café claim no warrant was shown and that the police harassed those inside. Further rumours suggest that the two plain clothes police completed a drugs deal before calling in their colleagues (conv. BM 18) or that the police were even smoking "ganja" in the café (conv. BM 20). Whether true or not, these perceptions indicate a general feeling about the illegitimacy of the police action.

Just as the police initially arrived, Cabot School, behind Grosvenor Road, had broken up for Easter. As the children went home they saw the beginnings of the police action and hence the news spread very rapidly. Moreover several people who had been in the café during the raid were allowed to leave. They, too, passed on word of what was happening. Over the hour from 3.30 p.m. to 4.30 p.m., as the police stacked liquor outside the Black and White, a crowd gathered. It was a warm day and people hung around watching.

(b) At about 4.30 p.m. the mood changed. It is impossible to point to one incident which sparked off the initial bout of violence. At least eight different accounts have been given of the initial flare up. Indeed it is false to believe that there is a single "real" story of what happened. For most individuals, not at the front of the crowd, all they knew was that a commotion was going on and the rumours they received provided a basis for their action. What is significant, therefore, is that all the accounts contained as a central theme an unjustified and unprovoked police attack on the Black and White—seen by many as the central focus of the St. Pauls' community. Apart from one set of stories, which centre on a man whose trousers were ripped by the police and whose requests for compensation were rudely rejected (how a row over torn trousers led to . . .FLASHPOINT: *Daily Mirror* 5 April 1980), most stories centre on three police who came out of the Black and White with drug exhibits. According to some, they struck out calling the crowd "black bastards" (conv. BM 18); according to others they had a man with them who made a break for it and dogs were set on him (radio BM age unknown); according to one witness the police ran after a black youth and beat him up (*Guardian* 5 April 1980).

Whatever the exact flashpoint the three police and others in the area were pelted with bricks. The windscreen of the police car to which these three fled was smashed, as was that of a civilian "who had smiled when the

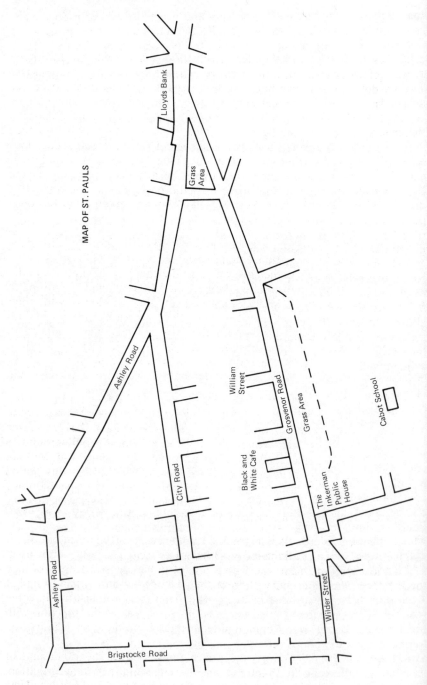

MAP OF ST. PAULS

police hassled us" (conv. BM 24). One police motorcyclist and a police dog-handler were hit in the face by bricks.

(c) As the police came under attack a help call went out and many police vehicles flowed into the area. By about 5 o'clock the situation had calmed down. The police began to leave again. The last of the beer was loaded into a police van. As this van drew off the police came under attack again. The van tried to get away but was stopped opposite the Inkerman pub, overturned and the beer was stolen. Several police who had been outside the Black and White fled, but a number were trapped inside. Two police cars parked further down Grosvenor Road, opposite William Street, came under attack and were turned over. Police officers from one of the cars turned it back over and drove off—the occupants of the other fled leaving it upside down. More help calls went out and about 30 to 40 police regrouped behind the Inkerman pub.

(d) At about 5.30 p.m. the police marched up Grosvenor Road from the Inkerman in close formation, intending to relieve their colleagues inside the Black and White. As they drew near to the café they again came under attack. This attack intensified as they reached the café and, according to one witness (conv. WM 30), smashed in the windows with their truncheons. Some police defended themselves with milk crates and with the help of dogs made forays into the crowd which they managed to disperse. At about this time the police car that had been left, upside down, opposite William Street, was set on fire—a group of three or four youths (including at least one white) ran up to it and threw a burning match in the petrol tank.

(e) At about 5.45 p.m. the situation was calm again. Some police withdrew back to the Inkerman pub, others patrolled the grass area opposite the Black and White with dogs. Yet others stood around in groups. A fire engine came to extinguish the burning car—it was not impeded and children helped unroll the hoses. All through this period people were coming home from work and large numbers of people lined the streets to watch what was going on. Although calm, there was a feeling of tension, of "I don't know what is going to happen next" (conv. WF 26).

(f) The police had called a removal van to tow away the burnt out car. It arrived at 6.30 p.m. and the car was hitched up to it. The police drew up in formation in front of the van with a line of police dogs in front. As they started to move the crowd withdrew, then a stone was thrown and a hail of 30 to 40 stones descended on the police. They began to scatter, in some disarray, up Grosvenor Road towards the grass area at the junction with Ashley Road, all the way coming under attack from the crowds lining the streets.

At the same time as this, the police regrouped at the other end of Grosvenor Road, by the Inkerman, and marched up the road in formation. They too came under a fierce barrage of sticks, stones and bottles. They retreated by the side streets onto City Road where, for the first time, riot shields were issued.

(g) For the next 30 minutes, from about 6.45 p.m. to 7.15 p.m., there was a running battle between the police and the crowd. It had two centres, one being the junction of City Road and Ashley Road, the other being the junction of Grosvenor Road and Ashley Road (around the grass area). The numbers involved are unclear—estimates varying from 300 to 3000. A reasonable estimate seems to be that a total of about 60 police faced two groups of between 200 and 300 people actively attacking them with a total of 2000 in the area (cf. Cotterill, 1981).

As the first group of police reached the grass area there was a pause. Then an old man walked up to a parked Panda car and kicked in its lights. There was a loud cheer and missiles were flung at the police, who were exposed on all sides and after a while were so fiercely pressed that they were forced to fall back towards City Road. On City Road itself the police seemed to be fairly disorganized—marching up the road in a phalanx protected by shields and then falling back as they came under attack and then again marching forward.

During this period two noticeable events occurred involving police cars. The first incident concerned three police cars which came in from lower Ashley Road. Outside Lloyds Bank they were blocked by the crowd. The occupants got out and fled. The crowd converged on the cars, stoned them (in so doing breaking windows of the bank), turned them over, and later set fire to them.

The second incident involved two cars that sped into the area from the west end of Ashley Road. According to one witness (tape WM 35) they were doing 70 to 80 mph; according to another (tape WF 25) 50 to 60 mph. The first car was met by a barrage of bricks, the windscreen shattered, the driver was hit, his face covered in blood. (He later needed nine stitches in the head.) The car swerved wildly nearly going into the crowd, then raced on and out of the area. The second car braked hard and reversed as fast as possible away from the crowd.

Despite all this, throughout this time traffic was flowing through the area, people were coming home, some were shopping, many were watching.

(h) By about 7.15 p.m. all the police were deployed on City Road. They had formed a cordon at the end, but were so badly exposed that they were forced to retreat. As they retreated the crowd surged forward flinging missiles at them. Skips along the road provided ample ammunition. As the police retreated some people came out of their houses joining in the attack, others came from the side streets to stone the police from behind. Outnumbered and outflanked the police line disintegrated and they retreated in disarray, some were chased up the side streets. Officially, the police "withdrew" at 7.26 p.m. By about 7.30 p.m. they were back at Trinity Road Police Station.

(i) After the police had left, the crowd did not stray beyond the boundaries of St. Pauls. Indeed, as soon as the last officer had been chased beyond the junction of City Road and Brigstocke Road, nobody followed after them. Moreover with the police gone, the crowd then moved apart to let the traffic back through and even helped direct it in order to ease congestion.

2.2. The Limits of Behaviour: Some Problems for Explanation

In this section three themes will be drawn out from the foregoing account. The first will be to show that the "riot" was marked by uniform behaviour showing distinct *social* limits (in addition to the geographical limits already described). The second will be to demonstrate that the event was not pre-planned, but rather, that the behaviour was spontaneous. The third theme will explore the ways in which participants had a clear social understanding of their actions, as well as a conception of themselves as social actors.

1. In his survey of the American urban riots of the 1960s Fogelson (1971) was moved to write: "restraint and selectivity were among the most crucial features of the riots" (p. 17). The same statement holds true for the present study. Indeed, perhaps the most remarkable feature of the whole episode was the backdrop of normality on which the so-called "Battle of Bristol" (*Bristol Evening Post* 3 April 1980) was played out. As police cars were burnt and officers stoned, cars flowed through the area, people walked home, families did their shopping, neighbours watched and chatted about the events.

Apart from the police who, without exception, seem to have been targets of attack, the only victims of intentional violence were T.V. and other camera operators and photographers. This seems to have been simply a function of the fact that people in the crowd were afraid of the film being used by the police (tape WM 35, conv. WM 30). Of the 60 odd police in the area, 22 were injured and 27 received minor injuries. In all, 21 police vehicles were damaged, eight by fire with six completely destroyed (these figures, from the official police report, include the period up to 11.05 p.m. when the police re-entered the area, most of the injuries and damage, however, occurred in the period under consideration). At the same time not a single individual was attacked on the streets nor a single private house maliciously damaged. However, it is important not to over-simplify the case. During this time ten civilians were hurt, five private vehicles were damaged and a number of windows were broken. Apart from the photographers, all the civilians seem to have been hurt either by the police or in the cross fire of stones between police and crowd. Similarly, some windows were broken as missiles aimed at the police or police cars missed their target. This is certainly true of the Black and White, Lloyds Bank, and the Criterion Pub. The case of the damaged cars is slightly more complicated. First, of all, as mentioned above, one car belonging to a man who was seen to approve of alleged police harassment was attacked. Secondly, there was a suspicion that several cars coming into the area shortly after 7.30 p.m. were unmarked police cars which were therefore attacked (tape WM 17). This may explain why one or two private cars were stoned as they drove down City Road (one such story told by the driver, Kathleen Lee, is reported in several papers). However, there is also an important general point to be made. What is of interest is not so much isolated individual acts, as acts which became rapidly generalized and which appear normative. Thus, if a single person throws a stone it cannot be considered as crowd behaviour unless many others join in. Indeed, it is only possible to see the boundaries of crowd action by seeing what acts are not followed or condemned. Thus it is possible to contrast the reaction to a number of acts involving different targets.

Take the following accounts of acts directed against the police or police-related targets:

[Of the second flare up described in Section 2.1(c).] All hell was let loose, after the first brick had gone in. This policeman dodged behind this van, was getting pelted by bricks. (tape WM 30)
[As the police drew away with the first burnt out car.] A few bricks went in and then people closed in the road and everyone started doing it. It just needed that initial encouragement. (tape WM 17)
[Of the same incident.] As soon as one brick went a sudden shower of about 30 to 40 bricks came sailing over. (tape WM 30)
[Of the police cars attacked outside Lloyds Bank, c.f. Section 2.1 (g).] A police car came through and someone started yelling "brick it!" All hell seemed to let loose and everyone started throwing bricks. (tape WM 20)

However, when other targets were attacked there was a very different response:

It was definitely against the police, because nothing or nobody else got hurt, except a bus—that got one window smashed. That could have been deliberate but I think it was probably not. Everyone went "Ugh," "Idiots." (tape WF 25)
[In reply to a question about whether private cars got stoned.] There were a few but people that had done it were told off and forcibly stopped from doing it. One boy said the object was the police, direct your antagonism that way. (tape WM 35)

Apart from clear limits in terms of targets, there were also clear geographical limits to the action. As described in Section 2.1(i), once the police had been chased out of St. Pauls they were not followed. The only area involved consisted of City and Grosvenor Roads and the streets backing off them. As the *Sunday Times* commented (6 April 1980), even later during the looting, the participants did not stray a yard beyond the boundaries of St. Pauls. Not only that, but once the police were drawn out no one else was stopped from entering the area, indeed crowd members even helped organize the traffic flow.

2. The most obvious explanation of the clearly discernable form taken by the "riot" and the concerted behaviour of crowd members is in terms of a pre-existing plan carried out by leaders. Indeed the "agitator" theory of crowds is as old as crowd action itself. Such ideas were also proposed in the present case. According to one local councillor (conv. WM approx. 55)) people were phoning each other up before the trouble started and busloads came down from Coventry and Birmingham with guns. According to a conversation with one senior police officer, (conv. WM approx. 55), the participants were a mix of "emotional psychopaths and subversive anarchists." Furthermore, shortly after the 2 April, a rumour was circulating in police ranks that Tariq Ali had been present on the day of the riots—in fact Tariq Ali had been there but he arrived on the afternoon of the 3 April in order to report for the left-wing paper *Socialist Challenge.*

An examination of the events reveals no pre-planning or leadership. Those involved in the events stress the spontaneity of the crowd's behaviour:

There was no organization or anything like that. It was just totally spontaneous, but it was . . . I don't know, just a feeling they were invading—bringing a hundred coppers down to St. Pauls. Obviously looking for trouble. (tape WM 17)
Well it just got around [referring to the police raid] then the niggling started it and we just got carried away (conv. BM 17)
It just burst into a great big riot. It burst like a small balloon first, then a gigantic one. (Script BM 11)

A similar description was given of the decision not to move out of St Pauls and to allow traffic back in.

Cars coming down City Road, they were getting stuck because people were blocking the road. People just moved apart and people stood there directing the cars through. It just seemed really strange, like you'd taken over control of the streets. (tape WF 25)
[In answer to the question "Did you consciously decide not to go outside the limits of St. Pauls?"] No, there was just that feeling. I think it was just an assumption by everyone in the crowd—get them [the police] out. (tape WM 17)

Of course it is possible that all those interviewed were intent on concealing some plot, but given their openness on various other matters that could have incriminated them, this is most unlikely. Another possibility is that although people were unaware of being led there were a number of individuals inciting violence both verbally and by example. When questioned about those individuals who initiated actions, subjects gave the following types of response:

> *Subject:* Somebody yelled police cars, pigs or something. I saw three cars come in and pull up outside the bank. Everyone charged towards them. . . .
> *Interviewer:* Those guys who had yelled, were they leaders or just anyone?
> *Subject:* Anyone. Everybody down there. I saw kids and their parents out, like a family outing. (tape WF 25).
> *Subject:* All it needed was the catalyst of one person throwing a brick and all hell let loose. (tape WM 35)

Hence it seems that, at least in the eyes of those involved, the initiators were simply any other local participants. Of course this still does not absolutely disprove the *agent provocateur* thesis. Yet, even in the unlikely eventuality that such people were present, it would still be necessary to explain why some actions were generalized and some not, given that the participants were neither aware of following a pre-arranged script, nor obeying predetermined leaders.

Despite the lack of a formal leadership, several witnesses report a "sense of leadership".

> A lot of the older black Rastas had come in and they seem to be looked up to by the youths and they, in a sense, took control to a certain extent. Not the extent of the whole operation but to the extent of looking at them as in a sense the leader. (tape WM 35)
> A few kids would run out to throw stones, followed by a surge . . . It didn't seem to be planned. The leaders seemed to be the most agile and most accurate stone throwers. (conv. WM 30)

It seems then that the older, more daring, black youths were looked up to by other participants, not as individuals with a directing role but rather in the sense that they represented a respected section of the community. Moreover, their influence was clearly limited in the ways already discussed.

3. While there is no evidence to support the notion of preconceived planning, subjects described their actions in terms of a clear purpose.

> [Talking about the police.] What I think they were trying to do was draw us out into the centre. They could have completely got us but it wasn't like that. We were just getting them out of St. Pauls. (tape WM 17)
> I think it was quite honestly a case of us against them. Us, the oppressed section of society, if you like, against the police, against authority, basically. (tape WM 25)

In other words, participants saw themselves as ridding St. Pauls of an illegitimate and alien police presence. In raiding the Black and White café, which was the one meeting place for the black residents which had not been closed down by previous raids, the police were seen as making a fundamental attack on the right of this community to control its own existence. (The concept of control is central to the response of all sections of the community. Time after time it was stressed that there is no point in spending money *on* St. Pauls unless it is spent *with* the residents.) Moreover, when Desmond Pierre was asked, on behalf of the St. Pauls' defence committee, to tell a television audience why the committee was set up, he replied, "We are defending ourselves on a lot of issues, but the main one is just the right to lead a free life" (TV Eye, 9 April 1981). To quote Roy de Freitus, one of the more widely respected figures in St. Pauls:

> The message I was getting last night and this morning in the area was: 'They've closed down this, they've closed down that, and if they close this particular one [the Black and White] where do we go from here?, (BBC Points West, 3 April 1980).

Or in the words of two youths outside the Black and White:

> Man can't take oppression, man gotta fight. Them police is bastards. (conv. BM 17 (a))
> Man can't just sit around all day smoking ganja—we just can't take it. Police think just because you're black they can do anything. (conv. BM 17 (b))

As well as having a well-formed idea of the events as purposeful action, it is clear that crowd members participated as social actors: that is to say as members of a social category rather than as private individuals. There are three types of data that support this contention.

Firstly, subjects described their own participation and that of other crowd members in the following terms:

> It was everybody, the whole community. (conv. BM 25)
> It was St. Pauls you know . . . this was just St. Pauls. You know the place and the coppers didn't. (tape WM 17)
> Just everybody came out of their houses, just everybody local. (tape WF 25)

Or more simply, from a large group outside the Black and White, the day after the riots: "Everybody." (BBC Points West, 3 April 1980).

Thus, participants viewed themselves as the St. Pauls' community, defined in opposition to the police as outsiders. This conclusion can be explained in two ways. Firstly, it is not meant to imply that all the community was involved (although participants did stress the breadth of involvement, exemplified by the probably apocryphal story of a woman who came home around 4 o'clock to find her daughter in bed after an all night party. "Get out of bed and go on the streets," the mother is quoted by various respondents as saying, "there's a riot going on)." Moreover, as Ken Pryce showed in his intensive study of St. Pauls (Pryce, 1979), it is probably false to speak of a single community in the area. Nonetheless, crowd members did see themselves as representing the entirety of St. Pauls, in the sense of an independent community, fighting for its right to survive. That is to say, the notion of community was a real, albeit ideological, creation for participants. Secondly there is the question of race. Over the days following 2 April, press and politicians conducted a debate over whether the events constituted a race riot or not. After the first day when numerous papers talked of black mobs and black riots, the tendency was to stress the multi-racial composition of the crowd and to down-play racial elements. Empirically, there is no doubt that both black and white were involved in stone throwing and burning police cars, and in that sense it is true that the "riot" was multi-racial. Yet in many accounts of the riots it is specifically the oppression of blacks that is seen as causing and guiding the riots. The police were seen as picking on black people, especially with reference to arrests on suspicion of possession of cannabis (smoking ganja being specifically a black cultural symbol). The Black and White itself is predominantly frequented by black people. Thus there is a potential problem in the use of the concept of community. Many respondents used it to denote people suffering oppression because of their blackness: this will be especially clear when the reactions of participants to the riots are examined. Several subjects refer to a new relationship with the police both as people from St. Pauls and as black people. If this is so, then it may seem difficult to reconcile the notion that there was a homogeneous crowd having a single social conception of themselves with the fact that whites participated. However, while it seems true to say that the concept of community was defined in terms of black experience, this does not mean it cannot be adopted by whites either because of a direct identification with blacks or because the black experience provided a potent frame for understanding their own problems: lack of jobs, poverty, problems with the police. Hence the concept of community can signify both black experience and coming from St. Pauls. As one witness observed of the crowd, "politically they were all black" (conv. WF 28).

The second way of showing how participants saw themselves as a community against the police comes from examining social relations within the crowd in contrast to those between crowd and police and other outsiders. For the press, and many outsiders, the event was marked first and foremost by aggression and fear:

I had a bit of wartime experience but then you had a foxhole or something to get into, you were inside here. (Shopowner on BBC Radio Bristol, 3 April 1980)
I am afraid I and my family are going to be killed. The youngsters,

hundreds of them, are out of control. They are going wild. They are setting fire to houses and shops and damaging cars. (Publican quoted in *Guardian*, 3 April 1980)

Perhaps the best illustration of the way in which outsiders viewed the event is contained in an account of the BBC radio car. It was seen reversing furiously with a look of terror on the face of the driver, alongside a large Rastafarian was running, banging on the roof. As the car passed by, my informant heard what the Rastafarian was saying: "play us a request, play us a request . . ." (conv. WM 28). Crowd members tell a very different story:

It was good, very good—everyone felt great. (conv. BM 20)
It was lovely, I felt free. (conv. BM 16)
All the atmosphere was against the police. It wasn't like the papers say. This absolute mad mob. Everyone was together. They were looking at each other the whole time. It was black and white and all ages and that was fantastic. (tape WF 25)
People were so warm: they said "glad to be with you brother," and put their arms around you. (conv. WM 35)
It was really joyful, that's what they [the media] all leave out, the "joy." (conv. WM 30)

The warmth of intra-crowd feeling thus contrasts strongly with outsiders' perception and with the violence of inter-group, that is, crowd–police interactions. What is more, the basis of this warmth was mutual membership of the "community" as described above:

It was due to police harassment. Everyone seems to be bound together against it in some way. (tape WM 20)
You were just grinning at everyone because everyone was from St. Pauls. (tape WM 17)

Thus intra-group cohesion seemed to exist as a function of a common identification.

The final piece of evidence which is the third pointer to a common, collective self-definition adopted by participants relates to their description of the effects of the "riot."

We took on the police and beat them. They will never again treat us with contempt. . . . They will respect us now. (BM quoted in *Sun*, 5 April 1980)
We feel great, we feel confident it was a victory and we were worthy of the victory. (BM quoted in *Socialist Challenge*, 10 April 1980)
You go to school, you learn and then—nothing. The colour of your skin determines everything. We can't beat them in the court but we defeated them on the streets. (BM quoted in *Socialist Challenge*, 10 April 1980)

One witness (tape WM 17) tells how the next day there was something akin to a victory dance on the grass opposite the Black and White. He goes on: "There were songs like 'Beat down Babylon' and all this lark, they were singing. Everyone was sort of smoking, like joints and stuff, in the open air and the coppers just never coming near us."

The song "Beat down Babylon" (Babylon signifying the land of oppression and, sometimes, more specifically, the police) once banned in Jamaica, goes as follows:

"I an' I going' beat down Babylon,
I an' I going' beat down Babylon,
I an' I mus' whip them wicked men,
    O what a wicked situation,
    I an' I starvin' for salvation,
    This might cause a revolution,
    and a dangerous pollution . . ."

Thus it seems that participants viewed the events of the 2 April as a collective statement and themselves as a collective mouthpiece. It is significant that two individuals, the local parish priest and a local Commission for Racial Equality spokesperson reminded the media of Martin Luther King's assertion that riots are the voices of the unheard. The priest went on to explain: "The community has stood up to say, very loudly, 'I am'." (Keith Kimber in *Daily Telegraph*, 5 April 1980)

2.3   Towards an Understanding of Crowd Process

A close examination of the events of 2 April has revealed a picture of spontaneous social behaviour with the twin characteristics of uniformity across individuals and of clear social limits. It is difficult to see how classic theories of the crowd could deal with these. Group mind theory would have to explain limits in terms of a racial unconscious, though how such an "unconscious" could determine, say, geographical limits to the events is unclear. Allportian individualism has a similar problem. It is hard to see individual attributes determining that people should not go beyond the junction of City and Brigstocke Roads. Nor does emergent norm theory fare much better. Firstly, the onset of certain action sequences seems to be immediate, and to preclude the process of keynoting which, for Turner & Killian (1972) is essential for the formation of group norms. Secondly, the theory cannot explain why certain actions (stoning the police) become generalized and others (stoning private cars) do not.

One of the most striking aspects of the data that was collected concerns the correspondence between the limits of behaviour and the definition of "community" in terms of which participants described themselves. The central elements of "community" comprised a geographical basis (St. Pauls), an opposition to the police, and a desire to be in control of their own life style. It is interesting to note how these themes became accentuated in accounts of how the disturbances started. Nearly all interviewees stress the unnecessarily large police presence, talking of an "invasion" of the area. In describing police conduct in the Black and White the impression given is that the police acted like "a cross between the Sweeney and Kojack" (tape WM 35), in refusing to show warrants and brutalizing the clientele. The notion of control comes through with reference to the importance of ganja (cannabis). Ganja is at once an important symbol of an independent culture and of conflict between the police and locals. Crowd members' perception of the hypocrisy of the police in suppressing that independent culture is brought out in a number of accusations: that the police regularly sell ganja in St. Pauls; that the plain clothes police made a deal in the Black and White on the 2 April; that police were smoking ganja inside the Black and White. For present purposes the importance of all these assertions lies not in their truth or otherwise, but rather in what they reveal about the meaning of the concept of community to participants. The attributes of this concept are clearly reflected in the crowd's behaviour. The geographical basis is translated into the decision of crowd members not to move beyond St. Pauls. The opposition to the police is seen in the selection of police officers and vehicles as the sole targets of collective violence. The notion of control is reflected in the way in which participants took over the area once the police had left, directing traffic through and, before they left, advising traffic not to go down certain roads and checking obvious strangers in the area.

Not only is there a match between the social identity used by participants and their actions but also actions unrelated to this definition were those that were not generalized. Thus acts, such as attacking cars or buses, which do not represent specific outgroups for the "community," stopped here rather than spread.

These relationships, then, require an explanation. One obvious possibility is that the various descriptions of self and purpose were a post-hoc construction used to explain and justify the "riot." There are, however, a number of weaknesses to this explanation. Firstly, there is evidence that a concept of community comprising the elements already outlined existed in St. Pauls prior to 2 April 1980 (cf. Pryce, 1979). Secondly, while it is almost impossible to assess a cognitive construct like identity during a crowd episode, the evidence of ingroup cohesion, as a function of perceived mutual "community" membership, even between Blacks and Whites, seems strong enough to suggest that crowd members were reacting to each other on the basis of social rather than individual factors.

The other possibility is that the participants' social self-definition plays some part in directing their behaviour. This is the conclusion canvassed by Reddy in the study of riots over a 100-year period in Rouen. As he puts it, "the targets of these crowds thus glitter in the eye of history as signs of the labourer's conception of the nature of society" (Reddy, 1977, p. 84).

Putting together these various considerations it is possible to outline a number of criteria that any adequate account of crowd behaviour must fulfil. First of all, this account must explain the genesis of spontaneous behaviour, secondly it must explain the uniformity of behaviour across crowd members, and thirdly it must explain the way in which a social ideology can affect the limits of crowd behaviour. If it is to meet this last criterion, the theoretical approach must accept how social factors may mould crowd actions, and therefore, must examine the social context in which these actions occur.

These are precisely the aims of the social identity model of the crowd developed by Reicher (1982a; forthcoming). What is unique about this model is that it provides a completely new way of approaching the question of the relationship between an individual and the social group—one of the basic questions of social psychology. As has already been pointed out, this question has hitherto been approached in one of the two ways, both derived from crowd theory. On the one hand, the "group mind" theory of Le Bon suggests that the individual disappears in the group and behaviour is guided by a collective mentality, which is above and distinct from the minds of group members. On the other hand, there is the approach of Allport who rejects any difference between individual and group behaviour. Group psychology, he says, "is a part of the psychology of the individual" (1924, p. 6). Despite their opposition, they both deny the social determination of behaviour.

In contrast to this the social identity model argues that there is a difference between "individual" and group behaviour but that this difference can be explained in terms of social parameters feeding into individual psychological processes. The model proposes that each individual's action is controlled by a cognitive construct—identity—but that the content of that identity is socially determined. When individuals join a group, say a group of "socialists," what happens is that the focus of their identity shifts from their own unique "personal identity" to a "social identity" determined by the nature of the group. Their behaviour is still cognitively controlled by the self but the meaning of the self, that is, of being a socialist, cannot be understood except in a historical and social context.

Applied to the present case, the social identity of a "St. Pauls' community member" adopted by crowd members provides the criterion for legitimate action. In the entirely unprecedented and rapidly evolving events, participants would seek appropriate responses by reference to this criterion: that is, they would be asking what do we, as the St. Pauls community, do now? Possible answers are provided in the actions of others, seen clearly as ingroup members, and thus certain classes of person seen to exemplify the social category, such as "older black youths" (that is aged 18–25) are looked to. However, actions can only be seen to translate social identity into specific situational norms if they are congruent with that identity. Hence, the limits of crowd behaviour.

While the data provided cannot be used to *prove* this model, it does exclude previous accounts except the social identification approach and it does explain the various characteristics of the data and relationships between those characteristics.

If the model is accepted it has two implications which are of considerable importance for an assessment of the significance of crowd behaviour. Firstly, not only is crowd behaviour moulded by social identity but, conversely, crowd behaviour may mould social identity. This is clear in the new found feelings of pride expressed by many resulting from the "riot," feelings which echo the black man who said after the Watts riot of August, 1965: "for the first time in Watts people feel a real pride in being black. I remember when I first went to Whittier I worried that if I didn't make it there, if I was rejected, I wouldn't have a place to go back to. Now I can say: 'I'm from Watts'" (Milgram & Toch, 1969, p. 516). Hence, crowd behaviour may play a crucial role in developing the nature of social ideologies. The second implication is closely related to this. Not only on the right but also on the left, there is an assumption that crowd episodes are inferior in some way. Thus the *Morning Star* referred to St. Pauls as a "primitive uprising" and *Socialist Worker* called for a "proper campaign." However, the present perspective stresses how sophisticated crowd actions are in the sense of being an accurate expression of an ideological understanding of the social world.

Put together, it suggests that, far from being a negative abberation, crowd behaviour provides not only one of the few contexts in which subjects act as historical subjects, but also that crowds play a central role in the development of social ideas.

THE PSYCHOLOGIST AS A RESOURCE FOR OTHER PROFESSIONS

We look now at the way psychologists make their knowledge available to other agencies or people that might have a use for it. In the past, other professionals have had to glean what they could from the psychological literature for their own purposes. Psychologists have now started to acknowledge that other professions use psychological insights and have at last taken it upon *themselves* to communicate relevant information rather than let their professional colleagues flounder amidst incomprehensible detail and theory.

Thus the work of Breakwell and Rowett (1982) provides informed guidance for social workers; the work of Saks and Hastie (1978) examines the relationship between psychology and the law; and that of Kent and Dalgleish (1983) focuses on doctor–patient relationships. The paper we have chosen to reprint here is an example of psychologists attempting to educate doctors to communicate more effectively with their patients. You will note, however, that the problem is seen in terms of the patient's inability to communicate so that the emphasis is upon the doctor needing to acquire better skills to get through to the patient. The knowledge is being given to the professional establishment and not to the patient, who is not seen as an equal partner in the exchange between patient and doctor. We may well wonder whether this is really what Miller meant by "giving away psychology." As a preamble to Kent and Dalgleish's paper, we have included an extract by Michael Argyle, an established authority in the social psychology of social skills, in which he emphasizes the need for social skills training in a wide range of jobs.

Reading XV.   Social Skills and Health, edited by M. Argyle—Extract from the Introduction

By 'social skills' we mean the styles of social behaviour used by interviewers, nurses or others in dealing with their clients. . . . To study social skills, the effectiveness of different performers must somehow be measured or assessed. Sometimes there are objective indices of success, as in the case of selling; sometimes it is necessary to resort to ratings by supervisors or colleagues. The second step is to compare the styles of social behaviour used by effective and ineffective performers of the skill to discover what they do differently and eventually to define the optimum style of social performance. The adoption of different social skills can have a considerable effect on the attainment of goals. The differences in effectiveness between good and bad performers, or between those at different ends of skills dimensions, are quite often fivefold in terms of measurable goals, e.g. the amount sold by salesmen. At the lower end of the scale, performance can be completely useless: supervisors of groups who produce nothing, psychotherapists whose patients get no better (or get worse), and selection interviewers whose selections are no better than chance. These are all jobs where social performance is of crucial importance; there are plenty of other jobs where it is much less so, such as research and technical positions, though here too it is necessary to be able to communicate and co-operate with other people.

When the optimum social skill has been discovered it can then be taught to trainees on training courses. An implication of the social skills approach

Source: Argyle, M. (Ed.) (1981). *Social Skills and Health*. London: Methuen, pp. xi–xvi.

is that specific styles of social behaviour will be taught—as opposed to attempts at increasing general sensitivity or insight, as in some other approaches to the problem. In the early stages of social skills training and research, emphasis was placed on the correct amount of use of elements of behaviour such as smiling, gaze, headnods, etc.—and socially inadequate people do make less use of these non-verbal (NV) signals or use them in the wrong way (Trower 1980). Emphasis has been placed on NV signals, since they are important and since trainees are often unaware of the NV signals they are sending, or which are being sent by others. However, verbal behaviour is also highly important, and training can be given for this also.

Awareness of the importance of social skills is fairly recent. The first skill to be studied was probably the supervision of working groups. During the early 1950s, field studies by research workers at the University of Michigan and elsewhere showed some aspects of the most effective style of supervision (Likert 1961). These studies were extensively replicated in several parts of the world and were rapidly incorporated in training courses (Argyle 1980). More details of these skills are given in Argyle (ed.) 1981, Chapter 5. At first such courses used the lecture and discussion method, but this was soon found to be ineffective, and was replaced by more powerful training methods (see Chapter 8). The result must surely be that supervisory skills have been changed throughout much of the western world.

The skills of teaching were discovered at a rather later date, but have been if anything even more widely promoted than supervisory skills (Dunkin and Biddle 1974). . . . Some . . . other skills . . . have been studied more recently, and some of them need a good deal more investigation. For example, doctor–patient skills are still not taught in some British medical schools, though nearly all those in America do so. Parent skills are as yet taught on a very limited scale, and here too more research is clearly needed.

While knowledge of particular social skills was developing, intensive laboratory research was being conducted into the basic processes of social interaction of which skilled performance consists. Research at Oxford in the early 1960s into social interaction led to the formulation of the social skill model, which draws on the similarities between social behaviour and the performance of motor skills (Argyle and Kendon 1967). Later research on social interaction at Oxford and elsewhere elaborated that model—for example, by showing the importance of non-verbal signals (Argyle 1975). Some of this research is quite recent—e.g. into sequences of interaction and the analysis of social situations—and it has not yet been fully used by those engaged in the study and teaching of specific skills. Research in other areas, such as the analysis of social relationships, is newer still and has scarcely been applied at all. Research in the applied field, however, often makes fundamental contributions to our knowledge of skills. For example, research on sequences of interaction in the classroom (Flanders 1970, and others) has made an important contribution to the study of sequences of behaviour. . . .

. . . Social skills are very important for nurses, doctors, psychotherapists and social workers; indeed much of their work consists of social performance in relation to patients. Although social skills are of central importance for all these professions, they are not the *only* kind of skill needed; doctors and nurses must know about medicine. The relative importance of social skills and technical skills and knowledge varies widely, but the importance of social skills has been greatly underestimated. The social skills of patients themselves are also important, and . . . poor social skills [contribute] to mental disorder. . . .

Social skills training (SST) for patients and for other kinds of clients, especially in the USA, has often taken the form of assertiveness training (Rich and Schroeder 1976). However, it must be pointed out that the skills used in making friends and influencing people are quite different. Many socially skilled tasks require forms of influence which have nothing to do with assertiveness. Further, there are cultural differences in the extent to which assertiveness is valued. . . .

An important problem in using all social skills is the need to vary social behaviour for different clients and in different situations. Research in several areas has shown how skills should vary in this way, and basic research in dyadic interaction has shown how to control the behaviour of others, in interviews or other settings. Recent research into the properties of social situations has shown how skill needs to vary with the social setting. Patterns of social behaviour also vary with class and culture. . . .

The social skills which are needed in jobs and elsewhere in society are different at different times and places. The same job may have to be done in different ways as the result of technological or other social changes. The power of industrial supervisors is reduced by the extension of industrial democracy and was much greater before the appearance of trade unions. There may be changes in the law which affect the power and responsibilities of social workers and others. Selection interviewers have a different relation to candidates depending on whether jobs are scarce or good applicants are scarce. There have been general changes in social relationships so that a less hierarchical and less authoritarian style of behaviour is now expected in most organizations.

Social changes also create new social roles, which require new social skills. Technological changes have created the roles associated with television, e.g. anchor men, political interviewers and performers at chat shows; other technological changes have led to the appearance of air hostesses—a role that was deliberately created, and for which training is given.

The activities of psychologists led to the roles of psychotherapist, T-group leader and social skills trainer. Now that we know more about social skills, the social skills requirements of new organizational structures should be remembered so that new roles can be carefully designed and appropriate training given.

The use of SST has grown very rapidly during recent years—e.g. for mental patients, prisoners, teachers, managers and doctors—though it has not yet become easily available to the general public. Early forms of training, by lecture and discussion, were soon found to be ineffective, and were replaced by role playing, usually with videotape playback. There have been many follow-up studies of SST, and we can now specify in some detail the form the training should take. These findings are reviewed in [Argyle, 1981, Ch. 8]. Curiously, those responsible for administering training, in industry and Government for example, have been rather uncritical, have not made greater demands for follow-up studies before commissioning training schemes, and have sometimes approved unsatisfactory forms of training.

The rapid growth of SST has sometimes led to a low-grade, watered-down form of training consisting of rather amateurish role playing. SST is a sophisticated affair and will be successful only if full use is made of knowledge of the skills to be taught and of the best techniques of teaching them. Clearly, however, social skills are not the whole story: in addition to the technical knowledge and skills needed, certain kinds of 'personal growth' are needed for those who are going to hold responsible jobs and make difficult decisions.

Several criticisms have been made of the social skills approach. It is sometimes said that leaders are born and not made, and similar remarks are made of other social skills. Whether there is any *genetic* component of social competence is not known; certainly by the age of 20 some people are very much more socially competent than others, but this is probably from informal, unplanned and chance social learning experiences. However, people can undoubtedly be trained to be more effective performers of social skills, though everyone probably has limits to what he can be trained to do. The same is true of motor skills like performance at sport, though the limiting factors here are chiefly muscular strength and other aspects of physique.

It may be said that a person's effectiveness depends on his power, or other favourable and unfavourable aspects of his situation. These factors are obviously very important, but unfavourable situations can be coped with by using appropriate skills. Fiedler's research (1967) has suggested that a leader whose group does not accept his authority should resort to a different style of supervision. There may be *role conflicts* if conflicting demands are made by other people; doctors, for example, may experience a conflict between looking after their patients and participating in research trials. These require special skills of role bargaining to keep both parties happy. In some roles a number of different people with different points of view must be dealt with; these may be difficult to reconcile, as for social workers who have to deal with the police, doctors, teachers and parents, as well as with their clients.

It is often said that training people in social behaviour encourages deception: pretending to have attitudes and feelings which are not truly felt. Part of the answer is that the rules in some situations and the rules governing a number of professional roles require people to control not only their behaviour but also their emotional states and their attitudes to other people. This can be done by controlling the expression of emotion and by controlling other bodily states, e.g. by relaxation, and control of thoughts and images (Hochschild 1979). Even if such control of feelings and attitudes is unsuccessful it can be argued that teachers, doctors and others should still treat well, i.e. give the appearance of liking, those clients whom they do not like. There is some evidence that real feelings change to fit those which are expressed (Laird 1974).

Another objection to the social skills approach is that people may be made self-conscious by being instructed in the details of social performance. The experience of trainers is that this is only a temporary phenomenon; after the second training session most trainees focus their attention once again on the job in hand and the behaviour of the others present rather than on their own performance. Finally it is sometimes objected that the use of skilled social techniques is a form of 'manipulation' of others. This is a curious point: if a teacher teaches effectively, or a doctor cures patients, this would not be regarded as manipulation, which presumably refers to successful social influence of a kind which is thought socially undesirable. Perhaps the use of subtle, or non-verbal, social skills is regarded with more suspicion than the use of more obvious, or verbal, skills. The social skills approach extends the range of social techniques beyond those which are familiar. It must be hoped that the new skills will be used more for desirable social ends than for undesirable ones.

Reading XVI. The Consultation, by G. Kent and M. Dalgleish

Interviewing

There are several reasons why skill in interviewing is important for the practising doctor . . . consideration of the patient's obligations and perceptions of the illness are significant. Insofar as these are related to outcome, an understanding of these factors is an important aspect of medical care. There is a more general reason for competent interviewing, however, having to do with the satisfaction that a patient feels about the consultation. Roughly speaking, satisfaction with care has cognitive and emotional components, although they are often related to each other. Cognitive satisfaction appears to be associated with the doctor's verbal behaviour. In general practice consultations, the opportunity to ask questions and to gain information about illness and treatment is predictive of patients' satisfaction with interviews. Emotional satisfaction, on the other hand, seems to be related more closely to the doctor's non-verbal behaviour. The ability to show care and concern by tone of voice, body movements and body posture is significant in this respect. Both verbal and non-verbal aspects of interviewing are discussed below.

Source: Kent, G., & Dalgleish, M. (1983). *Psychology and Medical Care*. Wokingham, Berks.: Van Nostrand Reinhold (UK) Co. Ltd., pp. 303–316.

Verbal Behaviour

That there is room for improvement in doctor's interviewing skills has been shown in studies by Peter Maguire . . . it seems that physicians often have the expectation that patients have *either* a social/psychological difficulty *or* an organic complaint. Physical illness is often missed in psychiatric patients, and surgeons and general practitioners often do not inquire about personal difficulties associated with physical diseases. Although much of the work on interviewing skills has involved medical students (rather then practising physicians) there is little evidence that length of training or experience are in themselves related to interviewing ability. For example, Helfer [1970] compared the interviewing skills of senior medical students with those of students just entering the medical course. He found that senior students fared worse at eliciting important problems besides those presented by the patients themselves. They obtained less information about personal difficulties than did the new students, suggesting that medical training actually had a detrimental effect on some interviewing skills. Further, the senior students often inhibited the patient's communication by the use of medical jargon.

Maguire and Rutter [1976] have outlined the deficiencies in interviewing skills commonly encountered in this research. It should be noted that their concern was with history-taking, a situation in which emphasis is placed on the collection of information. The same emphasis may not be appropriate to consultations in which the doctor and patient have met several times before, although many of these points are relevant. In this research, the students were allowed about 15 minutes for an interview with a psychiatric patient. They were asked to concentrate on current problems and to write up the history afterwards. The students were close to their final examinations. Seven of the common deficiencies were:

1. Insufficient information obtained. The students obtained only one-quarter of the information an independent judge considered important and easily obtainable. One-third of the students failed to elicit the patients' main illnesses or problems, and relevant psychological and social aspects were most commonly neglected. The students were unaware of the paucity of information they obtained, seriously overestimating the amount of useful information they had recorded. In another study [Maguire et al. (1978)], 80% of the students avoided personal aspects of the patients' problems, particularly sexual or marital problems. When these topics were raised by the patients, the students avoided any further inquiry, perhaps because they were concerned not to appear intrusive or perhaps because these topics were personally embarrassing.

2. Failure to control the interview. The students often allowed the patients to talk at length about matters apparently unconnected to the problem at hand. Realizing that the patients' communications seemed inappropriate, the students felt unable to either re-direct the interview or to examine the reasons why they were being given this information.

Although Maguire suggests that the patient should be encouraged to be relevant, it can also be argued that re-direction of the interview is not always suitable when the purpose is not primarily history-taking. Stiles et al. [1979] note that patients' emotional satisfaction with general practice consultations is associated with the opportunity to tell their own story in their own words.

3. Lack of systematic procedure. The interviews were conducted in a rather haphazard way, with little obvious connection between consecutive topics. This lack of procedure often resulted in important gaps in the history, and patients were sometimes left confused about the purpose of the interview.

4. Premature focus on problems. The students often assumed that the problem first presented was the only relevant one and focused the interview prematurely. Usually, this focus took either a social or organic direction. In Maguire's study, the students tended to assume that the patients would have only one problem and concentrated on this to the exclusion of related problems or unconnected but equally important difficulties.

5. Lack of clarification. Students were reluctant to ask for clarification on vague or contradictory information. In a similar study [Maguire et al. (1978)], only 22% of the students attempted to clarify what patients meant by such vague phrases as 'feeling run-down' or 'tense'. Given that most people are unable to specify the position of many of their internal organs or to understand the meaning of many common medical terms such as constipation or palpitation, the need to clarify what each patient means by such statements is important. Students were also unlikely to establish the medications currently used by the patients or to encourage accurate dating of symptoms, even though the patients often possessed the necessary information.

6. Deficiencies in style. Two main deficiencies in the way students asked questions were found. One concerned the use of leading questions (questions that make an assumption about the patient). The use of leading questions may be helpful in inquiring about topics that the patient may find too embarrassing to volunteer. For example, renal dialysis often has considerable effect on patients' sexual relations. In such an instance it may be more appropriate to ask 'In what ways has dialysis affected your sexual relationship? (which assumes that it has) than 'Has dialysis affected your sexual relationship?' (which may be too embarrassing to acknowledge). On the other hand, leading questions can restrict the information gathered: the above question may provide information on sexual matters, but perhaps not on feelings of dependency on the dialysis machine, another common anxiety. Asking too many leading questions can easily bias the interview towards what the doctor feels is important, and not what the patient wants to say.

A related deficiency involved the use of several questions at once, without waiting for an answer to each one. For example one student inquiring about feelings of depression asked 'You were losing weight? . . .

and what about sleeping?. . . waking early?. . . I mean, how did all this affect you?' The patient responded to one question, but the student did not follow up on other aspects.

7. Failure to prepare the patient. After the interviews, patients often reported that they wished the students had made some effort to explain the kinds of information they required and the time they had available. Most of the students began immediately by asking questions about the patients' main complaints. Maguire et al. [1978] reported that only 8% of the students explained the purpose of the interview and only 4% mentioned the time available. Only 10% of the students ended the interview within the time specified: perhaps more co-operation between the participants could have been gained if patients understood the restrictions and the intentions of the interviewer.

These findings suggest that doctor–patient communication could be improved by providing students with a model for conducting an interview. This protocol could point out many of the deficiencies listed above and suggest remedies. Maguire has conducted a series of studies examining such a model. He has shown that students are able to increase the amount of information they acquire by seeing and hearing themselves interview a patient and by following a systematic procedure during the interview. In one typical study, students were divided into two groups. Those in the experimental group were first videotaped while interviewing a patient. They were then presented with a handout explaining the model, and the course tutor asked the students to consider the problems the consultation presented while referring to the model and to the videotaped interview. Students in the control group also interviewed a patient, but were not given a handout or any other feedback.

When the students in both groups interviewed a second patient a week later, those in the experimental group obtained three times as much relevant and accurate information as those in the control group. Further, the patients of the experimental group rated their student interviewers somewhat more favourably than did patients of the control group, suggesting that the patients benefited as well.

In his model, Maguire makes a distinction between content (what information should be collected) and technique (how it might best be gathered). Students hearing themselves on audiotape learn the skills related to content adequately, but in order to develop a good interviewing technique, videotape seems to be particularly helpful. A synopsis of his model is presented below. . . . Similar training programmes have been found to be helpful in improving the interviewing skills of practising physicians [Verby, 1979].

Content. (i) Details of the main problems. The interviewer should be particularly aware that a patient may have several problems and that these may be physical, social and psychological in nature. After establishing the primary difficulty, the interviewer should ask whether there are any problems the patient would like to mention: in fact, the interviewer should assume these problems exist. For the problems that there is time to explore, the date of onset, the subsequent development of the problem, precipitating or relieving factors, the help given to date and the availability of support should be discussed.

(ii) Impact of the problem on patient and family. It is unlikely that physical complaints have no social and psychological consequences. The patient's ability to do his job, his ability to pursue leisure activities and the quality of his relationship with the family are all relevant here.

(iii) Patient's view of his problems. . . . The patient's beliefs about his illness and treatment are often better predictors of his behaviour than medical views. By obtaining a clear understanding of these beliefs, the physician is in a better position to provide effective reassurance and to correct misconceptions. Maguire provides an example of a patient who had been admitted to hospital with myocardial infarction. Having been led to believe by a staff member that it was of a minor nature, he was unwilling to follow his doctor's advice to restrict his activities. The doctor failed to realize the reason for the lack of compliance because he did not understand the patient's view of the illness.

(iv) Predisposition to develop similar problems. The patient's background is significant here, both psychologically and organically. Details of the family of origin, occupation, the patient's early development and childhood, sexual development, interpersonal relationships and previous health may be noted.

(v) Screening questions. Finally, the content of the interview should include an exploration of areas not yet covered. If the consultation has been primarily concerned with physical complaints, then it is appropriate to inquire about social and psychological difficulties; if the interview has been biased toward personal problems, then the physical well-being of the patient should be considered.

Technique. (i) Beginning the interview. The interviewer should take particular care to greet the patient both verbally, using the correct name and title, and non-verbally (e.g. by shaking hands, moving toward him). The interviewer should also indicate clearly where the patient is to sit and to introduce himself if they have not met before.

(ii) Discussing the procedure of the interview. As aids to understanding and remembering, a short explanation of the time available and the procedure to be used is in order. For example, if the interviewer plans to take notes, this should be mentioned and the patient's feelings about it should be elicited. Although note-taking may improve the accuracy of the doctor's memory, it may also inhibit the patient. If the interview is to be conducted in public (e.g. a hospital ward), the patient should be given the opportunity to voice hesitations about talking of personal matters and to move somewhere with more privacy. The theme of this aspect of the consultation is that doctors should make every attempt to put the patient at ease. In the section on non-verbal behaviour (which follows), other ways in which the doctor can contribute to feelings of comfort in his patient are discussed.

(iii) Obtaining the relevant information. After the opening of the interview, the patient should be encouraged to outline his important difficulties. Perhaps an open-ended question such as 'Can you begin by telling me what problems brought you here today?' could be used. The doctor could encourage the patient to continue by saying 'Go on' or 'Can you tell me more about that?' One technique, termed reflection, involves simply repeating, with a flat non-evaluative voice, a few words spoken by the patient. The repeated words appear to direct the patient's attention towards his feelings about a topic.

Most commonly, questions will be used to gain information. As mentioned above, asking several questions at once is not conducive to good communication. Nor are questions that restrict the range of possible answers always appropriate. To ask 'Was it because you walked too quickly or ate too much?' forces the patient to choose between two alternatives: perhaps both or neither seem correct to him. A distinction can also be made between open and closed questions. Open questions (e.g. 'How do you feel about your mother coming to stay?) allow the patient considerable latitude in his reply, whereas closed questions (e.g. 'Will there be enough room?') narrow the possibilities considerably. Frequent use of closed questions will elicit answers to the questions asked, but suffers from the problem that the doctor may not ask the most appropriate questions. This is particularly likely when social and psychological information is being sought.

Listening is another important skill in interviewing. Rather than determining the direction of the interview entirely, it is often important to allow the patient to say what he wants in his own way. Silence is often needed by patients (and doctors) to consider what has gone on before, or to formulate questions.

(iv) Terminating the interview. Students report that ending an interview is often difficult. Two or three minutes should be left at the end to review the information given, to ask if any important information has not been transmitted and to provide the patient with an opportunity to ask questions.

Non-verbal Behaviour

Although verbal behaviour is important in the consultation, the understanding of the relationship between doctor and patient requires consideration of non-verbal behaviour as well—'While we speak with our vocal organs, we converse with our whole body.' [Abercrombie, 1968, p. 55]. The gestures and bodily movements that surround a verbal statement modify its meaning. For instance, the comment 'Come in, Mr Smith' can give very different impressions depending on the speaker's non-verbal behaviour. If the speaker looks at his visitor, rises to greet him and perhaps shakes his hand, friendliness is indicated, but if he continues to look at his desk and issues the invitation in a routine manner, indifference is the likely impression. Several experimental studies support the notion that non-verbal aspects of conversation are mainly responsible for the emotional quality of the relationship between two people, whereas verbal communication is more relevant to their shared cognitive tasks and problems. For example, non-verbal signals have a greater impact than verbal ones on assertiveness and friendship [Argyle, Alkema & Gilmore, 1972]. Much of the work on social skills training . . . is based on the idea that inadequate non-verbal behaviour is responsible for many of the difficulties that various groups of patients encounter. The aim of this section of the chapter is to explore the importance of non-verbal behaviour in doctor–patient communication.

Broadly speaking, researchers in this area have taken one of two positions. One group of workers has maintained that every expression or bodily movement is part of a larger context that will influence its meaning to a large extent. For example, eye gaze can have two distinct and almost incompatible meanings, depending on the circumstances. When two people know each other well and the circumstances are friendly, long periods of looking at each other suggests intimacy, but when issues of status are at hand, gaze may indicate aggression [Exline, 1972]. Similarly, depending on the relationship between the participants, touching may indicate caring or dominance [Whitcher & Fisher, 1979]. In adopting this position, the behaviour of both participants must be taken into account, since they both contribute to the context.

A second group of researchers has suggested that many expressions bear a close relationship to emotional state. They are concerned with the relationship between behaviour and emotional feelings—that looking downwards is a sign of embarrassment, for example. This approach is often associated with either psychoanalytic or evolutionary traditions. One of the lines of evidence that Freud gave for his contention that emotions are often repressed and find expression in ways that the ego does not monitor . . . comes from his observations of patients in analysis:

When I set myself the task of bringing to light what human beings keep hidden within them, not by the compelling power of hypnosis, but by observing what they say and what they show, I thought the task was a harder one than it really is. He that has eyes to see and ears to hear may convince himself that no mortal can keep a secret. If the lips are silent, he chatters with his finger tips . . . [Freud, 1953].

It may be inappropriate to ask which of these approaches is the correct one. As in many areas of psychology, one model does not account for all observations, and in this case both provide insights into the reasons why people behave as they do. In the outline of research given in this section, both approaches are used and their implications for doctor–patient communication considered.

Vision. One way to explore the importance of various non-verbal cues is by experimenting with various combinations and testing for general principles. For example, the amount two people look at each other and the distance between them appear to be inversely related. Argyle and Ingram [1972] reported that people look at their fellow conversationalists more frequently when they are separated by a large distance than when they are close together. They suggest that eye gaze and distance can substitute for each other as signs of intimacy, so that in order to keep a constant level of intimacy people will look at each other less often and for shorter periods of time as they come closer together. An example of a similar situation to this experiment can be found in crowded buses—everyone is standing close together and studiously looking out of the window or at the advertisements.

Eye gaze is not necessary for person-to-person interaction (talking over the telephone is possible, for instance), but it does play an important role. When a person is speaking, he will tend to look at his partner infrequently and for short periods of time, presumably because he is concerned with formulating what he is going to say. Attention is mainly focused on thinking. However, speakers do look at their partners occasionally, apparently to gain information as to whether they are being understood. Observation of conversations indicates that it is during these times that listeners provide feedback, nodding their heads and murmuring agreement. (When conversationalists cannot see each other, the pause between the time when one speaker stops and the other begins is longer and there are fewer interruptions [Argyle, Lalljee, and Cook, 1968].) When a person is listening, he will spend most of his time looking at the speaker, showing attention to what is being said. Listeners who do not look and who do not nod their heads are often judged to be unfriendly and uninterested in the speaker. Whether speaking or listening, the amount of gaze a person gives appears to affect others' perceptions of friendliness and warmth [Exline and Winters, 1965].

A patient who is visually ignored by his doctor may well feel that the physician is not especially warm or caring towards him. Maguire and Rutter [1976] place considerable emphasis on non-verbal communication in their interviewing model, particularly stressing the importance of looking at the patient while he is talking. Several examples of the practical importance of these considerations are given by Byrne and Heath [1980]. They videotaped consultations and related the physicians' behaviour to the patients' reactions. In several cases, patients hesitated or fell silent when their doctors began to read or write on the medical records. In the following example, the patient stopped talking about her problem at line 3, just when the doctor began writing. Only at line 4, when the doctor looked up, did the patient begin again:

1. Patient: No, well, even the training centres for the unemployment . . . unemployed . . . they don't like them after a certain age to return there 'cos they say it's . . . they're too old . . . you see.

2. Doctor: I see.
3. Patient: So . . .
               (3.5 s)
4. Patient: So I don't think there's . . .

It seemed that the shift of eye gaze and attention away from the patient and towards the records effectively suspended the consultation.

It is also important that both interactants have an equal opportunity to see the other's face and eyes during conversation. Argyle et al. [1968] compared conversations in which both participants could see (or not see) each other equally well with those in which one participant could see the other better than he could be seen. This latter condition resulted in more feelings of discomfort and difficulty in the person who was seen but who could not see the other. The person with more visual information tended to dominate the encounter and felt more comfortable.

This result provides another pointer for doctor–patient communication. It is usual for a doctor to place his desk near a window, because of the light it throws. Yet a disadvantage of this position is that the doctor often sits between the window and the patient, with the light behind. This seating arrangement can result in the doctor's face being cast in shadow while the patient's face is well lit, a situation similar to that of the experiment described above. In such circumstances, the patient may be unable to see the doctor's face clearly, and therefore may be unsure of facial expressions and the direction of gaze.

Posture and gestures.   The posture assumed by interactants is important for conversation. A slight forward lean has been shown to be associated with perceptions of warmth [LaCrosse, 1975]. Although closed arm positions appear to indicate coldness, rejection and inaccessibility, moderately open arm positions convey warmth and acceptance [Smith-Hanen, 1977]. Changes in posture can convey a wealth of information. They often accompany a change in topic and can be used to signal the end of a conversation. If people are seated while talking, for instance, when one participant stands up the aim is often to finish the exchange. A conversationalist may serve notice that he wants to say something important by changing position or becoming restless. It is important that physicians recognize the significance of movements not only in their patients but also in themselves. A doctor who finds himself changing position constantly and keeping his arms closed around his body might reflect on his feelings toward the patient. Movement is also used to emphasize a point or to demonstrate an idea. The representation of size with the hands is a common occurrence: people often hold them far apart when describing a large object, close together when describing something small.

Facial movements comprise perhaps the most expressive non-verbal signals. Many appear to be common to all cultures, since people of very different upbringings smile, laugh and cry in similar ways. That the congenitally blind show these expressions to some extent suggests there may be an innate basis. Paul Ekman is an important researcher in this field, taking as his starting point Darwin's observations about the cross-cultural nature of many facial expressions. Ekman presented photographs of models portraying various expressions to people from very different cultures. There was considerable agreement in identifying the nature of emotions shown (happiness, surprise, anger and so forth) [Ekman, 1973].

This is not to say that everyone uses these expressions to the same extent, even within cultures. Women are generally more expressive than men, and part of the reason why some people seem to be warmer than others is due to their expressiveness. Counsellors who smile frequently and who show interest by nodding their heads frequently are often rated as being more facilitative than counsellors who show little emotional involvement [Tepper and Haase, 1978].

Proximity. One way of describing the distance between people is in terms of 'personal space'—a kind of bubble of territory that surrounds people. In order to find out the size of this space, several strategies can be used. One method is to simply observe conversationalists and measure the distance between them. When standing or talking casually, interactants usually keep about 2–2½ feet between them. A way of testing the validity of this observation is, simply, to walk closer to someone and measure the distance at which he or she begins to move backwards. The point at which this occurs is the edge of the bubble. It seems, from experiments of this type, that the bubble is not round: people will tolerate more proximity at their sides than at the front or back.

The boundaries of personal space vary according to several situational factors as well. Intimacy of topic is one variable, as is the relationship between the participants (e.g. friends or strangers) and cultural background (e.g. Mediterranean peoples generally stand closer together than Anglo-Saxons). Hall [1969] categorized proximity into four zones: Intimate (0–18 inches), Personal (18 inches–4 feet), Social (4–12 feet) and Public (greater than 12 feet). The topic of conversation and the relationship between the participants using these different zones varies. For example, two people standing or sitting between 4 and 12 feet apart are more likely to be speaking socially than personally or intimately.

Status is also related to proximity. Those with high status are observed to have more territory than those with low status [Argyle, 1969]. Not only will a director of a company have a larger office than those working for him, he will also have a larger desk that will serve to maintain a large space around him. The way in which a person enters another's office is a good example of how non-verbal behaviour can indicate relative status. Burns [1964] reports a study in which subjects were asked to fill out questionnaires indicating which of the people in various situations was superior to the other in status. Three of these situations are represented in Fig. 4.1.

To some extent, a patient entering a doctor's office is entering territory that 'belongs' to the physician. The way in which the patient acts may

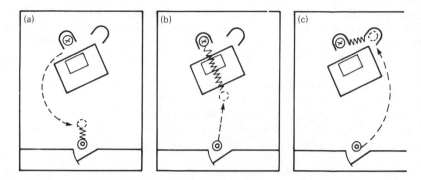

FIG. 4.1   Three examples of the way one person could enter another's office. In (a), person O steps into the office while person X rises and greets him: O was considered to have higher status than X. In (b), O moves towards X, who remains seated: O was seen as being of lower status than X. (c) illustrates one situation in which both were considered to be of equal status: O moves towards X and sits beside him without hesitation. (Reproduced from T. Burns, *Discovery*, 1964, 25, 30–37.)

provide a good indication of how comfortable or uncomfortable he feels in the doctor's presence. Conversely, the way the patient is greeted may give him an indication of the doctor's concern with status. If the doctor stays seated and waits for the patient to come to the desk, the patient may consider the doctor to be asserting higher status. Although many other variables (e.g. clothing, tone of voice) are important in the real-life consultation, this example of the role of non-verbal behaviour provides an indication of how the participants' behaviour at the beginning of the consultation can have an effect on the whole interview. Another feature associated with status is height, in that those of higher status often have higher and more comfortable chairs. Ley and Spelman [1967] suggest that one reason why patients do not follow doctors' advice is because they do not understand it and are diffident about asking questions. It may be that any feature of the consultation that emphasizes a difference in status may not be conducive to good communication.

Associated with proximity are studies on touching. Just as the distance between interactants depends on their cultural background, touching is associated with culture. Jourard observed the frequency of touching between couples in restaurants in various countries. In France, it was 110 contacts per hour, in the United States 2, and in England none. The nature of the relationship between two people is also relevant to touching. Jourard [1966] asked his subjects to indicate who touched them (e.g. mother, father, same-sexed friend) and how frequently they were touched on various parts of their bodies. As would be expected, only the hands were touched by everyone and the trunk of the body and the genitals were touched infrequently. The relevance of this study to doctor–patient communication is that touching and intimacy seem to be closely related to each other, such that if touch occurs the relationship is interpreted as a close one. Johnson [1965] reported that nurses often find their patients

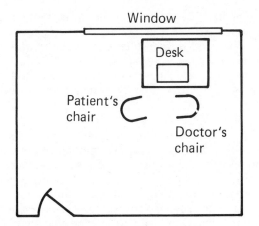

FIG. 4.2   A suggested office design consistent with research in social psychology. The window is at the side of the doctor and patient, rather than behind the doctor. Both participants are seated on the same side of the desk, so that the distance between them can be varied and so that the situation is likely to be considered co-operative rather than competitive. The chairs are of similar height and comfort.

begin disclosing very personal information during intimate forms of touching. Conversely, patients may feel violated when being physically examined by a doctor who has not taken time to establish some rapport.

Arrangement of furniture in the surgery.   The research discussed above indicates that the non-verbal behaviour of conversationalists has considerable effect on their relationship. The environment in which an interaction takes place also has an influence on the encounter.... Although there is little research specifically concerned with the arrangement of furniture in the consulting room, it is possible to suggest a setting that is conducive to good communication and not at odds with it. Fig. 4.2 illustrates one possibility. Since people become uncomfortable if they are unable to see the face of a fellow conversationalist yet can themselves be seen, the desk in this room is sited beside the light source, so that the doctor's face is not lost in the window's glare. Both doctor and patient are seated on the same side of the desk for two reasons. First, the distance between them can be varied to suit the requirements of the situation. It may be that the common practice of placing a desk between the doctor and the patient restricts the degree of intimacy between them, keeping them always about 4 feet apart and outside the personal zone. Typically, conversationalists move between zones as their relationship and topics of conversation change: greater proximity may be needed in times of distress than the intervening desk may easily allow. Secondly, there is some evidence that the positions people take up around a desk reflect the nature of their encounter. Sommer [1965] reported that individuals who are asked to interact casually prefer corner seating, cooperating individuals prefer to sit on the same side of the desk and competing individuals choose to sit opposite one another. It may be that people are more likely to regard the situation as competitive if they are asked to sit opposite one another, an expectation inappropriate to the consultation. Finally, in order to minimize differences in status—perhaps encouraging patients to be less diffident and ask more questions when they do not understand a doctor's recommendations—chairs are similar in height and comfort [Editorial, 1980].

Sensitivity.   Probably the most important of the non-verbal factors is the physician's sensitivity to the behaviour and feelings of the patient. Part of this sensitivity involves an awareness of patients' non-verbal behaviour, such as hesitations, restlessness and signs of embarrassment. It is not possible, as yet, to specify the 'best' way to communicate with all patients, particularly about a poor prognosis. Psychology has been able to provide some guidelines—it is important not to assume that once a patient has been informed the information has been understood or that further information is unnecessary—but studies in this area do not indicate that all patients should be treated in the same way. What might be appropriate for one person may be hurtful or shocking for another. In many of the studies on preparing patients for hospitalization and surgery mentioned elsewhere in the book, providing information about procedures and sensations they are likely to experience has been useful for most patients, but not all. Perhaps because people under the care of doctors are given the same label—patients—there is a tendency to consider this heterogeneous group as being very similar to each other.

An example of a difficult communication is telling parents that their child is handicapped. Parents of Down's Syndrome children have complained that they were not told together (one spouse being left to inform the other), that they were not told soon enough, that they were told in front of a large group of people rather than in private and that they were not given enough information [Cunningham, 1979]. Svarstad and Lipton [1977] reported a significant relationship between parental acceptance of mental handicap in their child and the nature of professional communication to them about the condition. Parents who received specific, clear and frank communication were more likely to accept the diagnosis than those who received vague and hurried information. Coming to terms with the disability was not related to any measured characteristics of the child (age, sex and IQ), the parents (social class) or the professional who informed them (age, sex and level of experience).

These findings do not, however, indicate that all parents could be informed in the same way. Although 60–80% of parents would have liked to have been told together, there remains the 20–40% who would not have wished this. Although some were glad that they had been told about the mental handicap straight away, others report that they would 'prefer to wait until the diagnosis is confirmed' or 'glad they waited a week—we might have rejected him' [Armstrong, Jones, Race & Ruddock, 1980, p. 24].

Another aspect of sensitivity is a recognition that the physician's own behaviour will be studied and interpreted by patients particularly when they are unsure about diagnosis and treatment. To take Down's Syndrome as an example again, Cunningham [1979] describes how it was the changes in hospital routine and reactions of the staff that had made some parents concerned about their children:

> I knew something was wrong as soon as he was . . . born. They all looked at each other and went very quiet. Some other people then came in . . . but when I asked was he all right, they said he was fine and not to worry . . . but I knew they knew all the time, so why didn't they say something instead of keeping me wondering and worrying all that time?

and:

> I guessed she wasn't all right. She was always the last baby brought up from the nursery after feeding and people—doctors, students and nurses and all that—kept popping in to see us but never seemed to want anything. [Cunningham, 1979, p. 314]

There has been considerable emphasis on the concept of 'accurate empathy', particularly in the literature on psychotherapy. It has been defined as 'the ability to be sensitive to another's current feelings and the verbal facility to communicate this understanding in a language attuned to the patient's present feelings'. Thus, empathy requires an ability not only to understand feelings but to *express* this understanding as well. There is recent evidence of its importance in doctor–patient communication. DiMatteo and Taranta [1979] focused on patients' perceptions of the rapport they had with their doctors and on the characteristics of physicians that contributed to this rapport. They found that the ability of physicians to understand the emotions of others and the ability to communicate this understanding was associated with patient satisfaction. There is also evidence that medical training does little to encourage empathy, in that final-year students have no greater skill than first-year students, and the level of empathy remains low throughout [Poole and Sanson-Fisher, 1979]. Attempts to increase sensitivity have been described by DiMatteo and Taranta [1979] and Kent, [Clarke & Dalrymple-Smith (1981)]. Teaching programmes often include an opportunity for trainees to role-play a consultation and then the patients (who are sometimes actors and actresses and sometimes patients living nearby) provide information on how they felt about the interview. Although assessment of such training is difficult, some studies (e.g. Poole and Sanson-Fisher [1979] have shown that sensitivity can be improved through these kinds of experiences.)

THE PSYCHOLOGIST AS AN AGENT OF CHANGE

The paper by Haley (1967), which is our chosen extract here

is an example of the way in which the psychologist can work within the system, not to maintain the *status quo* but to subtly change it. The paper explores how new directions in the work of psychotherapists (some of them psychiatrists, some of them having been trained as psychologists) have led to a questioning of existing assumptions about mentally disturbed people and their place in society.

Both psychiatrists and psychologists have begun to shift their focus from locating the need for psychotherapy from "causes" residing "inside" the person to locating them in the context in which the patient lives. The paper acknowledges the social nature of knowledge on which therapeutic interventions are based, indicating that the "facts" are determined by the ways they are collected: in other words, they are socially constructed. Some clear instances of this in the family therapy situations are given.

The Haley paper is an important example of the manner in which psychology can work towards breaking out of the role that for many years psychologists had been prepared to accept, if not at an ideological level, certainly for the purposes of getting on with their jobs and obtaining funds for further research. This paper marks the beginning of a movement (which started in psychiatry) that emphasized the focus of the problem to be not the individual, but the whole system of relationships of which the person was a part. In western society generally and in psychiatry until fairly recently, people who were psychiatrically "ill" were seen as failures or weak. Moreover their failure was seen as located within them. The whole of psychiatry and clinical psychology had adhered to this ideology and used the extent to which people adapted to the social structure as its own particular yardstick of success. The move from focusing on the individual to focusing on the system or systems of relationships that were the fabric of their lives was revolutionary. In the past, the professional psychologist or psychiatrist "colluded with" society in stamping the problem as an individual one. Hayley's paper is an example of a new wave in therapy, it spelt hope for the psychologist who wanted to address him- or herself to the problems implicit *in society*. For it was but a small step from looking at families and the relationships within the family to seeing a family's pathology as related to the strains and stresses of the broader social system.

Reading XVII.   Towards a Theory of Pathological Systems, by J. Haley

At this time psychiatry would appear to be undergoing a basic change in orientation. Quite possibly the change is a discontinuous one, which can mean that the knowledge and training necessary for the previous orientation is not helpful in dealing with the developments yet to come. To describe a change of this kind while it is happening is difficult, but the emerging ideas are becoming sufficiently clear to be contrasted with the past point of view.

Method

In the past it was assumed that a science of man could be developed by studying a man in isolation from his fellows, by examining him as he dealt with strangers in artificial group situations, or by analyzing the ideology of the society he inhabited. Primarily man as an individual has been the focus of study; the goal has been to describe and classify the individual in terms of his body type, character, personality, clinical diagnosis, and so on. The nature of this focus has severely limited the possible explanations about people and why they do what they do. Putting the individual person alone in a frame, the investigator attempted to explain all there was to know about him without including other people in the picture; to explain "why" someone did what he did, it was necessary to postulate something inside the person, such as instincts or drives or emotions. . . . The influence of psychiatric ideology upon social theorists usually led them more in the direction of the individual and further from a social orientation. Within psychiatry there was an absolutely basic assumption that the problem was how to diagnose and treat the individual patient.

In the last decade in psychiatry the frame around the individual has been broken, and questions about "why" a man does what he does are being answered in terms of the context of relationships he creates and inhabits. The reasons for this change have been continuing emphasis upon interpersonal relations over the years and the recent development of ideas about systems. The change is a shift in focus from the individual and his nature to the habitual and systematic patterns of behavior men develop when dealing with their intimates. The direct manifestation of this change is in the field of family research and family therapy.

In the last few years, for the first time in history, married couples and whole families are being brought under systematic observation. Family members are observed actually dealing with one another. The research problem is how to conceptualize the repeating, responsive behavior in this

Source: *Family Therapy and Disturbed Families*. (1967). Edited by G. Zuk and I. Boszormenyi-Nagy. Palo Alto, Calif.: Science and Behavior Books, pp. 11–27. Reprinted by permission of the author and publisher.

ongoing social network in such a way that statements about regularities in the interchange will hold true over time. The problem is no longer how to characterize and classify these individuals; it is how to describe and classify the habitual patterns of responsive behavior exchanged by intimates. Can one categorize the typical processes in the group, describe changes if they occur, and differentiate one organization from another? With this focus the "cause" of why someone does what he does is shifting from inside him to the context in which he lives. The question of whether a family containing a psychiatric patient is a different type of organization from another family is a question of whether there is a system of interactive behavior which provokes, or requires, one or more members of the system to behave in a way that could be classified as psychopathological. A similar question is whether there are discernable trends in relationships that predictably lead to violence or divorce and the dissolution of the family. These questions have relevance beyond the family research field. Insofar as any group of men have a history and a future together (for example, research groups or business organizations), the type of exchanges generated in the system may determine whether there will be amiable relations and productive work or a disturbed and unhappy group of participants. In the larger social scene, the family of nations may develop patterns of exchange that predictably lead to disruption and war. For inquiry into these questions, the focus must be shifted to the exchange of acts in a relationship and away from the description of man as if he were autonomous. This means breaking new ground.

If we take seriously the accusation often made that the psychological and social sciences, as contrasted with the physical sciences, are still in the dark ages, there is an analogy between what is happening today and what happened in the physical sciences in the seventeenth century. . . .

Today in the field of social relations we appear to be in a remarkably similar situation. Some people have begun to doubt the past theories about human beings, such as the idea that men are driven by instincts, and yet there are few factual observations of people in "orbit" in their intimate relationships. Many people are even uncertain whether such observations are necessary. We also have no conceptualization of laws of social relationships, if such regularities exist, as a framework in which to place the few observations that we do have. In addition, our current establishment of knowledgeable people has a large investment in the past theories of the individual as an autonomous being.

In that earlier scientific endeavor, there were several steps necessary before the problem could be solved. First of all, it was necessary to make a bold shift in the focus of attention. Copernicus did this when he suggested that planets orbited around the sun rather than the earth. To take this necessary step, men had to revise basic assumptions about man and the universe. The current shift of focus in psychiatry from the individual to the social network he inhabits could be said to be comparable to the shift from the earth to the sun as the center of the universe. It is a bold step, and many people react almost religiously against the idea that man is not the focal point but is rather helplessly responding within his network of ongoing relationships. Those who protest say the importance of the individual is being overlooked and he is being made a mere element in the system, just as they said man was diminished if his planet was not the focal point of the universe.[1]

The natural scientists' second step was to begin to doubt the statements and observations of the ancients and to collect accurate observations of the movements of the planets. . . . Today we have begun to doubt the statements and observations of our own "ancients" but we have hardly begun the task of collecting our observations. Despite the large number of books on marriage and the family, which describe what families are supposed to be like, it is only in the last few years that investigators have actually begun to bring families together and to observe the members dealing with one another. We have a great many opinions, which are adaptable to any causal explanation, but we will need many years of observing and testing families in operation before we have sufficient observations to refute a theory.

The final step of the men of earlier times was to derive from their new observations new generalizations sufficiently broad to include the idea that what occurred in the heavens also occurred on earth. In this way they delineated laws of nature that had wide application in many fields of endeavor. Now we, too, are beginning to assume that the idea of a coalition between family members is relevant to coalition patterns in any ongoing social group and that patterns in a marriage could be relevant to those of international relations. That is, we are beginning to seek laws, or regularities, which hold true in any system of relationships with a past and a future. It is this possibility that makes research on the family appear potentially so rewarding.

We can hope that it will not take as long to develop a science of human relationships as it did to develop the physical sciences, because we have that vast attempt to guide us. However, we should also not assume that we can jump the preliminary steps necessary and have a sophisticated theory of human relationships appear full blown in all its grandeur. Over time, we will need the three factors necessary in any scientific endeavor: (1) we must have a collection of facts—observable events which either occur or do not occur, (2) we must be able to formulate those facts into patterned regularities, and (3) we must devise theories to account for these regularities and be willing to discard past ideas if they handicap us in our efforts.

---

[1] A similar response was made to Freud when he suggested that the idea of man's being unable to control his own mind was the third great blow (after a sun-oriented universe and a descent from animals). Freud argued that man was driven by unconscious forces within himself which he was helpless to control. The current family-oriented view in psychiatry would also argue that man is helplessly driven, but by the people around him in the system he inhabits. Perhaps this diminishes man even more, since the "cause" of his behavior is no longer even located within him but in the outer context. However, this point of view also implies that he participates in creating that context.

Regarding the collection of facts, in family research it is not yet clear what the relevant "facts" are or what the best method is of collecting them. When studying families, if we confine ourselves to observable events we have only the behavior of family members as they respond to one another: their bodily movements and vocal intonations, their words and acts. If we extend our "facts" to include unobservable events, then we have the emotions, attitudes, expectations, and thought processes of the participating family members. Agreement has not yet been reached as to which of these types of data are most appropriate. Additionally, we face the problem that our "facts" are determined by the ways in which we collect them; there is not agreement about how to proceed in family research. There are three general methods of collecting data: (1) using the self-report of family members about their families obtained either by questionnaire or by interview, (2) bringing family members together to study them in operation, with the data consisting of observations by human observers who attempt to reach agreement on what they see happening, and (3) placing families in communication networks where their behavior is recorded on instruments. These three different schools of family research are obviously going to collect different "facts" about families.

A further difficulty in family research is the problem of formulating some sort of theory as a guide for the type of observations to make and the kind of methodology to use. We need to conceptualize formal patterns of human relations in such a way that we can ultimately collect data which will verify whether or not certain patterns actually occur. At this time we must conceptualize with only a minimum number of observations of families in operation. Yet we must speculate on the basis of what we have and then decide what sort of approach might support or refute our speculations. A speculation will be offered here about a characteristic pattern which appears evident in pathological systems.

Although men have not focused upon the systematic study of relationships, they have observed each other in action for many years and we might assume that if some aspect of ongoing relationships was truly important it would be emphasized in past literature. There exists a formal pattern that has been noted so often that it has been given a name. "The Eternal Triangle," and has been the focus of man's attention to psychiatry, religion, and politics, as well as in the fiction he has created to express his life experiences. It seems, in fact, to be the only relationship pattern that has been named in folk speech. Perhaps its importance is based on the fact that the essential learning context of the human being is triangular: in the usual biological family unit, two people unite to create and rear a third.

In the family research of the last decade there has been a progression from descriptions of individuals to descriptions of dyads (such as mother and child) to triadic descriptions (such as parents and disturbed child). Larger family groupings, for example a quadrad, have not been emphasized, despite a move toward studying the entire family network. The extended family is usually discussed in terms of the smaller units. For example, the influence of the grandparent generation is usually discussed in terms of the influence on a parent of *his* mother and father. This focus on a maximum unit of three people would seem to be partly because of the complexity of larger units and partly because the triangle appears to be a "natural" unit.

The Perverse Triangle

If we take the triangle as our unit of study in a family or in any ongoing social system, we can raise the question of what sort of triangular arrangement will generate what could be called a pathological system. In this case "pathological" means a system that will lead to the dissolution of itself or to violence among the elements, or indicates elements which behave in ways that appear peculiar and inappropriate. In terms of the family, a pathological system is one resulting in continual conflict, in divorce, or in the kind of symptomatic distress in one or more family members that requires community attention. If we examine the past literature and activities of man, we find that there is a triangle of this sort—it can be called a perverse triangle—that has long been taken for granted without being made explicit. These are its characteristics:

1. The people responding to each other in the triangle are not peers, but one of them is of a different generation from the other two. By "generation" is meant a different order in the power hierarchy, as in a human generation of parent and child or in an administrative hierarchy such as manager and employee.

2. In the process of their interaction together, the person of one generation forms a coalition with the person of the other generation against his peer. By "coalition" is meant a process of joint action which is *against* the third person (in contrast to an alliance, in which two people might get together in a common interest independent of the third person).

3. The coalition between the two persons is denied. That is, there is certain behavior which indicates a coalition which, when it is queried, will be denied as a coalition. More formally, the behavior at one level which indicates that there is a coalition is qualified by metacommunicative behavior indicating there is not.

In essence, the perverse triangle is one in which the separation between generations is breached in a covert way. When this occurs as a repetitive pattern, the system will be pathological. This concept is not being offered as something new but rather as a more precise formulation of what is becoming commonly assumed in the literature on pathology and the family.

As an illustration, in the area of administration it has been taken for granted that a breach of generations will make difficulty in an organization. It is said if a manager "plays favorites" among his employees the organization will be in distress. Put in terms of a triangle, the manager in such a case is forming a coalition across generation lines with one person against his peer. If he merely forms an alliance with an employee, the problem does not necessarily arise, but at the moment he sides with one *against* another while simultaneously denying that this is happening, the system will become pathological.[2]

This illustration is a rephrasing of a point made in most administrative manuals: the administrative levels in the hierarchy must be kept separate for the proper functioning of an organization. There is one other point assumed in good administrative procedure: communication should not jump levels. That is, an employee should not be allowed to "go over the head" of his immediate superior and contact a higher superior. Once again, this idea can be rephrased in terms of a breaching of generations: a coalition between a higher and a lower level against a middle level in the power hierarchy. It is assumed that such breaching should not take place and that if it occurs secretly as a consistent pattern, the organization will be in distress.

One would expect that if this perverse triangle were causal to pathological systems it would not only be avoided in organizations but it would be assumed to be important in the field of psychopathology, and this is obviously so. In psychiatry, one finds the perverse triangle, slightly rephrased, as the central thesis in psychodynamic theory. In psychoanalytic theory and in much of psychiatry it is argued that the Oedipal conflict is a focal point in the cause of psychiatric distress. The origin of this idea is particularly pertinent here. Sigmund Freud at one time proposed that hysteria was the result of a sexual assault on the patient by an older relative. In this sense he proposed that there was a breaching of generations which should not have occurred and, insofar as it was a secret act, could be considered a covert coalition across generations. However, he then discovered that in certain cases the sexual incident could not actually have happened, and he shifted from the idea of a familial cause of this malady to an intrapsychic cause—a fantasied wish for the sexual act. This was the birth of the Oedipal conflict, the wish of the boy to have sexual relations with his mother and the consequent fear that his father would not take this coalition kindly and would castrate him. The Oedipal conflict became a universal explanation of the neurosis.

In essence, this conflict, as in the play from which Freud drew the name, can be seen as a coalition across generation lines which is covert or denied. The action of the play *Oedipus* consists of the lifting of the secrecy of this breaching of generations. . . .

---

[2]If one seeks a "cause" of the distress in terms of the individual, it could be put in terms of an unresolvable conflict, or paradox, for the person coalesced against. A generation line or administrative level is implicitly a coalition among peers; employers are in coalition with others on their level and employees are in coalition with others on their level. Within that framework, if an employer and employee form a coalition against another, the other is faced with two conflicting definitions of the situation: (a) his fellow employee is in coalition with him as part of the natural framework of administration, but within that framework (b) his fellow employee is siding with the employer against him. Being forced to respond when there is a conflict between these two different orders of coalition creates distress.

In the psychiatry of the past, which focused upon the individual, the triangle was considered of basic importance, and when we turn to the newer approach of the relation of pathology to the family we find a similar emphasis common in the literature. Many family descriptions are cast in a framework of individual description, but implicit in them is a view of pathology nestling in a perverse triangle. For example, it has long been suggested that a disturbed child is a product of parents who are in conflict: the child is caught between them by being in coalition with one or the other. When the mother is described as overprotective and the father as passive, the implication is that mother is siding with child against father, who remains withdrawn. The mirror picture is presented, where father and child are in covert coalition against a difficult mother. Generally, the inability of parents of a disturbed child to maintain a common front to enforce discipline is a reflection of their inability to maintain a separation between the generations. A similar breach of generations appears in the case of the disturbed child who associates with his parents but avoids his peers.

It is also becoming more common to read in the descriptions of the extended family a similar pattern occurring in the next generation in disturbed families. . . .

The existence of a coalition between a disturbed child and a parent occurs so often in conjunction with a coalition of one of his parents with a grandparent that one might suggest they are inseparable. That is, it could be stated as a hypothesis that a breaching of generations with the child will coincide with a breaching at the next generational level. (Often, too, it will coincide with a coalition of child and grandparent against parent.) If such a triangle at one generation always accompanies a similar one at the next generational level, we can suspect a regularity in networks of family relations where the patterns in any one part of the family are formally the same as those in some other part.

Anyone who has observed or treated abnormal families assumes that the ways the parents form coalitions with the child against one another appears "causal" to the disturbance in the child. The idea is also present, with a slight translation, in the studies of the hospitals where patients are sent for treatment. Some years ago Stanton and Schwartz noted in their study of the mental hospital (Stanton and Schwartz, 1954) that a conflict between an administrator and a therapist was a "cause" of a patient erupting in a disturbance. This result can also be seen when one staff member sides with a patient against another staff member in a perverse triangle.

If we use the triangle as a unit of study and break down a family network into its triangular components, a rather awesome complexity appears. In an average-size family where there are two parents and two children, and each parent has two parents, this group of eight people composes 56 triangles. Any one person in the family is involved in 21 family triangles simultaneously (and this does not include aunts and uncles, neighbors and employers). Every one of the 21 triangles in which parents and children are involved carries the possibility of a coalition across generations. If the occurrence of a secret coalition across generations is indeed pathological, the potentiality for disturbance is exceedingly high in any family.

An analysis of a family network in terms of triangles also reveals that any one person in the family is at the nexus of a large number of these triangles. He is also the *only* person at this particular nexus. The fact that no two people are in the same position in a context, even in the same family, raises profound questions about whether individuals can be compared. . . . The family evidence being gathered indicates that different individuals live in quite different worlds.

If we assume that an individual's behavior is adaptive to his intimate relationships, it follows that he must not behave in one triangular group in a way which will disrupt another triangular grouping in which he is involved. For example, his behavior in the triangle with his parents will have repercussions in the triangle with his grandparents. In fact, the way a person relates to any one pair in the network will influence the response to him of any other pair. In a family where all the triangular groups consist of amiable members, the situation does not appear complex. But let us suppose that a child is at the nexus of two triangles, or groups, which are in conflict. Suppose, for example, that if he pleases his mother and her mother he will disturb his relationship with his father and his mother because the two groups are in conflict. To behave adaptively, the child must maneuver in such a way that his behavior in one group does not disrupt the other. If one imagines that all 21 of the triangles the child inhabits are in conflict with each other, and if the child is at the nexus of all these conflicting groups, then to adapt and survive in such a network he must exhibit strange and conflictual behavior. It is possible to explain the symptoms of schizophrenia as adaptive to this kind of conflicting set of groups. In fact, it appears that this way of looking at the family system could ultimately lead to a social description of any symptomatic behavior—a translation of psychopathology into the language of social behavior.

Schizophrenia as a Conflict of Groups

A way of explaining schizophrenia was offered some years ago by a research group in which I participated. It was noted that schizophrenia could be described as a disorder of levels of communication: the patient qualified what he said or did with an indication that he was saying or doing something else, and then qualified this meta-message with yet another which conflicted (Haley, 1959). . . . The idea proposed was that the schizophrenic had been raised in a situation where he faced conflicting levels of message from a parent or a combination of both parents with an injunction against commenting on this conflict or leaving the field [Bateson et al. 1956].

At that time I was particularly interested in attempting to correlate more precisely the behavior of the schizophrenic with his situation in his family to investigate whether schizophrenia was a form of adaptable, responsive behavior. To collect data on this point, it was necessary to accept the reports of the family members about what had happened in the past during a psychotic episode. Alternatively, one can observe the occurrence of psychotic symptoms in the patient during the course of family therapy and examine the situation in which the symptoms erupted. Such an incident can be used here to illustrate the familial context of a schizophrenic.

A schizophrenic daughter improved sufficiently to be sent home from the hospital on a trial visit, and her parents responded to this situation by separating. Mother left father (but called him and told him where she was going) and she asked her daughter to go with her (even though at the time she was saying she could not tolerate her daughter's company). When her mother made this request, the daughter faced a situation in which she had to choose between her parents and either stay with father or go with mother. The daughter's solution was rather complex. She went with her mother, but when they arrived at their destination, her grandmother's home, she called her father. The mother then protested that this meant she was siding with the father against her, and the girl said she had only called the father because when she said goodbye to him she had given him an odd look. A characteristic symptom of this daughter was her "odd looks" and the question was whether this behavior was irrational or adaptive, given this situation. The girl's behavior became more extreme when the father came and reclaimed the mother. The girl was asked by her mother to go to the store, and declined. The grandmother did the errand, and while the mother and father were in the other room discussing the girl's refusal, the girl began to scream. She was then rehospitalized.

At one time, the daughter's behavior might have been explained as adaptive to a situation where there was a conflict of family rules. The rule was that the daughter was not to form an open coalition with either father or mother, and yet the separation forced her to break her rule. She could not merely do nothing because that would have meant staying with her father. Her solution was to have a symptom—the odd look—which solved the problem of how to avoid siding with either parent.

In terms of the larger family context, it is possible to see a family "rule" in a somewhat new way. Repetitive behavior between two people can be seen as not merely the following of an arbitrary rule that has developed between them but as a product of responses in other parts of the family. That is, a rule not to have an open coalition with mother or father can be seen as a response to the consequences among other family members if the coalition occurs.

Examining the large context in which this girl was living, and focusing upon only the most important people in her life—her parents and two grandmothers—we see that she was involved in a group of ten cross-generational triangles. It would be possible that none of these triangles would involve cross-generational coalitions. The grandmothers might keep out of the parental difficulties, the parents might maintain a separation between themselves and the daughter, and the daughter might not attempt a coalition with either parents or grandparents but would confine her associations to her peers. Quite the opposite extreme was apparent in this situation. Impressions from family interviews indicated that all family members were involved in a consistent pattern of perverse triangles. The two grandmothers bid against each other for the daughter, the father's mother sided with him against the wife (she had once offered the wife a cash bribe to leave her son because she could take better care of him), and the daughter was constantly siding with her mother's mother against her mother and staying with her on visits home from the hospital. The most apparent and persistent cross-generation coalitions occurred in the triangle of the girl with her parents. Father accused mother and daughter of being against him, which they denied. Mother accused daughter of being in coalition with father against her and cited sexual play between them, among other activities, as proof of this. Generally the parents behaved as if there were no generational differences with the daughter.

The amount of struggle and conflict between the different family triangles appeared extraordinary and was complicated even further by the mother's sisters, who were also continually intervening in the family affair. When the girl was forced by this physical separation to choose between her parents, her response carried repercussions throughout the wider network of family triangles. If she went with her mother or if she did not, she was faced with a situation where her response would not only be condemned but she would provoke open disruption in the extended family. For example, to go with her mother also meant joining the mother's family against the father's family, joining one grandmother against another, and joining grandmother against father. At the nexus of warring family factions, what would be an "appropriate and normal" response to this situation? It would seem to be one in which the girl should behave in one way to satisfy one faction and another way to satisfy another, and then disqualify both ways by indicating she was not responsible for what happened in any case. Such conflicting communication would be diagnosed as schizophrenic behavior.

Persisting Triangles

Assuming for the moment that a pathological family system consists of a network of perverse triangles, questions arise about how a family got that way, why the members persist in behavior that is disturbing, and how one may go about changing such a system. It seems doubtful that the "cause" can be sought in the behavior of any single individual or even that of a set of parents. The pattern undoubtedly is passed down over many generations. However, the pattern must be continually reinforced if it is to continue. At a minimum, two people each of a different generation must cooperate to perpetuate it.

One might look upon the situation as one in which at least two people are dissatisfied with the status quo. If a wife is pleased with her association with her husband she is not likely to attempt to join child or parent against him. In a sense, such a coalition is an attempt at a change. Yet there is a perduring quality even in this attempt at change, because to breach generations in an attempt to change continues the family situation which leads to dissatisfaction. However, if one examines the question of "cause" in terms of dissatisfaction, he is focusing once again upon the individual. Such a focus usually indicates an avoidance of looking at the larger context. When one shifts to the larger view, alternative explanations appear that make "cause" appear more complex. For example, it is possible that the wife joins child against husband not merely because of internal dissatisfaction but as an adaptive response to her relationship with her parents. To maintain stability in relation to her parents, she may find it necessary to join child against husband because an amiable relationship with her husband would have repercussions in the way she is dealing with her parents and the way they are dealing with each other. In this sense, "cause" is a statement about regularities in larger networks.[3]

The argument that the extended family has less influence today because many generations do not live under the same roof is not necessarily valid. Young people may marry and settle in their little box in the suburbs, but they are not out of contact with their extended families. Anyone who has dealt with disturbed couples or families knows that communication takes place and repercussions occur in the extended family no matter how geographically distant the members may be.

When one examines an idea of this sort and thinks about how to verify it with more than impressionistic data, the basic problems of family research arise. Suppose we wished to test the hypothesis that families which exhibit violence, dissolve in divorce, or produce members suffering from psychopathology all characteristically exhibit covert cross-generation coalitions. In the past we might have assumed that we need only ask the family members the right sort of questions in order to determine whether the perverse triangle is more frequent in "abnormal" than in "normal" families. Now it is becoming more accepted that the self-report of family members can be used, at most, as an indicator of an area of research and not as a means of validating a hypothesis. (This is particularly so when one is concerned with levels of behavior that involve denials.) It seems necessary to bring the family members together and study the network in operation. One must precisely define "coalition" and "generation," and devise a context that will generate an opportunity for coalitions while providing a means of denying their existence. Then one must place family members in this context to determine whether or not such coalitions occur in a variety of family triangular groupings, and do this with a sufficiently large sample of families to be able to make statements about differences at some designated level of significance. If one uses human observers to observe families and guess whether coalitions are occurring there is always

---

[3]It would seem superfluous to bring to the question of "cause" of psychopathological behavior anything about the person's history, past conditioning, or internalized images. An adequate description of the present family network should be sufficient.

the possibility of bias. If one does not use observers, he must devise a situation where instruments will record the results—and the use of instrumentation to record multiple levels of communication is difficult. Yet ultimately if we are to bring rigor to this sort of study we must provide the opportunity for convert coalitions as they are defined in that context (Haley, 1962). Devising such an experimental procedure and testing an adequate sample is, let us say, a challenging task. . . .

Family Therapy

The tightness and rigidity of the family network become particularly evident to therapists attempting to bring about change in whole families. As with individuals, family studies indicate that flexibility is synonymous with normalcy and rigidity with pathology. It would seem to follow naturally that the more severe the disturbance, the more rigid the family pattern; change appears to be brought about more easily with minor pathologies than with families of schizophrenics. Had we more elaborate theories of the technique of family therapy, we might have more success with severely disturbed families. It would appear, however, that such theory will only be built over time.

The various methods of family therapy that have appeared would seem to have one factor in common: a focus on the problem of coalition both within the family and between therapist and family members. It is generally assumed that it is unwise for a therapist to join one member of a family against another. Yet it also appears that members of disturbed families are exasperatingly skillful at provoking a therapist to side with them and at antagonizing him to side against them. . . . One way to analyze family therapy is in terms of a process of the therapist constantly disinvolving himself from coalitions with family members as these occur in all their subtle variations. The art of family therapy seems to be that of developing ways of siding with all family members at once, or of clearly taking sides with different factions at different times while acknowledging this, or of leaving the coalition situation ambiguous so that family members are uncertain where the therapist stands. Family therapists seem to recognize, either consciously or by intuition, that generations should not be breached, and that denial should not take place if a breach does occur.

The tightness of organization in the disturbed family also indicates new possibilities in family therapy appearing on the horizon. If all parts of a family network are responsive to change in any one part because of the tightness of the organization, then a certain freedom appears with regard to which set of family relationships to focus upon in family treatment. Certain factions of a family might be more accessible to change than others. In schizophrenia, for example, the parents and schizophrenic child might be the triangle most resistant to change so that treatment of another section of the family could produce better results. Yet to suggest this possibility indicates how rapid a change has been taking place in psychiatry. Not many years ago, it was thought a waste of time to attempt psychotherapy with a schizophrenic. More recently, it has seemed pointless to treat *only* the schizophrenic, because of his involvement with his parents (and the hospital staff), who should also enter treatment. Now it is conceivable that the schizophrenic could be treated without ever entering therapy since a change in him is assumed to be brought about if another part of the extended family in which he lives is changed. . . . Recently it has been so taken for granted that the disturbed child is a "product" of the marital problems of the parents that the child is excluded and only the parents treated. This shift toward assuming that the "cause" of an individual's behavior resides in the context in which he is living reflects the extensive changes that have taken place in the basic orientation of psychiatry in less than a decade. . . . The consequences of this different point of view must inevitably permeate psychiatric thinking. In diagnosis, the change will be toward including more than one person in the diagnostic category. In treatment, the assumption is developing that one person cannot change unless the context of a relationship in which he lives also changes, which leads to more treatment of marital pairs and whole families as a natural consequence.

A NEW MODEL FOR PSYCHOLOGY

In what we have said so far, we have implied that psychologists can concentrate on the individual or society or, hopefully, on both as they plan and undertake interventions of various kinds. This view, however, is seen as too simplistic by Susan Llewelyn and John Kelly (1980). They argue for a new role for the psychologist on the social stage:

It is important to look at the ideology of psychology (an exercise which necessitates stepping outside the discipline itself) because of what it reveals about both values and science, and about the nature of psychology's subject-matter. This is generally understood to be the individual organism, behaving either independently of or dependently on its environment. Yet it is our view that this notion is itself open to question and has resulted from a reliance on positivism which has blinded psychologists not only to its value-laden aspects, but also to both the historical specificity and the limitations of psychology as a discipline. Whilst other social sciences, particularly sociology, have come to recognize the need to explain not only their chosen subject-matter, but their own existence, psychology has apparently perceived such reflexivity to be unnecessary (at least until very recently, see Buss, 1975).

Individualism

Psychology as it has been constructed in the past has strenuously resisted questions about values and the nature of science, because some of the questions, if answered, might undermine the entire discipline. The concept of "the individual" for instance is seen to be inviolable and sacred *as a concept* because it is central to the whole notion of psychology *as a discipline*. Yet the relatively recent historical development of psychology as an autonomous entity, devoted to the understanding of behavior and experience, suggests that its concepts are also historically specific, and that its methods and assumptions are perhaps less grounded in self-evident truths than its practitioners like to believe (cf. Gergen, 1973; Sampson, 1977).

This suggestion is amply confirmed through an historical examination of the components of *individualism*, a task recently performed by Lukes (1973). In pre-capitalist European social thought the most pervasive image of society was that of the biological organism whose parts (individuals) were constituted only in relation to the whole. Physical individuals were the bearers or occupants of pre-given social positions and characteristics, rather than their creators. Only with the disintegration of feudal societies and the rise of industrial capitalism did there emerge in Europe coherent philosophies centred on the relations between individual attributes and the social and political order. Increasingly, once the individual was constituted, theoretically, as separate from this order, the path was then cleared for the contraposition of these elements, and for the assertion of individual rights and freedoms against those of "society," increasingly epitomized (especially in liberal thought) by the political form of the State. Paradoxically, as society and social intercourse became more highly elaborated and developed, philosophies of individualism flourished simultaneously. . . . Psychology emerged as one of the clearest disciplinary expressions of individualism at the end of the 19th century, an outcome undoubtedly moulded by numerous social and economic developments, such as the growth of public education.

Psychology sees it as possible and logical to talk about the human individual as an autonomous unit which in some circumstances may be influenced by social factors. Thus, it works with a *biological* conception of individuality, in which the form of individuality is physically bounded within the limits of the individual organism. Just as organisms "have" physical organs, systems of organs and so on, i.e. interconnected physical structures, so too do individuals "have" personalities, needs, aspirations, etc. But as Sève (1978) argues very clearly, this conception of human individuality is fundamentally inadequate: psychological "structures" are fluid and capable of modification through interaction and experience in ways that are simply unavailable to physical, bodily organs. Hence, ". . . the human essence does not have the 'human form'. . . The personality is not at all to be reduced to individuality or to the ensemble of the particular formal characteristics of an individual's psychism . . ." (pp. 444–451).

Once we draw a conceptual distinction between concrete individuals and the *form* of individuality (a task rendered difficult by their apparent coincidence), we can then relocate what Sève calls "the human essence" in the social relations between individuals rather than as properties of individuals per se.

When we consider psychology in this way, it becomes clear, as Shotter (1975) has argued, that its subject-matter is at present inadequately constituted as discrete, structural entities. The domain of psychology is thus populated by individuals moving in and out of interactions in much the same way that Newtonian atoms careered about the universe. . . .

It is still possible to read of research that ignores the crucial social determinants of behaviour and concentrates entirely on psychological determinants. For example, in industrial psychology, several studies have examined industrial conflict in terms of individuals' "attitudinal militancy" (e.g. Alutto & Belasco, 1974). In another field, it might be thought that the history of the attempt to find significant personality variables which account for more than about 10 per cent of the variance between situations would have led to this attempt being abandoned. But the studies, with more and more refined methodologies, proliferate as any research journal will show, and strenuous efforts are made to explain away the mere 90 per cent of the variance unaccounted for, as resulting from extraneous variables or poor experimental design.

This research tradition perhaps marks the clearest testimony to the fetishism of method within psychology (recently criticised also by Levy) and to its tendency to substitute problems of method for theoretical and conceptual problems. In yet another field of inquiry, the clinical, it has been very clearly demonstrated that social factors are of considerable importance in the epidemiology of mental illness.

The reason psychology hives off the individual as subject-matter from the social, is generally thought to be pragmatic—we have to start somewhere. Yet the apparently sensible convenience of separating individual and social factors for analysis has an important and unfortunate consequence which is to obscure the nature of their relationship.

Sociologism

. . . It becomes clear that "society" is not an independent entity set over and against "individuals" merely as the social aspect of psychology, but is embodied within, or permeates the structure and relationships of individuals, i.e. it is both exterior and interior to individuals.

The ways in which forms of individuality are socially constituted have stood at the centre of the works of two of the greatest thinkers—Marx and Freud. As Jacoby (1977) argues in the case of Freud, the structure of the psyche and the contents of the unconscious were not merely repressed biological drives, but the results of generations of accumulated social experiences. Equally, Sève (1978), a Marxist psychologist, has endeavoured to trace the connections between economic structures and psychic structures and to locate the determinants of the latter in relations of production and technological developments.

We need, therefore, a working model for psychology that takes into account social and personal structures, as well as the dynamic relationships between them. Such a model should also throw some light on the confused question of causality (which we have not had the space to elaborate upon here), and the question of values. Such a model might well be a dialectical "psychology." (Llewelyn & Kelly, 1980, pp. 408–410)

5

Psychology in the Popular Imagination

Officer Krupke,
You're really a square,
This boy don't need a judge,
He needs an analyst's care,
It's just his neuroses that ought to be curbed,
He's psychologically disturbed.
(West Side Story)

THE CASE FOR STUDYING
"POP" PSYCHOLOGY

Until now we have concentrated on the way in which psychologists define and carry out their various professional roles. In the course of this investigation we have seen how academic and applied psychologists relate to other professionals (e.g., doctors, lawyers, social workers), to government officials (e.g., civil servants, judges, public administrators), and to pressure groups. Viewed in this fashion, psychology may seem rather remote from the lives of ordinary people. It is probably true to say that most people live their entire lives without ever having direct contact with psychologists and they are equally unlikely to read academic psychology journals or textbooks. This state of affairs seems to support Miller's assertion in his 1969 American Psychological Association presidential address that the task that faces the profession is to find some way of giving psychology away (Miller's article is in Chapter 1). However, the fact that most people do not have immediate access to psychology does not mean that the public are ignorant of or indifferent to its research and theories. Quite the opposite is true. The general public is in turn fascinated, suspicious and sceptical of psychological research and pronouncements. Clearly then the proverbial man or woman on the street has some conception of what psychology is all about.

241

We think that one of the aims of social psychology ought to be the understanding of these popular images (or what are sometimes called "shared" or "collective" representations). How people perceive psychology, is, we believe, a worthwhile topic of research. Likewise it is important to ask about the ways in which the public acquires its fund of images or collective representations and the topics which are likely to excite or capture the popular imagination. But what, you might wonder, do such matters have to do with the dialogues and debates we have been tracing? Questions such as these are all relevant to this book because they alert us to the fact that one of the ongoing debates within social psychology concerns the nature of the subject matter. What it boils down to is whether the task of speculating about the origin and impact of ideas should be undertaken by social psychologists or whether it should be left to social theorists, philosophers, and historians. Some have argued, as we saw in Chapter 1, that social psychology is an appendage of general experimental psychology, borrowing its concepts and methods from the parent discipline. As such its focus is individual behaviour and experience. Others have quarrelled with this definition and sought to disengage social psychology from the psychology of the individual. This debate may be traced back to Wundt, the German founder of experimental psychology, whose ideas laid the foundations for what some have perceived as two distinct social psychologies—a psychological social psychology and a sociological social psychology. Psychological social psychology starts from the assumption that the object of study is the individual, albeit within a social context. By contrast, sociological social psychology tries to make sense of social relationships and collective ways of thinking. Asking questions about psychology and popular consciousness forces us to think about where the boundary lines lie between social psychology, sociology, and social philosophy. It also highlights some of the differences between North American and European social psychology.

American academics wished to promote social psychology as a scientific enterprise and were anxious to rid the discipline of all philosophical vestiges. They were uneasy about studying something as vague and unquantifiable as "consciousness," let alone "group mind." For them the individual was the only reality. Hence, they were quite happy to leave the study of popular or mass culture and public opinion to sociologists and literary critics. Influential as this view was, it did not lead to the total demise of the other tradition. By and large the major figures in sociological social psychology have been European academics. Lindesmith and Strauss (1968) suggest that this was because in Europe social psychology was not hived off as a separate discipline in the early years of this century. Influential European sociologists, following in the footsteps of Durkheim and Weber, took it for granted that social psychological issues were legitimate topics of sociological concern. And similarly, European psychologists remained more aware of developments in sociology and in the humanities.

In America, before the appearance of the radical movement, those who wished to create a social psychology that was less preoccupied with individuals and artificial laboratory groups and more concerned with society than with "social stimuli," turned in one of two directions. Some were attracted to the theory of symbolic interaction because it seemed a promising way of linking the inner world of psychological experience and awareness to the world "out there" (without relegating either to second place). While others sought to create a sociological social psychology that revolved around the study of attitudes, public opinion, and mass media. Some hoped that this work on collective ways of experiencing the world would put an end to sterile individualism. However, much of the American work on attitude formation and change remained rooted in the individualistic approach and failed to bridge the gap between studies of individual and collective modes of thought.

Armistead (1974) makes this point most tellingly by quoting from the work of Lana (1969), a traditional social psychologist.

While working in the area of persuasive communication for several years, I became increasingly aware of what I thought to be a curious fact about research in this area, including my own work. We were almost always concerned with aspects of the communicative situation which had little to do with the content, that is, with the empirical and logical aspects of the message that was being communicated: Most of us were interested in one or more of the following variables: the controversiality of the issue referred to in the communication, the awareness by the subject of the manipulatory intent of the communicator, the style by the communicator, his prestige, the length of the communication, the medium used to transmit the communication. . . . This research focus was not an accident of the interest patterns of the various psychologists doing work in communication. Of that I was convinced. Was it a natural by-product of American behaviourist tradition to focus on just about everything but meaning . . .? (Lana, 1969, quoted in Armistead, 1974, pp. 14–15)

It was this seeming inability of North American social psychology to deal with real human beings living in society that contributed to the rise of radical psychology.

In Chapter 1 we explained that the radical critics of social psychology were dissatisfied with what they perceived as the individualistic bias to much of mainstream social psychology. What they sought to do was to reorient the discipline, to make it more social and more critical of its assumptions. They attempted to persuade their peers that it was important to ask questions about the ideological foundations of the discipline. This concern with problems of ideology suggested two possible lines of inquiry. On the one hand there was the task of examining what kinds of topics psychologists study, their reasons for selecting certain topics, and the way in which their findings or knowledge is applied. On the other hand a separate line of investigation was suggested, which radical social psychologists did not pursue, and that was to examine the way in which "pop" psychology is disseminated, via the media, to the widest audience.

. . . social psychology rationalises and reinforces the deep assumptions of popular consciousness . . . [yet] the fact remains that there is no systematic research on the diffusion and dissemination of social psychology . . . the broader cultural role of social psychology, which I think can be documented by studies in the diffusion and translation of knowledge—particularly between academic fields and popular guide-to-living books, and newspaper, magazine, and television presentation—remains virtually unexplored. (Wexler, 1983, pp. 161–162)

It is this popularization of psychology which is the focus of the material chosen for the present chapter. Given the fact that much of the work on mass media, mass culture, and ideology has been initiated by sociologists, historians, and social theorists, the articles and extracts included here are not drawn exclusively from social psychology. We regard this then as a very preliminary attempt to deal with questions that cut across the various social sciences and which are best thought of as issues within the sociology of knowledge, an approach we have discussed in Chapter 3. Thus, we do not claim that this chapter is a representative set of readings on "pop" psychology. What we hope to achieve with these selections is to convey the flavour of "pop" psychology and to encourage you to seek further examples. We should also point out that on the whole we shall refrain from making detailed critical comments on these readings. The reason for not evaluating the extracts is that we are not concerned so much with the particular points of view the authors express as we are with the hints that they provide as to the process by which psychology becomes part of the culture. It is, we acknowledge, quite a different but equally worthwhile matter to decide whether this diffusion of psychological knowledge is in the best interests of the profession and of the public.

THE RISE OF "POP" PSYCHOLOGY AND ITS IMPACT

We start with an extract from a book written by the American social historian Donald Napoli (1981), entitled *Architects of Adjustment*, which looks at the history of the American psychological profession this century. Napoli's claim is that modern Americans are predisposed towards psychological ways of thinking about events in the world, which in turn makes them receptive to psychology in all its different guises. Admittedly, at first this sounds like a rather circular argument, but when you read Napoli you will realize that he tries to demonstrate a link between social and economic conditions and the rise of "pop" psychology. His examination of post-war psychology begins with a description of a scene from a play in which psychological tests were administered to air force recruits. A number of the themes that Napoli raises in his book are taken up in the extracts from works by other writers presented in this chapter. For example, there is the question of the role played by the mass media in creating and diffusing images of psychology. Also, the attempt to identify post-war social conditions that gave rise to a generation preoccupied with matters concerning personal growth and self-fulfillment is a topic taken up by other social critics and observers.

Reading XVIII.   Applied Psychology in the Postwar Period, by D. S. Napoli

As the curtain rose, ten young cadets stood facing the mechanical testing apparatus. The examiner told them to be seated and gave them their instructions. Each cadet was to grasp the rod in front of him and hold it so steadily that it did not touch the sides of the metal aperture surrounding it. A light would flash every time a cadet made an error by allowing the rod to bump its enclosure. Each cadet was required to keep an accurate count of his mistakes. Before beginning the test the examiner explained that its purpose went far beyond simply gauging muscle control:

The test that you are to take now will measure your ability to remain steady under pressure. The pressure will consist of your anxiety to succeed in Air-Crew training. It will consist of your own fear that you will be eliminated. It will consist of your own weakness and secret doubts. It will consist of jumping nerves that you cannot control.

This test will pit you against yourself. Every man has fear. Every man has tenseness. Every man has weakness and jumping nerves and secret doubts. But not every man can control these things.

Then the first trial began. For ten seconds the cadets tried to keep their arms steady, but the lights continued to flash. Tension mounted as the examiner reminded the cadets that each mistake brought them closer to failure. There were four more trials exactly like the first. Then the test was over. The stage lights faded, and the curtain fell. [Hart, 1943, Act I, Scene 4, pp. 42–45.]

This scene, probably the first ever to depict the dramatic aspects of psychological testing, marked the high point in Moss Hart's semidocumentary Broadway play of 1943, *Winged Victory*. One critic declared that "the scene in which the cadets are undergoing the steadiness-under-pressure test, the test of the winking lights, is an ordeal for every person in the audience, and I doubt if many passed" (Morehouse, 1943, pp. 216–219). A year later, when Hollywood made a film version of the play, all Americans got a chance to agonize with the young cadets who

Source: Napoli, D. S. (1981). Reprinted from *Architects of Adjustment: The History of the Psychological Profession in the United States* by permission of Associated Faculty Press, Inc Port Washington, N.Y.: Kennikat Press Corp. Pp. 134–138, 142–144.

were trying to overcome the diabolical challenge to their competence and self-esteem.

It may not be too far-fetched to suggest that the testing scene from *Winged Victory* marked the point at which applied psychology became serious business for the American public. The scene's message was clear: everyone had a realm within his personality that lay beyond his immediate understanding and control. The requirements of a technological society, however, demanded that each person mobilize his innermost resources. No one could be spared a probing of his "weaknesses and jumping nerves and secret doubts" if social needs were to be met effectively. The scene in short, made a striking case for the necessity not only of adjustment itself but of sophisticated methods to achieve it. The scene did not invite skepticism, although some was warranted. Even before the play opened, air force psychologists had abandoned an improved version of the steadiness-under-pressure test, determining that it had not proved effective in predicting which cadets would succeed in aviation training.

The scene from *Winged Victory* heralded an era in which psychology came to have a greater impact on the American consciousness than it ever had before. In the period after World War 2 movies, books, and magazines would grow less satisfied with moral or sociological explanations and would turn to psychological interpretations of human behavior. Characters, whether real or fictional, would appear more fascinating when their psyches were opened for public examination. Psychology would, however, provide more than mere diversion and amusement. It would also become a large-scale enterprise, and the public would pour countless millions of tax dollars into psychological research and training. One of the chief beneficiaries of the great popular fascination with psychology would be the psychologists themselves: as people concerned themselves increasingly with the psychological aspects of living and working, the demand for psychological services would reach unprecedented dimensions.

The movies were one area of popular culture in which the war marked the beginnings of a trend toward broadly psychological themes. Films about psychology had emerged in the 1920s, observes film critic Leslie Halliwell but "the subject took its firmest hold in the middle of World War 2. . . ." [Halliwell, 1974, p. 624.] Characters suffering from various mental derangements appeared with increasing frequency. Beginning with sexual repression in *Lady in the Dark* (1944), audiences examined a full range of cases from amnesia (as in *Spellbound* with its surrealistic dream sequences) to homicidal schizophrenia (as in *The Dark Mirror*). Maladjusted protagonists soon became familiar figures on the silver screen—and later on the television tube as well.

Applied psychologists received only secondhand benefits from these films, however, for the psychotherapists depicted in them were almost always psychiatrists. Psychologists could not view a movie about themselves until 1952, when Stanley Kramer produced *My Six Convicts*. The story concerned a psychologist's efforts to set up a testing program in a federal penitentiary. Although the plot lacked the unpredictable twists of the usual psychological melodrama, it maintained interest by describing the growing friendship between the psychologist and the prisoners who worked for him. The film downplayed the importance of the psychologists research and emphasized his ability to foster trust and self-esteem in the prisoners. While audiences gained only a vague notion of what psychological work entailed, they could easily have concluded that psychologists were sympathetic people with a deep faith in the decency of their fellow men.

Generally psychological themes carried an element of mystery and even insidiousness. This proved especially true in the realm of social criticism. Through the 1950s, at least, critiques of American society became analyses of the American psyche. The titles alone told of psychological troubles: *The Lonely Crowd, The Organization Man, The Hidden Persuaders.*

Further evidence of the nation's psychological degeneration seemed to come from Korea, where American prisoners of war fell victim to something called "brainwashing." It was a sign of the times that Americans discounted duress and conversion in seeking an explanation of the prisoners' behavior. They saw instead, in the words of *Life* magazine, "an effort, as finely organized as any battle plan, to capture the minds of American prisoners. . . ." [Brinkley, 1953, p. 108.]

By the early sixties America's preoccupation with psychic deficiencies had begun to give way to a new interest in social problems. War, poverty, racism, and other issues became topics of public concern and scholarly inquiry. Psychologists did not suffer from the seeming deemphasis of personal problems, however, for each social issue had psychological ramifications. The prime example came in the struggle for civil rights, where psychological testimony on the deleterious effects of segregation influenced both the courts and the public. By the late sixties social protest came increasingly from college campuses, where demands for societal change mixed with the more personal goals of "relevance" and "doing your own thing." Psychology courses enjoyed unprecedented popularity; among established disciplines only anthropology showed a higher rate of increase in college majors.

Further evidence that interest in psychology did not decline in the late sixties came in the growing success of the popular monthly *Psychology Today.* Founded in 1967, the magazine offered simplified accounts of behavioral research in an illustrated slick-paper format. Bona fide psychologists, psychiatrists, and other experts wrote most of the major articles. Unlike its predecessors of thirty years before, *Psychology Today* aimed at a well-educated audience that did not seek facile advice on successful living. Though not a scholarly journal, the magazine did provide reliable information on the psychological aspects of important topics. Its popularity may be measured by its circulation, which had soared beyond 900,000 by 1974.

At the same time Americans continued their long-standing quest for a more satisfying life. Advocates of pseudoscientific or quasi-religious approaches still had their followers, of course, but to an increasing extent people turned to genuine psychologists for advice. Readers of paperbacks, for example, could catch the latest word from notables like Erich Fromm, learn about the newest therapeutic techniques ("reality therapy," "scream therapy," etc.), or discover how to renew self-esteem in books with snappy titles like *I Ain't Much Baby but I'm All I've Got*. The electronic media had their psychologists too, led by Joyce Brothers, the ebullient former quiz-show winner who had become something of a national celebrity by the mid-seventies.

Although postwar interest in psychology had some aspects of a popular fad, it also received strong backing from the federal government. The contacts that psychologists had made with federal agencies did not fade as had happened after World War 1. Instead, military programs continued on a reduced scale, and the Office of Naval Research provided funding for basic research in psychology as well as other sciences. Postwar aid, especially for clinical psychology, came from the Veterans Administration and the Public Health Service. While psychologists received only about 1 percent of the government's science dollar, the level of financing still dwarfed prewar figures. In the thirty years after World War 2, the federal government spent over $1.2 billion on psychological research. By 1972 over half the members of the American Psychological Association were receiving government subsidies for their work . . . .

Psychologists could count on a continuing interest in their field and a strong demand for their services . . . even more than teachers and researchers the public wanted practitioners—experts who could help individuals with personal problems and aid administrators in the efficient management of students and employees. School officials, businessmen—even psychiatrists—turned to applied psychologists in growing numbers after World War 2. As American society grew more complex, the need for expert assistance in adjustment became more acute. By the early fifties the need for applied psychologists had grown so large that practitioners outnumbered academicians for the first time. The three major fields of applied work—industrial, educational, and clinical—each enjoyed unprecedented prosperity in the postwar era. . . .

Of the three applied fields clinical psychology underwent the most changes in the postwar period. . . .

In the sixties traditional psychotherapy received two serious but widely differing challenges. One was behavior modification, a system that derived from the principles of John B. Watson and his most energetic postwar disciple, B. F. Skinner. . . .

The other challenge to traditional psychotherapy came from "humanistic psychology," a term used by Abraham H. Maslow and others who doubted that people should be used as objects of scientific inquiry. More protesters than systematizers, the "humanists" became associated with a wide variety of developments. Especially important were sensitivity groups in which participants sought "self-actualization" through "altered states of consciousness." Existentialism, Eastern mysticism, and equipment to measure brainwaves all became part of humanistic psychology, which an article in *Psychology Today* in 1972 proclaimed as "the erratic heart of the counter-culture." [Criswell and Peterson, 1972.] This was not the position that many psychologists envisioned for themselves, and they thus believed that "humanism" threatened both their science and their profession. Nevertheless, the movement promised to broaden psychology's clientele considerably. Its ideas and techniques attracted members of the middle class who, rather than showing clear signs of maladjustment, experienced only vague feelings of discontent that had previously been outside the purview of clinical work. . . .

POP PSYCHOLOGY AND
CULTURAL CHANGE

Freedman (1971), an American psychologist, dates the rise of pop psychology somewhat later but his interpretation of the set of social conditions that led to the upsurge of interest in psychology and the other social sciences is similar to Napoli's.

During the 1960s, college students gradually and then more rapidly lost interest in the physical sciences and turned instead to the biological and social sciences. In the last few years the turn to the social sciences has been pronounced. This fascination with the social sciences is also evident in the population as a whole. *Psychology Today,* admittedly a rather jazzy middle-brow magazine, has attained a circulation of 700,000 in a few years. A glance through the list of articles in mass readership magazines such as *Reader's Digest, Look, Life, Woman's Day,* and so on, reveals a strikingly high percentage of articles dealing with some aspect of the social sciences. Sex is still popular, but articles by social scientists or pseudo social scientists on topics ranging from the nature of prejudice to the structure of public corporations provide strong competition. The eager and often undiscerning public avidly reads and does not distinguish among the mush of Charles Reich's *The Greening of America*, the cute notion underlying L. J. Peters' and R. Hull's *The Peter Principle*, the careful observations and sloppy generalizations in Konrad Lorenz's *On Aggression*, and the mixture of science and nonsense in Desmond Morris's *The Naked Ape* and Lionel Tiger's *Men in Groups.*

It is not surprising that dissatisfaction with and interest in the social sciences have increased at the same time. As people have found that technology and the traditional physical and biological sciences do not have the answers to mankind's burning questions, and as they then turn to the social sciences only to find that the latter do not now have the answers either, it is natural that there should be dissatisfaction. [Freedman,1971, pp. 710–711]

What role has psychology played in the cultural upheavals

of the twentieth century? This is a difficult, and perhaps unanswerable question. Has popular psychology set the scene for a radically different way of thinking about the individual's role in the social order or have people turned to psychology because the old ways of thinking no longer seemed adequate? Which came first, popular psychology or cultural change? Posed in this way, the question seems far too simple minded. Surely, it must be the case that psychology has been both a cause and an effect. People turned to psychology to provide them with insights or guidance because the changes in the social order meant that the traditional answers to the timeless questions (Who am I? What is the meaning and purpose of existence? What does it mean to be a good person?) were no longer satisfying or sufficient. But at the same time, as more and more people became aware of the ideas and theories of "pop" psychology, as they formed some impression of what the gurus of the day were preaching, psychology became not simply a part of the cultural changes, but a *catalyst for social change.*

Popular psychology, then, seems to flourish during times of social upheaval. This has implications for the types of topics or issues which capture the popular imagination. Judging by the books that have become best sellers, the individuals who have become known outside the confines of the academic environment, and the concepts that have become part of the general vocabulary, what the public wants to learn about is personal life and intimate social relations. Books on friendships, love, sexual relations, marriage, divorce, parenthood, personal growth, and change have a guaranteed audience.

THE POPULAR APPEAL OF PSYCHOLOGY

Freedman (1971) makes the point that social science knowledge, by its very nature, is more accessible to the public than are the findings and theories of the natural sciences.

The social sciences differ from most of the other sciences in that the layman can usually understand enough about a problem in the field to feel that he can evaluate its importance;. . . When someone in chemistry or physics describes his area of interest to a layman, most of us listen with awe but little understanding. We hardly feel competent to decide whether he is working on an important problem in the field. In contrast, everyone is to some extent an expert in the social sciences. Freeman, 1971, p. 730]

Without cataloguing all the different themes of "pop" psychology, we shall look in this section at some examples of psychology's popular appeal and influence. One sphere of social life where popular versions of psychological theory have had a great impact is child-rearing. There is now an extensive literature which traces the way in which images of parenthood and childhood are socially determined and also documents how they may alter over time. Many writers have focused on the way in which expert advice is put across to mothers.

The first extract is by Christina Hardyment (1983), and comes from her book *Dream Babies*, which analyzes child-care advice from the time of John Locke to modern authorities such as, Freud, Dr. Spock and Jean Piaget. In the piece reprinted here, she develops the argument that in the post-war years baby came to rule the home. In Britain, she suggests, the time was ripe for new ideas about child care because normal domestic life had been disrupted by the war. In particular, the mass evacuation of children from urban areas had given people first-hand knowledge of the psychological traumas of childhood separation.

Reading XIX.   Baby Rules, O.K.?, 1946–81, by C. Hardyment

The Second World War certainly had the effect, in Britain at least, of turning thoughts towards children and their mothers. The disastrously clumsy evacuation at the start of the war is remembered with amusement by some of the organizers. It must have shattered the psyche of many of the evacuees, particularly the last to be chosen of the groups of children foisted on half-hearted country matrons. Perhaps the experience of evacuation opened the minds of that generation of mothers to the ideas of the Freudians about 'separation anxiety'. In *The Problem of Anxiety* (1936)

Source: Hardyment. C. (1983). *Dream Babies: Child Care from Locke to Spock.* London: Jonathan Cape, pp. 235–240. Copyright © 1983 by Christina Hardyment.

Freud wrote that anxiety in adults and older children was analogous to that experienced by the infant separated from or frustrated by its mother; if no anxiety of this sort occurred in infancy, then in later life the child would be more resilient to distress. Erikson extended this more positively, setting the mother's importance in a social matrix, not only as guardian, but as interpreter of the culture:

> Mothers create a sense of trust in their children by that kind of administration which in its quality combines sensitive care of the baby's individual needs and a firm sense of personal trustworthiness within the trusted framework of their culture's lifestyle. This forms the basis in the child for a sense of identity which will later combine a sense of being 'alright', of being oneself, and of becoming what other people trust one will become. (Quoted by Kagan [et al., 1978], *Infancy*)

Logically, interest should have been stimulated at this point in establishing mother's 'firm sense of personal trustworthiness', but attention continued to be directed predominantly to Erikson's other requirement, 'sensitive care of the baby's individual needs'. The man most responsible for establishing the concept of 'maternal deprivation' in the popular mind was John Bowlby.

Dr Bowlby was asked by the World Health Organization at the end of the Second World War to study the mental health of 'children who were homeless in their native country'. His original report, *Maternal Care and Mental Health* was reprinted in abbreviated form; a paperback *Child Care and the Growth of Love* in 1953. From that time on, most important manuals on baby-care mentioned or used his findings. 'Mother-love in infancy is as important for mental health as are proteins and vitamins for physical health,' he wrote. Birds hatched and cared for by human beings will fall in love with human beings in later life. One cannot be sure of the loyalty of a chow unless one has reared it from birth—any attempt to start after a few months would fail. 'These examples are perhaps sufficient to introduce the reader to the basic notion that what occurs in the earliest months and years of life can have deep and long-lasting effects.'

The main purpose of Bowlby's book was to make people look again at the assumptions and methods of institutions looking after homeless children, and to consider the possibility that even a bad parent was better than no parent. But it also had implications for ordinary family life. 'The absolute need of infants and toddlers for the continuous care of their mothers will be borne in on all those who read this book, and some will exclaim. "Can I then never leave my child?" ' Admitting that 'far more knowledge is required before a proper answer can be given, Bowlby advised that 'the holiday whilst granny looks after the baby, which so many mothers and fathers pine for, is best kept to a week or ten days'. Leaving a child under three years of age was a 'major operation, only to be undertaken for good and sufficient reason, and, when undertaken, to be planned with great care'. Moreover, leaving a baby to scream for hours 'because the baby books tell her to do so' was 'a common cause of partial deprivation'.

Maternal deprivation was as positively damaging in the first three years of life as German measles in the first three months of pregnancy. Once the baby's 'psychic tissue' became fixed, no recovery could occur—irreparable scarring remained. The baby might well not recognize its mother on reunion. This could imply a genuine injury to its power of abstract thinking, the loss of the capacity to identify. Or the child might have suffered so much that it was unwilling to give its heart again—it would withdraw and take up a lone-wolf attitude. In later life, its 'affectionless' character would ensure difficulty in forming meaningful relationships, and in all likelihood the child thus deprived would become a 'bad parent' itself.

Bowlby cannot be blamed any more than Freud for the fact that the meat of both men's findings has been borrowed from the world of the abnormal, where they were established, and applied over-enthusiastically to everyday life. Taken literally, these ideas meant that mothers had to devote themselves wholeheartedly to their babies to ensure their inoculation against the danger of emotional hang-ups and unfulfilled intellectual potential in later life. Kagan has summarized the duties of the modern mother as 'physical affection, sacrifice of the self's interests for that of the child, consistency of care, and enjoyment of interaction with the child'. This recalls Wolfenstein's perception of the obligatory nature of the new 'fun morality'. It is hardly plausible, except for the most saintly, to enjoy interaction with one's child while sacrificing one's own interests. But Kagan's analysis is correct—that is what mothers were, and are still, asked to do. Compare Buxbaum with one of the newest baby-care experts, Penelope Leach. In 1951 Buxbaum wrote:

> The young infant is completely dependent on his mother, she is his one means of survival. As soon as he recognises her and looks forward to her smile, to her handling, he is looking to her for the satisfaction of his most fundamental needs. He will be dependent on her love and be willing to do for her what she asks him to do. This relationship of the mother to the child is the very foundation of the child's existence.

Buxbaum's compensation to the mother for her maternal solicitude was infant obedience, 'he will . . . be willing to do for her what she wants him to do'. She made no mention of the two-way emotional satisfaction and reinforcement that more modern theorists have offered. For Penelope Leach love is far more than a means of survival. It is 'the means through which the new-born, wrapped in mystery, unfolds' (*Baby and Child* [1977]). Leach is of course a cuddler. . . . 'Loving a baby is a circular business, a feedback loop. The more you give, the more you get, and the more you get the more you feel like giving' (tiddley pom). She advocates 'sensitively concentrated attention', and admits that:

> bringing up a baby in this flexible, thoughtful way takes time and

effort. It involves extremely hard work as well as high rewards. But what worthwhile job does not? Bringing up a baby is one of the most creative, most worthwhile and most undervalued of jobs. You are making a new person, helped to be as you believe a person should be.

Although maternal deprivation could take place even if a mother spent all day in the same house as her baby, the crucial practical issue it involved was the question of day care, of mother substitutes, ultimately of whether a mother could have a job outside the home, or whether—as Leach clearly believed—no other job was possible. As the Women's Movement increased in strength and more and more women found the solitude of the servantless household between eight in the morning and six in the evening unbearable, mothers scuttled out of their homes as fast as psychological or financial necessity could carry them. How the manuals have coped with these unalterable facts is the subject of a later section on day care. Here it is enough to recall the standard assumption of earlier manuals that baby would have a nurse. They might have discussed whether to train her or to acquire her trained, how to dress her and how much to pay her, how to ensure she neither gassed the baby at bedtime nor infected it with loathsome diseases while flirting with her boyfriend in the park; but none of them questioned her existence, or the necessity of having help with children. Bowlby's requirement of 'constant attention night and day, seven days a week and 365 days a year' from mother or 'permanent mother substitute—one person who steadily "mothers" him, would have been tossed aside as lunatic. Handed from nursemaid to under-nursemaid, from monthly nurse to permanent nanny to nursery governess—what chance did any such unfortunate child have of growing up with a normal personality?

There have been enthusiasts who have asserted that several upper-class generations went to the emotional dogs because of such treatment. Jonathan Gathorne-Hardy's collection of scurrilous anecdotes about *The British Nanny* [1972] left one with little to hope for from them, although it did explain Churchill's excellence as the result of an exceptionally good nanny. Dr Mia Kellmer Pringle clearly believed the same, although she offered no specific evidence, when she wrote:

In fact, among the upper middle classes in Britain in the nineteenth and early part of the twentieth century, parental involvement with children was quite circumscribed, being delegated first to nannies and then to boarding schools. That this markedly affected emotional and social development is strongly suggested by the available evidence, which however, is mainly biographical and autobiographical. (*The Needs of Children* [1975])

Nor, Pringle continued, did 'the nanny's modern substitute', the au pair girl make matters any better. 'Most are young, and may have little understanding of a small child's needs. Perhaps worst of all, since they usually stay for a few months only, the child suffers the bewildering, if not traumatic experience of being looked after by a succession of such girls who inevitably bring with them the differing expectations and habits of their own national culture.' Mothers were thus left with no alternative but to devote themselves body and soul to their children.

I have dwelt on 'maternal deprivation' at some length, because it seems to be a fundamental issue still, and one which is closely linked to the Freudian assumptions—many of them, as Kagan has pointed out . . ., not proven—underlying recommended child-care practice since the last war. It concerns feeding, sleeping, leaving to cry, and so on.

PSYCHOLOGY AND THE
CONSTRUCTION OF IMAGES

The extract that follows from Rapoport, Rapoport, and Strelitz (1977) deals with the same theme as the Hardyment extract but looks more closely at the way in which the psychoanalytic writings of Bowlby and Winnicott laid the foundations for a very psychological, child-centred form of family life in the 1950s and 1960s. It has been suggested that one consequence of this popularization of psychoanalytic theories of children's nature and needs was that it justified the notion that women's place was in the home. Another was that it reinforced the assumption that the first five years leave permanent and irreversible effects upon later personality and behaviour. (It was against this backdrop of ideas that the Clarkes (1976) wrote their book *Early Experience: Myth and Evidence,* see Chapter 4.)

Reading XX.   Social Expectations of Parenting:
The Impact of Experts, by R. Rapoport,
R. N. Rapoport and Z. Strelitz

Expectations Deriving from Psychoanalytic
Writings in the 1950s and 1960s

First we consider the expectations about parenting that have arisen from

Source: Rapoport, R., Rapoport, R. N., & Strelitz, Z. (1977). *Fathers, Mothers and Others: Towards New Alliances.* London: Routledge & Kegan Paul, pp. 36–46.

the psychoanalytic writings of the 1950s and 1960s and the assumptions contained in those writings about the requirements of mothers, fathers and children in relation to one another. We use Bowlby and Winnicott to represent this arena, as they have been highly influential in the general population. The use of their work does not constitute a review of more modern psychoanalytic theory on this topic.

Bowlby worked essentially with fellow professionals and care-givers rather than with parents themselves; whereas Winnicott based his work on direct clinical experience and directed his later work in particular to ordinary parents. Bowlby's work focused on the consequences of extreme deprivation and the situations he wrote about do not relate directly to ordinary family life. He himself indicated that he would one day produce a book which would deal with issues of partial deprivation more closely related to the processes of everyday life, but his work was taken up in the meanwhile, became very popular and was generally applied to ordinary life as well as to special situations. Winnicott's work, however, specifically excluded special situations, and disturbed cases, and was addressed to the processes in ordinary family relationships. Nevertheless, the basic position of both writers is very familiar, and their influence has been in the same general direction.

Both writers emphasized the crucial importance of mothering. Major works which were widely influential were Bowlby's *Child Care and the Growth of Love* (1972 edn, based on a report for the World Health Organization in 1951 and first published by Penguin in 1953); and Winnicott's *The Child, the Family and the Outside World* (1973 edn, based on two volumes published by Tavistock Publications in 1957 and first published by Penguin in 1964).

It is important to note that in presenting an abbreviated statement of complex and important works, an element of caricature inevitably occurs. We feel, however, that we present a fairly accurate picture of what has filtered through to general public awareness and to care-givers' conceptions of these writers' views; these in turn affect the expectations parents have of themselves as a consequence of the work of these writers. Along with others like Salter Ainsworth (1972) and Rutter (1974a), who have clarified some of the original issues by further research, Bowlby refined and developed his contribution in his later work (Bowlby, 1969/1971, 1973) but these have not yet had the widespread and historical impact of the earlier work that we present here. It is the more historic writing, rather than the contemporary state of knowledge, that we believe still has a considerable influence on parents.

Neither Winnicott nor Bowlby dealt much with parenting as a joint enterprise; they saw it in terms of fairly rigid sex-role conceptions, in which the mother was intimately and continuously involved in child-care—a response which came naturally—and the father was seen to have a secondary and supportive role. This orientation relates in part to their heavy focus on child-care in the early stages, a focus consistent with the psychoanalytic emphasis on the primacy of a child's early experience for his or her later development. It follows from this perspective of infants' early needs as paramount, that parents are required to give their infants' needs top priority. The negative outcome of irreversible damage to children's development became a widely feared alternative.

Both Bowlby and Winnicott saw 'good' parenting as best undertaken by children's biological parents and in the family setting. This is the context which they saw as facilitating continuous relationships, and conducive to 'intensity of feelings and richness of experience' (Winnicott, 1973 edn, p. 175). Both called for support to ordinary families as a starting point to improved standards of child-raising.

Within this family context the mother–infant relationship was distinguished from the parent–child relationship—and from the parent–parent relationship, and given special prominence. Winnicott wrote in his introduction to his book: 'It is about mothers and babies, and about parents and children, and in the end it is about children at school and in the wider world' (Winnicott, 1973 edn, p. 9).

The mother–child relationship, was portrayed as having intimate, loving, dedicated, and similar characteristics. Bowlby visualized it like this:

> What is believed to be essential for mental health is that an infant and young child should experience a warm, intimate and continuous relationship with his mother (or permanent mother-substitute—one person who steadily 'mothers' him) in which both find satisfaction and enjoyment. It is this complex, rich and rewarding relationship with the mother in early years, varied in countless ways by relations with the father and with the brothers and sisters, that child psychiatrists and others now believe to underlie the development of character and mental health (Bowlby, 1972 edn, p. 13).

> A child needs to feel he is an object of pleasure and pride to his mother; a mother needs to feel an expansion of her own personality in the personality of her child; each needs to feel closely identified with the other. The mothering of a child is not something which can be arranged by rota; it is a live human relationship with alters the character of both partners. The provision of a proper diet calls for more than calories and vitamins; we need to enjoy our food if it is to do us good. In the same way, the provision of mothering cannot be considered in terms of hours per day, but only in terms of the enjoyment of each other's company which mother and child obtain (Bowlby, 1972 edn, p. 97).

Winnicott sensitively conveyed the feelings involved in this conception of the mother–infant relationship and gave prominence to his view of the *naturalness* of the mother's response as follows:

> you found yourself concerned with the management of the baby's body, and you liked it to be so. You knew just how to pick the baby up, how to put the baby down, and how to leave well alone, letting the

cot act for you; and you had learnt how to manage the clothes for comfort and for preserving the baby's natural warmth. Indeed, you knew all this when you were a little girl and played with dolls. And then there were special times when you did definite things, feeding, bathing, changing napkins, and cuddling. Sometimes the urine trickled down your apron or went right through and soaked you as if you yourself had let slip, and you didn't mind. In fact by these things you could have known that you were a woman, and an ordinary devoted mother.

I am saying all this because I want you to know that this man, nicely detached from real life, free from the noise and smell and responsibility of child care, does know that the mother of a baby is tasting real things, and that she would not miss the experience for worlds. . . .

If a child can play with a doll, you can be an ordinary devoted mother, and I believe you are just this most of the time (Winnicott, 1973 edn, p. 16).

We shall return to the way in which ordinary mothers were thus told just how good and devoted they are—or should be. Meanwhile, what was the psychoanalytic conception of the 1950s about fathers? Even in his chapter 'What About Father?' Winnicott did not deal with the meaning of the parenting experience to fathers, or the possible feelings it invokes. Though he ordinarily wrote far more about feelings than about roles, the element that he dwelt on was the *supportive role* that he saw the father playing in relation to the mother and baby.

I am trying to draw attention to the immense contribution to the individual and society which the ordinary good mother with her *husband in support* makes at the beginning, and which she does simply through being devoted to her infant (Winnicott, 1973 edn, p. 10; italics ours).

Describing the mother's need for freedom to grow in her parenting job, and in the richness she finds in her minute-to-minute contact with her baby, Winnicott amplified:

This is where the father can help. He can provide a space in which the mother has elbow-room. Properly protected by her man, the mother is saved from having to turn outwards to deal with her surroundings at the time when she is wanting so much to turn inwards, when she is longing to be concerned with the inside of her circle which she can make with her arms, in the centre of which is the baby. This period of time in which the mother is naturally preoccupied with the one infant does not last long. The mother's bond with the baby is very powerful at the beginning, and we must do all we can to enable her to be preoccupied with her baby at this, the natural time (Winnicott, 1973 edn, pp. 25–6).

And he encouraged mothers: 'Enjoy the way in which your man feels responsible for the welfare of you and your baby' (Winnicott, 1973 edn, p. 26).

This perspective on fathering was shared by Bowlby. His explanation for not considering the father–child relationship in any detail is now widely quoted:

> The reason for this is that almost all the evidence concerns the child's relationship with his mother, which is without doubt in ordinary circumstances by far his most important relationship during these years. It is she who feeds and cleans him, keeps him warm and comforts him. It is also to his mother that he turns when in distress. In the young child's eyes the father plays second fiddle and his value increases only as the child becomes more able to stand alone. Nevertheless, as the illegitimate child knows, fathers have their uses even in infancy. Not only do they provide for their wives to enable them to devote themselves unrestrictedly to the care of the infant and toddler but, by providing love and companionship, they support the mother emotionally and help her maintain that harmonious contented mood in the atmosphere of which her infant thrives. In what follows, therefore, while continual reference will be made to the mother–child relation, little will be said of the father–child relation; his value as the economic and emotional support of the mother will be assumed (Bowlby, 1972 edn, pp. 15–16).

The child's early needs were seen as paramount, but they were also seen to change as the child developed. By implication, the requirements of parents were also seen to change, with demands on parents believed to be most intense in the early years, tailing off after several years until adolescence.

Bowlby identified developmental phases in terms of the child's vulnerability in his capacity to develop human relationships. He accordingly defined the phases in terms of the supposed requirements of the child for the mother's presence.

> a) The phase during which the infant is in the course of establishing a relationship with a clearly identified person—his mother; this is normally achieved by five or six months of age.
> b) The phase during which he needs her as an ever-present companion; this usually continues until about his third birthday.
> c) The phase during which he is becoming able to maintain a relationship with her in her absence. During the fourth and fifth years such a relationship can only be maintained in favourable circumstances and for a few days or weeks at a time; after seven or eight, the relationship can be maintained, though not without strain, for periods of a year or more (Bowlby, 1972 edn, p. 61).

Intrinsic to this definition is the view that the mother's constant presence is critical to her child's satisfactory development, and hence the expectation that she must observe this if she is to succeed as a mother. But the *goals of parenting* were not discussed explicitly. Winnicott came closer to making explicit the rationale for constant personal mothering:

> The mother takes trouble because she feels (and I find she is correct in this feeling) that if the human baby is to develop well and to *develop richly* there should be personal mothering from the start, if possible by the very person who has conceived and carried that baby, the one who has a very deeply rooted interest in allowing for that baby's point of view, and who loves to let herself be the baby's whole world (Winnicott, 1973 edn, p. 88; italics ours).

He, too, saw the intense interaction tailing off with the life-cycle:

> Tremendous forces are at work in the small child, yet all you need to do is to keep the home together, and to expect anything. Relief will come through the operation of time. When the child is five or six, things will sober down a lot, and will stay sobered down till puberty, so you will have an easier few years, during which you can hand part of the responsibility and part of the task over to the schools, and to the trained teachers (Winnicott, 1973 edn, p. 102).

Both Bowlby and Winnicott dramatized the importance of the early years of mother–child relationship in sharp contrast to later periods, even though they differed in their views on the degree to which early experiences are irreversible and the inevitability of atypical experiences catastrophic.

This created an enormous onus on parents in the children's early years, an expectation often specially difficult to live up to, because the writers concerned did not always concretize what constituted or contravened adequate parental response. Bowlby, for example, posed the question 'Can I then never leave my child?', but his answer—'better safe than sorry'—is equivocal in relation to concrete situations.

Bowlby strongly held the view that lasting emotional ill-effects followed early negative experiences, a process he likened to the lasting biological harm in infants that followed early physical damage. The fact that the critical factors he isolated in this process related to extreme situations unlikely to occur in most families, seems not to have lessened the application of his views by others. In part this may have related to his emphasis to care-givers of the importance of the early years. An example was his recommendation that in the provision of child guidance and counselling services on a large scale, priority should go to those with young children, because it is very difficult to reverse a bad early start (Bowlby, 1972 edn, pp. 105–9).

The underlying ideas became well known in Bowlby's familiar cycle of deprivation thesis, that the impoverished child becomes a socially incapable adult and depriving parent.

> Thus it is seen how children who suffer deprivation grow up to become parents lacking the capacity to care for their children, and how adults lacking this capacity are commonly those who suffered deprivation in childhood. This vicious circle is the most serious aspect of the problem and one to which this book will constantly revert (Bowlby, 1972 edn, p. 79).

He also wrote of a positive cycle, which confirmed for him 'that deprived and unhappy children grow up to make bad parents' (Bowlby, 1972 edn, p. 96). Whilst the kind of evidence used would not be considered scientifically acceptable now (e.g. Bowlby, 1972 edn, p. 118), it seems to have been powerfully persuasive in relation to parental expectations.

Winnicott was less consistent about the absolute primacy of early experience. Sometimes he asserted that the child's experiences in early years were not inevitably decisive:

> It should not be concluded that every baby who is sensitively fed and managed by a devoted mother is necessarily bound to develop complete mental health. Even when the early experiences are good, everything gained has to be consolidated in the course of time. Nor should it be concluded that every baby who is brought up in an institution, or by a mother who is unimaginative or too frightened to trust her own judgment is destined for the mental hospital or Borstal. Things are not as simple as this. I have deliberately simplified the problem for the sake of clarity (Winnicott, 1973 edn, p. 106).

Yet it is the simple rather than the complex form of the message that is remembered, especially when addressed to other care-givers and parents, rather than fellow professionals. This explains the discrepancy between what is credited to people like Winnicott and what they may actually believe. And whilst Winnicott did suggest that the influence of early experiences was limited, he also emphasized their overriding importance. In *The Child, the Family and the Outside World,* he said: 'the foundation of the health of the human being is laid by you in the baby's first weeks and months' (Winnicott, 1973 edn, p. 16).

There are other examples of Winnicott's writing, sometimes telling mothers both that they are not totally responsible for their child's development, and sometimes suggesting that they are.

> Mothers reading what I have written must not be too upset if they have failed in their first contact with one of their children. There are so many reasons why there must be failures, and much can be done at a later date to make up for what has gone wrong, or has been missed. But the risk of making some mothers unhappy must be taken if one is to try to give support to those mothers who can succeed, and who are

succeeding, in this the most important of all mothers' tasks. At any rate, I must risk hurting some who are in difficulties if I am to try to convey my opinion that if a mother is managing her relation to her baby on her own, she is doing the best that she can do for her child, for herself, and for society in general.

In other words, the only true basis for a relation of a child to mother and father, to other children, and eventually to society is the first successful relationship between the mother and baby, between two people, with not even a regular feeding-rule coming between them, nor even a rule that baby must be breast-fed. In human affairs, the more complex can only develop out of the more simple (Winnicott, 1973 edn, p. 34).

Further on, he wrote:

It is not my intention to say that the baby's whole life is wrecked if there has been a failure actually at the breast. Of course a baby can thrive physically on the bottle given with reasonable skill, and a mother whose breast milk fails can do almost all that is needed in the course of bottle-feeding. Nevertheless, the principle holds that a baby's emotional development at the start is only to be built well on a relationship with one person, who should ideally be the mother. Who else will both feel and supply what is needed? (Winnicott, 1973 edn, pp. 91–2).

For many people this kind of writing promotes the tendency to think of parents as either 'good' or 'bad'. Bowlby's book, for example, was structured in terms of this polarity. Because he considered only 'complete deprivation', and not 'partial deprivation', as he called the situation where children lived with their parents who have some negative feelings towards them, he implicitly overlooked anything less than complete loving or complete deprivation. The idea that parents also have mixed feelings, or ambivalence, towards their children was integrated in his work. This lack of attention to feelings of ambivalence was a curious inconsistency for Freudian psychologists, and one which we believe was taken over widely by care-givers. This contributed to setting up idealized expectations for parents who may find them impossible to attain. (Bowlby recognized a range of feelings and motivations in relation to parents of illegitimate and adopted children but did not apply them to 'ordinary' parents.)

Winnicott's writings also suggested that ordinary mothers should express only positive feeling for their children. Whilst he wrote elsewhere on the topic of ambivalence (Winniccott, 1958), and his own conception of mother's love did allow for some negative elements, the latter loomed very small in his writing to parents.

A mother's love is a pretty crude affair. There's possessiveness in it, appetite, even a 'drat that kid' element; there's generosity in it, and power, as well as humility. But sentimentality is outside it altogether, and is repugnant to mothers (Winnicott, 1973 edn, p. 17).

Winnicott was concerned above all with the things a devoted mother does just by being herself:

It is surely tremendously important for a mother to have the experience of doing what she feels like doing, which enables her to discover the fullness of the motherliness in herself . . . (Winnicott, 1973 edn, p. 25).

The expectation arose here, however, that the ordinary good mother, in being herself, would be all loving. The exceptions are few and special. For example, he wrote of women who had not yet begun to want their babies, and whom he saw as possibly having feelings of resentment at the babies' interference in their own lives, though the 'yet' implied that they would eventually come around to wanting them. And whilst Winnicott recognized that child-care did not always entail joy for the mother:

What cannot be taken for granted is the mother's pleasure that goes with the clothing and bathing of her own baby. If you are there enjoying it all, it is like the sun coming out for the baby. The mother's pleasure has to be there or else the whole procedure is dead, useless and mechanical (Winnicott, 1973 edn, p. 27).

He explained away this observation: 'This enjoyment, which comes naturally in the ordinary way, can of course be interfered with by your worries, and worry depends a great deal on ignorance' (Winnicott, 1973 edn, p. 27). So, the argument came across, natural good will prevail unless disturbed:

The stomach . . . is a muscle, rather a complicated one, with a wonderful capacity for doing just what mothers do to their babies; that is, it adapts to new conditions. It does this automatically unless disturbed by excitement, fear, or anxiety, just as mothers are naturally good mothers unless they are tense and anxious (Winnicott, 1973 edn, p. 36).

Accordingly, when the ordinary good mother does have any negative feelings, they do not involve her child, and are not expressed to him or her:

The mother does not involve her baby in all her personal experiences and feelings. Sometimes her baby yells and yells until she feels like murder, yet she lifts the baby up with just the same care, without revenge—or not very much. She avoids making the baby the victim of her own impulsiveness. Infant care, like doctoring, is a test of personal reliability. Today may be one of those days when everything goes wrong. The laundryman calls before the list is ready; the front door bell rings, and someone else comes to the back door. But a mother waits till she has recovered her poise before she takes up her baby, which she does with the usual gentle technique that the baby comes to know as an important part of her. Her technique is highly personal, and is looked for and recognised, like her mouth, and her eyes, her colouring and her smell. Over and over again a mother deals with her own moods, anxieties, and excitements in her own private life, reserving for her baby what belongs to the baby. This gives a foundation on which the human infant can start to build an understanding of the extremely complex things that is a relationship between two human beings (Winnicott, 1973 edn, p. 87).

The major tenets portrayed here have two underlying values: that the conventional division of labour in parenting (mother the primary care-giver and father providing secondary support for the mother–child couplet) is the natural and preferred one; and that the ideal patterns of child-raising be geared to the facilitation of the child's psychological as well as physical developmental needs. The latter has led to the expectation that families should provide maximally favourable conditions for child development.

As we emphasize throughout this review of influential psychoanalytic writings, there has been considerable clarification of the research content of this work. Michael Rutter's *Maternal Deprivation Reassessed* (1974a) offers a thorough review of the experimental research relevant to the 'maternal deprivation' umbrella in purely research terms. His main conclusions, as they pertain here, are that: 'the very existence of a single term "maternal deprivation" has had the most unfortunate consequence of implying one specific syndrome of unitary causation' (Rutter, 1974a, p. 122).

The concept of 'maternal deprivation' has undoubtedly been useful in focussing attention on the sometimes grave consequences of deficient or disturbed care in early life. However, it is now evident that the experiences included under the term 'maternal deprivation' are too heterogeneous and the effects too varied for it to continue to have any usefulness. It has served its purpose and should now be abandoned. That 'bad' care of children in early life can have 'bad' effects, both short-term and long-term, can be accepted as proven. What is now needed is a more precise delineation of the different aspects of 'badness' together with an analysis of their separate effects and of the reasons why children differ in their responses (Rutter, 1974a, p. 128).

There is also discernible amongst psychologists and psychiatrists like Rutter (1974b) and others (e.g. Hoffman, 1974 and Maccoby and Jacklin, 1974) a shift of professional attitude reflecting changing values. The 'unproven' elements of the case for the maternal deprivation hypothesis are now taken by many to open the way for new experimentation in parenting, rather than—as previously—to close the door to it. . . . While we note in passing the impermanence of the value content of the most influential psychoanalytic writings of the 1950s, our intention here is not to trace dimensions of change in professional thinking, but rather to explore the prevalent influences on recent and current expectations of parents. The earlier work of Bowlby and Winnicott in this respect embodies many assumptions and values which are still widely held by parents today, even though the 'leading edge' of professional thought, has been moving on.

FROM SELF-SACRIFICE TO SELF-ACTUALIZATION

These psychoanalytically derived prescriptions for good mothering were challenged by feminists in the late sixties. Psychology was attacked as a form of disguised ideology that plays a key role in women's oppression. Very often such critics failed to distinguish between the actual research and conclusions of academic psychologists and the way in which such research was reported and interpreted. Nonetheless, feminists, along with radical psychologists, made psychologists aware of their many taken-for-granted assumptions about the nature of the social world.

According to two provocative and original American feminists Ehrenreich and English (1979), the pendulum has now swung full circle, from what they call the "masochistic" motherhood of the 1950s (motherhood = self-sacrifice) to the present notion that children should not interfere with women's freedom and independence. In their book, *For Her Own Good*, they try to show how social values relating to the family and personal life have shifted over the past 150 years. They maintain that in recent years there has been a wholesale rejection of the psychoanalytic ideal of mothering, along with its underlying moral premise that women have the primary responsibility to care for children. In the 1960s, they argue, there was a reaction against monogamy and a rejection of motherhood as a career because these old cultural ideals were at odds with the new cultural imperatives of fun, fulfilment, and freedom. The ready availability of new forms of birth control meant that a whole generation of women found themselves able to choose when to become mothers or whether indeed they wished to be mothers at all. As Ehrenreich and English point out, the massive shifts in social values that occurred in the late sixties brought in its wake new uncertainties about how to live one's life, what choices to make, how to use one's new found freedom. Women were receptive to oracles and sages.

In the extract that is reproduced here, Ehrenreich and English offer a critical appraisal of what they call the "human potential movement," a form of "pop" psychology which flourished in the late 1960s and in the 1970s. You will find that they are extremely hostile to the underlying premises of much of this "pop" psychology of self-actualization and self-fulfilment. What they consider to be particularly objectionable about the whole approach to social relations promoted by the counter-culture is its egoistic, individualistic philosophy. You should ask yourself as you read this extract whether Ehrenreich and English have overstated their case. In reacting against a certain form of "pop" psychology have they failed to distinguish between the academic tradition of humanist psychology and those who have exploited the movement for financial gain?

Reading XXI. For Her Own Good: 150 Years of Experts' Advice to Women, by B. Ehrenreich and D. English

With the spread of the "singles lifestyle" in the sixties and seventies, the media rushed to celebrate the "liberation" of the American woman. The kitchen and the nursery no longer beckoned as the unique arena for female creativity. Babies were no longer the self-evident climax of adult life. Work was crowding out of the peripheries of women's lives and into what had once been the peak years of reproductivity. And sex, once supposed to be the glue of perpetual matrimony, had become detached from any commitments—it was something a woman did for *herself.* Hip men and "sensitive" advertisers congratulated the sexy, self-supporting woman:

Source: Ehrenreich, B., & English, D. (1979). An extract taken from *For Her Own Good: 150 Years of Experts' Advice to Women.* London: Pluto Press, pp. 268–281.

"You've come a long way, Baby."

But for women it was an ambiguous kind of liberation. After the old dependency came the new insecurity of shifting relationships, a competitive work world, unstable marriages—an insecurity from which no woman could count herself "safe" and settled. There was a sense of being adrift, but now there was no one to turn to. The old romantic ideology, buttressed by 150 years of psychomedical theory, was transparently useless, and the old experts were increasingly discredited. The post-romantic era called for a new ethos, a new ideology, new rules of "right living."

Popular Psychology and the Single Girl

. . . [It was not long] before an entirely new school of experts made their dashing entrance on the scene. The proponents of the new popular psychology, or "pop psychology," broke with Freud, with medical science, and ultimately with science itself. They made few claims to "data," laboratory studies, or clinical experience. The new psychology would become, openly and without intellectual pretension, the mass ideology of the consumer society, the lore of the adman and the Market researcher, condensed into easy-to-read guidelines for daily living.

The new "marketplace psychology" was of course aimed at men and women—anyone who could pay fifteen to thirty dollars for a group-therapy session or $2.95 for a paperback. But its most revolutionary message was for women. The pop psychologists took the step which the neo-Freudians had drawn back from: they accepted permissiveness as a program of universal liberation—not only for infants, teen-agers and work-weary dads—but for women too. The new psychology was distinctly, and vociferously, *antimasochistic*. Suddenly the epidemic of "rejection of femininity" went the way of hysteria and other obsolete diseases. The new experts were concerned with a new and equally widespread syndrome: "femininity" itself. Women had been "brainwashed" (by their mothers, said the experts) to be passive and submissive. Taking a tip from Helen Gurley Brown, the experts now revealed that men weren't interested in the old "stereotypes," as they were now called. "Men don't want relationships with frail baby-dolls," announces the title page of an assertiveness training manual, "they want the excitement of a fully grown woman." [Baer, 1976.] And trusted popular writers like Dr. Joyce Brothers brought the message back from the frontiers of urban experimentation to the backwoods of middle American marriage: the time had come even for wives to "put themselves first." [Brothers, 1972, p. 190.]

The new pop psychology was invigorating, even lifesaving, news to the millions of women it reached through therapy groups, talk-show experts, self-help books and magazine articles. So they hadn't been crazy all along to blow up at that inverted bowl of Rice Krispies on the floor and the dirty socks on the coffee table. So it was all right for a woman to want something for herself, whether it was better sex or a higher salary or a little bit of recognition. Pop psychology amplified the youthful voice of the new feminism: It's OK to be angry; it's OK to be a woman; it's OK to be *you*. Summing up her own transformation by the new psychology, one woman wrote:

I'm entitled. That's what I learned . . . I'm entitled to a life of my own. I don't have to do everything *they* want. I'm not bad for wanting to do what they don't approve of—my mother, my husband, my sons. [Coleman, 1972, p. xii.]

But ultimately the new psychology turned out to be as misogynistic as anything that might creep out from under the fallen log of sexual romanticism. Romanticist ideology, finding no place for the values of love and nurturance in the Market, had fastened them onto woman. More precisely, nailed them into her flesh. Women would love in a world that did not honor love, so, as it was put in the final neo-Freudian debacle, women would have to love *pain*. But the new ideology was willing to accept the values of the marketplace as *universal* principles; in the world of the marketplace psychologists there was *no* place for the old "human" values of love and caring—not even on the backs of women. In a flash all the feminine traits which had been glorified as natural and instinctual were exposed as the trappings of a "socialized sex role," which—almost overnight—had become obsolete.

The marketplace psychology that would set guidelines for the new woman of the sixties and seventies was first born in the expansive, almost rebellious atmosphere of the Human Potential Movement. The HPM grew out of the broad spectrum of psychological methods and styles which flourished together in the iconoclastic atmosphere of the nineteen sixties. The thrust of the movement grew from the work of "Third Force" ("humanist") psychologists—neither Freudians nor behaviorists— optimistically dedicated to the "self-actualization" of a psyche presumed to be possessed of an almost infinite capacity for expansion. By the mid-sixties, psychotherapists from every kind of professional background were becoming excited by the mass appeal of the movement, its dramatic techniques (such as group work, physical touch, and direct expression of feelings) and its utopian vision of mass psychological transformation.

Because it was concerned with the "expansion of human potential," the new psychology was for everyone. "If there is one statement true of every living person it must be this: he hasn't achieved his full potential." [Schutz, 1967, p. 15.] HPM methods were not about "making sick people well"—they were about "making well people better." In fact, the new techniques worked best on people who were "healthy" and "open" (encounter group leaders learned that psychotics and neurotics had to be screened *out* or the new "expansion" techniques would only worsen them by bringing up "unmanageable material").

The point of achieving one's full potential, according to HPM ideologues, was not to be able to get more work done, or make a greater contribution to society, or any other old-fashioned "inner-directed" goal—but simply to have more fun. In *Joy*, an early manifesto of the HPM, Dr. Schutz tells us that the worst aspect of unfulfilled potential is that it "robs us of pleasure and joy in living." With the techniques he recommends (developed in experiments in the Air Force and various corporations) as well as at Esalen, the institutional mecca of the HPM, he promises a return to the bliss of childhood: "Perhaps we can recapture some joy, regain some of the body-pleasures, share again the joy with other people that was once possible." [Schutz, 1967, p. 10.] Schutz looked at his own newborn son as a creature who was in danger of losing his infant joyousness as he grew up, unless *Joy* techniques were widely practiced: "We'd better hurry," he warned, "The culture is already getting to him—Ethan looks as if he is beginning to feel frightened and guilty." [Schutz, 1967, p. 12.][1]

A major theme of the HPM and the various schools of pop psychology which followed it was that you didn't *have* to grow up, at least not in any old-fashioned, repressive, Freudian sense. Why be forced to give up the pleasures of a permissive childhood at any age? Characteristically, pop psychology sought psychic liberation through sensual indulgence, peer-group closeness, sexual experience, and other characteristic discoveries of adolescence transported to the world of adults. It gave a place of honor to "the child within us" as a permanent inhabitant, as if the Gesellian infant "with all his inborn wisdom" remained within each of us in a state of perfect preservation, lovable and hedonistic. While the birth rate fell throughout the sixties and seventies, more and more adult Americans were looking within themselves to find the "child" that they would nurture.

But the fact that you didn't have to grow up didn't mean you didn't have to *change*. HPM theory implied that it is not only a pleasure to expand oneself but almost an obligation: Who could be sure that their personality didn't need improvement? Any rejection, any dead-end relationship, any failure to advance at work could point to the need for psychological help.

In the context of the singles culture, with its rapid-turnover "relationships," compulsive sexiness, and nervous pressure to have "fun," this message took on special urgency. People were easily convinced that their personalities did need work, and hundreds of thousands of seekers from every kind of background converged at the sites of the new psychological practices. HPM workshops of every stripe flourished in locations as disparate as suburban community centers, college and high school campuses, corporation boardrooms, in every conceivable type of

---

[1]Writing in the sixites, Schutz had political ambitions that HPM techniques could be useful in containing youthful radicalism. He hoped that what he had to teach would ease the "current 'credibility gap' . . . that is eroding a political administration," and that it would answer "youth's demand that we 'tell it like it is.' " He even went so far as to suggest that the new techniques might match the joys of the drug culture.

professional and semiprofessional training program, in political organizations, and even in churches. Speaking of encounter groups alone, psychiatrist Joel Kovel writes:

> . . . such groups constitute a major social phenomenon, albeit one that seems, like acid rock, to have peaked in the late Sixties. It had to. At the rate it was growing then, the movement would have engulfed all other forms of social organization by now had it not slowed. I recall being told during a visit to Palo Alto, California, in 1969 that that modest-sized town sported something like 360 ongoing groups. [Kovel, 1976, p. 166.]

When encounter groups peaked, other therapies had already begun to fill the gap, including Psychodrama, Gestalt, Transactional Analysis, Primal Therapy, more unorthodox new ones (such as "est") and even "traditional" methods—like Jungian, Reichian, or Sullivanian approaches—plus a hundred "eclectic" variations on all of them. In addition there were "theme" groups—groups for the married, or the divorced, groups for smokers, or overeaters, or insomniacs. "Joy is burgeoning" exulted Schutz prophetically in 1967, exclaiming that if things kept going right, all of our institutions and even "the establishment" would soon be hooked on joy. [Schutz, 1967, p. 223.]

With this mass demand for psychological counsel, psychotherapy became a growth industry in itself, and soon a degree in psychology became one of the best bets for a college graduate looking for guaranteed status and money. But "pop psych" was too much of a bonanza to be contained by any mere academic discipline. Only a psychoanalyst can psychoanalyze you, but lots of people can be "marriage counselors" or "group leaders," and just about anyone with a typewriter can write a book advising millions of people on how to live. A horde of new psychological experts, loosely educated with a few inhalations of HPM doctrine, rushed in to meet the demand for guidelines in the confusing new singles culture. Frontrunners in the psychological gold rush were the veterans of the manipulation industries (marketing and advertising) who, recognizing that this was their natural turf, began the mass production of self-help books in the nineteen seventies. Jean Owen, whose background is in television audience and opinion research is the interviewer-editor of the best-selling *How to Be Your Own Best Friend. I Ain't Much, Baby—but I'm All I've Got*, a popular book followed up with *I Ain't Well—but I sure Am Better* were written by Jess Lair, who had a successful career as a marketing and management consultant before getting a Ph.D. in psychology.

Success Through Transactional Analysis, by Jut Meininger, applies TA directly to business. *How to Say No Without Feeling Guilty* was co-authored by Dr. Herbert Fensterheim and Jean Baer (his wife) the former public relations director of *Seventeen* magazine. After the success of *How to Say No*, Jean Baer broke into the psych market on her own with *How to Be an Assertive (Not Aggressive) Woman*.

Soon even the strongholds of academic psychomedicine, finding themselves left holding the old bag of romantic-masochistic formulas, had to stoop to learn from the paperback book racks. Jean Baer co-led an assertiveness training pilot study program at the Payne Whitney clinic of the New York Hospital. Eric Berne, who was denied admittance to the American Psychoanalytic Association in light of his Transactional Analysis theories, would, had he lived, have had the satisfaction of seeing TA taught in medical schools and Ph.D. programs. Freud was relegated to the back shelves while the more progressive M.D. and Ph.D. programs rushed to catch up with Gestalt, TA, "behavior mod" and their more overtly commercial variations.

With the seventies' boom in self-help book sales, modern market-place psychology, composed of one part HPM philosophy (drawn eclectically from the burgeoning new pop psych tendencies) and two parts sheer hardheaded marketing cunning, really took off as a mass cultural phenomenon on its own. Marketplace psychology took the cheerful expansiveness of the HPM and transformed it into a philosophy of ruthless self-centeredness. In the post-romantic world, where the old ties no longer bind, all that matters is *you*: you can be what you *want* to be; you *choose* your life, your environment, even your appearance and your emotions. Nothing "happens to" you. There are no "can'ts," only "won'ts." You don't have to be the victim even of your own emotional reactions: you choose to feel what you *want* to feel. "You are free when you accept the responsibility for your choices," write Newman and Berkowitz in *How to Be Your Own Best Friend*, adding that the only obstacles they know of are that "people cling to their chains." Similarly, Transactional Analysis is "realistic," according to popularizer Thomas Harris, M.D., ". . . in that it confronts the patient with the fact that he is responsible for what happens in the future no matter what has happened in the past," [Harris, 1967, p. 14.] In pop psychology logic it followed that the only thing that held women back was a "negative mental set": ". . . women don't think of themselves as equal to men so they don't act equal; consequently men, employers, relatives, society do not treat them as equal." [Baer, 1976, p. 12.]

The corollary of the proposition that you are totally responsible for your feelings is that you are *not* responsible for anything else: "You don't have to live up to anyone's expectations." Selfishness is not a "dirty word"—it is merely an "expression of the law of self-preservation." [Greenwald, 1973, p. 19.] A behavior-modification book warns you that when you embark on their program people will accuse you of being selfish, egotistical, or egocentric. Don't worry. The person who does this "is himself self-centered and is merely saying, indirectly: You are not centering enough on ME." [Newberger & Lee, 1974, p. 25.] Book after book assumes that the one way to avoid being "stepped on" is to "put yourself first." They promise to help you look out for Number One, or to help the person you love the most—yourself!: "Selfishness (self-ness) is simply the recognition and acceptance of the reality that each person is the

most important person in the world to himself." [Greenwald, 1973, p. 26.]
The flip side of "Don't be a victim" is "Don't rescue" any other victims.
The "Gestalt Prayer" which found its way onto thousands of posters,
greeting cards, and coffee mugs, puts it best:

> I do my thing, and you do your thing.
> I am not in this world to live up to
>   your expectations
> And you are not in this world to live
>   up to mine.
> You are you and I am I, and if by chance
>   we find each other, it's beautiful
> If not, it can't be helped. [Perls & Stevens, 1969, p. 4.]

If you are not responsible to anyone but yourself, it follows that
relationships with other people are merely there to be exploited when
(emotionally) profitable, and terminated when they cease to be profitable.
The primary assumption is that each person in a relationship has a set of
emotional, sexual, or other "needs" which he or she wants met. If they are
no longer being satisfied by a friend or sexual partner, then that bond may
be broken just as reasonably as a buyer would take his business away from
a seller if he found a better price. The *needs* have an inherent
legitimacy—the *people* are replaceable.

Thus, a bad relationship is one where you "put in" more than you "get
out." Relationships—especially marriages—are in reality financial/
emotional "contracts" in which rights and responsibilities should be clearly
agreed on, and preferably spelled out in writing, down to the last intimate
expectation. With this the veil of sentimentality is finally torn away
from what Charlotte Perkins Gilman had called the "sexuo-economic
relation." Marriage, it is revealed, is a deal like any other which begins
when two people "sell" themselves to each other. Robert Ringer (former
real estate salesman and author of *Winning Through Intimidation* and
Looking Out for Number One) sets forth these four steps for successful
personal "selling":

1) Obtain a product to sell (e.g., a woman's "product" could very well
   be *herself*—as a wife),
2) Locate a market for the product (in the above example this would
   consist of available men who would meet her standards),
3) Implement a marketing method (put into effect a procedure for
   selling herself), and
4) Be able to close the sale (get the stiff to sign on the dotted line and
   hand over the ring). [Ringer, 1974, p. 96]

Once you're in a relationship, according to another advice book, its
success will be based on such conditions as "the desire and ability of both
partners to reinforce the expectations of each in a trade negotiation

sufficiently balanced to maintain consonance." For example, an assertiveness training manual recommends that couples follow certain rules for "behavior exchange contracts" in which couples alter their behavior for each other. Some of the rules include:

> a. Each partner gets something he/she wants from the other. For instance, you contract to "wear a nice robe in the morning instead of that torn one." He agrees to "come home for dinner on time instead of drinking with the boys." You start with simple behaviors and progress to more complex ("She should initiate more sex . . ." "He should kiss me more.") . . .
> d. Whenever possible, keep track of the target behavior with graphs, charts, points, or tokens.
> e. Avoid disagreements about the contract by writing it out. Keep it in a spot where you both can see it easily. Many couples put it on the refrigerator or bedroom door. When you effect one Behavior Exchange Contract to your mutual satisfaction, go on to another. [Baer, 1976, p. 208.]

Should such negotiations break down, according to a different book, there can be a "successful divorce,"—by no means to be thought of as a failure—but one which "has been pre-considered in terms of personal upward mobility, with stress laid not nearly so much on what is being left, and may therefore be lost, as on what lies ahead that may be incorporated into a new and better image." [Newberger & Lee, 1974, p. 25.] After the successful divorce, this behavior-modification book tells us, "Little Affairs" may be useful for many reasons including "the opportunity to replace lovers who have contributed sexual dissonance with others more able to contribute consonance." The person with a "Positive Self Image" need not worry about promiscuity. *All* these affairs will be "meaningful" because they will all contribute to the "self's reservoir of experiences."

If relationships are business transactions, the Self is now an owner, an investor, and a consumer. One can almost hear the scratching of pencil on paper as the "strokes" are counted and the tabulations of love-given/love-received are totaled up. In the language of psycho-business, we are smart to capitalize on our assets and cut our losses, maximize the return on our (emotional) investments, and in general put all our relationships—whether with lovers, co-workers, or family members—on the psychic equivalent of a cash 'n' carry basis.

From the business metaphor for relationships, it's a quick leap to the "game" metaphor—already so stylish in the real business world. Marketplace psychology divides the world into two categories of people—"winners" and "losers." The *Winner's Notebook, Born to Win, Winners and Losers,* and *Winning Through Intimidation* are only a few titles from the self-help book rack. (In the nineteenth-century economy, everyone knew that most people would be "losers." But in the modern consumption-centered economy, where "winning" doesn't necessarily mean gaining wealth and power, but having fun—suddenly everyone can be a "winner": it just takes the right frame of mind.) "What is called for is concentration on the forthcoming material and the desire to minimize losing streaks while maximizing winning ones," says *Winners and Losers.* "In poker, it's done every day in the week: Cut your losses; throw in the bad or "maybe" hands and bet big on the good ones." [Newberger & Lee, 1974, p. 192.] And don't get too upset about anything—it's only a game!

As an abstract system, marketplace psychology postulates an emotional "economy" in which standardized "players' interact, like real business-men, according to definite rules of possession and exchange. Standardizing the players is the hard part, since they are, of course, human. The first step is to dismiss, as much as possible, the unique personal past. Almost all the marketplace psychologists pride themselves on their avoidance of time-consuming and confusing history: One Gestalt book dismisses the past with the words, ". . . reality exists only in the present. A person's memory of the past (despite his sincere denials of this fact) is a collection of obsolete distortions and misperceptions." With their personal autobiographies eradicated, people do appear more similar, and can be analyzed in terms of their needs and their behavior in the here-and-now: "What we do and how we function *is* our self." [Greenwald, 1973, p. 10.] The conception of the self is simplified, and whenever possible, mechanized. "The brain functions as a high-fidelity tape recorder" says Harris. "The Adult [ego-state] is a data-processing computer." When they're not tape-recorders or computers, people most often appear as robots whose "programming" keeps them from taking in "positive input" or from stopping other robots, who are looking for "negative payoffs," from pushing their "anger buttons." "Freedom," is, of course, "standing at your own controls."

The rules of possession are clear: First of all, concentrate on "owning yourself" and "owning your feelings," because everyone else will be busy doing the same. No more will love be sung to the tune of romantic bondage—"we belong to each other," "I gave my heart to him," "I'm going to make her mine" and so forth. No, in the new game you never give yourself away completely:

> . . . an adult, when he loves, does not risk his whole identity. That he already has, and will have however the other responds. If he loses his lover, he will still have himself. But if you look to someone else to establish your identity for you in some way, losing that person can make you really feel destroyed. [Newman, Berkowitz, & Owen, 1971, p. 74.]

To this self-possessed adult in a universe of standardized "selves," not even death makes too much of an impact. One of the psychiatrist-authors of *How to Be Your Own Best Friend* recalls:

I once was seeing a man who was grieving deeply. The person he had been closest to had died, and he felt utterly desolate. I sat with him and could feel the depths of his sorrow. Finally, I said to him, "You look as if you had lost your best friend." He said, "Well I have." And I said, "Don't you know who your best friend is?" He looked at me, surprised. He thought a moment, and tears came into his eyes. Then he said, "I guess it's true—you are your own best friend." [Newman et al., 1971, p. 88.]

In the world of standardized, interchangeable "players," all relationships are governed by the marketplace principle of equivalent exchange. If the two of you can establish an equitable stroke exchange: beautiful. If not, it can't be helped: move on to another player. The old hierarchies of protection and dependency no longer exist, there are only free contracts, freely terminated. The marketplace, which had long ago expanded to include the relations of production, has now expanded to include *all* relationships.

The new psychology recognized at once that women were entering the expanded emotional-economic marketplace with a special handicap: they had been prepared since childhood for a life of unqualified *giving*, in a framework of stable, protective relationships. This handicap called for a special sort of mass therapy—something which could provide women with the "survival skills" they would now need in a world dominated by the singles culture. Assertiveness Training, as the new therapy was labeled, called for nothing short of a complete psychological make-over. According to the introduction to one manual women were recognizing that "there was a kind of disability in our femininity" [Bloom, Coburn, & Pearlman, 1976, p. 11] and that if they were not going to go under in the fierce personal and occupational race, they would have to change—fast.

With very little hesitation, the assertiveness-training books fastened on male behavior as the model. They observed that most men don't have assertiveness problems; their socialization has given them the proper degree of self-centeredness. But "Society has never impressed on women as it has on men the absolute necessity of putting yourself first." [Brothers, 1972, p. 190.] The assertiveness training books enviously praise the emotional upbringing of boys in stark contrast to the experiences of girls:

Had you been born a boy, you'd probably have been welcomed warmly, with expectations of either following in Father's footsteps (if they're big ones) or of surpassing him. As a girl, however, your greeting may be more subdued—particularly if you already have an older sister. "Oh well, maybe we'll try again," Dad might say. "She is a pretty little thing." . . . If you have in fact put yourself first you've learned to feel guilty afterward, in contrast to boys, who can assert themselves, say what they want—and even fight to get it! [Bloom et al., 1976, p. 11.]

The fortunate men have no trouble with the marketplace or with marketplace psychology—but women have to unlearn their socialization and imitate the male style. One book on how women can make it in managerial jobs counsels: "Above all, don't show emotion and *never* cry in front of a male co-worker. Men have spent their lives learning to repress tears; women have a lot of catching up to do." [Bernay, 1977, p. 80.]

Assertiveness training, like popular psychology generally, is meant to be applied to all situations—work, sexual relationships, friendships. One assertiveness-training book opens with the following illustration of how to be "assertive" with a woman friend: In the story, "you" are at home alone, the housework done. You have some free time—two hours "just for yourself." Then the phone rings. It's a friend asking if you would please, as a very special favor, watch her two-year-old daughter Alison for the morning while she goes out to a meeting. You have a "familiar sinking feeling in your stomach." You *really* wanted those two hours for yourself:

> If you were non-assertive you could simply deny your own wishes, and agree to care for Alison: "Well, I was going to do something else, but it really doesn't matter. O.K., bring her over."
>
> Or you could say, *assertively,* "I know it's a drag to take Alison with you, but I've set aside two hours for myself this morning, so I won't be able to take her today." [Bloom et al., 1976, pp. 24–25.]

The book promises to help you learn to do what you want to do. Neatly evaded is the annoying question of what is *right* to do. There is no room here for you to balance Alison's mother's need to go to the meeting against your need to have two hours alone; nor of Alison's mother's relative hardships against your own. The only possible reason to take care of Alison is because you *want* to do it (which in fact the authors assume you don't). The acknowledgment, "I know it's a drag to take Alison with you" is nothing but a psychological "technique" intended to make the friend *feel* that you sympathize, even as you refuse to help. One is left to wonder what will become of Alison's mother when she arrives at her meeting, child-in-tow, only to be told—assertively—that they really don't want children at the meetings any more.

But in the dog-eat-dog sexual marketplace no woman can afford an old-fashioned sense of responsibility to other women. One assertiveness-training book lists a series of single women's rights, including the right to—"date a married man":

> Do you want this right? It's a decision only you can make. Today, in these days of urban renewal, Back Street has practically ceased to exist. The Other Woman is alive, well, and living everywhere from one-room efficiency to posh pad ... today's OW may suffer some guilts, but she ... does not consider herself immoral; she sees herself as a moral, self-respecting woman who is in the Other Woman situation. [Baer, 1976, p. 173.]

Like a boomerang, this denial of the existence of any moral values comes back to strike at all women. The marketplace model purports to be egalitarian or even feminist. But in fact it assumes a false equality, and denies that women have any special needs or experience any special discrimination as women. Even the ideal object of marketplace psychology, the single girl with no family responsibilities, has "handicaps" which can't be overcome by any amount of psychotherapy or paperback self-help. Assertiveness training doesn't remove the hazards of contraception, the risks of pregnancy, the price of an abortion.

But it is over the issue of children that marketplace psychology completely breaks down as a practical philosophy for women. The relationships in the pop psychology books are never relationships with children, and when a child appears, like little Alison, it is assumed that *nobody* wants her. After all, how can you run a relationship with a child on the principle of equivalent exchange? Do you ignore the infant who doesn't give you enough "strokes"? Refuse to make breakfast for the two-year-old who peed on its sheets last night? Desert a child who doesn't meet your needs (kindly reciting the Gestalt Prayer as you go)? When confronted with the problem of children—always introduced as a "problem," an obstacle to women's mobility—the marketplace psychologists suddenly become rigid, judgmental and even scolding:

> I'm not against day care or careers for women. But having children is—or ought to be—a choice. If women want to have babies, they should. If they don't want to raise children, they shouldn't have them . . . They can lobby for day-care centers if they like, but they shouldn't feel like victims. [Newman et al., 1977, p. 34.]

And in *Winners and Losers*, the authors ask themselves: "Aren't divorced men better off, because they're usually without children, involved in work, and also freer to find social and sexual partners?" and answer:

> If men are better off in any area of divorce, it's because they choose to be better off; if women are worse off, it's because they've chosen to be worse off . . . As for freedom from children, the best way to be free from children is not to conceive them. . . . [Newberger & Lee, 1974, p. 25.]

Psychological ideology had swung 180 degrees from the neo-Freudian theories of libidinal motherhood and female masochism. From being the only source of fulfillment in a woman's life children had become an obstacle to her freedom. From being a symbolic act of submission, sex had become a pleasurable commodity which women as well as men had a right to demand. The old rationalist promise that the forces of the Market would break the ancient ties of the family seemed to be coming true, and the ideology of sexual romanticism at last began to crumble. But if the rules imposed by sexual romanticism had denied women any future other than service to the family, the new psychology seemed to deny human bonds altogether—for women or for men. Pop psychology, which had begin with the effusive evocation of universal joy, ended up with the grim "realism" of the lifeboat strategy: not everyone can get on board, so survival depends on learning how to fight it out on the way to "getting yours." Despite their radical break with sexual romanticism, the experts of marketplace psychology ended up promoting an ideal of women's nature which was no less distorted and limiting than the ideal which had once been advanced by nineteenth- century gynecology.

THE ANTI-PSYCHIATRIST AS CULTURE CRITIC

In Britain, as in America, the late 1960s was a period of experimentation, of seeking for new life styles and social philosophies. American writings on humanistic psychology made an impact on British culture. Encounter groups and other spin-offs from the "human potential movement" became fashionable. In Britain there was also a great deal of interest in the topic of mental illness, kindled by the writings of Laing, Cooper and Esterson, all of whom came to be identified with the anti-psychiatry movement. It is hard to define precisely what this movement represented. In a book called *The Radical Therapist,* Steiner outlined four beliefs (1974, pp. 16–17) that were widely endorsed and they are summarized here:

1. The first principle of radical psychiatry is that in the absence of oppression, human beings will, due to their nature or soul . . . live in harmony with nature and each other.
2. The second principle is that alienation is the essence of all psychiatric conditions. Everything diagnosed psychiatrically, unless *clearly* organic in origin, is a form of alienation.
3. All alienation is the result of oppression. The oppressed are mystified or deceived about the origins of their oppression. As a result, people feel that their alienation is their own fault.
4. Psychiatry as it is predominantly practised today has a great deal to do with the deception of human beings about their oppression.

Although various ideas expressed by the anti-psychiatry movement had been current in intellectual and academic circles for a decade or more, it was Laing who succeeded in popularizing and promoting them to a much broader audience. His books were widely read and his influence spread far beyond the academic environment. In the Preface to a book that examined Laing's contribution to anti-psychiatry, Boyers (1972) had this to say about his influence:

He is . . . a psychiatrist who first made his reputation by writing about his experience in treating psychotic, more specifically schizophrenic, patients, but his audience is hardly a professional one, and many who applaud his psychiatric researches can be said to know very little indeed either about mental illness or the history of psychoanalysis . . . one must suppose, it is as a culture critic, a new species of psychiatrist as prophet, that Laing [should] be known, for he has chosen in his most recent writings to combine the examination of severe mental disorders with a more general assault on the foundations of Western civilization. This is a project that has attracted a large following among philosophers, sociologists, literary people, religionists, practically any group interested in the history of ideas and the dimensions of contemporary culture, with the possible exception of Laing's own colleagues in the psychiatric profession (p. 7).

In his early writings, Laing concentrated on schizophrenia and family life. His self-professed goal was to give an existential account of madness which was in plain English. The extract that follows is from *The Politics of Experience and the Bird of Paradise,* (1967), a book that introduced many people to Laing's ideas. The book is comprised of a series of essays and papers that were published separately during the 1960s. The selection that we present is taken from Chapter 4 and is based on a paper which originally appeared in *New Left Review.* We think that this paper conveys the flavour of Laing's early work, and shows him in his most social-psychological phase. He tackles the complex problem of how human action is built up from our personal experience, from our perceptions or assumptions about other people's experience, and from how we think other people perceive our reality. Alienation is the end product of misperceptions and communication breakdowns. When you read Laing you may form your own conclusions as to why he enjoyed such a tremendous popular following.

Reading XXII.   Us and Them,
by R. D. Laing

. . . once certain fundamental structures of experience are shared, they come to be experienced as objective entities. These reified projections of our own freedom are then introjected. By the time the sociologists study these projected-introjected reifications, they have taken on the appearance of things. They are not things ontologically. But they are pseudo-things. Thus far Durkheim was quite right to emphasize that collective representations come to be experienced as things, exterior to anyone. They take on the force and character of partial autonomous realities, with their own way of life. A social norm may come to impose an oppressive obligation on everyone, although few people feel it to be their own. . . .

Them

Gossip and scandal are always and everywhere elsewhere. Each person is the other to the others. The members of a scandal network may be unified by ideas to which no one will admit in his own person. Each person is thinking of what he thinks the other thinks. The other, in turn, thinks of what yet another thinks. Each person does not mind a coloured lodger, but each person's neighbour does. Each person, however, is a neighbour of his neighbour. What They think is held with conviction. It is indubitable and it is incontestable. The scandal group is a series of others which each serial number repudiates in himself.

It is always the others, and always elsewhere, and each person feels unable to make any difference to Them. I have no objection to my daughter marrying a Gentile really but we live in a Jewish neighbourhood after all. Such collective power is in proportion to each person's creation of this power and his own impotence.

This is seen very clearly in the following inverted Romeo and Juliet situation.

John and Mary have a love affair, and just as they are ending it Mary finds she is pregnant. Both families are informed. Mary does not want to marry John. John does not want to marry Mary. But John thinks Mary wants him to marry her, and Mary does not want to hurt John's feelings by telling him that she does not want to marry him—as she thinks he wants to marry her, and that he thinks she wants to marry him.

The two families, however, compound the confusion considerably. Mary's mother takes to bed screaming and in tears because of the disgrace—what people are saying about the way she brought her daughter up. She does not mind the situation 'in itself', especially as the girl is going

Source: Laing, R. D. (1967). *The Politics of Experience and the Bird of Paradise*. Harmondsworth; Penguin, pp. 65–82.

to be married, but she takes to heart what everyone will be saying. No one in their own person in either family ('. . . if it only affected me . . .') is in the least concerned for their own sake, but everyone is very concerned about the effect of 'gossip' and 'scandal' on everyone else. The concern focuses itself mainly on the boy's father and the girl's mother, both of whom require to be consoled at great length for the terrible blow. The boy's father is worried about what the girl's mother will think of him. The girl's mother is worried about what 'everyone' will think of her. The boy is concerned at what the family thinks he has done to his father, and so on.

The tension spirals up within a few days to the complete engrossment of all members of both families in various forms of tears, wringing of hands, recriminations, apologies.

Typical utterances are:

MOTHER *to* GIRL: Even if he does want to marry you, how can he ever respect you after what people will have been saying about you recently?

GIRL (*some time later*): I had finally got fed up with him just before I found I was pregnant, but I didn't want to hurt his feelings because he was so in love with me.

BOY: If it had not been that I owed it to my father for all he had done for me, I would have arranged that she got rid of it. But then everyone knew by then.

Everyone knew because the son told his father who told his wife who told her eldest son who told his wife . . . etc.

Such processes seem to have a dynamism divorced from the individuals. But in this and every other case this process is a form of alienation, intelligible when, and only when, the steps in the vicissitudes of its alienation from each and every person can be retraced back to what at each and every moment is their only origin: the experience and actions of each and every single person.

Now the peculiar thing about Them is that They are created only by each one of us repudiating his own identity. When we have installed Them in our hearts, we are only a plurality of solitudes in which what each person has in common is his allocation to the other of the necessity for his own actions. Each person, however, as other to the other, is the other's necessity. Each denies any internal bond with the others; each person claims his own inessentiality: 'I just carried out my orders. If I had not done so, someone else would have', 'Why don't you sign? Everyone else has', etc. Yet although I can make no difference, I cannot act differently. No single other person is any more necessary to me than I claim to be to Them. But just as he is 'one of Them' to me, so I am 'one of Them' to him. In this collection of reciprocal indifference, of reciprocal inessentiality and solitude, there appears to exist no freedom. There is conformity to a *presence* that is everywhere *elsewhere.*

Us

. . . Some families live in perpetual anxiety of what, to them, is an external persecuting world. The members of the family live in a family ghetto, as it were. This is one basis for so-called maternal over-protection. It is not 'over'-protection from the mother's point of view, nor, indeed, often from the point of view of other members of the family.

The 'protection' that such a family offers its members seems to be based on several preconditions: (i) a phantasy of the external world as extraordinarily dangerous; (ii) the generation of terror inside the nexus at this external danger. The 'work' of the nexus is the generation of this terror. This work is *violence*.

The stability of the nexus is the product of terror generated in its members by the work (violence) done by the members of the group on each other. Such family 'homeostasis' is the product of reciprocities mediated under the statutes of violence and terror.

The highest ethic of the nexus is reciprocal concern. Each person is concerned about what the other thinks, feels, does. He may come to regard it as his *right* to expect the others to be concerned about him, and to regard himself as under an obligation to feel concern towards them in turn. I make no move without feeling it as my right that you should be happy or sad, proud or ashamed, of what I do. Every action of mine is always the concern of the other members of the group. And I regard you as callous if you do not concern yourself about my concern for you when you do anything.

A family can act as gangsters, offering each other mutual protection against each other's violence. It is a reciprocal terrorism, with the offer of protection-security against the violence that each threatens the other with, and is threatened by, if anyone steps out of line.

My concern, my concern for your concern, your concern, and your concern for my concern, etc. is an infinite spiral, upon which rests my pride or shame in my father, sister, brother, my mother, my son, my daughter.

The essential characteristic of the nexus is that every action of one person is expected to have reference to and to influence everyone else. The nature of this influence is expected to be reciprocal.

Each person is expected to be controlled, and to control the others, by the reciprocal effect that each has on the other. To be affected by the others' actions or feelings is 'natural'. It is not 'natural' if father is neither proud nor ashamed of son, daughter, mother etc. According to this ethic, action done to please, to make happy, to show one's gratitude to the other is the highest form of action. This reciprocal transpersonal cause-effect is a self-actualizing presumption. In this 'game', it is a foul to use this interdependence to hurt the other, except in the service of the nexus, but the worst crime of all is to refuse to act in terms of this presumption.

Examples of this in action are:

Peter gives Paul something. If Paul is not pleased, or refuses the gift, he is ungrateful for what is being done for him. Or: Peter is made unhappy if Paul does something. Therefore if Paul does it he is making Peter unhappy. If Peter is made unhappy, Paul is inconsiderate, callous, selfish, ungrateful. Or: if Peter is prepared to make sacrifices for Paul, so Paul should be prepared to make sacrifices for Peter, or else he is selfish, ungrateful, callous, ruthless, etc.

'Sacrifice' under these circumstances consists in Peter impoverishing himself to do something for Paul. It is the tactic of *enforced debt*. One way of putting this is that each person *invests in the other*. . . .

It is just as well that man is a social animal, since the sheer complexity and contradiction of the social field in which he has to live is so formidable.

MENTAL ILLNESS AS A METAPHOR FOR MODERN LIFE

How can we explain the popular success that Laing enjoyed for more than a decade? Despite his intention of writing in plain English, his writings are not easy to read, consisting as they do of a curious blend of phenomenology, existentialism, psychiatry, mysticism, and Marxism. Peter Sedgwick (1982) offers the following interpretation of why the anti-psychiatry movement gained momentum and why Laing became a recognized spokesman of the counter culture and the new left.

Reading XXIII.   Psycho Politics, by P. Sedgwick—Extract 1 from Chapter 3 (R. D. Laing: The Radical Trip)

The anti-psychiatry movement required a whole train of concurrent, convergent influences before it could gather force. Some of these factors lay in the changing age structure of Western societies, as the prolongation and intensification of active life span, extending back into the teen-years as well as onward into maturity, encouraged unprecedented strains at the boundaries of dependency, both in youth and old age. The expansion of welfare facilities as part of the price of working-class consensus in all the capitalist democracies had encouraged a flow of expectations, mingled with rising disappointments, in matters affecting the public health—and, within this complex of recently assembled social rights, the standing of psychiatric provision was due for some serious challenge and scrutiny. Mental illness became an urgent source of welfare politics, but at the same time touched on deeper, more intimate political structures: the relations of authority between doctor and patient, between administration and clientele, between parent and child, between woman and man became open to fresh and simultaneous collisions in the post-war boom years, even as the authority relations between employer and worker became continually and

---

Source;   Sedgwick, P. (1982). An extract taken from *Psycho Politics*. London: Pluto Press, pp. 66–69.

centrally challenged in the politics of the factory. The sixties, in most countries of the West, constituted the high-water mark in the assertiveness of the various discontented classes.

But before the swing into counter-revolution which we have experienced since, consciousness was raised, and confidence was still relatively intact. The confidence arose from the strong trading position of a labour force and an electorate able to extract substantial benefits either from employers or from politicians. Consciousness changed partly through diffuse spontaneous changes in ideas refracted from altered circumstance, and partly through the propagation of militant alternatives to the status quo. Militancy in argument, in mood, in manners was the work of groups and leaders who offered, in various models and images, the outline of a logic that could vanquish the hallowed syllogisms of everyday banality. The movement for a critical psychiatry had (and still has) its leaders, its world-historic individuals who gathered the questionings and forged them into questions, who became prophets and sages. And amid the succession of psychiatric prophets who compelled attention through the sixties and early seventies it was R. D. Laing who dominated the scene longest, as arch-seer and prophet-in-chief. 'After Freud and Jung, Now Comes R. D. Laing. Pop-shrink, rebel, yogi, philosopher-king? Latest reincarnation of Aesculapius, maybe?' trilled the headline over *Esquire*'s interview with him in January 1972. On his college lecture tour of America later that year, one university billed him as 'The Controversial Philosopher of Madness', and at another his arrival was greeted with bumper-stickers proclaiming 'I'm Mad About R. D. Laing'. 'Two chicks who dig Coltrane, The Dead and R. D. Laing' advertised for compatible guests to meet them at a party, in a back-page column of the New York *Village Voice* in the previous year: and Laing's assumed connection with the life-style of popular music had been earlier instanced in the assertion by a book reviewer (*Library Journal*, 1 June 1969) that he 'is reputed to have treated the Beatles'.

More serious and sustained attention was accorded to Laing by an unusual range of publics and specialists. The paperback editions of his main writings have been reprinted in most years since their first appearance, and the invocation of his name and work by philosophers, creative writers, and co-workers in the field of abnormal psychology was unabated even during periods when the mass media were angling their spotlights towards other celebrities. The reputation and rumour which has surrounded Laing has both eased and impeded his accessibility to intellectual audiences. The hundreds of thousands of young readers who bought and absorbed the scraps of psychedelic autobiography in *The Politics of Experience* found, for the first time in their lives, an apparently medical authority who, unlike most doctors and scientists, was not afraid of philosophising, or of quoting or writing poetry, or of expressing powerful and deep emotions that could variously either excite or shock his listeners. Others, from a more established vantage-point, felt outraged: one group of pro-medical polemicists even queried his right to speak as an accredited member of his profession:

How much more serious he would seem if he gave up his medical identity . . . If Laing wishes to be a guru or a philosopher, there is no doubt a place for him, but young people who are suffering from schizophrenia may prefer to entrust themselves to a doctor who will treat their illness as best as he can. [Siegler, Osmond & Mann, 1969, p. 957.]

The resistance to Laing's ideas was not simply a matter of professional pique; the very idiom in which he couched his early contributions, a blend of psychoanalytic and existentialist concepts interspersed with close reportage on the inner experience of deranged patients, presented obstacles for those not fully attuned to these rather particular sensibilities. Professor Roger Brown, an experimental social psychologist from the Harvard laboratory, has remarked of *The Divided Self* that 'In the course of several years I read it three times—that is, all the pages passed my eyes, but nothing happened that I would call "understanding".' The fact that Brown's fourth reading was much more successful, leading him to his choice of Laing's work to round off an introductory undergraduate psychology textbook, and to the conclusion that 'there is a sense in which Laing better than anyone else enables us to "understand" schizophrenia' [Brown & Herrnstein, 1975, pp. 686–689], is a tribute to the power of Laing's ideas to work their way past what were clearly the entrenched methodological defences of a sceptical scientist. This experience of illumination, whether into mental illness or into a more general human situation, was common among those who followed Laing's writings. Equally frequent, though, was a blockage of comprehension like Brown's earlier response, or an irritated rejection either of Laing's own positions or of the manner in which they were being construed and used by his following. . . .

The second difficulty [in surveying Laing's intellectual history] arises from [his] habit of offering all at once several lines of enquiry which, pushed to any sort of conclusion, would yield obvious inconsistencies. . . . In one particularly expansive phase of his development, roughly from 1964 to 1970, his writings and public activity consorted with a number of vanguard trends in society and politics—Marxism, the counter-culture, psychedelic experimentation, romantic-expressionist literature, the critique of the mental institution, the critique of the family, transcendental meditation, Sartrean existentialism, Freudian psychoanalysis—which are normally, for quite good reasons, taken to be to a certain extent divergent or even dissonant. Laing's utterances held these disparate trends in intellectual suspense, counterbalanced in a kind of equilibrium that was bound to collapse once he advanced one particular element or argument to preclude certain others. During his lengthy balancing act he was continually misunderstood by those who saw him as more committed to one item—to Marxism, let us say, or to meditation—than he was.

Extract 2 from Chapter 1 (Anti-psychiatry, Illness and the Mentally Ill)

The thrust of Laingian theorising accords so well with the loose romanticism and libertarianism implicit in a number of contemporary creeds and moods that it can easily generate support and acquire plausibility. It is only four years since I walked into a gathering of 30 or 40 postgraduate trainees in social work, to introduce them to two parents of schizophrenic children, both of them activists with me in a local pressure group for the welfare of schizophrenia sufferers. Much to the surprise of the parents and myself, this audience of social-work trainees directed a barrage of hostile questions and comments at us. Was not psychiatric diagnosis just a means of labelling awkward people just like in Russia? How could we be sure that we were talking about a real illness, and not something that was the product of faulty family handling? Faced with these attacks, which might have been quite uncomfortable for the morale of ordinary parents outside the gamut of the doubts and guilt that afflict the families of the handicapped, the three of us from the support group became increasingly more defensive, conventional and lame in our replies. We left an audience that had been sympathetic to Laing before we entered the room and was now more Laingian than Laing himself: for had they not witnessed the evasiveness and inauthenticity of a repressive and authoritarian parenthood left in charge of an innocent deviancy? Musing on the experience afterwards, one of the parents, a robust and good-humoured mother who had to look after her seriously ill black adolescent son in a suburban neighbourhood not distinguished for its racial tolerance (and still less for its mental-health liberalism), remarked that she could quite understand the reactions of our interrogators. 'We must have looked very conservative and square; and besides, only a few years ago, I read Laing and accepted his story completely—before we had any knowledge at home of what these things were really like.'

BEHAVIOUR UNDER EXTREME CONDITIONS

All of the selections we have examined so far in this chapter have suggested that the reason why "pop" psychology has prospered in recent years is because it either offers assurances as to how we can live our lives or it provides an analysis of social reality. People are seeking both of these when they are

Source: Sedgwick, P. (1982). An extract taken from *Psycho Politics*. London: Pluto Press, pp. 6–7.

confused or uncertain about their personal lives. By and large, what attracts people's attention and what "pop" psychology provides are guidelines on how to conduct their lives: advice on marriage, personal changes in circumstance, family life, child rearing or sexual relations.

It would, however, be misleading to suggest that the public is *only* interested in psychology in so far as it relates to personal life and everyday experiences. Curiously enough, we find that as well as displaying an interest in topics that touch upon everyday experience, the public is also inquisitive about human reactions to experiences that are quite remote from ordinary lives. Themes such as brainwashing, propaganda, torture, interrogation, and captivity have long gripped the popular imagination. Also, there is a perennial fascination with madness, neurosis, and deviance.

Peter Watson, a British psychologist and journalist, has written a book *War on the Mind* (1980) dealing with the military uses and abuses of psychology which exemplifies this other side of pop psychology. In a sense, Watson's book may be seen as the latest in a tradition of British books on the topic of behaviour under extreme conditions, all of which have enjoyed a popular acclaim. In 1957, William Sargent, a British psychiatrist, wrote *Battle for the Mind*, a book about indoctrination, brainwashing, and thought control. Another work by a British psychiatrist, J. A. C. Brown, *Techniques of Persuasion* (1963), covered much the same ground, as well as religious conversion and advertising; it continues to be widely read. How can we explain the popularity of both of these books? One guess is that both appeared at a time when the general public was still puzzling over the events of the Second World War. Moreover, the issues of mind control and indoctrination remained in the news throughout the Cold War years. In particular, the Korean War and the Chinese Revolution, with its emphasis on "thought reform," kept the issues topical and worrying. In more recent years, kidnapping and hijacking have aroused a great deal of general and scientific interest in the question of how captors and captives relate to one another.

Watson's book contains a chapter on the dynamics of captivity. *War on the Mind* grew out of Watson's journalistic work investigating the uses of psychological warfare by the

British in Northern Ireland. It is unusual because it combines first-rate journalism with a thorough understanding of the psychological issues. The chapter of the book that we reprint here deals with the psychological consequences of captivity. Watson describes four different examples of captivity—a German concentration camp, a Japanese and Korean prisoner-of-war camp, and the experiences of the crew of the U.S. spy ship, the *Pueblo*, who were held by the Koreans for 11 months. The final section of the chapter moves from real world events to the research of academic social psychology. Watson gives details of Zimbardo's controversial prison study. (This study has already been referred to in Chapter 4 where extracts from the work of Savin and of Philip Zimbardo himself were presented, both of which considered some of the ethical issues raised by such a piece of research.) Zimbardo's study, like Milgram's famous obedience to authority research (also discussed in Chapter 4), has generated much interest and fuelled debate, both within and without the profession. These two studies have been the subject of television documentaries and have been written up in many non-academic magazines.

A point worth noting about Watson's book, which does not apply to most of the other examples we have looked at, is that he spends considerable time describing and evaluating specific pieces of research. This is significant because it offers the reader a chance to form his or her own view of the evidence. What is also noteworthy about this book is the author's caution in his conclusions:

We live at a time when the military uses of science are of immense concern to everyone. . . . With such a background it is perhaps understandable that so many books about science and its applications to military affairs in the last ten years have been written with a marked anti-military slant. . . . Researching and writing this book, I felt very keenly this kind of "anti-military" reaction myself on several occasions. Taking the evidence in the book as a whole, however, and considering the more humdrum experiments alongside the controversial ones, is it fair to judge all military psychology as provocative and dangerous? (Watson, 1980, pp. 330–331)

Watson does not directly answer the question, but he does give the impression that people have exaggerated the effectiveness of the various forms of "mind control" that have been researched.

Reading XXIV.   Captivity, by P. Watson

For our purposes we shall consider three aspects of captivity as psychologically distinct. First, there is the capture itself as a result of which the soldier has to live usually in cramped circumstances, undergoing physical hardship and a boring routine existence, always surrounded by the uncertainty of his fate and having to obey the superior position of his captor(s). Next there is interrogation and possibly torture in which this captor–captive relationship is heightened; when special techniques, some physical, some psychological, are used to try to extract crucial information from him. Third, there is what is called 'brainwashing'—basically the use of interrogation and other psychological techniques not merely to extract information but also to manufacture a confession on the part of the POW for public consumption and which has been claimed at times to 'rework' a man's mind, to create a new set of beliefs.

No one seems to have carried out the obvious study of whether there are any psychological differences between the men who get captured and those who do not. One study by the British in Malaya found that a group of captured *and* defecting guerrilla soldiers were of lower intelligence than the population from which they were drawn, but that is as far as it went. [Lakin, 1965.]

There have been several studies about captivity behaviour itself. These range from A. L. Vischer's *Barbed Wire Disease: a Psychological Study of the Prisoner of War*, published in 1919, through 'The prisoner of war mentality', an article in the *British Medical Journal* in January 1944, to a major book by W. C. Bradbury and A. D. Biderman, *Mass Behavior in Battle and Captivity*, published in 1962. The latter is probably the most comprehensive account for the interested reader. Here I want simply to describe captivity in four situations: under the Germans in the Second World War; under the Japanese in the Second World War; under the Koreans and Chinese in the Korean War; and later under the Koreans in 1968, when the crew of the *Pueblo* spy ship was captured and held for eleven months. These provide a range of experiences which enable us to see how much captivity varies and what its salient features are. Finally, we examine an attempt to reproduce experimentally the experience of captivity, which shows how it affects the behaviour of both captives and captors.

Internment: A German Concentration Camp

The camp of Terezin was situated in Theresienstadt in Northern Bohemia. It served as an internment camp for Jews from November 1941 until the

Source: Watson, P. (1978). *War on the Mind: The Military Uses and Abuses of Psychology.* Harmondsworth: Penguin, pp. 187–197.

end of the war—139,666 people being sent there, 33,468 of whom died. The average population was 30,000–40,000. Dr V. A. Kral [1951], a psychiatrist, observed that the normal reaction to the camp was initial shock, 'the severity and duration of which was rather uniform in the average adult of both sexes'. This was characterized by depression and retardation, loss of initiative (even for washing and eating), and accompanied by anorexia, sleeplessness, constipation and, in most of the women, loss of the menstruation period. Suicide or panic, however, were *not* observed. Many experienced feelings of unreality, as if surrounded by ghosts.

This initial phase usually subsided after about two weeks without any treatment. Young children did not go through this phase, and old people were often unable to overcome it. Women, it seems became adjusted earlier and better than men. Level of intelligence did not appear as decisive as other personality factors: people 'educated to fairness . . . and trained to control their emotions . . . became better adjusted than those with higher intelligence and not so trained.' Religion also helped, as did being allowed to practise a profession, such as medicine. Some were unable to accept the reality of camp life, were given to boasting of past achievements and to day-dreaming; they adjusted less well than those who accepted the camp for what it was and set to to make the best of it.

Regardless of this, however, the degree of starvation did produce psychological sequelae. The vitamin deficiency, for example, caused memory deficits for recent events, most marked in the aged, but present even in adolescents. Orientation at night was affected, as were attention and the ability to concentrate. In the longer term, indifference and instability set in, leading to occasional temper outbursts. It became characteristic that such things as the death of a relative met only superficial sympathy, whereas trifles grew in importance. Thousands could be shipped east by ten SS officers without any trouble.

Food governed everyone's thoughts, day-dreams and night-dreams; sex became less necessary. The only thing to interfere with this was political discussion, which was sometimes capable of breaking the otherwise chronic indifference and apathy.

Japanese POW Camps

Reactions in German POW camps are reported as roughly similar in most studies. With the Japanese one difference was that they were often wholly unprepared to manage a large body of prisoners of war. As a result the individual guards seemed to be given free rein in the treatment of prisoners. They were capricious and unpredictable. When orders were not promptly carried out they could be vindictive and cruel.

A study by Major Stewart Wolf and Lt-Col. Herbert Ripley [1947] considered soldiers from several nationalities, including British, Americans and Dutch, who had survived three years of imprisonment and torture by the Japanese. The Japanese camps were just as crowded, dirty and as short of food as the German ones, but they were also far more disorganized, according to Wolf and Ripley. The Japanese, according to this study, divided the men into groups of ten, and indicated that should any one of the ten escape, the remainder would be killed. This effectively stopped escapes and the fact that officers had to enforce this policy also drove a wedge between them and their men.

Tortures used included beatings, standing to attention in the sun for hours, having hair or fingernails pulled out and the 'water treatment' in which the prisoner had his stomach distended with water via a long tube down his throat. In the 'sun treatment' prisoners had their eyelids kept open with sticks and were then left to look into the sun for hours on end.

Reactions were more extreme than in Germany. Some prisoners developed cravings for tobacco, others gave it up and traded what they had for food. None thought of home—just of work. To have thought of home, report Wolf and Ripley, would have meant the end.

During captivity most of the men were 'seclusive and taciturn'. There were few group activities though many cliques held mock 'classes' in which someone would describe in detail the preparation of some especially delicious dish. Sex was a topic of conversation for the first few months only and when extra food was available. At such times homosexuality and masturbation were common, giving rise to guilt feelings. The Americans took it out on their officers more than the British, no doubt due, say Wolf and Ripley, to cultural differences: the Americans were more prone to 'speak their mind' and needed to stress their masculinity. Yet they could not do this and survive. So it was redirected on to their own officers.

There was a lowering of moral standards: food was often stolen. Depression was common in the early months, plus anxiety arising from the unpredictable behaviour of the guards. These disappeared with time to be replaced, say Wolf and Ripley, by 'hysterical suppression of resentments and conflicts with loss of function . . . Some eventually became unable to cry or laugh.' Several later reported that they could stand the torture because they could 'turn off the pain'. Hysterical blindness or deafness was reported, in most cases similar to those seen in people with gross vitamin deficiency.

Wolf and Ripley report that the survivors said that the men who succumbed usually did so because they allowed themselves to be dominated by thoughts about home, developed a distaste for food, and died. Difficulty in concentration and loss of memory were also reported as widespread. Other studies on captivity under the Japanese (for example, that by Nardini) confirm Wolf and Ripley's findings though there is some doubt about the effects of self-image on survival. Nardini [1952] found that people who persistently told themselves that they were 'a soldier, a Texan, a father' survived. But how one does this *without* thinking of home is not made clear. Nevertheless, there emerges a basic picture of captivity reactions as due to two things: physical hardships and the unpredictability and cruelty of the captors.

Captivity in the Korean War

The North Koreans and Chinese took the process one step further in the Korean War. There they put their POWs through extreme physical hardship, including forced marches, and developed their own unpredictability to a high degree; but they also applied chronic pressures on the men to collaborate and to give up existing loyalties in favour of new ones. This was the brainwashing process. . . .

The Chinese systematically destroyed the prisoner's formal and informal group structure. Men were segregated by race, nationality and rank. [Schein, 1957.] Any group meeting was banned, the lower ranks were put in charge of the higher ranks. Harvey Strassman, an American psychiatrist, reports that the only way the men could keep from either collaborating or resisting to the point of eliciting punishment 'was to withdraw as much as possible from any but routine interactions with either the Chinese or *other* POWs'. This was not the 'apathy' that characterized concentration camp victims but a more conscious attempt not to collaborate. [Strassman, et al., 1956.] There was no element of resignation: 'The men were waiting and watching rather than hoping and planning,' says Strassman.

We shall see in chapter 15 how these studies have been fitted into training techniques to help men survive prison camps and brainwashing. But before that we consider the *Pueblo* incident—which occurred in peacetime, making it psychologically different from what has been considered so far.

The Pueblo Incident

The US spy ship, the *Pueblo*, was seized off the Korean coast on 23 January 1968. A long-term follow-up of the crew is still being carried out by the US Navy, so severe were the psychological sequelae of this ordeal: but what is already available is very interesting. [Ford, 1975.] The *Pueblo* was a small intelligence ship and when she was attacked one crew member was killed and two others sustained substantial injuries. The ship was then boarded, captured and sailed into Wanson Harbour. The crew of eighty-two was transferred to Pyonfyang by rail, where they were imprisoned in a building known to them as 'the barn'. The commanding officer was separated from the others who were quartered three or four to a room. They were threatened with death and beaten. Forced 'confessions' about criminal aggressive acts were obtained from all crew members as a result. Subsequently, they were transferred nearer to military installations, where officers got their own rooms and the men were eight to a room. They were later given lectures, field trips and written material by the Koreans in an effort to convince them that the US government was imperialist and unjust. Despite this and despite the 'confessions', the crew attempted to communicate to the world their lack of sincerity. In letters home they referred to dead relatives and used uncharacteristic phrasing: and in the propaganda photographs which they were forced to take part in they could be seen making obscene gestures.

After eleven months they were suddenly released, arriving in California on Christmas Eve. They were immediately examined both physically and psychiatrically. A psychiatric investigation was carried out not only to assess current functioning at the time of release but also to explore how the men had got on as captives. The psychiatrists probed the men's psychological defences, their ability to contribute to group support and morale and to provide realistic resistance to their captors.

Half the men admitted they had experienced serious worries but all said this was due to the unpredictability of their treatment; sixteen reported they had been chronically depressed, most saying that separation from their families upset them most of all, though four were upset by the fact they had 'confessed'. Suicide ideas were uncommon though three said they had made attempts. On average they had lost about 30 lb, twenty-seven complaining of anorexia during their confinement. Disturbances of sleep had been common and related to mood; dreams were common and included wish-fulfilment dreams of wanting to be back home and of escape. Many men fantasized that the US government would seek retribution by killing the *Pueblo* crew for its breach of discipline and loss of ship.

It was clear that some men had acted as informal group leaders in each room, where talk was found to resemble group therapy—there was ample time for discussion of lives, hopes and so forth. Sex was also a popular discussion topic though there was no reported homosexuality.

Chuck Ford [1975], one of the psychiatrists studying the crew, was able to divide the men into three groups according to how well they had coped with the captivity. Comparing the upper third (twenty-four) men with the bottom third (twenty-seven) he found no differences in age, military service, educational level or psychiatric or legal history. There was little difference in marital status, though among the bad captives there were three who were divorced or separated as opposed to none in the upper group.

There were, though, definite differences in personality. More than a third of the bottom group had passive–dependent personalities, whereas two thirds of the good captives were either healthy or 'schizoid'. As regards ego defence mechanisms, Ford says, the higher group used an average of 5 whereas the poorer group managed only 2.4. The better captives also used different types of mechanism—reality testing, rationalization, faith, denial and humour, most noticeably, whereas the poorer captives were more likely to defend themselves with 'obsessive ideation'.

So some neat results appear to be emerging from the *Pueblo* study (Ford revealed the latest details at a NATO conference in 1975) and from which counter-capture training could benefit quite handsomely. . . . [H]owever. . . it is by no means certain that those men who stand up well to the experience of capture are those who adjust back to normal life most readily when the conflict is over.

... [Finally], let us look at a study of the captive–captor relationship that has been carried out in the laboratory. It lacks some of the credibility of wartime studies, yet it does enable more systematic manipulation of the captor–captive situation. And this can provide some equally striking insights.

Zimbardo's Prison Study

The foremost researcher in the area of captivity has been Dr Philip Zimbardo. In his work for the US Office of Naval Research, Dr Zimbardo and his colleagues were especially interested in captivity behaviour. Their most colourful study was carried out in 1972–3, the methods and results of which are highly controversial. Let us look first at the experiment itself and then come back to the implications. [Haney, Banks, & Zimbardo, 1973b.]

Ostensibly, Zimbardo wanted to study the group dynamics of a prison: he was interested in whether abuses in prison arise because, for example, the prisoners are a group who have a long record of disregard for society, or whether the power inherent in the prison officer's job made him especially vindictive. Accordingly, Zimbardo advertised in his local newspapers for some healthy males to help him in an experiment into 'prison life'. Out of seventy-five people who applied, the twenty-four most emotionally stable men were picked; none of them had a previous history of either criminal or any other deviant activity—they could not be seen as disadvantaged in any way. Half of the subjects were arbitrarily assigned the role of 'guards' and the other half were designated the 'prisoners'. The prisoners were told to be available on a certain Sunday when the experiment would begin. The guards were called to a meeting before the experiment started where they met the 'prison superintendent' (Zimbardo) and a 'warden' (one of his assistants). They were told that within the limits of moral and pragmatic considerations, it would be their job to maintain a degree of reasonable order within the prison, although how this specifically might be done was deliberately not explored. They were made aware of the fact that although there might be escape attempts and so on, their job was to make sure that these did not come off. They were to work in shifts, and had to fill out shift reports and critical incident reports. They were intentionally given only minimal guidelines on their treatment of the prisoners though it was made clear that all forms of physical punishment were ruled out. To make it even more realistic the guards helped to construct the final part of the prison.

This was designed to be a functional prison but not necessarily life-like in every detail (it was in fact built in the basement of Stanford University psychology department). There were three 6 × 9 ft cells with black, barred doors. There was a strong door at the entrance to the cell block and an observation door. A small room represented the enclosed prison exercise yard and a much smaller room (2 × 2 × 7 ft), which was unlit was used for solitary confinement. The entire prison was fitted out for video and audio surveillance.

The experiment proper began without warning when the subjects who had been assigned the role of prisoner were 'arrested'. Zimbardo was successful in getting the cooperation of the Palo Alto City police department and a police car called at their homes. The officer said that he was arresting them on suspicion of armed robbery or burglary, advised them on their legal rights, handcuffed them and gave them a thorough search (often in the presence of curious neighbours). They were then driven to the police station where they were photographed and their fingerprints were taken. Then they were placed in a detention cell before being blindfolded and driven by one of the experimenters to the 'prison'. Throughout the entire arrest sequence the police officers maintained a restrained attitude; they gave no indication that the arrest was anything to do with the mock prison study. On arrival, the prisoner had all his clothes taken from him, was sprayed with what was supposed to be a de-lousing chemical (but was in fact merely a spray deodorant), and had to remain alone and naked in the 'yard' for a while. He was again photographed and then given his prison tunic.

The guards wore khaki shirts and trousers, and had a police whistle, a night stick, and reflecting sunglasses which made eye-contact impossible. Each prisoner wore a loose-fitting muslin smock with an identification number stamped front and back, no underclothes (which forced him to sit in feminine poses), a light chain and lock around one ankle, rubber sandals and a cap made from a nylon stocking to remove differences in hair length (in some prisons, inmates' heads are shaved). When all the cells had been filled, the warden greeted the prisoners and read them the rules of the institution (developed together by the guards and the warden) which they had to memorize and follow. From then on prisoners were only referred to by number.

The prisoners were fed three bland meals a day, were allowed supervised toilet visits and two hours daily for the privilege of letter writing and reading. They were given work and received an hourly wage to make up the $15 a day that they had been promised. Two visiting periods a week were to be allowed, as were film nights and exercise periods. Three times a day prisoners were lined up for a count—these parades coinciding with the beginning of a new shift for the guards.

The results of this experiment were shattering. Right from the start the prisoners were found to adopt a passive attitude whereas the guards became more and more aggressive. Forbidden to give physical punishment, they came increasingly to rely on the use of verbal aggression.

Extreme signs of stress emerged in five of the prisoners as early as the second day. The pattern was similar in four of these and included depression, fits of crying, bursts of anger and acute anxiety. The fifth subject had to be released prematurely after he had developed a skin rash due to his harsh treatment. Of the remaining prisoners, only two said they would not forgo their pay for being let out early. When the experiment was in fact terminated a few days before schedule, all remaining prisoners were delighted. In contrast the guards seemed distressed by the decision to stop. None of them had ever failed to come to work on time and indeed, on several occasions, guards remained on duty and uncomplaining for hours extra without any additional pay.

There can be little doubt that the simulation became a very real experience for much of the time (and a very unpleasant one for the prisoners). Zimbardo and his colleagues monitored guards and the prisoners without them being aware of it. Ninety per cent of the prisoners' private conversation was directly related to immediate prison conditions—food, privileges, harassment. Only one tenth of the time did they talk about their lives outside the prison. As a result the prisoners got to know surprisingly little about each other, says Zimbardo, and the excessive concentration on the vicissitudes of their current situation helped to make the prison experiences more oppressive for them, because instead of escaping from it when they had a chance to do so in the privacy of their cells, they continued to allow it to dominate their thoughts and social relations. And when prisoners were interviewed they spent a lot of time deprecating one another.

Similarly, the guards spent a lot of their free time talking about 'problem' prisoners. They also had the tendency to be even more cruel when they thought they were not being watched by the experimenters. They continued to intensify their aggressive behaviour even when it had become obvious to everyone that the prisoners' deterioration was marked and visible.

A measure of how real the experiment had become to most of the participants is that when the prisoners were visited by a real priest, many referred to themselves by their number and not by their names; some even asked him to get them a lawyer to get them out. And when some of them appeared before a 'parole board', three said they would be willing to forgo their pay in order to be released. Yet when the chairman of the board (Zimbardo himself) said that their requests would be considered, the prisoners all allowed themselves to be led quietly back to their cells even though they were in reality able to leave just for the asking.

Undoubtedly a powerful study. The question is, however, what was its real aim? At the end of his paper, Zimbardo rightly says that his experiment shows the powerful dynamic built into the prison situation and that it might provide a basis for a new type of prison guard training—presumably to allow guards to see the dangers of arbitrary power. This is plausible: but it is by no means the only interpretation that can be placed on this study—nor is it the one which fits most of the facts of the experiment.

Starting from the premise that the US Navy does not really need to spend a lot of money in training its stockade guards in how to understand their role, let us first remember that the study is part of a Navy inquiry into the basic psychological principles underlying aggression. We can be forgiven perhaps for assuming that the Navy is more interested in the warlike uses of aggression than the behaviour of prison guards. We can then note that there were some crucial psychological aspects to the experiment which made it much *less* like a prison than it could have been. The prisoners had no record: yet it surely is a psychological fact of life that prisoners by and large end up in jail because they deserve to. To make the prison experience realistic, there must be some measure of feeling in the prisoners that they took a risk, and failed. A consequence of this should be that a real prisoner would feel much less outraged at the arbitrary nature of his arrest than was the case in the experiment. Next it would have been relatively easy to make the Stanford basement physically much more like a prison yet the experimenters seemed to prefer the idea of a compromise: it was a temporary prison, something which at other times had other uses. Then there was the symbolic shaving of the heads of the men; in truth this is done very rarely in western prisons, but—and this is perhaps the most overt clue to the experiment's purpose—it *is* done to prisoners of war. Next there was the admission by Zimbardo that his guards were given khaki uniforms—to make them look as much like military men as possible?

Whatever the ostensible purpose of this research, its implications for prisoners of war are clear. The psychological situation facing the 'prisoners' was similar in many respects to that facing a prisoner of war: the surprise of the arrest, the blindfolding on the way to prison, the corporate aspect of the greeting. In prison men are still known by their name *and* number; only prisoners of war usually are referred to by their number.

Many armies now prepare their soldiers to be able to withstand interrogation. Zimbardo has in effect developed a method to teach people how to cope with the experiences of capture and imprisonment. The fact that 90 per cent of the conversation by prisoners was about prison, and that it made matters worse, suggests that POWs should not talk about prison, but should use every opportunity to escape from it mentally. The tendency to deprecate fellow prisoners and its security hazards should be pointed out. Continually dwelling on their immediate circumstances prevented the men from becoming a group and suggests that POWs should attempt to get talking and form themselves into a group straight away. Zimbardo's prisoners were strangers to one another, paralleling the POW situation. The fact that small guards can make large prisoners act foolishly and childishly is dramatically brought home; Zimbardo found that subjects mainly felt that the selection of guards had been on the basis of height—bigger men became guards—but in fact there were no physical differences between the two groups. At times in the experiment prisoners were encouraged to belittle each other publicly, during the counts, perhaps an experimental version of public confessions which were so infamous during the time of brainwashing.

On many matters, therefore, the Zimbardo experiment seems as much an exploration for a course in how to train soldiers or sailors to cope with the stresses of captivity as an experiment to find out how prison guards and prisoners behave, and perhaps that was Zimbardo's initial intention.

Zimbardo's experiment is but one of many that, since the Korean War in particular, have begun to examine captivity, torture and interrogation on a more scientific basis. The Korean War itself spawned a whole series of studies into who collaborated and into the thorny question of treason and loyalty. But laboratory experiments have not been lacking either, including many studies on forced compliance, how to threaten, the psychology of suffering and much else. . . .

THE DISTRIBUTION OF "POP" PSYCHOLOGY

In our analysis of "pop" psychology up to this point we have highlighted the social conditions that give rise to "pop" psychology and we have considered the range of topics dealt with by "pop" psychologists. What we have not treated in any detail is the process by which "pop" psychology is distributed. Undoubtedly, a process of selection operates. Certain research is more likely to be noted, reported, and commented upon by the mass media than is other equally sound or important work. As a result of this filtering process, some parts of academic psychology are brought to public notice and other areas go unheeded.

Once results have been published, says Shipman (1976), they are often used in ways that suggests that they have either been misunderstood or deliberately distorted: "The cautions of the researcher and the conditions and contexts originally circumscribing the evidence are often ignored by the public and the media. Researchers are frequently misunderstood and many suffer as their work is used selectively to support political positions that they personally reject" (Shipman, 1976).

This leads us to speculate upon the role of the mass media in creating and sustaining images of the social sciences. Although social psychologists have been active researchers in the field of mass media and mass communications, unlike sociologists, they have shown little interest in studying the manner in which the concepts and theories of their own discipline are diffused. Sociologists seem much more alert to the handling of their findings by the mass media. One reason for this, as mentioned at the beginning of this chapter, is that for sociology it is quite acceptable to study collective forms of experience. As a result, critical social theorists have attempted to understand popular consciousness. In Britain, much work on mass media, ideology, and popular culture has been initiated by the Centre for Contemporary Cultural Studies at the University of Birmingham. Their focus of interest has encompassed such varied topics as trade unions, sport, and women's social status.

In a very bitter account in the British Sociological Association Newsletter, Jennifer Platt (1984) reports the way in which a paper she and Jennifer Clarke gave to the British Association on the subject of children's packed lunches was trivialized and misrepresented by the press, radio, and television.

Reading XXV.   The Media Make a Meal out of it, by J. Platt

We all probably agree in principle that it's a good idea to get mass media publicity for sociological research of a practically useful kind: I'm not sure, however, that my recent experience doesn't lead me to have some second thoughts on this. With a dietician colleague, I presented a paper to the recent meeting of the British Association on children's school packed lunches (Jennifer Platt and Jennifer Clarke 'Social factors affecting the composition of children's school packed lunches'), and this aroused considerable media interest, stories relating to it appeared in *The Times*, *The Guardian*, *New Society* and local papers, it was picked out as one of the highlights by *New Scientist*, and we were interviewed for radio and television. But just what did all this have to do with the diffusion of research?

First, it was clear that the general level of interest in the work arose partly from the fact that the topic of what children eat is one of obvious practical concern, and much more accessible than most natural science topics reported on at the British Association, and so is of relatively wide interest. To that extent it was entirely consistent with our purposes. Second, however, it was also clear that school lunches are seen as intrinsically funny, so that research on them lends itself to easy humorous stories. Some minor features of the paper facilitated that kind of story. An anecdote about one child who regularly swapped his orange for a Mars bar was repeated *ad nauseam* and even, I am told, appeared as a headline item in one Radio 2 news bulletin; it only illustrated one minor point in the argument. One is not surprised when a brief item in *The Times* diary is jokey, but I was disconcerted to find a summary in *New Scientist* played for laughs. This picked out of the methodological appendix a passing reference to the coding problem created by one child's claim to eat each day 'one blue thing and one brown thing' and referred to it in the headline, the summary and the conclusion: '. . . the great question from this year's

Source: *Network* (Newsletter of the British Sociological Association). (Jan. 1984), No. 28, pp. 4–5.

BA—what *is* the blue thing that one Sussex schoolgirl eats for lunch every day?'

A similar sensitivity to the sociologically significant detail was shown by the comment that 'the most meaningful sociological information from the report is that Platt had never encountered the cheese-and-salad cream sandwich prior to the survey . . .' To this I personally prefer the TV interview where the reporter with simple frankness declared that he had a copy of the paper but hadn't read it, and that anyway I would only end up with 90 seconds on the programme so there wasn't any scope for detail.

Other modes of making a story were suggested by some efforts by less posh media to create a factitious 'controversial' angle; the local evening paper tried to suggest to me, on no evidence at all, that teachers might have been reluctant to co-operate in the data-collection, and Radio Belfast attempted to create an argument between my dietician colleague and a Belfast dietician. (Radio Belfast, incidentally, gave me what may be the only opportunity I shall ever have to intersperse a live presentation of my research with pop records. To set against which—if I had been a senior *male* academic, would the presenter have called me by my Christian name?)

How did Radio Belfast hear of the research? From a 2-line mention in a news agency report. It was quite clear that some sources picked up the story from others: *The Times'* diary version repeated minor errors from *New Society*, and one local paper reporter who asked to talk to me about it over the phone then said she didn't need to because she had found a story about it in the other local paper.

Why did media so essentially uninterested in getting a correct firsthand version of what the paper said report it at all? One reason appears to me to have been that by virtue of being reported elsewhere it had become 'news'. The oddity of the conception implied is shown by another experience. The only short-term topical feature of our paper was that it was publicly given on one particular day. Very shortly after the paper was given I went abroad for a fortnight. On my return I found two messages asking me to ring reporters about it; in both cases I politely did so, found them out and left a message saying that I was now available—and heard no more of the matter.

From my point of view, and my colleague's, the point of the paper was that it had some systematic findings which suggested a sociological conclusion and drew from it some implications for practical policy. The paper was written in a technically careful but not, I think, esoteric or jargon-laden style, and a factual abstract of the main points (with no jokes or anecdotes), covering less than one side, was available as a press release. I do not think, therefore, that the presentation of the paper was in any obvious way responsible for its treatment, and some personal effort by reporters was necessary to get the versions most presented. (As far as I know, none came to the oral presentation of the paper; certainly no one spoke to me there.) What was the point from their point of view? I infer that it was (a) to print anything, never mind precisely what, potentially interesting to readers because of its connection with an issue with political implications in their daily lives; (b) to find a funny story; (c) to find a 'story' that counted as such because it could be made 'controversial'; (d) not to be left out of something that must be a 'story' because it had appeared in other media.

Can one draw any conclusions about how to get sociological research diffused in an acceptable form? My experience suggests that it would be wise to try to ensure that anecdotes or funny bits are included only if they convey a central point in what one is trying to say, and to take special care that the *first* media coverage should be accurate and relevant. I am not confident, however, that non-specialist reporters will ever share our priorities enough to get things right. Even what aimed to be a straight factual summary in *The Guardian* managed to mention none of our main points. Should we be doing more to improve the mass media's understanding of sociology?

SOCIAL RESEARCH AS "NEWS"

In a similar vein, the sociologist Julienne Ford (1976) describes the publicity that her book on social class and comprehensive schools received. It appeared in 1969 and was based on fieldwork in three secondary schools, one grammar, one comprehensive, and one modern. The evidence collected from this very small sample suggested that the move to comprehensive schools was not leading to a fairer society.

Looking back on the reception her book received, Ford chronicles the way in which her research has been misquoted, quoted out of context, and cited to support political positions at odds with her own: "This is academic alienation. The theorist or researcher confronts his published statements as things apart from him, he no longer has autonomy over them, they exist in and of themselves ... He feels responsible for what he has said but impotent to intervene in the course of the dialogue" (1976, p. 59).

This experience left her feeling very cynical about the manner in which research is reported:

Just as the score at a football match is taken by newspaper readers as "evidence" of the outcome of the game, so are the "results" of research reported in the news media. Thus they become rumours of "evidence" in the ubiquitous sphere of polemical debate which we sometimes call "public opinion." But, whereas the rules of football are fairly well understood and the referee's decision is final, rhetorical rules are harder to apply, and there can be no question of umpires. Unless the news reporter is himself adept at scientistic critical dialogue, or unless he wishes to employ the reported "evidence" for his own polemical purposes, he will tend to accept the researcher's own conclusions, however tentatively these may have been expressed. These conclusions will thus tend to be reported as the "results" of the research. (Ford, 1976, p. 55)

Are Platt's and Ford's negative experiences typical of the way social science news is reported? We suspect that such treatment is more likely if the subject of the research is of topical concern, but we do not wish to suggest that the mass media necessarily and inevitably distort or misrepresent academic research. In psychology, we have a very remarkable instance where a journalist was responsible for actually uncovering a major fraud. We refer here to the discrediting of Sir Cyril Burt's research on the inheritance of intelligence. The most important piece of research evidence used to support the claim that I.Q. is a highly heritable trait was that of Sir Cyril Burt. In 1966, Burt published a study that was purportedly based on 53 pairs of separate identical twins. He claimed that he had found a higher I.Q. correlation between separated twins than had ever been reported previously in the literature. The American psychologist, Kamin, was the first to point out that there were various "absurdities, contradictions, evasions, ambiguities and dishonesties scattered throughout Burt's work" (Kamin, 1981, pp. 101–102). It was a British journalist, Dr Oliver Gillie, who followed up Kamin's suspicion that Burt's data was faked. In the following extract, Kamin gives details of Gillie's investigation and the ensuing debate.

Reading XXVI.   The Cyril Burt Affair, by L. Kamin

The *Sunday Times* Exposé

The argument about Burt's data might have been confined to academic circles, and might have tiptoed around the question of Burt's fraudulence, were it not for Oliver Gillie of the London *Sunday Times*. Dr. Gillie, the

Source: Eysenck, H. J. & Kamin, L. (1981). *Intelligence: The Battle for the Mind* London: Pan Books, pp. 102–105.

newspaper's medical correspondent (and incidentally also a geneticist), attempted to locate two of Burt's research associates—the Misses Conway and Howard. These two women had published papers, in collaboration with Burt and separately, in the psychological journal that Burt edited. They were the people who, according to Burt, had actually tested the twins and other relatives about whom he wrote so extensively. There was no documentary evidence to be found, anywhere, of the existence of either of these two "research associates". Burt's colleagues at University College, London had never laid eyes on them. Nor had his secretary or housekeeper seen them, or any correspondence from them. When asked about them, Burt had sometimes maintained that they had emigrated to Australia—*before* the time when they were supposedly testing separated twins in England! Dr Gillie's front-page article, written in 1976, flatly asserted that Burt had been guilty of a major scientific fraud and cited many of the absurdities in Burt's work that were by then becoming quite widely known in academic circles. The charge of fraud against Burt was supported by the testimony of two of his distinguished former students, Alan and Ann Clarke. The cat was now out of the bag, and the feathers began to fly.

Professor Jensen wrote to *The Times* to assert that I had "spearheaded the attack . . . to wholly discredit the large body of research on the genetics of human mental abilities. The desperate scorched-earth style of criticism that we have come to know in this debate has finally gone the limit, with charges of 'fraud' and 'fakery' now that Burt is no longer here to . . . take warranted legal action against such unfounded defamation."

Professor Eysenck leapt to Burt's defence as "Britain's outstanding psychologist for many years, who had been knighted for his service to education, and who had achieved world fame for his contributions . . .". The allegations against Burt, according to Eysenck, contained "a whiff of McCarthyism, of notorious smear campaigns, and of what used to be known as character assassination". While implying that he disapproved of smear and of character assassination, Eysenck nevertheless described Dr Gillie's behaviour as "unspeakably mean". The press, according to Eysenck, had discussed the Burt affair in an irresponsible way. The tone of the press coverage had been so debased that in 1977 Eysenck threatened (he did not, alas, follow through) to retire from public debate to the privacy of his scientific garden.

This swashbuckling attack on Burt's critics was mounted before many members of the psychological community were aware of the conclusions being reached by Burt's authorised biographer, Professor Leslie Hearnshaw. With publication of Hearnshaw's work impending, the tone of Burt's defenders became more muted. Thus, by 1978. Eysenck was writing of Burt: "On at least one occasion he invented, for the purpose of quoting it in one of his articles, a thesis by one of his students never in fact written; at the time I interpreted this as a sign of forgetfulness." This lapse of memory on Burt's part had evidently been forgotten by Eysenck when, one year later, he had attacked Burt's critics as McCarthyite character assassins. By 1978 Eysenck was beginning to cast his lot with the character assassins. Though Eysenck was not certain that Burt had engaged in "wholesale faking", he was now certain that Burt had behaved "in a dishonest manner".

The Final Blow: Burt's Biography

The last lingering doubts about Burt's faking have been put to rest by Hearnshaw's painstaking biography, published in 1979. The work was commissioned by Burt's sister, and Burt's diaries, letters and papers were made available to Hearnshaw. Professor Hearnshaw had delivered the eulogy at Burt's memorial service, and he began his work as an admirer of Burt. He could find no trace of Miss Conway, or Miss Howard, or of separated twins. He found many instances of dishonesty and of evasion and of contradiction in Burt's written replies to correspondents who had asked questions about his data. The evidence was clear in indicating that Burt had collected no data at all during the last 30 years of his life, when most of the twins were supposedly studied.

With obvious reluctance, Hearnshaw was forced to conclude that the charges made by Burt's critics were "in their essentials valid", and that Burt had "fabricated figures" and "falsified". Perhaps too charitably, he suggested that Burt might actually have collected some of his purported data when he was younger, but that, as an ailing and elderly man, he padded the data and engaged in various forms of deception. From the available evidence, however, it is reasonable to suggest that perhaps Burt never tested a separated twin, or calculated a genuine correlation between relatives, in his entire life.

There is now no doubt whatever, and no dispute, that in any discussion of IQ heritability the entire body of Burt's work must be discarded. The Burt data were by far the strongest and clearest in the entire field. The following pages will document how weak and inconclusive the data from other sources are. The remaining data cannot even establish that the heritability of IQ is significantly greater than zero.

What, however, are we to make of the fact that Burt's transparently fraudulent data were accepted for so long, and so unanimously, by the "experts" in the field? When I first criticised Burt's papers, as an outsider to IQ testing, Eysenck wrote derisively, in 1974, of my "novitiate status" and my "once-a-year interest" in a subject best left to the experts. The same Burt papers that I had first read in 1972 had been read many years earlier by Eysenck, who repeatedly quoted them as gospel.

A Sorry Comment

Perhaps the most important moral to be drawn from the Burt affair was spelled out by N. J. Mackintosh in a 1980 review of Hearnshaw's biography in the *British Journal of Psychology*:

> Ignoring the question of fraud, the fact of the matter is that the crucial evidence that his data on IQ are scientifically unacceptable does not depend on any examination of Burt's diaries or correspondence. It is to be found in the data themselves. The evidence was there . . . in 1961. It was, indeed, clear to anyone with eyes to see in 1958. But it was not seen until 1972, when Kamin first pointed to Burt's totally inadequate reporting of his data and to the impossible consistencies in his correlation coefficients. Until then the data were cited with respect bordering on reverence, as the most telling proof of the heritability of IQ. It is a sorry comment on the wider scientific community that 'numbers . . . simply not worthy of our current scientific attention' . . . should have entered nearly every psychological textbook . . .

To my mind . . . it is an equally sorry comment on the fraternity of IQ testers that, having lost Burt's data, they continue to assert that the remaining evidence demonstrates the high heritability of IQ.

THE PSYCHOLOGIST AS POPULARIZER

In reflecting upon the way in which psychology reaches the public, we should also consider the role that academic psychologists themselves play in the transformation of knowledge from laboratories and scholarly journals to a more popular form. "Pop" psychology is not just created by the mass media, but by professional practitioners, researchers and academics as well. Nevertheless, academics, as Shipman quite rightly points out, tend to use the term "popular" as an implied criticism:

The attempt to reach and influence a wide public seems to be justifiable if behavioural science has any contribution to make to improving the human condition. But the attempt can involve a loss of academic credence.

The conventional definitions of research separate basic and applied, conclusion-oriented and decision-oriented, hypothesis-testing and hypothesis-seeking, suggesting that there is a division which would justify the different status accorded to the academic and the practical. But these distinctions disappear in practice. Taylor has suggested that they are management concepts, helping those in charge of funds for research purposes to designate the kind of work they favour. But in practice all research has pure and applied aspects because the little evidence that exists has to be stretched as far as possible. (Shipman, 1976, pp. 150–151)

What we must not overlook is the fact that some psychologists seem to have the knack of popularizing their own work, directing it both towards their academic peers and towards a non-specialized audience. Many key figures in the history of psychology have written for both specialist and general audiences. One could argue that the first "pop" psychologist was Freud, who had a gift and the desire to communicate to scientists, doctors, and the intelligent lay reader. Strachey (1962) writes: "All through his life Freud was willing and ready to publish general accounts of his discoveries and views which should be non-technical and understandable by people of ordinary knowledge and intelligence. More than a dozen of these semi-popular accounts could be named, among them the very last of his writings" (p. 7). Some of these works, aimed at the general public, were based on lectures that Freud gave in Vienna and on his visit to the United States.

J. B. Watson, the founding father of behaviourism, also wrote for the general reader. He published a book on child care and various articles in women's magazines. And B. F. Skinner, who was designated by *Time* magazine as "the most influential of living American psychologists and the most controversial figure in the science of human behaviour," has always sought to interest and inform the public of the findings and implications of psychology. Like Watson, he has not been averse to writing for women's magazines. In the 1940s he wrote an article in the *Ladies Home Journal* in which he described the mechanical baby tender (the so-called "Skinner baby-box"), he had devised for his second child. In the early years of his career, Skinner (1948) also published a novel, *Walden Two*, which presents a behaviourist's view of a Utopian community. Of *Walden Two* Schellenberg writes:

It was three years before this book was published (several publishers had turned it down as being unlikely to arouse the interest of readers), but it soon became widely read, ultimately selling over a million copies. In this book a professor named Burris visits a scientifically planned Utopian society. The dialogue between Burris and Frazier, the leading architect of the planned society, represented the issues to be faced in a scientific reconstruction of society. It also represented, as Skinner later admitted, "a venture in self-therapy in which I was struggling to reconcile two aspects of my own behaviour, represented by Burris and Frazier" (quoted in *Time*,

September 20, 1971, p. 50). In the end the liberal academic Burris
swallows his doubts, and prepares to join the behavioural technologists at
Walden Two. (Schellenberg, 1978, pp. 92–93)

In the extract reproduced here we listen in on a conversation
between Frazier, the founder of Walden Two, and Castle, a
philosopher who is visiting the commune along with Professor
Burris. The theme is one that is frequently encountered in
Skinner's work—a questioning of traditional concepts of
freedom. What is particularly noteworthy about this passage,
however, is that it involves a comparison between a society
based on principles of behavioural engineering and one
derived from a political philosophy. Skinner has always been
dismissive of political theory and political solution. His critics
maintain that in his more popular writings Skinner reveals
political naivity by supposing that "answers" to factual
psychological questions could ever result in the demise of
politics. Unlike Skinner, many psychologists think that we
shall continue to have need of politics to resolve conflicts of
interest and the age old problems of justice and morality.

Reading XXVII.   Walden Two, by B. F. Skinner

[Frazier, the guiding light behind Walden Two, an
experimental community based on principles of behavioural
technology, explains his philosophy to two visitors–Burris and
Castle.]

". . . What is emerging at this critical stage in the evolution of society is a
behavioural and cultural technology based on positive reinforcement
alone. We are gradually discovering—at an untold cost in human
suffering—that in the long run punishment doesn't reduce the probability
that an act will occur. We have been so preoccupied with the contrary that
we always take 'force' to mean punishment. We don't say we're using force
when we send shiploads of food to a starving country, though we're
displaying quite as much power as if we were sending troops and guns.". . .
     "Now, early forms of government are naturally based on punishment.
It's the obvious technique when the physically strong control the weak. But
we're in the throes of a great change to positive reinforcement—from a
competitive society in which one man's reward is another man's

Source: Skinner, B. F. (1948) *Walden Two*. London: Macmillan, pp. 216–230.

punishment, to a cooperative society in which no one gains at the expense of anyone else.

"The change is slow and painful because the immediate, temporary effect of punishment overshadows the eventual advantage of positive reinforcement. We've all seen countless instances of the temporary effect of force, but clear evidence of the effect of not using force is rare. That's why I insist that Jesus, who was apparently the first to discover the power of refusing to punish, must have hit upon the principle by accident. He certainly had none of the experimental evidence which is available to us today, and I can't conceive that it was possible, no matter what the man's genius, to have discovered the principle from casual observation." . . .

"But what has all this got to do with freedom?" [Burris] said hastily.

Frazier took time to reorganize his behavior. He looked steadily toward the window, against which the rain was beating heavily.

"Now that we know how positive reinforcement works and why negative doesn't," he said at last, "we can be more deliberate, and hence more successful, in our cultural design. We can achieve a sort of control under which the controlled, though they are following a code much more scrupulously than was ever the case under the old system, nevertheless *feel free*. They are doing what they want to do, not what they are forced to do. That's the source of the tremendous power of positive reinforcement— there's no restraint and no revolt. By a careful cultural design we control not the final behavior, but the *inclination* to behave—the motives, the desires, the wishes. . . ."

[Frazier continued] "The question is: Can men live in freedom and peace? And the answer is: yes, if we can build a social structure which will satisfy the needs of everyone and in which everyone will want to observe the supporting code. But so far this has been achieved only in Walden Two. Your ruthless accusations to the contrary, Mr. Castle, this is the freest place on earth. And it is free precisely because we make no use of force or the threat of force. Every bit of our research, from the nursery through the psychological management of our adult membership, is directed toward that end—to exploit every alternative to forcible control. By skillful planning, by a wise choice of techniques, we *increase* the feeling of freedom.

"It's not planning which infringes upon freedom, but planning which uses force. A sense of freedom was practically unknown in the planned society of Nazi Germany, because the planners made a fantastic use of force and the threat of force.

"No, Mr. Castle, when a science of behavior has once been achieved, there's no alternative to a planned society. We can't leave mankind to an accidental or biased control. But by using the principle of positive reinforcement—carefully avoiding force or the threat of force—we can preserve a personal sense of freedom." . . .

"The government of Walden Two," [Frazier] continued, "has the virtues of democracy, but none of the defects. It's much closer to the theory or intent of democracy than the actual practice in America today. The will of the people is carefully ascertained. We have no election campaigns to falsify issues or obscure them with emotional appeals, but a careful study of the satisfaction of the membership is made. Every member has a direct channel through which he may protest to the Managers or even the Planners. And these protests are taken as seriously as the pilot of an airplane takes a sputtering engine. We don't need laws and a police force to compel a pilot to pay attention to a defective engine. Nor do we need laws to compel our Dairy Manager to pay attention to an epidemic among his cows. Similarly, our Behavioral and Cultural Managers need not be compelled to consider grievances. A grievance is a wheel to be oiled, or a broken pipe line to be repaired . . . Democracy . . . isn't, and can't be, the best form of government, because it's based on a scientifically invalid conception of man. It fails to take account of the fact that in the long run *man is determined by the state*. A *laissez-faire* philosophy which trusts to the inherent goodness and wisdom of the common man is incompatible with the observed fact that men are made good or bad and wise or foolish by the environment in which they grow."

"But which comes first," [Burris] asked, "the hen or the egg? Men build society and society builds men. Where do we start?"

"It isn't a question of starting. The start has been made. It's a question of what's to be done from now on."

"Then it's to be revolution, is that it?" said Castle. "If democracy can't change itself into something better—"

"Revolution? You're not a very rewarding pupil, Mr. Castle. The change won't come about through power politics at all. It will take place at another level altogether."

[. . .]

"I can think of a conspicuous case in which the change you're advocating is coming about at the level of power politics," [Burris] said.

Frazier sat up quickly, with obvious effort. He looked at [Burris] suspiciously.

"Russia," [Burris] said.

"Ah, Russia," he said with relief. He showed no inclination to go on.

"What about Russia, though?"

"What about it, indeed?"

"Isn't there a considerable resemblance between Russian communism and your own philosophy?"

"Russia, Russia," Frazier murmered evasively. "Our visitors always ask that. Russia is our rival. It's very flattering—if you consider the resources and the numbers of people involved."

"But you're dodging my question. Hasn't Russia done what you're trying to do, but at the level of power politics? I can imagine what a Communist would say of your program at Walden Two. Wouldn't he simply tell you to drop the experiment and go to work for the Party?"

"He would and he does."

"And what's your answer?"

"I can see only four things wrong with Russia," Frazier said, clearly enjoying the condescension. "As originally conceived, it was a good try. It sprang from humanitarian impulses which are a commonplace in Walden Two. But it quickly developed certain weaknesses. There are four of them, and they were inevitable. They were inevitable just because the attempt was made at the level of power politics.' He waited for [Burris] to ask him what the weaknesses were.

"The first," he said, as soon as [Burris] had done so, "is a decline in the experimental spirit. Many promising experiments have simply been dropped. The group care of children, the altered structure of the family, the abandonment of religion, new kinds of personal incentives—all these problems were 'solved' by dropping back to practices which have prevailed in capitalistic societies for centuries. It was the old difficulty. A government in power can't experiment. It must know the answers or at least pretend to know them. Today the Russians contend that an optimal cultural pattern has been achieved, if not yet fully implemented. They dare not admit to any serious need for improvement. Revolutionary experimentation is dead.

"In the second place, Russia has overpropagandized, both to its own people and to the outside world. Their propaganda is much more extensive than any which ever enslaved a working class. That's a serious defect, for it has made it impossible to evaluate their success. We don't know how much of the current vigor of Russian communism is due to a strong, satisfying way of life, and how much to indoctrination. You may call it a temporary expedient, to counteract the propaganda embedded in an older culture. But that need has long since passed, yet the propaganda continues. So long as it goes on, no valid data on the effectiveness of Russian communism can be obtained. For all we know, the whole culture would fall apart if the supporting attitudes were taken away. And what is worse, it's hard to see how they can ever be taken away. Propaganda makes it impossible to progress toward a form of society in which it is unnecessary.

"The third weakness of the Russian government is its use of heroes. The first function of the hero, in Russia as elsewhere, is to piece out a defective governmental structure. Important decisions aren't made by appeal to a set of principles; they are personal acts. The process of governing is an art, not a science, and the government is only as good or as long-lasting as the artist. As to the second function of the hero—how long would communism last if all the pictures of Lenin and Stalin were torn down? It's a question worth asking.

"But most important of all, the Russian experiment was based on power. You may argue that the seizure of power was also a temporary expedient, since the people who held it were intolerant and oppressive. But you can hardly defend the continued use of power in that way. The Russians are still a long way from a culture in which people behave as they *want* to behave, for their mutual good. In order to get its people to act as the communist pattern demands, the Russian government has had to use the techniques of capitalism. On the one hand it resorts to extravagant and uneven rewards. But an unequal distribution of wealth destroys more incentives than it creates. It obviously can't operate for the *common* good. On the other hand, the government also uses punishment or the threat of it. What kind of behavioral engineering do you call that?"

his hands with an exaggerated shrug and drew himself slowly to his feet. He had evidently had enough of Castle's "general issues."

A CAUTIONARY NOTE

At the outset of this chapter we warned that little work has been done on the process whereby psychology becomes a part of popular culture. Consequently, this treatment of "pop" psychology should be regarded as a tentative approach to mapping out the issues. Our reason for introducing this topic to the reader is because we think that, even though the popularization of psychological knowledge has not been thoroughly researched, nonetheless the issues surrounding it are very salient to social psychology. Writers of different persuasions agree that the results of psychology should be communicated to the general public. We do not disagree with this edict, but we think that it rather overlooks the fact that the public is not awaiting passively the transmission of psychological knowledge from psychologists. Although Miller's (1969) exhortation to his fellow professionals to attempt to give psychology to people may not have influenced academic practice, as we have seen in this chapter, there are already ways in which psychology becomes part of the popular imagination and culture.

Epilogue

Just before she died she asked, "What is the answer?" No answer came. She laughed and said. "In that case what is the question?" Then she died.

(Gertrude Stein, as recorded by her biographer, Duncan Sutherland)

The goal of the book has been to illustrate some of the tensions that have beset social psychology using historical evidence, research examples, theoretical papers, and the case study on desegregation to reflect the different ways in which practitioners approach their subject. As we have seen, early social psychology, on both sides of the Atlantic, was characterized by optimisim and its willingness to comment upon large-scale social issues. Although there may have been a dearth of empirical evidence upon which to base their conclusions, social psychologists were confident that their knowledge was of relevance to their society. By the late 1960s this confidence had been eroded to such an extent that it was commonplace to find writers speaking of the "crisis" in social psychology. Radical critics connected this crisis with the nature of the psychologist's social role and with the image of man embedded in the discipline. Mainstream commentators, such as Miller, also acknowledged that psychology needed to rethink its purpose.

It would be quite out of keeping with the spirit of this book to try at the finish to gather up all the loose ends and smooth over the inconsistencies so as to present you with a tidy picture of the discipline. But is there anything, you might wonder, that we can safely predict about likely developments over the next decade? One point seems certain: we cannot turn back the clock. We cannot regain the idealism of the early days. We now have to learn to live with the realization that our discipline does not provide us with a blueprint for redesigning

313

the social world. Our concluding paper by Sarason presents some ideas which may give you a new angle from which to examine the issues touched upon in this book. Sarason makes a point that has been implicit in much of what we have said. Psychology (and indeed all science), he maintains, lacks a sociohistorical perspective. For him the general crisis in social science stems from the fact that we refuse to accept that *certain problems may be intractable.* As long as we remain wedded to the idea that all problems have "solutions" in the scientific sense of the word, we shall, he insists, either retreat from the messiness of the real world or else continue to fashion problems in such a way that they fit our available solutions.

There are a number of striking similarities between what Sarason says in this article and Freud's thesis in *Civilization and its Discontents* (1930). Like Freud, he reminds us that all societies and all individuals are confronted with certain inescapable and unsolved problems. These are part of the human condition: (1) our sense of aloneness in the world; (2) our need for other people; (3) death.

You may not agree with what Sarason says; you may feel that, like Freud, he is unduly pessimistic. But whether or not you agree with his point of view, it should encourage you to explore the nature of the task confronting the social psychologist. If, as Gertrude Stein affirmed, we cannot have the answer, at least let us be clear what the question is.

Reading XXVIII. The Nature of Problem Solving in Social Action, by S. B. Sarason

ABSTRACT: *Science has never had a self-conscious social-historical stance. It uses narrow history in a narrow way, and to the extent that science solves problems, it renders that history obsolete. The nature of scientific problem-solving has been assumed to be appropriate to all problems, including those in the social realm. There are no intractable problems: problems you have to "solve" again, and again, and again. If problems in*

Source: American Psychologist (1978). 33, pp. 370–380.

the social realm seem intractable, it is assumed it is because they have not been formulated and attacked scientifically. Like the atomic scientists, the social scientists who entered the world of social action after World War II, armed with their theories and scientifically tested knowledge, found a world that would not bend to their paradigms. They had entered a world governed by values, not facts, where persuasion and power were in the service of different definitions of age-old questions, where the relationship between action and values was far more crucial to living than was the requirement that action lead to a solution. Many social scientists reacted either with petulance or bewilderment. They had not been content to study and explain the social world; they had wanted to change it. They fared poorly. A malaise set in, a crisis of confidence. How does one justify trying to cope with what may be intractable problems? The very nature of the question belies its origins in the assumption of science that one has to believe that all problems are solvable.

. . . What lends fascination to historical constructions and reconstructions is the process of deducing or intuiting what people in that era took for granted. But if the process is fascinating, it is inherently problematic. For one thing, there are many vantage points—so many, in fact, that it is literally impossible for one person or group to achieve them all. No less serious for those who have to believe that they are on the road to truth, and that the road has an end, is that reconstructions of the past always reflect what we from our present vantage points take for granted. Can you deduce what people in a far-off era took for granted without having what you take for granted affecting your conclusions in ways that you cannot know but that people in future eras will think they know? The process of historical reconstruction inevitably says as much about the present as it does about the past. If history strikes so many people as uninteresting and irrelevant, it is, in part, because they do not understand that what we call history is literally manufactured by the present. When Henry Ford, that self-made sage, said "history is bunk" he was saying a good deal about himself and many others in our society, far more than he was saying about the past. That was obviously less true, but still true, in the case of Gibbon's *Decline and Fall of the Roman Empire*.

The social-historical stance has not been a dominant feature of American psychology. An amusing but illuminating example—back in the late forties the American Psychological Association began to accredit graduate programs in clinical psychology. An APA committee came for a site visit to Yale, and part of their time was spent talking with our graduate students. At the end of the visit I talked with one of the committee members, who expressed satisfaction with our program with one exception. He had asked one of our graduate students if he had read Köhler's (1925) *The Mentality of Apes*, and the reply was: "No one reads that any more. That's old hat." We both laughed, very uneasily. Both of us were pre-World-War-II-trained psychologists and very much aware that as a result of the war, the face of psychology was being changed. For both of us, the Henry Ford type of statement by the graduate student presaged something disquietingly new in psychology, but it was hard to put into words. . . . But something told me that what the student said was very important, and I have been trying ever since to make sense of it. The first conclusion I came to was that there was really nothing new in what the student said. By virtue (among other things) of psychology's divorce from philosophy and its marriage to science, history in psychology became a lot of narrow histories depending on the particular problem that interested you. That is, if you were interested in reaction time to a type of stimulus, you had the obligation to know what others in the past had done and found. This obligation served several purposes: to deepen your knowledge of the particular problem, to avoid repeating what others had done, and to increase the chances that what you were going to do would shed new light on the problem. This might be called the rational justification of the use of history. But, as is always the case, there were nonrational factors at work. . . . One of them was that you were going to add something new to an understanding of the problem precisely because you were building on knowledge provided by others from the past.

In the scientific tradition, knowledge is cumulative: You either add a new brick to the edifice of knowledge so that it looks different or, better yet, you destroy the edifice and present your colleagues with a foundation for a new and better structure. One part of this tradition says that knowledge is cumulative, the other part says that your contribution is proportionate to how much past knowledge you have rendered obsolete. You use history, so to speak, with the hope of destroying its usefulness. This kind of attitude or hope is subtly but potently absorbed by young people entering scientific fields, and I believe it has been particularly strong in psychology, less because of psychology's youth as a scientific endeavor and more because of its self-conscious desire to identify with that endeavor. This has tended to produce still another belief: If a study was done 10 years ago, it is unlikely that you will learn much from it; if it was done 20 years ago, the chances are even smaller; and if it was done before World War II, don't forget it but be prepared quickly to do so. Put in another way, it would go like this: "We have come a long, long way in a relatively short period of time and there is not much from the past that is usable to us now. What is more worrisome than whether we are overlooking anything from the past is whether someone in the present is rendering what I am doing as wrong or obsolete." Köhler studied apes during World War I. Obviously, the odds are small that he has anything to say that is important to the here and now of psychology! Yes, he probably belongs in the Museum of Greats but you only go to museums when you are not working.

My purpose is neither to discuss nor question the implicit and explicit uses of history in scientific research. What I wish to suggest is that these uses (and, therefore, perceptions and conceptions of the past) have been very influential in shaping people's attitudes toward the significance of history in general. That is, among all those who think of themselves as scientists, there has been a noticeable tendency to view the social world as having been born a few days ago. This should not be surprising when one considers the status and functions society has given to science. Within the confines of its own traditions, science long has been on an onward–upward trajectory in the course of which it has displayed a seemingly boundless capacity to solve its problems. This did not go unnoticed by society as it saw that in solving its problems science could also contribute to the welfare of society. Scientists and the public came to agree that the deliberately impractical goals of science (knowledge for knowledge's sake) had very practical implications. No one ever said it, and perhaps no one ever thought it, but the agreement between science and society contained a "message": Society had problems *now* and science could be helpful in solving them *now* or *in the foreseeable future.* There was no disposition to recognize that the relatively ahistorical stance of science might be mischievously inappropriate to social problems. Put in another way, the pride that science took in rendering past scientific knowledge obsolete, the view of its past as more interesting than it was usable, the concentration on now and the future—these stances fatefully determined the degree to which, and the ways in which, society's problems would be placed in a historical context. The type of influence seemed proper and productive as long as the findings of science had two types of consequences: one was of the technological, thing-building or thing-creating variety, and the other was of the illness-prevention or the illness-curative variety. It may be more correct to say that the nature of the influence went unnoticed as long as there was near-universal social acceptance of what science seemed to be able to do. As long as society posed essentially nonhistorical questions for science, science came up smelling technological roses. Agriculture, industry, medicine, the military—they asked the kinds of here-and-now questions to which the findings of science could be applied.

It is hard to overestimate how total identification with science eroded whatever significance social history had for psychology. For one thing, it seriously limited the capacity of the field to examine its past in order to illuminate its present, that is, to try to fathom how its view of the past (and its projections into the future) might be a function of the myth-making present. For another thing, it blinded psychology to the obvious fact that any field of human endeavor is shaped by forces beyond its boundaries and that its structure and contents can never be wholly explained by that endeavor's narrow history. For example, can one understand the history of behaviorism or psychoanalysis by restricting oneself to what behaviorists and psychoanalysts did and said? Boring did his best to sensitize psychologists to *zeitgeist*, but his efforts have been honored far more in the breach than in the practice. "The spirit of the times" is such an apt metaphor because it warns us that what we think and do, what we think we are, what we say the world will be—all of these in part reflect influences that are time-bound and hard to recognize. The word *spirit* (an uncongenial one in psychology), like the concept of the unconscious, reminds us that as individuals or fields we are affected by forces near and far, known and unknown, inside and outside.

At its best, social history serves the purpose of reminding us that we, like those of past eras, are very biased, time-bound organisms. We differ in all kinds of ways from those of past eras, but one thing we clearly have in common: We breathe the spirit of our times. If we use social history for the same purpose that we do a table of random numbers, we stand a little better chance of avoiding the worst features of uncontrolled bias. At the very least, sensitivity to social history makes it hard to ignore several things. First, despite all the diversity among human societies, past and present, each dealt with three problems: how to dilute the individual's sense of aloneness in the world, how to engender and maintain a sense of community, and how to justify living even though one will die. Second, each society defines and copes differently with these problems, and as a society changes, as it inevitably does, the nature of the definitions and copings changes. Third, these changes, more often than not, are not recognized until people see a difference between past and present definitions and copings. Fourth, the three problems are always here and there in the life of the individual and the society, but not in the sense that inanimate matter is here and there. Fifth, these are not problems that people have created, and they can never be eliminated or ignored. Sixth, any planned effort to effect a social change (as in the case of scientists who seek to apply their knowledge and skills for purposes of social change) that does not recognize and understand the history and the dynamics of these three problems will likely exacerbate rather than dilute the force of these problems.

Applying scientific and technological knowledge and skills in social action is not like applying paint on a wall, except as both applications literally obscure what one may not like to look at. Scientists who enter the world of social action like to think themselves possessed of the basic knowledge and problem-solving skills of their science, and they often have a feeling of virtue because they are applying these to practical social issues. What they fail to see is that because science does not start with the three problems, because it in no explicit way recognizes or is controlled by them, science *qua* science has no special expertise to deal with them. Everyone knows the old joke about the graduate student who had learned about Latin-square design and was looking for a problem that fitted it. There is a way of looking at science and seeing some similarity between it and this student. Science has learned a lot about problem solving, but when it looks beyond its confines to the arena of social problems, it has tended not to ask what the "basic" problems are there but rather to seek problems that fit its problem-solving style: clear problems that have unambiguously correct solutions. The separation of science from disciplines concerned with social history will always obscure from science that not all basic problems in nature can be molded to its problem-solving models.

Science and Solutions

Before World War II, academic psychology never quite made up its mind whether it was a social or biological science. The image of the laboratory was very attractive. After all, look at what had been discovered in laboratories, and wasn't society grateful? If psychology was to earn society's gratitude, and also be accepted by the older sciences, what was needed, among other things, was a certain kind of place where problems could be analyzed, dissected, and studied. A laboratory was a place where one solved problems. One could study problems outside of a laboratory but that meant that one had drastically reduced the chances of finding solutions to basic problems. . . . [It was generally thought that] not until the basic questions are clarified, studied and solved in the most rigorous ways can a foundation be provided for truly effective psychotherapeutic practice. It's like building bridges: Basic science had to solve a lot of basic problems before engineers could build bigger and better bridges . . .

Now, if one knew something about social history and had the courage, one could have asked: "Is it possible that these problems are of a human and social nature and are not solvable by science? Is it not obvious that in the chasm between your scientific findings and solutions, on the one hand, and the realm of human affairs, on the other hand, there is a mine field of values for the traversing of which your science provides no guide? If we can build magnificent bridges, or develop life-extending vaccines, is it only because of basic problem-solving research or is it also because society wanted those fruits from the tree of science? Just as technology depends on basic science, don't both depend on or reflect the wishes of the larger society? What will happen if and when the social world changes and the relation between society and psychology is altered so that psychology is asked and willingly attempts to solve social problems it never encountered, and never could encounter, either in the laboratory or through employment of any of its research strategies? Will psychology be found inherently wanting?

These were questions that could not be raised in psychology before World War II. Some of these questions were explicitly raised by one psychologist, J. F. Brown, in his 1936 *Psychology and the Social Order,* but no one paid him much mind. In the midst of a social catastrophe, the Great Depression, Brown saw the crisis in psychology. He was able to because social history in its Marxist version had become part of his conceptual framework. His was not a parochial mind—witness his attempt to bring together Marx, Lewin, and Freud. Lynd, a sociologist, raised similar questions in his 1939 book *Knowledge for What?* Having studied Middletown before and after the Great Depression, Lynd, like Brown, questioned the traditional directions of the social sciences and asserted their conceptual and moral bankruptcy.

In one crucial respect, Brown and Lynd were in basic agreement with an underlying assumption of science: All problems of society, like those in the rest of nature, had solutions. The problems might be of a different order, the ways of studying and controlling them might require new theories and methodologies, and their solutions might be a long way off, but they were solvable. Who would deny that the creativity and ingenuity that had unravelled the mysteries of the atom, exemplified in the work of Rutherford and Bohr, or that allowed Einstein to supersede Newton, would falter when faced with the problems of social living? But what if these problems were not solvable in the sense to which science was accustomed?

The concept of solution in science is by no means a clear one, and it is beyond my purposes to examine the different and overlapping meanings that concept has been given. In one respect, however, the lay and scientific understanding of a solution is very similar: A problem has been "solved": (a) when it does not have to be solved again because the operations that lead to the solution can be demonstrated to be independent of who performs them, (b) when the solution is *an* answer to a question or set of related questions, and (c) when there is no longer any doubt that the answer is the correct one. If there are competing answers, the problem has not yet been solved. So, when geneticists around the world were trying to "solve" the genetic code, they could agree on only one thing: Someone would find *the* answer. And the answer would be of the order of "four divided by two is two." There is or will be only one correct solution. There are times, of course, when the solution about which there is consensus is proved wrong, and then everybody is off and running to find the "really" correct solution. The correct solution always raises new questions, but at least the earlier question does not have to be solved again. The question was asked, the solution was found, and now for the next question. [Although psychologists have studied problem solving, they always begin with a problem that is solvable.] Why, for all practical purposes, is there nothing in this literature on how artists solve their problems? For example, what was the problem or problems Cézanne was trying to solve?

. . . What was the cognitive substance of the problem, how was he trying to solve it in a visual form, what made for such a long struggle, and did he solve the problem? Several answers could be given to these questions. One would be that we cannot be sure what the problem was, and even if he were alive we could not accept his version of the problem. How do you justify studying problems whose clarity and formulation you know ahead of time must be of dubious status and when there are no known ways of determining what the "real" problem is? If you are fuzzy about the nature of the problem, how can you ever state criteria by which to judge successful outcomes? And what would we do if Cézanne had said: "In this painting I solved the problem, in that one I did not." Do we accept his judgments, and what have we learned by doing that? And what do we learn from fellow artists who are awed by Cézanne's accomplishments? Their judgments permit no firm conclusions about the relationship between problem and solution. Besides, not every artist, then or now, agrees either about the substance of Cézanne's artistic problems or artistic solutions. A final answer might be: Cézanne is a great artist, but his problem-solving accomplishments cannot be understood and judged in the way the works of great scientists can be. In short, they would say Freud was right: Before the artist you throw up your hands.

. . . These are problems that are not science's cup of tea. There is problem solving that does not fit the researcher's requirements of a clear, manipulable problem and unambiguous criteria for the correct solution. So, science has always left that problem alone, albeit from a stance of superiority. The problems of social living were also left alone until the emergence of the social sciences, led by economics. Just as the natural sciences had developed laws about the nonhuman world, the social sciences would seek the laws of human society, not only for the purposes of explaining the workings of society but for controlling it. They would be the embodiment of Plato's philosopher-kings. Apparently they were not impressed with the fact that Plato saw the problems of social living as so difficult to understand and cope with, requiring of philosopher-kings such a fantastic depth of learning and wisdom, that one could not entrust social responsibility to them until they were well along in years. And to my knowledge, Socrates infrequently answered a question and never solved a problem. He was too impressed with man's capacity for self-justification and self-deceit. Neither Plato nor Socrates ever assumed that the accomplishments of Greek scientists reflected a model of question asking and problem solving that was appropriate to the development of the good society.

Social Action

Let us now turn to a moment in history when the workings of impractical science led to a most practical product, one that our scientists and society desperately wanted. It was a moment that simultaneously illustrated the fruitfulness of scientific problem solving and exposed its inappropriateness for solving social problems. I refer, of course, to the successful solution of all the problems, theoretical and technical, leading to the harnessing of atomic energy for military purposes. As soon as it became evident that a successful atom bomb was in the offing, some scientists began to ask themselves questions: Should it be used, how should it be used, and how could the seemingly endless uses of atomic energy be exploited for human welfare? They saw a problem, many problems, and as in the case of Cézanne, the substance of the problem was by no means clear. The end result of a successful solution seemed clear: a world in which the destructive uses of atomic energy were rendered impossible or nearly so and in which its uses for human welfare were maximized. But how do you go from here to there? What was the bearing of the scientific tradition on that problem?

As best as I can determine, none of the scientists thought they were dealing with a scientific problem. They recognized that they had been catapulted into a social world that was fantastically complicated, constantly changing, and seemingly uncontrollable. It was not even a maze, because that image conjures up entry points, stable pathways, and some kind of end point. The social world was not a maze. It was not even a cloud chamber, because that is a device rationally constructed to record and measure predictable events. It may be a world of facts and events but it is ruled by passions. It is ironic in the extreme that at the same time that the world saw these scientists as at the apogee of human achievement, the scientists saw themselves as angry, bewildered, impotent people. They became like most other people: passionate, committed, partisan, rhetorical, and irrational. Those are not characteristics foreign to scientific controversy and investigation, but the morality of science and the critical eyes of the scientific community are effective controls against the undue influence of these characteristics. If you suspect a fellow scientist of lying and cheating, or of just being a damn fool, you have ways of finding out and spreading the word. But that means there is consensus about the rules of the game. The social world is not the scientific world. As a physicist friend once said to me, ... "I can't deal with a world where everybody has his own definition of the problem, where facts are an intrusive annoyance and of tertiary importance, where who you are is more important that what you know, and where the need to act is more decisive than feeling secure about what the consequences will be." And he concluded with this: "I will stick to my world where there are answers, and if I don't find them, someone else will." When the atomic scientists entered the world of social action, that world could not be molded to fit the problem-solving strategies to which they were accustomed.

But, many social scientists thought, those were atomic scientists and one should not be surprised that when they left the world of minute matter and entered the world of human matters, they faltered. After all, they were not social scientists whose stock in trade was human matters. The fact is that up until World War II, the social sciences had contributed to our understanding of the social world, but, with one noteworthy exception, these contributions were mainly descriptive or analytic, or historical. They were not contributions stemming from the social scientist's effort to participate in and solve social problems. Like the natural scientists, the social scientists were the dispassionate observers, and deliberately so, who sought to formulate clear questions to which clear answers could be obtained. They saw their task as understanding the social world, not changing it. The one exception was economics, which for decades had an intimate tie with the practical world of government, business, industry, and finance. Early on, economists not only described the world as they saw it but they drew conclusions about what should or should not be done. They were listened to, and they took responsible positions in the social arena. Heilbroner (1961) has aptly called them the "worldly philosophers." They lived, so to speak, in two worlds: the scientific problem-solving world, and the world of social action.

It was the Great Depression that really made the world of social action accessible to increasing numbers of economists. The underlying assumption, of course, was that economists had knowledge and skills that could inform public policy and action. If, during the thirties, the atomic scientists had developed firm friendships with their university colleagues in economics (unlikely events in the community of scholars), they would have learned much earlier than they did that scientific knowledge as power in the social arena is of a different order than it is in the research community; that in the social arena one is always dealing with competing statements of a problem and there is no time or intention to experiment in implementation with one or another of the formulations; that the choice of formulation has less to do with data than with the traditions, value, world outlooks, and the spirit of the times; that the goal of social action is not once-and-for-all solutions in the scientific sense but to stir the waters of change, hoping and sometimes praying that more good than harm will follow; that the very process of formulating a problem, setting goals, and starting to act not only begins to change *your* perception of problems, goals, and actions but, no less fateful, the perceptions of *others* related to or affected by the process in some way. *In the phenomenology of social action, problem changing rather than problem solving is figure, and you know what that does to solutions regardless of how you define them!*

World War II opened up many opportunities for social scientists to be in social action or policy-related roles. It was truly the first global war bringing us into contact with scores of different cultures and peoples. So, as never before, anthropologists became socially important people. And sociologists and psychologists were even in short supply. World War II forever changed the social sciences. They were exposed to new problems, and much that they thought they knew was proved either irrelevant or wrong. More important, they tasted the heady wine of influence and action and they liked it. Government needs us, they said, and government seemed to agree. At least one noted psychologist (Doob, 1947) had his doubts and wrote a brief paper beautifully describing the naive scientist in the world of social action. Doob's paper is noteworthy in two other respects. First, his recognition that in social action, the scientist *qua* scientist is like a fish out of water—dead.

> Where social science data are inadequate or where social science itself can provide only principles or a way of approach to a problem, the social scientist must hurl himself into the debate, participate on an equal or unequal footing with men and women who are not social scientists, toss some of his scientific scruples to the winds, and fight for what seems to him to be valid or even good. A strict adherence to the scientific *credo* in such circumstances leaves the social scientists impotent and sterile as far as policy is concerned. (Doob, 1947)

Second, the fact that Doob early on learned that if he responded seriously to his and others' needs for mutuality and community, even if some of those others were opponents, social action could be rewarding despite the fact that one never knew whether one was having an intended pro-grammatic effect, that is, whether one was solving a problem.

In the aftermath of World War II, the government became both patron and employer of social science. After all, the argument ran, if the government respected and supported social science research, as it did research in the biological and natural sciences, the social atom might be split and its energies harnessed for the greatest good of the greatest number. For 20 years after World War II, the social sciences became, and with a vengeance, vigorous, quantitative, theoretical, and entrepreneurial. If you wanted to solve in a basic and once-and-for-all way the puzzles of individual and social behavior, you needed resources of the wall-to-wall variety. True, it would take time to learn to ask the right questions, to develop the appropriate methodologies, before you could come up with the right answers. What we were after were those bedrock laws of social behavior and process that would allow a society "really" rationally to diagnose and solve its problems. Give us time (and money) and you will not regret it. In the meantime, if you think we can be helpful to you with your current problems, please call on us. And call they did, and go they went. The results have been discouraging and shattering, discouraging because of the lack of intended outcomes, and shattering because they call into question the appropriateness of the scientific-rational model of problem definition and solution in social action. Nelson (1977), a noted economist, has summed it up well in his recent book *The Moon and the Ghetto.*

> The search for "the Great Society" entailed highly publicized efforts at turning the policy steering wheel. Broad new mandates were articulated—the war on poverty—and specific policies were designed to deal with various aspects of the problem. The histories of these departures clearly identify the key roles often played by research reports, social science theory, formal analytical procedures. More recent years have seen an increasing flow of proposals for organizational reform: vouchers for schools, health maintenance organizations, greater independence for the post office, a national corporation to run the passenger railroads, pollution fees, revenue sharing. It is easy to trace the intellectual roots of many of these ideas. The technoscience orientation has come later, and never has had the thrust of the others. Nonetheless the intellectual rhetoric has been strong, and has generated at least token efforts to launch the aerospace companies on problems of garbage collection, education and crime control, and programs with evocative titles like "Research Applied to National Needs."
>
> The last several years have seen a sharp decline in faith, within the scientific community as well as outside, regarding our ability to solve our problems through scientific and rational means. Those who want to get on with solving the problems obviously are upset about the loss of momentum. It is apparent that many of the more optimistic believers in the power of rational analysis overestimated that power. There are strong interests blocking certain kinds of changes. Certain problems are innately intractable or at least very hard. But the proposition here is that a good portion of the reason why rational

analysis of social problems hasn't gotten us very far lies in the nature of the analyses that have been done. John Maynard Keynes expressed the faith, and the arrogance, of the social scientist when he said, "The ideas of economists and political philosophers, both when they are right and when they are wrong, are more powerful than is commonly understood . . . I am sure that the power of vested interests is vastly exaggerated compared with the gradual encroachment of ideas." But surely Abe Lincoln was right when he made his remark about not being able to fool all of the people all of the time.

In addition to their clumsy treatment of value and knowledge (a problem that seems to infect analysts generally), analysts within each of the traditions have had a tendency to combine tunnel vision with intellectual imperialism . . . Members of the different traditions have had a tendency to be lulled by their imperialistic rhetoric. This has often led them to provide interpretations and prescriptions that the public, and the political apparatus, rightly have scoffed at. Failure to recognize the limitations of one's own perspective has made analysis of problems that require an integration of various perspectives very difficult. Indeed a kind of internecine warfare obtains among the traditions over the turf that lies between them. (Nelson, 1977, pp. 16, 17, 19)

Nelson illustrates his position using day care, breeder reactor programs, and the SST.

Nelson argues that there are inherent limitations to the scientific problem-solving model as the basis for social action, and he also suggests that there are problems that are inherently intractable. The very word *intractable* is foreign to the scientific tradition. In science, problems may be extraordinarily difficult, but they can never be viewed as intractable, and if some fool says a problem is intractable it is because he or she is not posing the problem correctly or does not have the brain power to work through to the solution. In science, fools are people who say problems are intractable. In the realm of social action, fools are people who say all problems are tractable.

The Challenge of Intractability

Why is it so difficult for people, particularly scientists, to entertain, let alone accept, the possibility that many problems in social living are intractable, not solvable in the once-and-for-all-you-don't-have-to-solve-it-again fashion. I have already given one part of the answer: Science has been such a success in solving so many of the problems in nature that people became persuaded that the dilemmas and puzzles of the human social world would likewise become explicable and controllable. In fact, people in Western society were so persuaded that it became an article of unquestioned faith. And when religion's hold on people's minds began to disappear and the scientific outlook and enterprise took its place, it tended to go unnoticed that one article of faith (the world is divinely ordered) had been supplanted by another (the world, animate and inanimate, is ordered, knowable, and controllable). And the tendency of science to be ahistorical in general, particularly in regard to social history, effectively obscured for people that the rise of modern science not only coincided with the Age of Enlightenment but was its major beneficiary. And few things characterized that age as did the belief in the perfectibility of man and society. As Becker (1932) so well described, the heavenly city of St. Augustine would be built on earth, not through divine inspiration but through human reason. Science could not recognize the possibility of intractable problems, and like the religions it supplanted, it purported to give clear direction and meaning to living.

What would happen if one accepted intractability, which is no less than to accept the imperfectibility of man and society? What would keep us going? How would we justify our individual strivings and our commitment to social action? What happens to the idea of progress? What will permit us to look forward to tomorrow? Do we seek, as some people do, new religious experiences that tell us we are not alone in this vast world, that there are solutions to the problems of living, and that mortality can open the door to immortality? And that last question, I submit, contains the substance of the real challenge of intractability to science in that it says that humans need to deal with three facts: They are inevitably alone within themselves, they need others, and they will die. These are facts that create problems, but they are not the kinds of problems that fit into science's problem-solving model. Leaving religion aside (although it is true for many believers) the problems created by these facts need to be solved again, and again and again. At different times in our lives, the same problem has a different answer.

It has not gone unnoticed that the wonders of science and technology have had little or no effect on society's capacity to help its members feel less alone in the world, to enjoy a sense of community, and to help them cope with anxiety about death. Some would argue that the failure of science to start with and to be governed by these facts of human existence has exacerbated the pain associated with them. And when value-free science entered the realm of human affairs, it exposed its naivete, its ignorance of social history, its hubris, and its blindness to man's need to deal with his aloneness, to feel part of and needed by a larger group, and to recognize and not deny his mortality. This is what the atomic scientists learned, or should have learned.

There is a malaise in all the sciences. For the first time in modern science, as well as in modern Western society, people are questioning whether the fact that science and technology can accomplish a particular feat is reason enough to do it. In psychology we have been brought up short by the fact that as adherents of science we do not have license to conduct research in any way we want. We are accountable, and that means that we should feel and nurture the bonds of similarity and communality between ourselves and the people we study. It is the difference between *knowing* that you are studying people, like yourself, and not "subjects." Society does not exist for the purposes of scientists. It is arrogance in the extreme to look at society from a *noblesse oblige* stance, expecting that the gifts you give it will be responded to with gratitude, not questions or hesitations. Today, both among scientists and the public, there is the attitude that one should look a gift horse in the mouth.

What bearing does this have on social action? Well, let us talk about Norway. As you know, several years ago they found a lot of oil under the Norwegian Sea. Far from this being greeted with hosannas and visions of a bountiful future, Norwegian leaders reacted with a kind of fear. What could happen to their society if they plunged into the development of the oil fields and began to collect the billions of dollars from the sale of oil? What would be the consequences for Norwegian culture, for their sense of continuity with their past, for their sense of community? A decision was made to go as slowly as possible, to give priority to what they regarded as the important issue in living! The Norwegians know that they live in a world they cannot control, and they will be subject to pressures within and without their society to develop the oil fields quickly and fully, that they may be unable to act in ways consistent with their needs and values. They may not be able to have it their way. Indeed, we can assume they will fall short of their mark. What will keep them going is what is wrapped in what a poet said: "Life takes its final meaning in chosen death." That may sound melodramatic but only to those who cannot understand that the fact of death informs the experience of living. We live each day as if we were immortal, although our rationality tells us how silly a basis for living that is. If our own rationality does not tell us, we can count on all sorts of events and experiences to shock us, not into the recognition of the fact that we will die, but into confronting how we justify why we have lived and how we planned to live (Becker, 1973; Sarason, 1977). And when scientists confront those questions, and each one does at one time or another, they frequently find that there was a lot they took for granted that they wish they had not. But that is the fate of everyone. At each vantage point in our lives we see our history differently.

As for the scientists who enter the arena of social action (and that may be in different roles), they would do well to be guided by the values they attach to the facts of living in much the same way that the amazing Norwegians are trying to do. This will present scientists with a type of problem (and transform their concepts of solution) for which their scientific models are inappropriate and may even be interfering. They will find themselves dealing in persuasion, not only facts; the problems will change before and within them; they will not be concerned with replicability because that will be impossible; there will be no final solutions, only a constantly upsetting imbalance between values and action; the internal conflict will be not in the form of "Do I have the right answer?" but rather "Am I being consistent with what I believe?"; satisfaction will come not from colleagues' consensus that their procedures, facts, and conclusions are independent of their feelings and values, but from their own convictions that they tried to be true to their values; they will fight to win not in order to establish the superiority of their procedures or the validity of their scientific facts, concepts, and theories but because they want to live with themselves and others in certain ways.

Most scientists who entered the arena of social action have left it bloodied, disillusioned, and cynical. They came with data and solutions, but even when they had neither, they assumed that their training and capacity for rational thinking and their ability to pose clear problems and find appropriate methods leading to solutions would establish their credibility as well as their right to an important role in rational social change. Most of them did not realize, if only for their lack of knowledge or respect for social history, that they were fully agreeing with Karl Marx, who had said that it was not enough to try to understand the world. You had to change it and in a scientific way! Marx considered himself a scientist, and the arrogance of scientism permeated his writings and actions. He had his theory, he stated the problems, collected his data, developed procedures, and had no doubt about the correct solution. And what scorn he had for his unscientific opponents! But Marx did not fool himself about what was behind his science, indeed prior to it. He saw man pathetically alone, separated from others, afraid of living and dying. Unfortunately, his dependence on his science led him to give priority to methods dictated by that science and not to what those methods meant *at that time* to man's plight. The solution to that plight was put off to the distant future. In the meantime, trust Marx's scientific theory and procedures. Look what it explained and promised!

The scientist is committed to seeking and saying his or her truths and must not be concerned with whose ox is being gored, an imperative that science has never questioned because to do so would be to destroy the enterprise at its foundation, which is, of course, moral in the sense of describing how scientists should live with each other. To the extent that they live together on the basis of that imperative, scientific problems can be solved. In the social arena, whose ox is being gored cannot be ignored. It can, of course, be ignored, but history contains countless examples of how bloody the consequences can be. And yet, there are times when one takes a position and acts, knowing that the oxes of other individuals and groups will be gored. But somewhere along the way one should be aware that as important as the desire to prevail over your opponents is, the need on both sides is to feel some bond of mutuality. Winning no less than losing can increase one's sense of loneliness and decrease the sense of belonging. In science, how you did something is no less important than what you say you found. Some would say that how is more important. There are hows in social action, but of a very different cast, so different that it becomes understandable why so many scientists who entered the arena of social action faltered. They could not unlearn fast enough to start learning that the nature of problem solving in the kitchen of social action bore no resemblance to what they had been accustomed to. It is not a kitchen for everyone. But as my favorite president liked to say: "If it's too hot in the kitchen, get the hell out."

Even if you can get out, you will still be dealing with the same issues in your personal life and social circle. But even as a scientist, a new problem has arisen. I refer, of course, to the growing sentiment, already reflected in certain legislation, that what science studies, and the ways it conducts its studies, will be determined by the larger society. And one of the diverse factors behind that determination is the feeling that despite our dazzling capacity to gain new knowledge and skills, to open new vistas for human experience, perhaps even to create new forms of life, we still feel alone, socially unconnected, unhappy in living and fearful of dying. It is a very hot kitchen, not one that the wonders of science and technology have been or will be able to air-condition.

What I have said is no excuse for inaction or pessimism, or any other attitude that only deepens the sense of aloneness, accentuates the lack of community, or makes facing the end an intolerable burden. Nor have I in any way intended to denigrate science or intellectual endeavor. There is a difference between science and scientism, between modesty and arrogance, between recognizing limitations and seeing the whole world from one perspective.

Social action takes on a very different quality when it is based on or controlled by certain facts and values. In a recent book, some colleagues and I (Sarason, Carroll, Maton, Cohen, & Lorentz, 1977) describe an effort over a $3\frac{1}{2}$-year period to develop and sustain a barter economy network of relationships, the purposes of which were to deal more effectively with the fact that resources are always limited and people have a need for a sense of community. I should emphasize that it was an effort not only to increase people's access to needed resources but to do it in a way that also widened and deepened their sense of belonging. The members of this network range from high school students to researchers from different colleges and universities. It is an ever-expanding network of human relationships that makes it a little easier, and sometimes a lot easier, to cope with personal and intellectual needs. Central to the story we tell is a remarkable woman we call Mrs. Dewar, whose distinctive characteristic is the ability to scan her world to see and create opportunities whereby people unknown to each other are brought together because each has something the other person needs. There is resource but no money exchange, and people stay together and have call on each other.

The problem-solving literature is not helpful in trying to understand a Mrs. Dewar or several others like her that we describe. None of these individuals has dealt with solvable problems defined in the traditional scientific sense, but they have transformed their worlds. How they did it is no less important than why they did it, but their distinctiveness in social action lies in the way they put the whys and hows together. In these days when social scientists, suffering from the burnt-child reaction, are either retreating from the world of social action or scaling down their claims to credibility, they would be well advised to pay attention to people like Mrs. Dewar who are not burdened by the concept of "problems" but whose thinking and actions are explicitly powered by the concepts of "opportunities" and "matching," concepts in the service of a clear vision of what makes learning and living worthwhile.

References

Abercrombie, K. (1968). Paralanguage, *British Journal of Disorders of Communication*, **3**, 55–59.

Ainsworth, M. D. (1962). The effects of maternal deprivation: a review of findings and controversy in the context of research strategy. In, *Deprivation of Maternal Care: a Reassessment of its Effects*. Geneva: World Health Organization.

Ainsworth, M. D. (1972) Further research into the adverse effects of maternal deprivation. In J. Bowlby (Ed.), *Child care and the growth of love*. (Part III, 2nd edn). Harmondsworth: Penguin.

Allport, F. H. (1924). *Social Psychology*. Boston: Houghton Mifflin.

Allport, F. H. et al. (1953). The effects of segregation and the consequences of desegregation: A social science statement. *Minnesota Law Review*, **37**, 429–440.

Allport, G. W. (1954). *Prejudice*. Cambridge, Mass.: Addison-Wesley.

Alutto, J. A., & Belasco, J. A. (1974). Determinants of attitudinal militancy among nurses and teachers. *Industrial and Labour Relations Review*, **27**, 216–227.

American Psychological Association. (1968). Bylaws of the American Psychological Association. *1968 Directory*. Washington, D.C.: Author.

American Psychological Association. (1973). *Ethical Principles in the Conduct of Research with Human Participants*. Washington, D.C.: Author.

Ames, C. (1978). Children's achievement attributions and self-reinforcement: Effects of self-concept and competitive reward structure. *Journal of Educational Psychology*, **70**, 345–355.

Ames, C., Ames, R., & Felker, D. W. (1977). Effects of competitive reward structure and valence of outcome on children's achievement attributions. *Journal of Educational Psychology*, **69**, 1–8.

Argyle, M. (1969). *Social Interaction*, London: Methuen.

Argyle, M. (1975). *Bodily Communication*. London: Methuen.

Argyle, M. (1980). The development of applied social psychology. In R. Gilmour & S. Duck (Eds.), *The Development of Social Psychology*. London: Academic Press, 81–105.

Argyle, M. (Ed.) (1981). *Social Skills and Health*. London: Methuen.

Argyle, M., Alkema, F., & Gilmour, R. (1972). The communication of friendly and hostile attitudes by verbal and non-verbal signals. *European Journal of Social Psychology*, **1**, 385–402.

Argyle, M., & Ingram, R. (1972). Gaze, mutual gaze and proximity, *Semiotica*, **6**, 32–49.

Argyle, M., & Kendon, A. (1967). The experimental analysis of social performance. In L. Berkowitz (Ed.), *Advances in Experimental Social Psychology: Vol. 3*. New York: Academic Press, 55–98.

Argyle, M., Lalljee, M., & Cook, M. (1968). The effects of visibility on interaction in a dyad. *Human Relations*, **21**, 3–17.

Armistead, N. (1974). *Reconstructing Social Psychology*. Harmondsworth: Penguin.

Armor, D. (1980). White flight and the future of desegregation. In W. G. Stephan & J. R. Feagin (Eds), *School Desegregation: Past, Present and Future*, New York: Plenum.

Armstrong, G., Jones, G., Race, D., & Ruddock, J. (1980). *Mentally handicapped under five*, Evaluation Research Group Report 8, University of Sheffield.

Aronson, E., Stephan, C., Sikes, J., Blaney, N., & Snapp, M. (1978). *The Jigsaw Classroom*. Beverly Hills, Calif: Sage.

Ashton-Warner, S. (1963). *Teacher*. New York: Simon & Schuster.

Baer, J. (1976). *How to be an Assertive (not Aggressive) Woman*. New York: New American Library.

Baers, M. (1954). Women workers and home responsibilities. *International Labour Review*, **69**, 338–355.

Bateson, G., et al. (1956). Toward a theory of schizophrenia. *Behavioural Science*, **1**, 251–264.

Becker, C. L. (1932). *The Heavenly City of the Eighteenth Century Philosophers*. New Haven, Conn.: Yale University Press.

Becker, E. (1970). The social role of the man of knowledge: A historical and critical sketch. In T. Shibutani (Ed.), *Human Nature and Collective Behaviours*. Englewood Cliffs, N.J.: Prentice-Hall.

Becker, E. (1973). *The Denial of Death*. New York: Free Press (Macmillan).

Bennis, W., Benne, K. D., & Chin, R. (1961). *The planning of change*. New York: Holt, Rinehart & Winston.

Bernay, E. (1977). *Growing up to be Chairman of the Board*. Ms, June, p. 80.

Bloom, L. F., Coburn, K., & Pearlman, J. (1976). *The New Assertive Woman*. New York: Dell.

Boring, E. C. (1929). A History of Experimental Psychology. New York: The Century Co.

Bowlby, J. (1951). *Maternal Care and Mental Health*. Geneva: World Health Organization.

Bowlby, J. (1953). *Child Care and the Growth of Love*. Harmondsworth: Penguin.

Bowlby, J. (1969/71). *Attachment and loss, vol. 1*. London: Hogarth Press. (And Harmondsworth: Penguin).

Bowlby, J. (1973). *Attachment and loss, vol. 2*. London: Hogarth Press.

Bowlby, J., Ainsworth, M. D., Boston, M., & Rosenbluth, D. (1956). The effects of mother–child separation: a follow-up study. *British Journal of Medical Psychology*, **29**, 211–247.

Boyers, R. (1972). Preface. In R. Boyers & R. Orrill (Eds), *Laing and anti-psychiatry*. Harmondsworth: Penguin.

Bradbury, W. C., & Biderman, A. D. (1962). *Mass Behaviour in Battle and Captivity*. Chicago: Aldine.

Bradley, L. A., & Bradley, G. W. (1977). The academic achievement of black students in desegregated schools: A critical review. *Review of Educational Research*, **47**, 399–449.

Brand, E. S., Ruiz, R. A., & Padilla, A. M. (1974). Ethnic identification and preference: A review. *Psychological Bulletin*, **81**, 860–890.

Breakwell, G., & Rowett, C. (1982). *Social Work: The Social Psychological Approach*. New York: Van Nostrand Reinhold.

Brinkley, W. (1953). Valley Forge GIs tell of their brain washing ordeal. *Life*, 25 May, 108.

Bronfenbrenner, U. (1968). Early deprivation: a cross-species analysis. In S. Levine, & G. Newton (Eds), *Early Experience in Behavior*. Springfield Ill.: Charles C. Thomas, 627–764.

Brothers, J. (1972). *The Brothers' System for Liberated Love and Marriage*. New York: Avon Books.

Brown, J. A. C. (1963). *Techniques of Persuasion*. Harmondsworth: Penguin.

Brown, J. F. (1936). *Psychology and the Social Order*. New York: McGraw-Hill.

Brown, P. (Ed.) (1973). *Radical Psychology*. London: Tavistock.

Brown, R., & Herrnstein, R. J. (1975). *Psychology*. London: Methuen.

Buckley, W. (1967). *Sociology and Modern Systems Theory*. Englewood Cliffs, N.J.: Prentice-Hall.

Bunde, T. (1919). *The Place of Science in Modern Civilization and Other Essays*. New York: B. W. Huebsch.

Burgess, T. (1975). Why can't children read? *New Society*, **32**, 10–11.

Burns, T. (1964). Non-verbal communications. *Discovery*, **25**, 30–31.

Buss, A. R. (1975). The Emerging Field of the Sociology of Psychological Knowledge. *American Psychologist*, October, 988–1002.

Buxbaum, E. (1951). *Your Child Makes Sense. A Guidebook for Parents*. (Foreword by Anna Fread, English edn.) London: Allen & Unwin.

Byrne, E. M. (1978). *Women and education*. London: Tavistock Press.

Byrne, P. S., & Heath, C. C. (1980). Practitioners' use of non-verbal behaviour in real consultations. *Journal of the Royal College of General Practitioners*, **30**, 327–331.

Campbell, D. T. (1969). Reforms as experiments. *American Psychologist*, **24**, 409–429.

Casler, L. (1961). Maternal deprivation: a critical review of the literature. Monographs of the Society for Reseach in Child Development, **26**, 1–64.

Cherns, A. (1979). *Using the Social Sciences*. London: Routledge & Kegan Paul.

Churchman, C. W., & Emery, F. E. (1966). In J. R. Lawrence (Ed.), *Operational Research and the Social Sciences*. London: Tavistock.

Clark, K. B. (1971). The pathos of power: A psychological perspective. *American Psychologist*, **26**, 1047–1957.

Clark, P. A. (1972). *Action Research and Organization Theory*. New York: Harper & Row.

Clark, K. B., & Clark, M. P. (1939b). Development of consciousness of self and the racial identification in Negro children. *Journal of Social Psychology*, **10**, 591–599.

Clark, K. B., & Clark, M. P. (1939a). Segregation as a factor in the racial identification of Negro preschool children: A preliminary report. *Journal of Experimental Education*, **9**, 161–163.

Clark, K. B., & Clark, M. P. (1940). Skin color as a factor in racial identification of Negro preschool children. *Journal of Social Psychology*, **11**, 159–169.

Clark, K. B., & Clark, M. P. (1947). Racial identification and preference in Negro children. In E. E. Maccoby, T. M. Newcomb & E. L. Hartley (Eds) (1958), *Readings in Social Psychology*. New York: Holt, Rinehart & Winston.

Clarke, A. D. B., & Clarke, A. M. (1954). Cognitive changes in the feebleminded. *British Journal of Psychology*, **45**, 173–179.

Clarke, A. D. B., & Clarke, A. M. (1959). Recovery from the effects of deprivation. *Acta Psychologica*, **16**, 137–144.

Clarke, A. D. B., Clarke, A. M., & Reiman, S. (1958). Cognitive and social changes in the feebleminded—three further studies. *British Journal of Psychology*, **49**, 144–157.

Clarke, A. M., & Clarke, A. D. B. (1976). *Early Experience: Myth and Evidence*. London: Open Books.

Coleman, E. (1972). *How to Make Friends with the Opposite Sex*. Los Angeles: Nash.

Coleman, J. S., Campbell, E. Q., Hobson, C. J., McPartland, J., Mood, A. M., Weinfield, F. D., & York, R. L. (1966). *Equality of Educational Opportunity*. Washington, D.C.: Office of Education, U.S. Government Printing Office.

Cook, S. W. (1979). Social science and school desegregation: "Did we mislead the Supreme Court?" *Personality and Social Psychology Bulletin*, **5**, 420–437.

Cotterill, M. (1981). *St Pauls riot opinion*. Confidential Report to Avon Regional Authority. (Unpublished.)

Criswell, E., & Peterson, S. (1972). The whole soul catalog. *Psychology Today*, **8**.

Cunningham, C. (1979). Parent counselling. In M. Craft, *Tredgold's Mental Retardation*. (12th Edn.) London: Baillière-Tindall.

Dale, R. R. (1974). *Mixed or Single-Sex School: Attainment, Attitudes and Over-view*, Vol. 3. London: Routledge & Kegan Paul.

Daniel, W. W. (1968). *Racial Discrimination in England*. Harmondsworth: Penguin.

Davie, R., Butler, N., & Goldstein, H. (1972). *From birth to seven: A report of the National Child Development Study*. London: Longman.

Davis, K. (1947). Final note on a case of extreme isolation. *American Journal of Sociology*,

45, 554–565.

Davis, K. (1967). The perilous promise of behavioural science. In, *Research in the Service of Man: Biomedical Knowledge, Development, and Use*. A conference sponsored by the Subcommittee on Government Research and the Frontiers of Science Foundation of Oklahoma for the Committee on Government, Operations of the U.S. Senate, October, 1966. Washington, D.C.: U.S. Government Printing Office.

Debord, L. W., Griffin, L. J., & Clark, M. (1977). Race and sex influence in the schooling processes of rural and small town youth. *Sociology of Education*, **50**, 85–102.

Dennis, W. (1973). *Children of the Crèche*. New York: Appelton-Century-Crofts.

Denzin, N. K. (1970). *The Research Act*. Chicago: Aldine.

Department of Education and Science. (1975). *Curricular differences for boys and girls*. Education Survey 21, London: HMSO.

Deutsch, M., & Gerard, H. B. (1955). A study of normative and informational influence upon individual judgement. *Journal of Abnormal and Social Psychology*, **51**, 629–636.

Deutscher, M., & Chein, I. (1948). The psychological effects of enforced segregation: a survey of social science opinion. *Journal of Psychology*, **26**, 259–287.

Dicks, H. V. (1972). *Licensed Mass Murder: A Socio-psychological Study of Some S.S. Killers*. New York: Basic Books.

DiMatteo, M. R., & Taranta, A. (1979). Non-verbal communication and physician–patient rapport. *Professional Psychology*, 540–547.

Doob, L. W. (1947). The utilization of social scientists in the overseas branch of the office of war information. *American Political Science Review*, **41** (No. 4), 649–677.

Douglas, J. W. B. (1975). Early hospital admissions and later disturbances of behaviour and learning. *Developmental Medicine and Child Neurology*, **17**, 456–480.

Dunkin, M. J., & Biddle, B. J. (1974). *The Study of Teaching*. New York: Holt, Rinehart & Winston.

Eckland, B., and Kent, D. P. (1968). Socialization and social structure. In, *Perspectives on Human Deprivation: Biological, Psychological and Social*. U.S. Dept. of Health, Education & Welfare.

Editorial. (1980). Non-verbal communication in general practice. *Journal of the Royal College of General Practitioners*, **30**, 323–324.

Ehrenreich, B., & English, D. (1979). *For her own Good: 150 years of the Experts' Advice to Women*. London: Pluto Press.

Ekman, P. (1973). *Darwin and Facial Expression*. London: Academic Press.

Epps, E. G. (1975). Impact of school desegregation on aspirations, self-concepts and other aspects of personality. *Law and Contemporary Problems*, **39**, 300–313.

Epps, E. G. (1979). Impact of school desegregation on the self-evaluation and achievement orientation of minority children. *Law and Contemporary Problems*, **78**, 57–76.

Exline, R. V. (1972). Visual interaction: the glances of power and preference. In J. K. Cole (Ed.), *Nebraska Symposium on Motivation*. Lincoln: University of Nebraska Press.

Exline, R. V., & Winters, L. C. (1965). Affective relations and mutual gaze in dyads. In S. Tomkins & C. Izard (Eds), *Affect, Cognition and Personality*. New York: Springer.

Eysenck, H. J. (1974). H. J. Eysenck in rebuttal. *Change*, **6**, 2.

Eysenck, H. J. (1978). Sir Cyril Burt and the inheritance of the I.Q. *New Zealand Psychologist*.

Eysenck, H. J., & Kamin, L. (1981). *Intelligence: The Battle for the Mind*. London: Pan Books.

Fiedler, F. E. (1967). *A Theory of Leadership Effectiveness*. New York: McGraw-Hill.

Field, F. (1974). *Unequal Britain: A Report on the Cycle of Inequality*. London: Arrow Books.

Fishbein, M. (1977). *Consumer beliefs and behaviour with respect to cigarette smoking: A critical analysis of the public literature*. Report prepared for the Staff of the US Federal Trade Commission.

Flanders, N. A. (1970). *Analyzing Teaching Behaviour*. Reading, Mass.: Addison-Wesley.

Fogelson, R. M. (1971). *Violence in Protest*. New York: Doubleday.

Ford, C. V. (1975). *The "Pueblo" incident: psychological responses to severe stress. Paper given to Nato Conference on Dimensions of Stress and Anxiety*. Oslo.

Ford, J. (1976). Facts, evidence and rumour: a national reconstruction of social class and the comprehensive school. In M. Shipman (Ed.), *The Organization and Impact of Social Research*. London: Routledge & Kegan Paul.

Frank, L. (1959). In D. Lerner (Ed.), *The human meaning of the social sciences*, (1973). Gloucester, Mass.: Peter Smith.

Freedman, J. L. (1971). Psychology as a science. *Social Research*, **38**, 710–731.

Freud, S. (1930). *Civilization and its discontents*. (Translated by J. Riviere.) Garden City, N.Y.: Doubleday Anchor Books.

Freud, S. (1933). *New Introductory Lectures on Psychoanalysis*. New York: W. W. Norton & Co.

Freud, S. (1936). *The problem of anxiety*. (Translated by H. A. Bunker). New York: W. W. Norton & Co.

Freud, S., (1953). Fragments of an analysis of a case of hysteria. In (1973), *The Standard edition of the Complete Works of Sigmund Freud, Vol. 7*. London: Hogarth Press.

Garfinkel, H. (1959). Social science evidence and the school segregation cases. *Journal of Politics*, **21**, 3, 37–59.

Gathorne-Hardy, J. (1972). *Rise and Fall of the British Nanny*. London: Hodder.

Gerard, H. B. (1953). The effect of different dimensions of disagreement on the communication process in small groups. *Human Relations*, **6**, 249–271.

Gerard, H. B. (1954). The anchorage of opinions in face-to-face groups. *Human Relations*, **7**, 313–326.

Gerard, H. B. (1983). School desegregation: The social science role. *American Psychologist*, **38**, 869–877.

Gerard, H. B., & Hoyt, M. F. (1974). Distinctiveness of social categorization and attitudes toward ingroup members. *Journal of Personality and Social Psychology*, **29**, 836–842.

Gerard, H. B., & Miller, N. (1975). *School Desegregation*. New York: Plenum.

Gergen, K. J. (1973). Social psychology as history. *Journal of Personality and Social Psychology*, **26**, 309–320.

Gilham, W. E. C. (1973). *The child psychologist's responsibility to his client. Paper presented to the British Psychological Society Division of Educational and Child Psychology*.

Gillie, O. (1976). Pioneer of IQ Faked his Research. *The Sunday Times*, 24 October.

Ginsberg, H. (1972). *The Myth of the Deprived Child*. Englewood Cliffs, N.J.: Prentice-Hall.

Goldfarb, W. (1943). The effects of early institutional care on adolescent personality. *Journal of Experimental Education*, **12**, 106–129.

Graziano, A. M. (1969). Clinical innovation and the mental health power structure: A social case history. *American Psychologist*, **24**, 10–18.

Greenwald, J. (1973). *Be the Person You Were Meant to Be*. New York: Dell.

Haley, J. (1959). An interactional description of schizophrenia. *Psychiatry*, **22**, 321–332.

Haley, J. (1962). Family experiments: a new type of experimentation. *Fam Proc.*, **1**, 265–293.

Haley, J. (1967). Towards a theory of pathological systems. In G. Zuk & I. Boszormenyi-Nagg (Eds), *Family Therapy and Disturbed Families*. Palo Alto, Calif.: Science and Behavior Books, pp. 11–27.

Hall, E. T. (1969). *The Hidden Dimension*, London: Bodley Head.

Halliwell, L. (1974). *The Filmgoer's Companion* (4th edn.), New York: Hill & Wang.

Haney, C., Banks, C., & Zimbardo, P. G. (1973). Interpersonal dynamics in a simulated prison. *International Journal of Criminology and Penology*, **1**, 69–97.

Hardyment, C. (1983). *Dream Babies: Child Care from Locke to Spock*, London: Jonathan Cape.

Hargreaves, D. N. (1967). *Social Relations in a Secondary School*. London: Routledge & Kegan Paul.

Harris, T. A. (1967). *I'm O.K.—You're O.K.* New York: Avon Books.

Hart, M. (1943). *Winged Victory*. New York: Random House.

Harvey, J. H., Cacioppo, J. T., & Yasuna, A. (1977). Temporal pattern of social information and self-attribution of ability. *Journal of Personality*, **45**, 281–296.

Hauser, P. M. (1967). In M. Leeds (Ed.), *Washington Colloquium on Science and Society*. Baltimore: Mono Book Corporation.

Hearnshaw, L. S. (1979). *Cyril Burt: Psychologist*. Ithaca: Cornell University Press.

Hechinger, G., & Hechinger, F. M. (1974). Remember when they gave A's and D's? *New York Times Magazine*, 5 May, 84, 86, 92.

Heilbroner, R. L. (1961). *The Worldly Philosophers*. New York: Simon & Schuster.

Helfer, R. E. (1970). An objective comparison of the paediatric interviewing skills of freshmen and senior medical students. *Paediatrics*, **45**, 623–627.

Helmreich, R., Bakeman, R., & Scherwitz, L. (1973). The study of small groups. In P. H. Mussen & M. R. Rosenzweig (Eds), *Annual Review of Psychology*. Palo Alto: Annual Reviews Inc., 337–354.

Hochschild, A. R. (1979). Emotion work, feeling rules and social structures. *American Journal of Sociology*, **85**, 551–575.

Hoffman, L. (1974). The effects of maternal employment on the child—a review of the research. *Developmental Psychology*, **10**, 204–228.

Horowitz, I. L. (1967). *The Rise and Fall of Project Camelot*. Cambridge, Mass.: MIT Press.

Horowitz, R. E. (1939). Racial aspects of self-identification in nursery school children. *Journal of Psychology*, **7**, 91–99.

Ingleby, D. (1972). Ideaology and the human sciences: some comments on the role of reification in psychology and psychiatry. In T. Pateman (Ed.), *Counter Course: A Handbook for Course Criticism*. Harmondsworth: Penguin.

Ingleby, D. (1974). The job psychologists do. In N. Armistead (Ed.), *Reconstructing social psychology*. Harmondsworth: Penguin.

Jacoby, R. (1977). *Social Amnesia: Conformist Psychology from Adler to Laing*. Brighton, Sussex: Harvester Press.

Jensen, A. R. (1976). Heredity and Intelligence: Sir Cyril Burt's findings. Letter to *The Times*, 9 December, 11.

Jessor, R., & Richardson, S. (1968). Psychosocial deprivation and personality development. In, *Perspectives on Human Deprivation*. U.S. Dept. of Health, Education & Welfare.

Johnson, B. S. (1965). The meaning of touch in nursing. *Nursing Outlook*, **13**, 59–60.

Johnson, D. W., & Johnson, R. (1975). *Learning Together and Alone: Co-operation, Competition and Individuation*. Englewood Cliffs, N.J.: Prentice-Hall.

Jones, G. N. (1969). *Planned Organizational Change*. London: Routledge, & Kegan Paul.

Jordan, B. (1974). *Poor Parents: Social Policy and the Cycle of Deprivation*. London: Routledge & Kegan Paul.

Jourard, S. M. (1966). An exploratory study of body accessibility. *British Journal of Social and Clinical Psychology*, **5**, 221–231.

Jourard, S. M. (1972). *Psychology for Control and for Liberation of Humans*. Paper presented to The British Psychological Annual Conference, Nottingham.

Kadushin, A. (1970). *Adopting Older Children*. New York: Columbia University Press.

Kagan, J., & Klein, R. E. (1973). Cross-cultural perspectives on early development. *American Psychologist*, **28**, 947–961.

Kagan, J., Kearsley, R. B., & Zalazo, P. R. (1978). *Infancy: Its Place in Human Development*. Cambridge, Mass.: Harvard University Press.

Kamin, L. (1981). The Cyril Burt affair. In H. J. Eysenck & L. Kamin, *Intelligence: The Battle for the Mind*. London: Pan Books, pp. 102–105.

Kardiner, A., & Ovesey, L. (1951). *The Mark of Oppression*. New York: Norton.

Katz, I. (1964). Review of the evidence relating to the effects of desegregation on the intellectual performance of Negroes. *American Psychologist*, **19**, 381–399.

Kay. H. (1972). Psychology today and tomorrow. *Bulletin of the British Psychological Society*. **25**, 177–188.

Kent, G., Clarke, P., & Dalrymple-Smith, D. (1981). The patient is the expert. *Medical Education*, **15**, 38–42.

Kent, G., & Dalgleish, M. (1983). *Psychology and medical care*. Wokingham, Berks: Van Nostrand Reinhold (UK) Co. Ltd.

Klineberg, O. (1935). *Negro intelligence and selective migration*. New York: Columbia University Press.

Kluger, R. (1976). *Simple justice*. New York: Knopf.

Köhler, W. (1925). *The mentality of apes*. New York: Harcourt, Brace.

Koluchová, J. (1972). Severe deprivation in twins: a case study. *Journal of Child Psychology and Psychiatry*, **13**, 107–114.

Kovel, J. (1976). *A complete guide to therapy: from psychoanalysis to behavior modification*. New York: Pantheon Books.

Kral, V. A. (1951). Psychiatric observations under severe chronic stress. *American Journal of Psychiatry*, **108**, 185.

Kuhn, T. (1962). *The structure of scientific revolutions*. Chicago: University of Chicago Press.

LaCrosse, M. D. (1975). Non-verbal behaviour and perceived counsellor attractiveness and persuasiveness. *Journal of Counselling Psychology*, **22**, 563–566.

Laing, R. D. (1967). *The Politics of Experience and the Bird of Paradise*. Harmondsworth: Penguin.

Laird, J. D. (1974). Self-attribution of emotion: the effects of expressive behavior on the quality of emotional experience. *Journal of Personality and Social Psychology*, **29**, 475–486.

Lakin, F. H. (1965). *Psychological warfare in Malaya 1952–55*. Paper presented to the 11th Annual U.S. Army Human Factors Research and Development Conference.

Lana, R. E. (1969). *Assumptions of Social Psychology*. New York: Appleton-Century-Crofts.

Larson, P. S., & Silvette, H. (1968). *Tobacco, experimental and clinical studies supplement I*. Baltimore: Williams and Wilkins.

Lazarsfeld, P. F., Sewell, W. H., & Wilensky, H. L. (Eds.) (1968). *Uses of Sociology*. London: Weidenfeld & Nicholson. (Originally published 1967 by Basic Books.)

Leach, P. (1977). *Baby and Child*. London: Michael Joseph.

LeBon, G. (1947). *The Crowd: A Study of the Popular Mind*. London: Ernest Benn (First published 1895.)

Levine, J. M. (1983). Social comparison and education. In J. M. Levine & M. C. Wang (Eds), *Teacher and Student Perceptions: Implications for Learning*. Hillsdale, N.J.: Lawrence Erlbaum Associates.

Lewin, K. (1944). Problems of research in social psychology. In D. Cartwright (Ed.) (1951), *Field Theory in Social Science: Selected Theoretical Papers of Kurt Lewin*. New York: Harper & Row.

Lewis, H. (1954). *Deprived Children*. London: Oxford University Press.

Ley, P., & Spelman, S. (1967). *Communicating with the patient*. London: Staples Press.

Likert, R. (1961). *New Patterns of Management*. New York: McGraw-Hill.

Lindesmith, A. R., & Strauss, A. L. (1968). *Social Psychology*. Holt, Reinhart and Winston, New York.

Lippmann, W. (1922). *Public Opinion*. New York: Macmillan.

Llewelyn, S., & Kelly, J. (1980). Individualism in psychology: a case for a new paradigm?

Bulletin of the British Psychological Society, **33**, 407–411.

Loxley, F. O. (1975–76). The child sterilisation case: some background issues. *Occasional paper of the Division of Educational and Child Psychology of the British Psychological Society*, Winter Issue No. 9.

Lukes, S. (1973). *Individualism*. Oxford: Blackwell.

Lynd, R. S. (1939). *Knowledge for what? The Place of Social Science in American Culture*. Princeton, N.J.: Princeton University Press.

Maccoby, E., & Jacklin, C. U. (1974). *Sex differences revisited: myth and reality. Paper presented at Annual meeting of American Education Research Association*. Chicago, Ill.

Mackintosh, N. J. (1980). Review of Cyril Burt: Psychologist, by L. S. Hearnshaw. *British Journal of Psychology*, **71**, 174–175.

Maguire, P. et al. (1978). The value of feedback in reading interviewing skills to medical students. *Psychological Medicine*, **8**, 695–704.

Maguire, P., & Rutter, D. (1976). Training medical students to communicate. In A. E. Bennett (Ed.), *Communication Between Doctors and Patients*. Oxford: Oxford University Press.

Mantell, D. M. (1971). The potential for violence in Germany. *Journal of Social Issues*, **27**, **4**, 101–112.

Marks, P. (1976). Feminity in the classroom: an account of changing attitudes. In J. Mitchell & A. Oakley (Eds). *The Rights and Wrongs of Women*. Harmondsworth: Penguin.

Marsden, D. (1970). How comprehensives missed the tide. In D. Rubinstein & C. Stoneman (Eds), (1970). *Education for Democracy*. Harmondsworth: Penguin.

McDougall, W. N. (1908). *Social Psychology*. London: Methuen.

McGregor, D. (1960). *The Human Side of Enterprise*. New York: McGraw-Hill.

Mead, G. H. (1934). *Mind, Self and Society*. Chicago: Chicago University Press.

Milgram, S. (1963). Behavioral study of obedience. *Journal of Abnormal and Social Psychology*, **67**, 371–378.

Milgram, S. (1965b). Some conditions of obedience and disobedience to authority. In I. D. Steiner & M. Fishbein (Eds), *Current Studies in Social Psychology*. New York: Holt, Rinehart & Winston.

Milgram, S. (1965a). *Obedience (a filmed experiment)*. Distributed by the New York University library.

Milgram, S. (1974). *Obedience to Authority*. New York: Harper & Row.

Milgram, S., & Toch, H. (1969). Collective behaviour: crowds and social movements. In G. Lindzey and E. Aronson (Eds), *Handbook of Social Psychology*. 2nd edn., Vol. 4. Reading. Mass.: Addison-Wesley.

Miller, G. A. (1969). Psychology as a means of promoting human welfare. *American Psychologist*, **24**, 1063–1075.

Morehouse, W. N. (1943). New York Sun, 22 November 1943 (as reproduced in *Winged Victory*). *New York Theatre Critics Reviews*, **4**, 216–219.

Morgan, P. (1975). *Child Care: Sense and Fable*. London: Temple Smith.

Moscovici, S. (1976). *Social Influence and Social Change*. London: Academic Press.

Murayama, G., & Miller, N. (1979). Re-examination of normative influence processes in desegregated classrooms. *American Educational Research Journal*, **16**, 273–284.

Murphy, G. (1965). The future of social psychology in historical perspective. In O. Klineberg & R. Christie (Eds), *Perspectives in Social Psychology*. New York: Holt, Rinehart & Winston.

Myrdahl, G. (1944). *An American Dilemma: The Negro Problem and Modern Democracy*. New York: Harper.

Napoli, D. S. (1981). *Architects of Adjustment: The History of the Psychological Profession in the United States*. Port Washington, N.Y.: Kennikat Press.

Nardini, J. E. (1952). Port Washington, N.Y.: Kennikat

Nardini, J. E. (1952). Survival factors in American POWs of the Japanese. *American Journal of Psychiatry*, **109**, 241–248.

Nelson, R. (1977). *The Moon and the Ghetto*. New York: W. W. Norton.

Newberger, H. M., & Lee, M. (1974). *The Art of Self-image Modification*. New York: David McKay.

Newman, M., Berkowitz, B., & Owen, J. (1971). *How to be Your Own Best Friend*. New York: Ballantine Books.

Nicholls, J. (1975). Causal attributions and other achievement-related cognitions: Effects of task outcome, attainment value, and sex. *Journal of Personality and Social Psychology*, **31**, 379–389.

Nicolaus, M. N. (1968). Sociology liberation movement. In T. Pateman (Ed.) (1972), *Counter Course: A Handbook for Course Criticism*. Harmondsworth: Penguin.

Niehoff, A. H. (Ed.) (1966). *A Casebook of Social Change*. Chicago: Aldine.

Orlando, N. J. (1973). The mock ward: A study in simulation. In O. Milton and R. G. Wahler (Eds), *Behavior Disorder: Perspectives and Trends*. Philadelphia: J. B. Lippincott.

Pepitone, E. A. (1972). A comparison behavior in elementary school children. *American Education Research Journal*. **9**, 45–63.

Perls, F., & Stevens, J. O. (1969). *Gestalt Therapy Verbatim*. Lafayette, Calif: Real People Press.

Platt, A. (1972). The triumph of benevolence: The origins of the juvenile justice system in the United States. In A. S. Blomberg (Ed.), *Introduction to Criminology*.

Platt, J., & Clarke, J. (1984). *Social factors affecting the composition of children's school packed lunches*. Paper presented to the British Sociological Association.

Platt, J. (1984). The media make a meal out of it. *Network (Newsletter of the British Sociological Association)*. No. 28, January, 4–5.

Poole, A. D., & Sanson-Fisher, R. W. (1979). Understanding the patient. *Social Science and Medicine*, **13A**, 37–43.

Porter, J. R., & Washington, R. W. (1979). Black identity and self-esteem: A review of studies of black self-concept. *Annual Review of Sociology*, **5**, 53–74.

Potter, J., & Mulkay, M. (1982). Scientists interview talk: Interviews as a technique for revealing participants, interpretative practices. In M. Bremner, J. Brown & D. Canter (Eds), *The Research Interview: Uses and Approaches*. London: Academic Press.

Pringle, M. K. (1975). *The Needs of Children*. London: Hutchinson.

Proshansky, H., & Newton, P. (1968). The nature and meaning of Negro self-identity. In M. Deutsch, I. Katz, & A. R. Jensen (Eds), *Social Class, Race and Psychological Development*. New York: Holt, Rinehart & Winston.

Prugh, D. G., Staub, E. M., Sands, H. H., Kirschbaum, R. M., & Lenihan, E. A. (1953). A study of the emotional reactions of children and families to hospitalization and illness. *American Journal of Orthopsychiatry*, **23**, 70–106.

Pryce, K. (1979). *Endless Pressure*. Harmondsworth: Penguin.

Rainwater, C., & Yancy, W. L. (1967). *The Moynihan Report and the Politics of Controversy*. Cambridge, Mass.: MIT Press.

Rapoport, R., Rapoport, R. N., & Strelitz, Z. (1977). *Fathers, Mothers and Others: Towards New Alliances*. London: Routledge & Kegan Paul.

Rathbun, C., Di Virgilio, L., & Waldfogel, S. (1958). The restitutive process in children following radical separation from family and culture. *American Journal of Orthopsychiatry*, **28**, 408–415.

Rathbun, C., McLaughlin, H., Bennett, O., & Garland, J. A. (1965). Later adjustment of children following radical separation from family and culture. *American Journal of Orthopsychiatry*, **35**, 604–609.

Reddy, W. M. (1977). The textile trade and the language of the crowd at Rouen 1752–1871. *Past and Present*, **74**, 62–89.

Reich, J. W. (1981). An historical analysis of the field. In L. Bickman, *Applied Social Psychology Annual, Vol 2*. Beverly Hills: Sage.

Reicher, S. D. (1982a). The determination of collective behaviour. In H. Tajfel (Ed.), *Social Identity and Intergroup Relations*. Cambridge: Cambridge University Press; Paris: Maison des Science de l'Homme.

Reicher, S. D. (1982b). *Crowd psychology and group process*. Paper given to Annual Conference of the British Psychological Society, York, April.

Reicher, S. D. (1984). St Pauls: a study in the limits of crowd behaviour. (First published in this volume.)

Reicher, S. D. (forthcoming). *The Crowd: A study in the Social Determination of Behaviour*. London: Academic Press.

Rich, A. P., and Schroeder, H. E. (1976). Research issues in assertiveness training. *Psychology Bulletin*, **83**, 1081–1096.

Ringer, R. J. (1974). *Winning Through Intimidation*. Los Angeles: Los Angeles Book Publishers.

Rogers, C. R., & Skinner, B. F. (1956). Some issues concerning the control of human behaviour: A symposium. *Science*, **124**, 1057–1066.

Rosenthal, R., & Jacobson, L. (1968). *Pygmalion in the classroom. Teacher expectations and pupil's intellectual development*. New York: Holt, Rinehart & Winston.

Rosenthal, R., & Rosnow, R. L. (1966). Volunteer subjects and the result of opinion change studies. *Psychological Reports*, **19**, 1183.

Runciman, W. G. (1972). *Relative Deprivation and Social Justice*. Harmondsworth: Penguin.

Rutter, M. (1970). Psychosocial disorders in childhood and their outcome in adult life. *Journal of the Royal College of Physicians of London*, **4**, 211–218.

Rutter, M. (1974a). *Maternal Deprivation Reassessed*. Harmondsworth: Penguin.

Rutter, M. (1974b). Dimensions at parenthood: Some myths and some suggestions. In, *The Family in Society: Dimensions of Parenthood*. Seminar held by Department of Health & Social Security. London: HMSO.

Rutter, M. (1975). *Helping Troubled Children*. Harmondsworth: Penguin.

Rutter. M. (1975b). Discussion In D. Barltrop (Ed.), *Paediatrics and the environment*. Report of the Second Unigate Paediatric Workshop. Fellowship of Postgraduate Medicine.

Rutter, M., & Madge, N. (1976). *Cycle of Deprivation*. London: Heinemann.

Saks, M. J., & Hastie, R. (1978). *Social Psychology in Court*. London: Van Nostrand Reinhold Co.

Sameroff, A. J., & Chandler, M. J. (1975). Reproductive risk and the continuum of caretaking casualty. In F. D. Horowitz, & M. Hetherington (Eds). Review of Child Development Research, 4. Chicago: University of Chicago Press.

Sampson, E. E. (1977). Psychology and the American Ideal. *Journal of Personality and Social Psychology*, **35**, 767–782.

Sanders, G. S., Gastorf, J. W., & Mullen, B. (1979). Selectivity in the use of social comparison information. *Personality and Social Psychology Bulletin*, **5**, 377–380.

Sarason, S. B., Carrol, C., Maton, K., Cohen, S., & Lorentz, E. (1977). *Human Services and Resource Networks*. San Francisco: Jossey-Bass.

Sarason, S. B. (1977). *Work, Aging and Social Change. Professionals and the One-life-one-career imperative*. New York: Free Press (Macmillan).

Sarason, S. B. (1978). The nature of problem solving in social action. *American Psychologist*, **33**, 370–380.

Sargent, W. (1957). *Battle for the Mind: A Physiology of Conversion and Brain Washing*. London: Pan Books.

Savin, H. B. (1973). Professors and psychological researchers: conflicting values in conflicting roles. *Cognition* **2**(1), 147–149.

Schaffer, H. R. (1958). Objective observations of personality development in early infancy. *British Journal of Medical Psychology*, **31**, 174–183.

Schein, E. H. (1957). Patterns of reaction to severe chronic stress in American army POWs of the Chinese. In *Methods of forceful indoctrination: Observations and interviews*. GAP Symposium No. 4. New York: Group for the Advancement of Psychiatry, Publications Office.

Schellenberg, J. A. (1978). *Masters of Social Psychology: Freud, Mead, Lewin and Skinner*. New York: Oxford University Press.

Schofield, J. W., & Sagar, H. A. (1977). Peer interaction patterns in an integrated middle school. *Sociometry*, **40**, 130–138.

Schutz, W. C. (1967). *Joy: Expanding Human Awareness*. New York: Grove Press.

Sedgwick, P. (1974). Ideology in modern psychology. In N. Armistead (Ed.), *Reconstructing Social Psychology*. Harmondsworth: Penguin.

Sedgwick, P. (1982). *Psycho Politics*. London: Pluto Press.

Segall, M. H. (1976). *Human Behaviour and Public Policy*. New York: Pergamon.

Seligman, M. E. P. (1973). Fall into helplessness. *Psychology Today*, **7**, 43–48.

Sève, L. (1978). *Man in Marxist Theory and the Psychology of Personality*. (Trans. from the French by J. McGrael). Brighton, Sussex: Harvester Press.

Shaw, J. (1976). Finishing school—some implications of sex-segregated education. In D. L. Barker & S. Allen, *Sexual Divisions and Society: Process and Change*. London: Tavistock.

Sherif, C. W. (1976). *Orientations in Social Psychology*. New York: Harper & Row.

Shipman, M. (Ed.) (1976). *The Organisation and Impact of Social Research: Six Original Case Studies in Education and Behavioural Sciences*. London: Routledge & Kegan Paul.

Shotter, J. (1975). *Images of Man in Psychological Research*. London: Methuen.

Siegler, M., Osmond, H., & Mann, H. (1969). Laing's models of madness. *British Journal of Psychiatry*, **115**, 947–958. (Reprinted in R. Boyers & R. Orril (Eds), (1972). *Laing and Anti-Psychiatry*. Harmondsworth: Penguin.)

Sighele, S. (1892). *La Foule Criminelle essai de psychologie collective*. Trans. from Italian by P. Vigny, Paris: Felix Alcan.

Skeels, H. M. (1966). Adult status of children with contrasting early life experiences: A follow-up study. *Monographs of the Society for Research in Child Development*, **31**, No. 3, Serial No. 105.

Skeels, H. M., & Dye, H. B. (1939). A study of the effects of differential stimulation on mentally retarded children. *Proceedings of the American Association on Mental Deficiency*, **44**, 114–136.

Skinner, B. F. (1948). *Walden Two*. New York: Macmillan.

Skinner, B. F. (1971). *Beyond Freedom and Dignity*. New York: Knopf.

Slavin, R. E. (1980). Cooperative learning. *Review of Educational Research*, **50**, 315–342.

Smith, D. J. (1974). *Racial disadvantage in employment*. PEP Broadcast No. 544.

Smith, M. B., Bruner, J. S., & White, R. W. (1964). (First published 1956.) *Opinions and Personality*. New York: John Wiley & Sons.

Smith-Hanen, S. (1977). Effects of non-verbal behaviour on judged levels of counsellor warmth and empathy. *Journal of Counselling Psychology*, **24**, 87–91.

Sommer, R., (1965). Further studies of small group ecology. *Sociometry*, **28**, 337–348.

Stanton, A. H., & Schwartz, M. S. (1954). *The Mental Hospital*. New York: Basic Books.

Steiner, C. (1974). Radical psychiatry: Principles. In the Radical Therapist/Rough Times Collective (Ed.), *The Radical Therapist*. Harmondsworth: Penguin.

Stephan, W. G., & Rosenfeld, D. (1978). Effects of desegregation on race relations and self-esteem. *Journal of Educational Psychology*, **70**, 670–679.

Stephan, W. G., & Feagin, J. R. (1980). *School Desegregation: Past, Present and Future*. New York: Plenum.

Stephan, W. G. (1978). School desegregation: An evaluation of predictions made in *Brown vs. Board of Education. Psychological Bulletin*, **85**, 217–238.

Stiles, W. B., Putnam, S. M., Wolf, M. H., & James, S. A. (1979). Interaction exchange structure and patient satisfaction with medical interviews. *Medical Care*, **17**, 667–681.

St. John, N. (1975). *School Desegregation*. New York: John Wiley & Sons.

Stone, J., & Taylor, F. (1976). *The Parent's Schoolbook*. Harmondsworth: Penguin.

Strachey, J. (1962). Preface to *S. Freud: Two Short Accounts of Psycho-analysis*. Trans. and ed. by J. Strachey. Harmondsworth: Penguin.

Strassman, H. D., et al. (1956). A prisoner-of-war syndrome: Apathy as a reaction to severe stress. *American Journal of Psychiatry*, **112**, 998–1003.

Suls, J., & Sanders, G. S. (1979). Social comparison processes in the young child. *Journal of Research and Development in Education*, **13**, 79–89.

Svarstad, B. L., & Lipton, H. L. (1977). Informing parents about mental retardation. *Social Science and Medicine*, **11**, 645–651.

Tajfel, H. (Ed.) (1979). *Differentiation Between Social Groups: Studies in the Social Psychology of Intergroup Relations*. London: Academic Press.

Tarde, G. (1890). *La Philosophie Penale*. Lyon: Edition Storck.

Taylor, N. C., & Walsh, E. J. (1979). Explanations of black self-esteem: Some empirical tests. *Social Psychology Quarterly*, **42**, 242–252.

Tepper, D. T., & Haase, R. F. (1978). Verbal and non-verbal communication of facilitative conditions. *Journal of Counselling Psychology*, **25**, 35–44.

Tew, M. (1979). The safest place of birth. *Lancet*, **1**, 1388–1390.

Thorton, D. A., & Arrowood, A. J. (1966). Self-evaluation, self-enhancement and the locus of social comparison. *Journal of Experimental Social Psychology, Supplement 1*, 40–48.

Tizard, B., & Rees, J. (1974). A comparison of the effects of adoption, restoration to the natural mother, and continued institutionalization on the cognitive development of four-year-old children. *Child Development*, **45**, 92–99.

Toda, M., Shinotsuka, H., McClintock, C. G., & Stech, F. J. (1978). Development of competitive behavior as a function of culture, age, and social comparison. *Journal of Personality and Social Psychology*, **36**, 825–829.

Trower, P. (1980). Situational analysis of the components and processes of behavior of socially skilled and unskilled patients. *Journal of Consulting and Clinical Psychology*, **48**, 327–339.

Tucker, R. (1961). *Philosophy and Myth in Karl Marx*. Cambridge: Cambridge University Press.

Turner, J. C. (1982). Towards a cognitive redefinition of the social group. In H. Tajfel (Ed.), *Social Identity and Intergroup Relations*. Cambridge: Cambridge University Press; Paris: Maison des Sciences de l'Homme.

Turner, R. H., & Killian, L. (1972). *Collective Behaviour* (2nd edn). Englewood Cliffs, N.J.: Prentice-Hall.

Varela, J. A. (1970). *Introduction to Social Science Technology*. New York: Academic Press.

Verby, J. E. (1979). Peer review of consultations in primary care. *British Medical Journal*, **1**, 1686–1688.

Vernon, P. E. (1964). *Personality Assessment: A Critical Survey*. London: Methuen.

Veroff, J. (1978). Social motivation. *American Behavioral Scientist*, **21**, 709 & 730.

Waddington, C. H. (1966). *Principles of Development and Differentiation*. New York: Macmillan.

Watson, P. (1980). *War on the Mind: The Military Uses and Abuses of Psychology*. Harmondsworth: Penguin.

Wedge, P., & Prosser, N. (1973). *Born to Fail*. Arrow Books.

Weigel. R. H., Wiser, P. L., & Cook, S. W. (1975). The impact of cooperative learning experiences on cross-ethnic relations and attitudes. *Journal of Social Issues*, **31**, 219–244.

Weinberg, M. (1975). The relationship between school desegregation and academic achievement: A review of research. *Law and Contemporary Problems*, **39**, 240–270.

Wexler, P. (1983). *Critical Social Psychology*. London: Routledge & Kegan Paul.

Whitcher, S. J., and Fisher, J. D. (1979). Multi-dimensional reactions to therapeutic touch in a hospital setting. *Journal of Personality and Social Psychology*, **37**, 87–96.

White, R. W. (1959). Motivation reconsidered: The concept of competence. *Psychological Review*, **66**, 297–333.

Williams, L. P. (1959). *The Politics of Science in the French Revolution*. In M. Clagett (Ed.), *Critical Problems in the History of Science*. Madison: University of Wisconsin Press.

Winnicott, D. W. (1973). *The Child, the Family and the Outside World*. Harmondsworth: Penguin.

Wolf, S., & Ripley, H. (1947). Reactions among allied prisoners subject to three years of imprisonment and torture by Japanese. *American Journal of Psychiatry,* **104**, 180–193.

World Health Organisation Expert Committee on Mental Health (1951). *Report on the Second Session*. Technical Report Series, No. 31, Geneva: World Health Organisation.

Wortman, C. B., Costanza, P. R., & Witt, T. R. (1973). Effect of anticipated performance on the attributions of causality to self and others. *Journal of Personality and Social Psychology*, **27**, 372–381.

Wylie, R. C. (1979). *The Self-concept: Theory and Research on Selected Topics* (Rev. Edn). Lincoln: University of Nebraska Press.

Young, K. (1945). *Handbook of Social Psychology* (2nd Edn). New York: Crofts.

Zimbardo, P. G., Banks, W. C., Haney, C., & Jaffe, D. (1973). The mind is a formidable jailer: a Pirandellian prison. *The New York Times Magazine*, 8 April, Section 6, 38–60.

Zimbardo, P. G. (1973a). On the ethics of intervention in human psychological research with special reference to the "Stanford Prison Experiment." *Cognition*, **2**, 2, 243–255.

Zimbardo, P. G. (1973b). Letter. *The New York Times Magazine*, 20 May, 123.

Author Index

Subject Index